W9-BAX-076

ARNULFO L. OLIVEIRA MEMORIAL LIBRARY
1825 MAY STREET
BROWNSVILLE, TEXAS 78520

THE KEY TO FAILURE

THE
KEY TO FAILURE

Laos and the Vietnam War

Norman B. Hannah

MADISON BOOKS
Lanham · New York · London

ARNULFO L. OLIVEIRA MEMORIAL LIBRARY
1825 MAY STREET
BROWNSVILLE, TEXAS 78520

Copyright © 1987 by

Norman B. Hannah

4720 Boston Way
Lanham, MD 20706

3 Henrietta Street
London WC2E 8LU England

All rights reserved

Printed in the United States of America

British Cataloging in Publication Information Available

Library of Congress Cataloging-in-Publication Data

Hannah, Norman B.
The key to failure.

Bibliography: p.
1. Vietnamese Conflict, 1961-1975—United States.
2. Vietnamese Conflict, 1961-1975-Laos.   I. Title.
DS558.H36   1987   959.704'3   87-22125
ISBN 0-8191-6440-2 (alk. paper)

All Madison Books are produced on acid-free
paper which exceeds the minimum standards set by the National
Historical Publications and Records Commission.

*This book is dedicated to
all the Americans who served in
Indochina*

Contents

Acknowledgments

/ /"W"ords pay no debts," said Shakespeare in *Troilus and Cressida*. Nevertheless, acting on the wisdom of the philosopher Seneca who, some 2,000 years ago, said that "he who receives a benefit with gratitude repays the first installment on his debt," I should like to make a small down payment to:

William F. Buckley, Jr. and Priscilla Buckley for their support and encouragement beginning in June 1975 with publication in *National Review* of my first article on Vietnam, from a paragraph of which I have taken the title of the Prologue;

Col. Harry G. Summers, whose application, in his *On Strategy: A Critical Analysis of the Vietnam War*, of the principles of Clausewitz demonstrated the theoretical basis for the thesis advanced in this book;

Robert Foulon and Charles Flowerree, my former Foreign Service colleagues who not only shared with me much of the experience which provided my grist but read and commented on my draft manuscript at various stages, as did Dr. Kenneth P. Landon, formerly of the Department of State and Mr. Alf R. Thompson of Effingham, Illinois.

Kevin Lynch, formerly an Associate Editor of *National Review*, now with the Voice of America, who first encouraged me to look beyond articles to a book and who then read the first tentative drafts of the early chapters;

Sol Sanders, my long-time friend with me in Southeast Asia, formerly with *U.S. News and World Report*, who read my outline and steered me to Madison Books;

Elizabeth Carnes, formerly with Madison Books, whose early interest and confidence opened the way to eventual publication, and her successor as Managing Editor, Charles Lean, who effectively completed the process;

Professor John Clark Pratt, author of *Laotian Fragments* and *Vietnam Voices* whose own experience in Indochina, coupled with his sharp but knowing editorial razor have contributed indispensably to the final result;

Sharon Holand Hannah, my daughter-in-law, who plowed through my voluminous drafts with her word processor, reducing them to neat legible chapters.

On another level are those whose contribution is immeasurable and inexpressible because it is crystallized in the virtue of patience. "They also serve who only stand and wait"—

My mother, Vivian Britton Hannah, who, at the age of 93 has waited a very long time;

My sons, Norman and Harry, and their mother—my late wife, Eddie, who shared with me the origins of this book and waited as long as she could;

My wife, Betty, who for fifteen years has waited and suffered the book's gestation and birth pangs and deserves some relief, now and in the future.

Foreword

For years the debate has raged over "Who lost Vietnam." And there has been no dearth of candidates—the Presidents who got us involved in the first place; the senior civilian and military leaders who were charged with formulating a winnable military strategy; the Congress which has the responsibility for providing the wherewithal with which to fight the war; and even the American soldiers, sailors, airmen, marines and coastguardsmen who actually fought the war in the jungles and in the air and seas of Indochina.

But while valid criticisms can be leveled at each of these groups, none satisfactorily explains the Vietnam debacle. President Lyndon Johnson, for example, certainly did not set out to lose a war, plunge his country into chaos, and ruin his political career. David Halberstam was not being sarcastic when he characterized Vietnam-era civilian and military leaders as "the best and the brightest" who were trying to do the right thing. The Congress, which appropriated billions of dollars for arms, equipment and material with which to prosecute the war, did not intend to engineer America's defeat. And it is pernicious to blame those who put their lives on the line on the battlefield for America's lack of success.

The answer lies elsewhere, and for years it avoided detection. It was hidden in what computer programmers call an "algorithmic error"—a defect in the intricate mathematical-logical rules in computer software that govern both wargaming and the operation of intricate defense systems. Although only recently given a name, such errors have not been uncommon in warfare.

One such algorithmic error was the Army Corps of Engineer's arbitrary decision in the 1920s to limit military bridging to ten tons. Ten years later when inventor J. Walter Christie tried to sell his revolutionary new tank to the Army it was rejected because at fifteen tons it was too heavy for Army bridging. Thus a seemingly minor and unrelated decision unintentionally became a limiting factor on development of American battlefield armor and almost lead to America's defeat in the opening battles of both World War II and Korea. At Faid and Kasserine passes in North Africa and again at Normandy American tanks were decidedly inferior to the German panzers and it was only by the weight of numbers and by the sacrifice of thousands of American lives that the United States was able to prevail. The pattern was repeated again in Korea, as initially American tanks were unable to stand up to the North Koreans' Russian-built T-34s which incorporated Christie's design.

A more recent example occurred in the 1982 Falklands War, when an algorithmic error was unintentionally programmed into the British air defense systems. The "logic" anticipated attack only by a single aircraft, and when two Argentine aircraft attacked the British destroyer HMS *Sheffield* simultaneously, the ship's air defense system was faced with a dilemma. Unable to differentiate it shut itself down, and the *Sheffield* was struck and sunk by an Argentine missile.

Now Norman B. Hannah has found the algorithmic error that lead to America's defeat on Vietnam. That algorithmic error—the "key to failure" as he accurately portrays it—was the inversion of the 1962 Geneva Accords on Laos. As Hannah describes it in convincing detail, the Laos Accords unwittingly became a critical limiting factor on America's ability (but not on North Vietnam's) to prosecute the war in Indochina.

American military commanders knew that isolating the battlefield— cutting the Viet Cong off from their sources of external supply—was essential if the war was to be won. To do that required cutting North Vietnamese lines of supply and communication both at sea and on the ground. With Operation Market Time the U.S. and South Vietnamese Navy established successful barriers to sea-borne infiltration of men, supplies and material. But the ground infiltration route—the so-called Ho Chi Minh trail—was never effectively interdicted.

Begun in May 1959 long before America became directly involved in the war, the Ho Chi Minh trail was North Vietnam's road to victory. It was their equivalent of the sea-bridge between the United States and Europe that made Allied victory possible in World War II. Beginning in North Vietnam the 16,000 kilometer [10,000 mile] "trail" with its 3,082 kilometer [1,925 mile] fuel pipeline ran southward through the Laotian panhandle and the eastern border regions of Cambodia, with spurs into North Vietnamese base areas in South Vietnam. With the success of Operation Market Time and especially after the Cambodian port of Sihanoukville was closed to the North Vietnamese in 1970, it became their main route for movement of men and supplies.

Not only did this "trail" give North Vietnam a logistical advantage, it gave them the tactical advantage of interior lines as well. South Vietnam is shaped like a bow, with the coastal transportation network available to South Vietnamese forces following the bow itself. Representing the bow-string was the relatively straight Ho Chi Minh trail. As a result North Vietnamese forces could move anywhere in South Vietnam faster than could their South Vietnamese counterparts, an advantage that proved crucial in North Vietnam's decisive 1975 blitzkrieg.

During the war the North Vietnamese launched a successful propaganda campaign to disguise the importance of the trail, going so far at times as even to deny its existence. After the war, however, they have publicly acknowledged its importance. A 1985 illustrated booklet, "The Ho Chi Minh Trail," published by the Foreign Language Publishing House in Hanoi, brags that two million people used the trail during the course of the war, and forty–five million tonnes of material were transported along its length.

Recognizing the trail's importance, the United States launched a major air campaign in 1965 to interdict the flow of men and material. But by 1967 it became obvious that air power alone could not do it. If the flow was to be stopped the trail would have to be physically cut on the ground by extending the so-called demilitarized zone (DMZ) across Laos into Thailand. But every request by the Joint Chiefs of Staff and by American commanders in the field to launch such an operation ran head on into the algorithmic error created by the inversion of the 1962 Laos Accords.

Hannah makes clear, that as an aftermath of these Accords the United States and North Vietnam reached a "tacit agreement" that North Vietnam would not launch ground attacks against western Laos so long as the United States did not launch ground attacks against the Laotian panhandle.

This proved to be a massive failure in logic. Western Laos was strategically insignificant, but because of the Ho Chi Minh trail which ran its length the Laotian panhandle was what the military would call key terrain—terrain so important that it conveys a major advantage to its possessor. With this algorithmic error the United States not only virtually guaranteed its own failure but sealed the fate of its South Vietnamese ally as well.

"War is only a branch of political activity," wrote the master theorist on war, Carl von Clausewitz, a century-and-a-half ago. "It is [political] policy that creates war. Policy is the guiding intelligence and war only the instrument, not vice versa."

Thus if a war is lost other than on the battlefield the place to look for the cause is in political policy. And that is precisely what Norman B. Hannah has done. While others searched for villains and demons on which to blame America's failure, Hannah searched for and found errors in the logic of the "guiding intelligence" that shaped and determined how America fought the Vietnam war.

The result is "The Key to Failure: Laos and the Vietnam War," one of the most incisive and thought-provoking books yet written on the Vietnam war.

Colonel Harry G. Summers, Jr.
Washington, D.C.
June 10, 1987

Author's Preface

A mong the "lessons of Vietnam" the one most often recited—and with reason—is the warning against "graduated military escalation." The problem is to know how and when to apply the lesson. Stated baldly, it gives no criteria or guidance to be used in application. As a result, its value is being progressively dissolved through thoughtless overuse. "No escalation" is becoming a mystic taboo used as a magical incantation requiring no reasoned explanation. Surely, it does not mean that there are no choices to be made between the extremes of turning the other cheek and nuclear obliteration. Choice and judgment in a moderate democracy require the ability to discriminate intelligently between degrees of action.

We all know what we want to avoid. We want to avoid escalation that leads on and on but never to a conclusive result within the limiting parameters set by our objective. "Conclusive" is the operative word. We want to avoid an inconclusive escalation. But how? Here, our Indochina experience does indeed have important lessons. But to extract them, we must immerse ourselves in the "how" of our entanglement in an inconclusive escalation. Our leaders did not set out deliberately to escalate inconclusively. That our entanglement was not a decision but a graduated process in itself is what we must understand. It was a complex process—not a single mistake which can be simply avoided by never taking a graduated step again. To apply the lesson, therefore, is an equally complex process requiring detailed examination of "how" it happened before.

Nor was it simply a military syndrome. In the United States, the military are supposed to take their policy cue from the civilian leadership and, throughout the Indochina war, they did. Military escalation was the handmaiden of civilian conceptual escalation. For this reason, I have used the term "incrementalism" to refer to a conceptual process that formed the common denominator of our decision-making, military and civilian, throughout the war.

What was "incrementalism?" It was the practice of reducing big choices into small incremental bits, each one of which could be taken singly without facing directly the ultimate big decision to which they led. Incrementalism was our standard operating and conceptual process during the war—in political as well as military terms. It ran from the top—the White House—downward, and outward, saturating the whole bureaucratic system, civilian and military. President Kennedy recognized the syndrome in its military, operational form, when speaking of the dangers of sending troops to Vietnam, as Arthur Schlesinger notes:

"The troops will march in; the bands will play; the crowds will cheer; and in four days everyone will have forgotten. Then we will be told we have to send in more troops. It's like taking a drink. The effect wears off, and you have to have another."[1]

But, in its political, conceptual guise, the President found the syndrome less easy to recognize and, indeed, succumbed to it himself. In 1961, he wisely decided to try to neutralize Laos and accepted Averell Harriman's judgment that if the Communists accepted neutralization, "they would have committed themselves to block the use of Laos against South Vietnam." Yet, eighteen months later, in early 1963, he had been incrementally brought to agree that Communist re-partition of Laos—which permitted continued invasion of South Vietnam through Laos—could, in the interest of the United States, be the basis of a "tacit agreement" between us.

But—logically—if the first decision in 1961 to neutralize Laos was in our interest, how could its reversal in 1963 be also in our interest? It could happen only through the alchemy of "incrementalism"—the conceptual syndrome of which graduated military escalation was a latter-stage, operational symptom. To shed some light on this process is my purpose.

I mean to focus on the "how" of incrementalism—the "why" is beyond the scope of this effort. To do this I have tried to present strategy in the process of gestation rather than an autopsy of a final decision. The final decision was never made—it just "growed"—like Topsy. At the same time, I have tried to present the process of "incrementalism" alongside—parallel, as it were—a different concept of our Indochina war, an opposed view which was fertilized by reaction to the official view. The object is not to prove the validity of the opposite proposal but to illuminate the process of incrementalism by contrasting it with the process of decisive choice. This process accounts for the organization and style of this book. It also accounts for a large amount of repetition. Incrementalism is essentially a repetitive process, and in the course of a twelve-year war the process became dismally repetitive.

This book is not a history of the whole drama of the American war in Indochina. Its focus is on the formulation and application of our strategic premise of counter-insurgency and on the gestation of an alternative strategy of territorial defense, similar to that which Col. Harry Summers had advanced in his book *On Strategy: A Critical Analysis of the Vietnam War*,[2] and which Stanley Karnow has scorned as an "autopsy" in his *Vietnam: A History*.[3] This period is covered in Chapters 1 through 18.

Chapter 19 is a reflection as seen during the Tet Offensive intermission. Except for the accident of a change of administration in America, that would have been the end of this book—although not necessarily of the war—because it would have been the end of any possibility of changing strategy.

The impending advent of a new administration, however, did provide one more chance to shift from a losing counter-insurgency to a strategy of territorial defense. Chapter 20 advances an outline of how that chance might have been realized in 1969 by a new strategy based on the fact that Laos—no neutral buffer—had been partitioned so that its eastern sector had become a strategic extension of North Vietnam. Chapter 21 describes how this chance was lost in the Cambodia incursion of May 1970 and in the political reaction in the U.S. From here on, the end was inevitable. Vietnamization would have worked had there been a barrier across southern Laos. The U.S. withdrew under cover of the Paris Treaty—no better than the failed Geneva Accords—and under cover of President Nixon's promise to intervene, if necessary. Watergate ended that.

I never served in Indochina. I made five visits of a couple of days each during the years of 1964 to 1970. Nevertheless, since January 1945, during a brief and uneventful sally by a U.S. Navy Task Force (of which my ship was a part) into the South China Sea between the Philippines and Vietnam, when Indochina first rose above my horizon of consciousness, it never completely disappeared. I remember a 1946 graduate course on Southeast Asia at the University of Minnesota. One of the early Southeast Asia scholars in America, Dr. Lennox Mills, described, in mocking good nature, the preposterousness of the demand for independence of a thin ribbon of South China Sea coast inhabited by people "quite unready for self-government." Indochina rose somewhat higher on my horizon during 5 1/2 years in Foreign Service posts in Shanghai and Bangkok from 1947 to 1953.

By the time of the Geneva Conference of 1954 which partitioned Vietnam I was in the Middle East at the beginning of a seven-year sabbatical from the Far East, a period which coincided roughly with the seven-year gap between the end of France's Indochina war in 1954 and the beginning of America's Indochina war in 1961. I had no measurable influence on the course of the war. Nevertheless, from 1962 onward the war was with me as Deputy Director of Southeast Asian Affairs in the Department of State, as Political Advisor to the Commander-in-Chief, Pacific (CINCPAC) in Hawaii, as Deputy Chief of Mission at the U.S. Embassy in Bangkok and finally as diplomat-in-residence at Haverford College, 1970 to 1971, in the wake of the Cambodia incursion. It still is with me.

I have a point of view to advance about how and why we failed and how we might have succeeded. I believed then (and still believe) that it was possible to discern the strategy being followed by North Vietnam and its allies, to estimate their prospects of success, to devise an American limited war strategy of containment that would have preserved South Vietnam's independence (and that of Cambodia as well as much of Laos). I believe it was also possible to make an early decision either to execute that strategy or, alternatively, to avoid involvement on a losing course. Many will disagree. I am accustomed to that. I do not expect now to convince those whom I failed to convince before. But I do believe that exposition of a strategic point of view thus far little examined could contribute to the rational discussion of the war and assist us to uncover our errors—not some presumed, fated sins.

Every American old enough to listen to the radio news on December 7, 1941, remembers where he was when he learned of the Japanese attack on Pearl Harbor. If, today, we could say the same regarding the beginning of our war in Indochina then we would have succeeded and South Vietnam would today still be an independent country, even as South Korea is. But North Vietnam's political and military strategists deserve great credit for managing to insinuate their invasion of South Vietnam in such a way that we—too cleverly trying to beat them on their own terms instead of ours—too subtly insinuated ourselves into the war so very gradually that we don't know ourselves when it started. One of the elements in understanding the war is to understand its structure well enough to know when we got into it. I date the beginning in 1961—more precisely, in the month of October. The reasons for this will emerge.

I have deliberately used extracts from some of my own memoranda written at the time. I have done so not to prove their rightness but to illuminate the process of incrementalism. I have my own perspective on the war which I have summarized in the Prologue and Chapter I. I believed Indochina was important and that South Vietnam should be insulated against North Vietnam's aggression. But learning the lessons of incrementalism does not depend on acceptance of this view. Others believed that Indochina was relatively unimportant to the

United States, that South Vietnam was not worthy of our defense and that we should never have appeared in Indochina in a military role. Although I disagree, I respect this point of view. We would have been far better off had we deliberately chosen one view or the other as our operating premise rather than doing what we actually did do— that is, incrementally split the difference between defending South Vietnam and not defending it.

"Once to every man and nation comes the moment to decide," wrote James Russell Lowell in his 1844 poem, "The Present Crisis." In Indochina, the United States missed this moment.

Prologue:
The Toreador's Cape

"In South Vietnam we responded mainly to Hanoi's simulated insurgency rather than to its real, but controlled, aggression—as a bull charges the toreador's cape, not the toreador."

"The Great Strategic Error," *National Review*, June 20, 1975.

The United States did not lose a war in Indochina. American forces consistently defeated North Vietnamese forces in South Vietnam. Our forces withdrew in an orderly planned process, completed two years before Hanoi launched its final aggression in 1975. When the U.S. withdrawal was completed there was no indigenous insurgency. The Vietcong were impotent—a contemptible parasite dependent on North Vietnam which quickly destroyed them as soon as its conquest of South Vietnam was complete. South Vietnam's political structure had been stabilized and its armed forces re-equipped and trained. A peace treaty had been signed.

So what went wrong? What happened was that when the U.S. departed, North Vietnam remained in position—contrary to the freshly signed treaty—to resume the attack when possible. South Vietnam was outflanked for 700 miles by North Vietnamese forces—regular and irregular—positioned in southern Laos and eastern Cambodia as well as in the adjacent mountains of South Vietnam. These were the forces which, two years later, would suddenly assault South Vietnam from their bases in Laos and Cambodia as well as directly from North Vietnam. They were forces of the same North Vietnam that launched the Tet Offensive of 1968—a military setback for Hanoi but a domestic political disaster for the United States—a disaster that triggered the beginning of the long U.S. withdrawal.

How was it possible to retire undefeated and lose totally the objective for which we fought? Although the process was vastly complex, the essential answer is quite simple. The U.S. won the wrong war by expending its effort against the wrong target. Confronted with a real aggression through Laos and a largely simulated insurgency inside South Vietnam, the United States built its strategy around the latter. Even though the war against the simulated insurgency was substantially won, the aggression which fed it continued. The aggression advanced from North Vietnam through Laos and Cambodia into South Vietnam where it emerged in the tactical guise of an indigenous insurgency.

On the recommendation of Averell Harriman, President Kennedy decided to negotiate with the Soviet Union to neutralize Laos. Behind the resultant protective screen of a neutralized Laos, we would then deal with the symptoms of insurgency within South Vietnam. Harriman articulated this strategy succinctly as early as October 1961, just a month after he had obtained a Soviet promise to ensure that Hanoi would comply with the neutralization of Laos—including the withdrawal of North Vietnamese forces from that country. Arguing that neutralization of Laos would help to solve the Vietnam problem, Harriman cabled the President on October 26 as follows:

"If agreement reached, both Soviets and [Premier] Souvanna have committed themselves to block use of Laos territory against South Vietnam, for what that may accomplish. Regardless of other considerations, I continue to feel that the South Vietnam problem can best be solved *in South Vietnam* rather than trying to find the solution by military action in Laos. . . . Introduction of forces into South Vietnam would not be as dangerous or without terminus."[1] (Emphasis added.)

Accordingly, the United States proceeded to develop two separate strategies for Laos and South Vietnam—rather than one integrated strategy for Indochina. The strategy for Laos was to neutralize it and thereby avoid the commitment of ground forces there. The strategy for South Vietnam was periodic injections of whatever resources were necessary, including—in due course—U.S. ground forces, to defeat what masqueraded as an internal insurgency. The two strategies became incompatible when the Communist side—with the Soviet Union's connivance—reneged on compliance with the agreed neutralization of Laos and instead converted eastern Laos into the route for invasion of South Vietnam. At this point, the United States should have formulated a new strategy based on the new set of facts. There were two choices—either to block the invasion through Laos or avoid commitment in South Vietnam. The U.S. chose neither.

Instead, the United States behaved like a bull confronted by a toreador bearing the usual two weapons—a sword with which eventually to dispatch the bull and a cape with which to distract and tire it. North Vietnam was the toreador whose sword—the controlled invasion over the Ho Chi Minh Trail through Laos—was concealed behind his red cape—the simulated insurgency in South Vietnam. Just as a bull is unable to grasp the operative linkage between the toreador's sword and cape, so the U.S. was never able to grasp the operative linkage between the real aggression through Laos and the simulated insurgency in South Vietnam. Or, if it grasped the linkage (as some did) it was unable to devise and apply an integrated strategy based on it. So, like a bull, the U.S. continued to charge the cape and made occasional demonstrative but ineffective feints at the toreador— carefully avoiding any chance to knock the sword from his other hand.

This was the theme of an article I wrote for *National Review* in the wake of North Vietnam's final invasion and conquest of Saigon.[2] The theme is distilled in the sentence quoted from the article at the head of this chapter. To extend the metaphor a bit further—gradually the bull wearied and became discouraged. When, in the Tet Offensive of 1968, North Vietnam, the toreador, charged with the Ho Chi Minh Trail sword, the bull knocked him on the ground. As the toreador picked himself up, still holding his sword, the world of spectators, led by the media, shouted, "Olé!" At times the bull fought fiercely and mauled the toreador severely, but always carefully avoided either goring him or knocking the sword from his hand. Because the bull's owners gradually pulled him out of the ring by 1973, neither the toreador nor the bull had an opportunity to administer the *coup de grace* in 1975, but an army of North Vietnamese toreadors and picadors proceeded to occupy the ring—Laos, Cambodia, and South Vietnam. And the world thundered, "OLÉ!"

The toreador's cape metaphor has been used by two historian-analysts of our Indochina war—one did so favorably, the other scornfully. In 1982, the U.S. Army's Col. Harry G. Summers used it (with appropriate attribution) to illustrate the origin of our Indochina disaster in the following paragraph:

> We could have taken the tactical offensive to isolate the battlefield. But, instead of orienting on North Vietnam—the source of war—we turned our attention to the symptom—the guerrilla war in the south. Our new "strategy" of counter-insurgency blinded us to the fact that the guerrilla war was tactical and not strategic. It was a kind of economy of force operation on the part of North Vietnam to buy time and wear down superior U.S. military forces. . . . "In South Vietnam we responded . . . as a bull charges the toreador's cape, not the toreador".[3]

More recently, the same figure of speech appeared in Stanley Karnow's comprehensive history, *Vietnam: A History*. Karnow picked it up from Summers, whose argument he summarizes fairly but dis-approvingly as follows:

> The basic mistake made by U.S. planners was to have focused on chasing Vietcong guerrillas, who were deployed to grind down the American forces until big North Vietnamese units were ready to launch major operations. In other words, the Americans exhausted themselves in a costly, futile counter-insurgency effort, "like a bull charging the toreador's cape rather than the toreador."[4]

Karnow discards this along with other theories on the origin of the U.S. failure. "Re-appraisals of wars," he says, "tend to be a litany of 'what-might-have-beens' which profit from the acuity of hind-sight, and the Vietnam experience is no exception."[5] Why Karnow, essaying the role of historian, casually discounts the value of 'profit from the acuity of hindsight' is curious. One would have thought that taking advantage of hindsight was a principal merit of history—unless perhaps, it reveals unwelcome lessons. "But," Karnow goes on, "such autopsies are academic exercises, like war games." This, however does not stop him from volunteering his own autopsy which is that the fanatically devoted and committed North Vietnamese were pre-pared to fight longer than the United States and to accept greater losses.

He is right in suggesting that the U.S. grossly underestimated Com-munist determination and endurance. But he fails to go on to probe the more important question: Why were the determination and en-durance of the United States relatively weaker? How important was Indochina to the United States? "Vital" according to one view. "Mar-ginal" according to another. The former was the position of the U.S. Government. But the actions of the Kennedy Administration—which shaped our policy—did not support its strong forensic posture. The operative criterion applied to the selection of measures in Indochina was that any proposed course not foreclose the possibility for the United States to "keep its options open" including the flexibility to withdraw gracefully at any moment. This criterion however, is not one of a vital interest, but one of marginality. When applied con-stantly, it will inexorably reduce any objective to marginality. The ironic fact that the United States gradually committed a ground force of over half a million men underlines the tragedy of a strategy which lost nearly 60,000 lives "to keep our options open."

I believed that Indochina was vital to the long range stability of Southeast Asia which is on India's flank, controls the sea-lanes through which 90% of Japan's oil passes, dominates U.S. access to the Indian

Ocean from the Pacific and is an important source of agricultural and mineral surpluses. More than that, it is the home of 400 million people of some of the oldest civilizations of the world. I believed that the definition of a clear geographic line of demarcation between the Communist and non-Communist worlds in Southeast Asia would be the logical and necessary conclusion of the strategy of containment which we had followed since World War II in order to restrain Soviet-sponsored Communist expansion. Since 1946, a rough perimeter between Communist and non-Communist worlds had been stitched—running from the Baltic Sea to Burma and from the Korean 38th parallel to the Vietnamese 17th parallel. Our object should have been, I thought, to deny Laos to the Communists. From my point of view, Indochina was vital, and worthy of a decisive effort.

The opposing view held that Vietnam was of marginal importance in an area which was of marginal importance to the U.S., whose interests were seen as being tied to those of Europe and Japan. I shall not repeat the arguments of this school of thought with which I disagree. It was a serious view and—if valid—should have required no U.S. military commitment at all, but instead needed only dexterous use of diplomacy and political maneuver. There was a case to be made for this choice, but the United States did not consciously choose it. Ironically, the political shape of the course the U.S. actually followed was better suited to this concept—the concept of marginality—than it was to the concept of a vital interest—as the result demonstrated.

Instead, the United States "opted" to describe South Vietnam as vital but not to block its invasion through Laos, thereby "keeping its options open." But it was impossible to defeat North Vietnam decisively in South Vietnam without stopping the invasion. As a result, U.S. determination eroded as the casualties mounted and the prospect of success receded. It was the paradigm of our disaster in Indochina— *the inability to choose.* Americans do not lack determination—or endurance, as the records of our fighting men and prisoners of war demonstrated. America did lack a strategy which could convert its efforts into decisive achievement. The determination and endurance of Americans were wasted—leaked through the sieve of a strategy of marginality.

A real choice between those two real alternatives should have emerged from a judgment as to South Vietnam's importance to us and a judgment as to the nature of the problem. If South Vietnam was not of critical importance to the U.S. *or* if the trouble there was *primarily* of an internal origin, then we should have stayed out. If South Vietnam was of vital importance *and* if the trouble was primarily of external origin, then we had sound ground to intervene against the *external* threat—*provided* that having looked ahead we were both able and determined to make our intervention decisive, prepared to meet all contingencies.

Either course—to stay out or intervene (and I favored the latter)—would have been better than the one we followed. If we had intervened on this basis we could have secured the independence of South Vietnam, Cambodia and much of Laos from North Vietnam's domination. If we had stayed out we could have avoided the large human, economic and political losses. There is sound argument for expending human and material substance to gain an important objective. There is no argument for expending great human and material substance and also losing the objective.

This book is an attempt to grasp and explain the way of thinking which underlay the drama of our disaster in Indochina.

Book I

The Establishment of the Facade

1

Two Plays—In One and Two Acts

"You can't tell the players without a program"

Everyone knows (or should know) that after World War II there were two Indochina wars. The first was a French one from 1946 to 1954 in which France sought to pacify a former colony, failed and departed in 1954. This French war is not my subject. The second war was an American one, from 1961 to 1975* in which the United States came to the aid of an independent ally. This American war is the subject of this book.

It is important to maintain the distinction between these two different wars. Failure to do so was part of our problem. Our leaders seemed sometimes confused as to whether to strike out on a distinctive American strategy suited to the defense of an ally or whether to do a better job than the French did at defeating an insurgency.

The First (French) Play—in One Act, (1945–1954)

The confusion appears in the habit of treating the French and American wars as Acts I and II of a single drama in which Ho Chi Minh, leading a Communist-dominated, but genuine independence uprising, defeated first the French and then the Americans. In fact, how-

---

*I date the end of the American war in 1975 because, even though our forces were withdrawn in 1973, and the Paris Accords had been signed, the structural relationship of the parties remained the same until 1975, when North Vietnam destroyed it with the conquest of Saigon.

ever, there were two quite separate dramas with different casts and different plots. The fact that some Vietnamese faces appear in both should not have confused us. From Hanoi's point of view it was useful—and quite effective—to simulate the first play (the French one) in the second (American) one. Some of the American directors allowed this deception to induce them to use and try to improve some of the old French scores, librettos and stage notes.

The first (French) drama was a one-act play, conceptually simpler than the second. France, the 100-year colonial ruler of Indochina, sought to reassert the rule it had lost during the Japanese occupation. To do this, France had to suppress an internal independence uprising (or insurgency) led by the Communist-controlled Vietminh under Ho Chi Minh whose imperial objectives included Cambodia and Laos as well as all of Vietnam. Ho's Vietminh waged a masterful insurgency— with some support from China after 1950. The French fought bravely but, in the end, withdrew in the face of the burdens and disadvantages which usually attend an attempt by a 20th century foreign power to suppress a popular independence uprising in a distant land. In 1954, both sides agreed to end the war with French withdrawal, partition of the country along a 17th parallel truce line and Vietminh withdrawal from the South. A nine-nation conference of Communist and non-Communist nations meeting at Geneva legitimized the partition (subject to possible later reunification) with some pieces of paper called the Geneva Accords of 1954. These documents recorded the promise of the signatories to observe the terms and specifically, not to move arms or forces in violation of the integrity of either North or South Vietnam, or of Cambodia or of Laos—where dissident forces (Pathet Lao) controlled by North Vietnam were supposed to reunify with the forces of the Lao Government. An International Control Commission composed of India, Poland and Canada was created to enforce the terms of the agreements.

North Vietnam anticipated that a combination of woes in the South, coupled with agitation by several thousand of their own subversive cadres left behind (illegally), would cause the rapid disintegration of South Vietnam which would then be quickly reabsorbed by the North— perhaps behind the curtain of a plebiscite. Distrusting Hanoi, South Vietnam refused to participate in elections without international supervision. Hanoi rejected such supervision. Reunification did not occur and, during the years 1954 to 1959, South Vietnam achieved a considerable degree of cohesion, making greater economic and social progress than did the North. Accordingly, Hanoi embarked on a progressive program to destabilize and take over South Vietnam, first by subversion, then by terrorism and eventually, by incremental invasion.

In May, 1959, Hanoi created Group 559 to enlarge and develop the infiltration trails to the South.* In 1961, North Vietnam decided to open still bigger routes further to the west in Laos and Cambodia. During this period, the United States provided economic assistance and military equipment and training which were generally increased in response to the intensifying North Vietnamese campaign.

This is the way things stood as the curtain rose on the second drama. Note how the players had changed. France was gone. What had been a Vietminh independence uprising against colonial rule had become the recognized government of a territorial state, protected by international guarantees and owing obedience to international obligations, including the Geneva Accords of 1954. This was an independent state— the Democratic Republic of Vietnam—one among many states, equal but not superior in status to the Republic of Vietnam in the south. True, much of the leadership of North Vietnam was the same as the leadership of the old Vietminh uprising against France but now they were no longer leaders of an internal insurgency. They had become the responsible leaders of a state.

Similarly, South Vietnam in 1961 was an internationally recognized state with just as full a claim to sovereign statehood as North Vietnam. Some South Vietnamese officials, both military and civilian, had served with the French, some had not, some had been with the Vietminh and many had fled from the Vietminh in the North. But, whatever their former roles, they were in 1961 occupying new roles as participants in an independent state.

I know—it is said that the partition was intended to be only temporary. The same could be said for the partitions of Korea and Germany. It is said that reunification of the whole Vietnamese nation was intended at Geneva, that South Vietnam refused to participate in plebiscitary elections in 1956. On the other hand, it can also be said that Hanoi never withdrew all its military forces from Laos in 1954, that Hanoi left a large clandestine, subversive apparatus in South Vietnam, that the North failed to cooperate with the International Control Commission in facilitating execution of the Geneva Accords. But none of these things changed the fact that both North and South were separate, independent, juridically-based, internationally recognized states. Neither of them was France or a Vietminh insurgency—the main characters of the first play.

Hanoi, of course, did not intend that the partition would last. The whole Communist world did not so intend—the Soviet Union, Com-

---

*General Vo Bam, of North Vietnam, who was given this assignment, confirmed on French TV, February 16, 1984, that some 20,000 cadres moved along this route in the early years. (*The Economist* Feb. 25, 1984)

munist China, Poland and their allies and sycophants. The United States did not sign the Geneva Accords, nor did South Vietnam for lack of a provision for international supervision of elections. But the United States accepted the partition of Vietnam, as established by the Accords, and agreed not to seek to overturn them. Partition, therefore, became the basis of our relations with Indochina and we were legally obliged to plan our relations and our strategy on that basis—not on the basis of some covert, contrary scheme which the Communist side secreted behind the facade of the 1954 Geneva Accords. Having accepted the new drama, we could have played it out within its own structure and according to its own script, not backsliding into the plot, scores or librettos of the old Franco-Vietminh drama. Or, alternatively, we could have stayed at home. Either would have been better than what we did do.

The Second (American) Play—in Two Acts (1961–1975)

What we did, in fact, was to enter on the stage without a clear-cut role in mind. Sometimes we declaimed in the role of the United States coming to the aid of a small, threatened independent ally. At other times we acted in an updated analogue of the French role in the first drama. At such times we talked of pacifying an internal insurgency, or reforming and encadring the South Vietnamese administrative structure, of "winning the hearts and minds of the people." As a new player in a new drama we needed a distinct role which could have been to hold back North Vietnam while South Vietnam coped with its internal problems—ending up with a Korea-like result.

There were two acts in the drama of the American war in Indochina. The first ran from 1961 to our militarily successful but politically disastrous defeat of Hanoi's Tet Offensive in January 1968. During this seven-year period American policy and strategy in Indochina were premised on the neutralization of Laos as negotiated by Averell Harriman. After the Tet Offensive it was no longer possible for the Administration to continue fighting the war on the old, failed escalatory scale. So, there ensued a parenthetical space of nearly a year during which the bombing of North Vietnam was first reduced and then ended. President Johnson withdrew from the presidential campaign. Harriman attended talks with the North Vietnamese in Paris. He finally agreed on the shape of a table which obfuscated the fact that, despite U.S. public protestations, the Vietcong were elevated to a status equal to the Republic of South Vietnam. During this intermission, the essential structure of the war did not change—based on the hypothetical premise that Laos was neutralized. But the script which had led us gradually into war was rewritten to lead us gradually out.

The second act, beginning in January 1969, included three scenes. First, there was Nixon's execution of a costly, strategic fighting withdrawal while trying (vainly as it turned out) to leave South Vietnam in a position to hold its own. Second, was a miscarried attempt to shift strategy in the 1970 Cambodia incursion. Finally, the third scene was Watergate, the numbing effect of which paralyzed the United States and encouraged Hanoi to accelerate its final attack in 1975.

2

The Bay of Pigs and Indochina

"The right deed for the wrong reason"

T.S. Eliot, *Murder in the Cathedral*

What had Cuba to do with Indochina? In a sense, the pattern of our failure in Indochina was set at the Bay of Pigs. Containment was a territorial strategy designed to restrain Soviet expansion into contiguous areas. But territorial restraint cannot prevent the Soviet Union and its advance men from "stealing" control of an internal upheaval in some distant country.

This is what happened to the Cuban revolution. Once the revolution had succeeded, Castro and his cohorts publicly—even proudly—announced what they had until then secreted—that contrary to the pure nationalist, reformist image they had cultivated, they had been Communists all along. Castro then proceeded, with the help of Russia, to fix a rigid, totalitarian Communist framework on his country which became an outpost of the Soviet Union 90 miles off the shore of Florida. This was a revolution literally "stolen" behind a screen of ambiguity, from the people in whose name it was made. Despite many important differences, this theft of power through contrived ambiguity was an early harbinger of the ambiguity by which North Vietnam disguised its assault on South Vietnam as an "insurgency."

What is the meaning of containment in such a case? If Soviet-supported Communists extend their power by theft over new territories does the strategy of containment reserve to the West the right to seek to restore the frontier of territorial containment? This would be active containment on the offensive. Or, does containment mean that any expansion of Communist-held territory, once completed, automatically creates a new *status quo* which becomes the new contracted frontier of containment? This would be passive, or purely defensive, containment which, in the long run, would make real containment impossible.

What was the United States to do? Both the Eisenhower and Kennedy Administrations believed that the U.S. was not bound to accept any Communist expansion as a one-way *fait accompli*. But, how to oppose without risking a widening war? Both Administrations opted to compete with the Communists on their own terms, i.e., by irregular warfare. As the Eisenhower Administration waned, it took two initiatives. It began to train and support anti-Communist Cubans who were organized to launch a counter-Communist guerrilla action in the hope of sparking a large-scale uprising. It also began to plan something called "counter-insurgency" to oppose increasing Communist guerrilla warfare supported by North Vietnam in South Vietnam. But the Eisenhower Administration ended before either concept had been developed and made ready for action. The Kennedy Administration developed these initiatives into significant parts of the New Frontier posture.

Although the two initiatives bore certain superficial similarities, they were fundamentally different. The plan for Cuba was an example of "offensive containment" designed to launch *a counter-Communist insurgency* in Cuba against a Communist regime that had stolen power. The concept for Vietnam was an example of "defensive containment" designed to *counter a Communist insurgency* already launched by North Vietnam against South Vietnam. The conceptual difference between the two concepts was as wide as the verbal difference was narrow. The plan in Vietnam was to *hold* the existing frontier of containment against a campaign by North Vietnam (supported by the USSR) to advance the frontier to include all of Indochina. The plan in Cuba was to *restore* the frontier of containment to the position occupied before the Cuban Communists (with Soviet connivance) stole the revolution.

And why not? Why, after all, should insurgency be the exclusive weapon of the Communists? Why could not insurgencies arise in Communist countries—say, for example, in the Moslem subject nations of the Soviet empire in Asia? These insurgencies the Free World could support in the same way that the Soviets, as Khrushchev had frankly told us only a few months earlier (January 6), would support insurgencies which he called "wars of national liberation," in countries beyond the Iron Curtain perimeter.[1]

For one brief shining moment in mid-April 1961, as anti-Castro insurgents landed at the Bay of Pigs, the New Frontier seemed to have earned its sobriquet. Then came the quick humiliating collapse. As my friend, Douglas Blaufarb, put it, the Bay of Pigs failed "to reverse the roles with the U.S., striking through a controlled indigenous force."[2] Quickly, after the Bay of Pigs, the focus of counterinsurgency narrowed to Vietnam where it did not mean supporting an insurgency against Leninist totalitarianism in North Vietnam, but defending, at enormous disadvantage, against Hanoi's attack on South Vietnam masquerading as an insurgency. So much for offensive containment!

Meanwhile, containment was being sorely tested in Laos which stretched along the western borders of North Vietnam and the northern portion of South Vietnam. In that remote, sparsely populated, undeveloped kingdom both state and society were torn by a three-way struggle between an ineffective, military-dominated right wing, a Communist left wing dependent on North Vietnamese army support and a semi-covert Soviet airlift of arms and, finally, a relatively weak neutral center in danger of being squeezed to death. Against this backdrop the events in Cuba took on a special meaning.

The disaster at the Bay of Pigs bent our initial steps with respect to Laos and South Vietnam in opposite directions. Having occurred only 100 miles from Florida, the failure in Cuba made it impossible for the Kennedy Administration to consider telling the American people they must undertake commitments 10,000 miles away—specifically in Laos, where, as detailed in Chapter 5, a major crisis was building. But, at the same time, the same Bay of Pigs disaster created a political need for Kennedy to compensate by demonstrating American vigor. How? By undertaking to oppose Communist expansion in South Vietnam. Imagine! Undertaking to protect a farm and undertaking to leave the gate untended!

The Bay of Pigs reflected a deadly combination of bold, imaginative tactics and thoughtless, short-sighted strategy. President Kennedy forthrightly shouldered the burden of the failure and then went on to set the stage for a similar error in Indochina. From the day after the Bay of Pigs disaster our course in Indochina began to be shaped to meet the Administration's need to offset public alarm, to bolster public confidence and to refurbish its own image, rather than to meet the strategic challenge of Indochina.

No one, however, deliberately intended events to work out that way. But, although the relation between our Bay of Pigs defeat and our Indochina strategy, set in 1961 and 1962, was not planned, it emerged dramatically from the events. How sharp the reversal precipitated in the Kennedy Administration's attitude toward Laos was is revealed by reference to the stirring clarion call to its collective defense, drafted for the Department of State on March 26, 1961 less than a month before the Bay of Pigs. In preparation for possible reference of the Laos question to the United Nations, and anticipating a Soviet veto, Under-Secretary of State Bowles asked the new Director of USIA, Edward R. Murrow, to begin drafting a U.S. statement to the Security Council. These words should be borne in mind when reading what follows them:

> We have sought nothing more and nothing less than to insure the independence, integrity and neutrality of Laos. . . . We will not permit that this small and peaceful nation shall be simultaneously talked to death at the conference table while forces, armed, commanded and nourished from abroad continue to chew their way through the jungle.
>
> If we flinch or falter in the face of tyranny in the jungle—if we regard Laos as a small nation of which we know little, then other small nations on other continents will face that same tyranny.
>
> Laos is either a dam or a floodgate. If we fail to hold the dam . . . if the forces of freedom falter here . . . the forces of tyranny will continue to press outward. . . . Whatever happens in Laos today may happen elsewhere tomorrow.
>
> We stand today upon a great pinnacle of history.
>
> We refuse to conclude that "things are in the saddle and ride mankind."[3]

Here, now, is the record of key Kennedy Administration participants in policy on both Cuba and Indochina. The connection between the two was recognized weeks before the Cuba adventure took place. Professor Schlesinger, Kennedy historian who, as Special Assistant to the President, attended Cabinet meetings on the planning of the Bay of Pigs operation has stated, "If we did in the end have to send American troops to fight communism on the other side of the world, we could hardly ignore communism ninety miles off Florida. Laos and Cuba were tied up with each other, although it was hard to know how one would affect the other."[4]

How the Bay of Pigs would affect the Laos problem (not the reverse) quickly became clear after the disaster in Cuba. Schlesinger reports his conclusion that "The Bay of Pigs finally destroyed any possibility of military intervention in Laos."[5]

He goes on to quote from a Robert Kennedy memo written two months after the Bay of Pigs. The President's brother wrote, "I don't think there is any question that if it hadn't been for Cuba, we would have sent troops into Laos. We probably would have had them destroyed. Jack has said so himself."[6]

The same thought was expressed directly by the President to Special Counsel Theodore Sorenson in September, 1961: "Thank God", Sorenson quotes the President, "the Bay of Pigs happened when it did. Otherwise, we'd be in Laos by now and that would be a hundred times worse."[7]

But if the President was glad the Bay of Pigs had precluded the United States' involvement in Laos at that time, it followed that perhaps the Soviets would perceive the interrelationship as well and detect the weakness behind it. So, to offset such a Soviet inference, the President started on the day after the Bay of Pigs to cast a bolder image. Speaking to the Society of Newspaper Editors on April 20, the President, chastened by criticism of his failure to use the Air Force to support the Cuba landing, warned that "We face a relentless struggle in every corner of the globe that goes far beyond the clash of armies, or even nuclear armaments. The armies are there. But they serve primarily as the shield behind which subversion, infiltration, and a host of other tactics steadily advance, picking off vulnerable areas one by one in situations that do not permit our own armed intervention. . . . We dare not fail to grasp the new concepts, the new tools, the new sense of urgency we will need to combat it— whether in Cuba or South Vietnam."[8]

On the same day he set a one-week deadline on completion of his Administration's first program of aid to Vietnam. A special annex was added to the program to offset the effects of the Laos decisions, including U.S. support for two new divisions in the South Vietnamese Army.

Moreover, on April 20, he ordered American military advisors in Laos to don their uniforms in place of the mufti they had been wearing. As reported by Roger Hilsman, a key advisor on Southeast Asia, "It seemed possible that the Communists might see his decision on Cuba as irresolution. Fearful of this, the President decided on at least a token introduction of American forces as a signal and he instructed the American military advisors in Laos to take off their civilian clothes, put on uniforms and quite openly accompany the Royal (Laos) Army's battalions."[9]

About a week later, as Vice President Johnson prepared for an official visit to Saigon, Kennedy authorized him, if necessary to allay President Diem's concern about Laos, to raise the possibility of a bilateral U.S.-Vietnamese treaty and even the stationing of U.S. forces in South Vietnam. In short, the President was ready to commit the United States to South Vietnam to offset his inability to act in Laos because of the Bay of Pigs debacle. Although the Vice President used this authority, Diem was not ready for such actions.

In this way did Cuba lead to Laos and Laos to South Vietnam in the shaping of our posture. In Laos, we avoided a commitment while in South Vietnam we embraced commitment to project a compensatory image of toughness. But what was actually happening was clear to an old hand Far East journalist such as Keyes Beech who wrote in *The Saturday Evening Post*: "What the President is engaged in is a tactical retreat under cover of a show of American strength, which may save face but will not save Laos."[10]

The point is not to argue in favor of a U.S. military entry into Laos at that time, which would have been entry into a political snakepit rather than an effort to stop the slow invasion of South Vietnam. The point is that the Administration's tactics grew out of a need to compensate for the Cuba debacle rather than out of a considered Indochina strategy.

Today, we may forget just how deeply the Kennedy Administration's confidence in its image, both at home and abroad, had been hurt. Secretary of State Rusk, then in Geneva trying to get the 14-nation conference on Laos started, cabled Washington his concern that "Neutrals . . . may abandon their neutrality if they believe we will shy away from confronting Soviet power when the chips are down. . . . The unfortunate Cuban episode has had far more effect on us in Washington than upon anyone else in the world. Our present task seems to me to be to shake off that affair and get on with our great central tasks."[11]

But we didn't shake it off. The Bay of Pigs continued to shake and shape the Administration's policy toward Indochina.

The post-Cuba image cultivated by the Administration was a low profile in Laos and a high profile in South Vietnam. Always a political realist, President Kennedy told John Kenneth Galbraith, "There are limits to the number of defeats I can defend in one twelve-month period. I've had the Bay of Pigs and pulling out of Laos and I can't accept a third."[12]

The obvious place to make a show of standing firm was South Vietnam.

Does this sound like too pat a formula? Down in Laos and up in South Vietnam? Well, just to put a fine point on it, Professor Schlesinger reports that "The President now made a *de facto* deal with the national security establishment; if it went along with neutralization in Laos, he would do something for resistance in South Vietnam."[13]

In this "deal" is the basic formula of our Indochina strategy from 1961 onwards—and the recipe for our ultimate failure. Two days after the Bay of Pigs disaster President Kennedy ordered an investigation of what went wrong. To head the inquiry, he recalled from retirement former Army Chief of Staff, General Maxwell Taylor, who then went on to become Chairman of the Joint Chiefs of Staff and later, Ambassador to South Vietnam.

I was in Kabul, Afghanistan, in April 1961 at the time of the Bay of Pigs fiasco. Nearly a year later, still in Kabul, I experienced a kind of cosmic irony in receiving a homespun lesson in *machtpolitik* from —of all people—the Indian Ambassador, a lesson worth all the Bay of Pigs post-mortems. Speaking in tones of reproof in cocktail conversation, the Ambassador criticized the Bay of Pigs action. Thinking he was criticizing the United States on moral grounds (as is the wont of some Indians) I reminded him of the hostility and subversion emanating from Castro's Cuba. I alluded also to India's recent sudden and unprovoked attack on Goa, which it quickly absorbed. But I was wrong. He did indeed question the justifiability of our action but that was not his main point. He assured me that he understood that nations sometimes must act unilaterally in their own interest even as India did when it seized Goa. What he found most unacceptable was our inconstancy. To start something important in our own security interest—something with international impact—and then not finish it was irresponsible. To reverse course because of world opinion or a bad press is not becoming to a Great Power embarked on protecting its own interests and it is destabilizing.

India was condemned around the world for taking Goa but pressed on in its own interest. Now, Goa is forgotten.* The Bay of Pigs cannot be forgotten. I do not recall the Ambassador's words but his meaning was that to behave in such an irresolute manner opened the United States to criticism from all sides and introduced an element of uncertainty into the equations of world politics. Amen.**

One could say that Indochina was lost at the Bay of Pigs. Of course that would be a bit of retrospective, not to say simplistic, impressionism. Ironically, there were powerful reasons, quite apart from the Bay of Pigs, to do what Kennedy did—that is, to avoid commitment in Laos at that time and to move toward commitment in South Vietnam—*provisionally*. Why provisionally? To gain time to test the value

---

*Indeed, on November 27, 1983, twenty-two years after India seized Goa, the Commonwealth nations met in Goa and solemnly issued the Goa Declaration which expressed alarm over the vulnerability of small states to external attack.

**A similar point was made to me by the Afghan Foreign Minister when I handed him a U.S. note replying to Afghanistan's protest against Eisenhower's announcement of Francis Gary Powers' U-2 flight which overflew Afghanistan. "All governments, including my own," he lectured me, "must carry out special operations in secrecy but it is absolutely unacceptable to announce openly the violation of Afghan sovereignty." Moral: If something must be done, do it, finish it and keep quiet. Don't parade one's good intentions as the cloak for failure.

of the Soviet Union's expressed willingness to neutralize Laos. The result of this test became known by the end of 1962—total failure. For the Communist side, neutralization of Laos was a screen for *de facto* partition which, in turn, became the screen for a slow invasion of South Vietnam.

3

Insurgency: What's in a Name?

Tsze-lu said, "The ruler of Wei has been waiting for you in order with you to administer the government. What will you consider the first thing to be done?"

The Master replied, "What is necessary is to rectify names."

"So, indeed!" said Tsze-lu. . . . Why must there be such rectification?"

The Master said, "If names be not correct, language is not in accordance with the truth of things. If language be not in accord with the truth of things, affairs cannot be carried on to success."

Analects of Confucius—No. 13 (III)

If the Bay of Pigs was the first impetus to the shaping of our Indochina strategy, the new doctrine of counter-insurgency was the second. If the U.S. was to balance its shyness in Laos with vigor in South Vietnam it would have to have a concept and a strategy on which to base its effort. The concept was that the problem in South Vietnam was primarily of indigenous origin, an insurgency abetted by infiltration from the North. The strategy for action was to become "counter-insurgency." The secondary infiltration factor was to be handled by the neutralization of Laos. What was urgently needed was a doctrine of "counter-insurgency."

"Insurgency" was a word with a respectable history. But what was "counter-insurgency"—a word barely heard before the winter of 1960–1961? In March, 1955, the Eisenhower Administration had instructed missions abroad to report on possibilities for U.S. assistance to police-type forces to deal with "Communist subversion" and, in immediately threatened countries, to the armed forces to deal with "Communist insurrection." Then, in the winter of 1960–1961, a program was being

ARNULFO L. OLIVEIRA MEMORIAL LIBRARY
1825 MAY STREET
BROWNSVILLE, TEXAS 78520

prepared which was called the "Counter-Insurgency Plan for Vietnam." Kennedy signed this plan one week after coming to office. But this was only the beginning. With New Frontier vigor he charged into the White House, demanding, "What are we doing about guerrilla war?" On the day after the Bay of the Pigs disaster he demanded an urgent program for South Vietnam. He got it.

Very quickly, counter-insurgency became the familiar logogram of the new Administration in the underdeveloped world from Vietnam to Afghanistan. By the summer of 1961, our Embassy in Kabul—where I was Deputy Chief of Mission—like others in developing countries, was hip-deep in a flood of instructions, questionnaires and interpretations and exhortations concerning counter-insurgency. Suddenly, not just Laos, South Vietnam and the Congo, but three fourths of the world had been blanketed under an American doctrine which was supposed to cope with incipient insurgency wherever its symptoms appeared. This included Afghanistan which had no insurgency but had an unmatched historical record of waging insurgency against external interlopers.

One of the official papers circulated in this period gave the approved official definitions. They are worth repeating because they foreshadow the shape of American strategy in Indochina:

> Insurgency—A condition resulting from a revolt or insurrection
> against a constituted government which falls short of civil war.
> In the current context, subversive insurgency is primarily
> Communist inspired, supported or exploited.
> Counter-insurgency—Those military, paramilitary, political,
> economic, psychological and civic actions taken by a
> government to defeat subversive insurgency.[1]

These are not definitions. This is spilled glue. What is wrong? Too many words meaning too many things. A definition should be simple. It would have been enough to define insurgency as, "an internal revolt against a constituted government." The insurgency is the revolt itself, not the widely varying conditions resulting from it. And why should it be assumed that a "subversive insurgency" must be "primarily Communist-inspired"? In Indochina itself in 1961, the very focus of our counter-insurgency doctrine, the most genuine insurgency was not of the Communist Vietcong against Saigon but of the anti-Communist Meo tribes in northern Laos against interloping North Vietnamese.

Another question. Where is the cut-off line at which an insurgency becomes a civil war? Is insurgency only a benchmark on a linear scale of violence? Or is the criterion of an insurgency simply the use of indirection and guerrilla tactics—regardless of who the parties are? Might not the word "insurgency" be better defined in terms of the structural relationship between the parties? When President Lincoln, in his second Inaugural Address, just a month before Appomattox, described the Confederates as "insurgents" was he revealing an appalling insensitivity to the unparalleled level of violence in our Civil War? Or was he perceptively reflecting the actual structural relationship between the parties? From a different angle, is a military campaign controlled, directed and often waged by outside forces against a separate state, a true insurgency at any level violence?

As for counter-insurgency, the approved definition encompasses virtually all of life and society. Pandora's box is open and out comes the whole "revolution of modernism" in the southern part of the world. All those adjectives elaborating the definition of counter-insurgency—"military, paramilitary, political, economic, psychological and civic"! This definition of "counter-insurgency" caused those U.S. embassies, in Kabul and elsewhere during the early 1960s to cast most of their programs artificially into the framework (and vocabulary) of "counter-insurgency" in order to get attention in Washington. Walt Rostow, then Chairman of the Policy Planning Council in the State Department, laid the framework clearly in words circulated to Foreign Service Posts around the world—including Kabul, where I first read them:

> To understand this problem [revolutionary war and guerrilla war] however, one must begin with the great revolutionary process that is going forward in the southern half of the world; for the guerrilla warfare problem in these regions is a product of the revolutionary process and the Communist effort and intent to exploit it.
>
> What is happening throughout Latin America, Africa, the Middle East and Asia is this: old societies are changing their ways in order to create and maintain a national personality on the world scene. . . . This process is truly revolutionary. It touches every aspect of the traditional life: economic, social and political. The introduction of modern technology brings about not merely new methods of production but a new style of family life, new links between the villages and the cities, the beginnings of national politics, and a new relationship to the world outside.[2]

Perhaps it was natural in the wake of the Bay of Pigs to concede "insurgency" as a Communist monopoly. But throughout the literature of counter-insurgency, Communism and insurgency are treated as symbiotic, if not organically related forces which can only be understood together. Rostow, indeed, said that, "Communism is best understood as a disease of the transition to modernization."[3] But, as the case of Afghanistan has demonstrated—twenty years later—an insurgency in an underdeveloped country can be virulently anti-Communist and anti-Russian. And, ironically, even as our counter-insurgency doctrine was being developed, the only valid insurgency in Indochina was that of the Meo in Laos against North Vietnamese invasion. And, even in South Vietnam, Hanoi finally had to throw off the disguise to conquer in 1975.

Fascination with irregular tactics and the calibration of levels of violence was endemic throughout the literature of counter-insurgency. To say that insurgency "falls short of civil war," reflected a widespread tendency in the early 1960s to generalize about kinds and levels of conflict as if they were all mere benchmarks on a linear scale of violence.* The scale was eventually stretched from barbed wire around a hamlet to heavy bombing of North Vietnam and a vast American fleet patrolling the coast. In a most important article of this period, entitled "Internal Defense and the Foreign Service," Deputy Under-Secretary of State, U. Alexis Johnson identified the problem as: "all forms of Communist-inspired indirect aggression, from subversion up through the spectrum of violence to outright insurgency and guerrilla warfare."[4]

Or, as Dr. Ralph Sanders, then of the Industrial College of the Armed Forces, had it, "Insurgency then represents a band in a spectrum of actions against constituted government, its distinguishing feature being the degree of physical violence."[5]

Also in 1962, President Kennedy told the graduating class at West Point, "This is another type of war, new in its intensity, old in its origins—war by guerrillas, subversives, insurgents, assassins; war by ambush instead of by combat; by infiltration instead of aggression, seeking victory by eroding and exhausting the enemy instead of engaging him. . . . It requires in those situations where we must encounter it . . . a whole new kind of strategy."[6]

These are important tactical questions but they are subsidiary to making a determination as to the strategic nature of a war. What is the generic structure of the war in which one is involved? Who are the sides? What are their respective objectives? What are their struc-

---

*For example, speaking of Laos in 1961, the editors of the *Pentagon Papers* remarked that, "since the war in Laos had moved *beyond* the insurgency stage, Vietnam was the only place where the Administration faced a well developed Communist effort—with an externally aided pro-communist insurgency." (Emphasis added) Reflecting the outlook of 1961, the editors failed to note the far more genuine insurgency by the Meo tribes.

tural relationships? Does the war arise essentially from within the body politic? Or does it originate from an external force outside the nation? If both elements are present they must be identified and distinguished, their relative weights measured and relationships mastered. These are not mere shades along a graduated spectrum. Priorities must be established—the order in which things must be done. First, the internal and then the external? Or vice versa? And is either possible without the other?

All military tactics and methods may have their uses in war, whether of an internal or external origin, but the first problem is to know what kind of war it is. Col. Harry G. Summers, in his seminal study, "On strategy: the Vietnam War in Context," quotes Clausewitz as follows: "The first, the supreme, the most far-reaching act of judgment that the statesman and commander have to make is to establish . . . the kind of war on which they are embarking; neither mistaking it for, nor trying to turn it into, something that is alien to its nature. This is the first of all strategic questions and the most comprehensive."[7]

Words are important. They are the tools of understanding. Wrong words lead to wrong thought. In South Vietnam, our doctrine, our definitions and our vocabulary focused our attention on matching the enemy's tactics of fighting rather than on whether the enemy came from Hanoi or from inside South Vietnam. This made it virtually impossible for us to make the supreme judgment which Clausewitz enjoined—"to establish the kind of war on which [we were] embarking."

We did not use the names "insurgency" and "counter-insurgency" correctly and our language was not in accordance with the truth of things—as Confucius had enjoined. And since our language was not in accord with the truth of things, our affairs in Indochina could not be carried to success.

One could say that Indochina was lost in the semantical crevice between "insurgency" and "conquest."

4

Something Other Than War

"An interesting example of one type of gambit in the politics of Washington policy-making."

Roger Hilsman, *To Move a Nation*

What was needed next was a way to solve the problem created by the use of the different words "insurgency" and "conquest." Subtly, it materialized in the form of what could be called "semantical incrementalism."

At the center of the problem was the Kennedy Administration's inability to resolve the following dilemma: opposite views of what was happening in Indochina.

Was it *essentially* a genuine internal insurgency against local grievances (aided on the side by sympathizers from North Vietnam)?

Or was it *essentially* a determined, though disguised, campaign of conquest by North Vietnam (which benefitted incidentally from elements of local ferment in the South)?

The Kennedy Administration never definitely accepted either premise nor did it successfully integrate the two. Instead, it often seemed to embrace both. The President continually received conflicting advice. Hilsman reports that, in the State Department "we fully agreed . . . that Vietnam was a political problem of winning the allegiance of the people rather than a military problem of killing Vietcong."[1]

On the other hand, General Earle Wheeler (later Army Chief of Staff and Chairman of the Joint Chiefs of Staff) said on November 7, 1962:

"Despite the fact that the conflict is conducted as guerrilla warfare it is nonetheless a military action. . . . It is fashionable in some quarters to say that the problems of Southeast Asia are political and economic rather than military. I do not agree. The essence of the problem in Vietnam is military."[2]

Not surprisingly the President's view of the war oscillated! Sometimes it appeared to him to be primarily a political issue as, at the November 15, 1961 meeting of the National Security Council, when he described the problem as "being more of a political issue, of different magnitude and . . . less defined than the Korean War."[3] He postponed action on a proposal to send ground forces to South Vietnam but did send two helicopter companies, the precursors of our eventual half-million man force.

Just a month later, on December 14, he wrote President Diem "the campaign of force and terror now being waged against your people and Government is supported and directed from the outside by the authorities at Hanoi."[4]

This was rapidly followed, in the President's State of the Union message of January 1962, by the flat statement that: "The systematic aggression now bleeding the country is not a 'war of liberation'—for Vietnam is already free. It is a war of attempted subjugation—and it will be resisted."[5]

And a year later, in the January 1963 State of the Union address, he told the Congress that "the spear point of aggression has been blunted."[6]

Still he was haunted by the "civil war" concept of the problem and, shortly before his death, in November 1963, he was so uncertain of the nature of the problem that he told his aide, Michael Forrestal, to "start a complete and very profound review of how we got into this country, what we thought we were doing and what we now think we can do . . ., I even want to think about whether or not we should be there."[7]

What did he believe? Aggression or civil war? Probably the best explanation is given by Roger Hilsman who, first as Director of Intelligence and Research in the Department of State and then as Assistant Secretary of State for the Far East, served Kennedy from the beginning of his term until his death. He writes that the "President preferred to treat the problem of Vietnam as something other than war."[8]

But what? Hilsman doesn't say nor does he explain how anyone— even a President of the United States—can make such judgments on the basis of preference rather than of the facts. This is the paradigmatic essence of "semantical incrementalism."

The same syndrome underlay Kennedy's thinking on Laos. Thus, at lunch with the President and Walter Lippman on March 20, 1961, Schlesinger heard JFK think aloud "that he hoped to steer the course between intervention and retreat and end up somehow with neutralization."[9]

In ordinary politics one can sometimes pursue compromise middle courses, but when war is one of the possible choices or prospects, the gray shadings must give way to definite choice. In this case, however, definite choice was finessed. Instead, the President adopted the practice of making small incremental decisions which were sufficient to meet the immediate need but did not, of themselves, involve strategic judgments from which it might be difficult to withdraw later. "Semantical incrementalism" was at the root of military "graduated response." The two made their Indochina debut on April 20, 1961, the day after the Bay of Pigs, when Kennedy ordered American military advisors in Laos to don their uniforms as a show of resolution which we had not reached.

Commenting on Kennedy's performance during the spring and summer of 1961, the editors of *The Pentagon Papers* remark that "Someone or other is frequently promoting the idea of sending U.S. combat units. Kennedy never makes a clear-cut decision but in some way or other, action is always deferred. . . . In general, we seem to be seeing here a pattern that first began to emerge in the handling of the Task Force Report and which will be even more strikingly evident in the President's handling of the Taylor Report."[10]

At the President's direction in October 1961, General Maxwell Taylor and Presidential Assistant, Walt Rostow made an extensive tour and intensive study in South Vietnam. In his report, Taylor recommended various internal reforms plus more aid to Saigon's counterinsurgency effort in the form of military advisors and squadrons of specially equipped, slow-flying U.S. Air Force aircraft suitable for small-scale guerrilla warfare. He also recommended sending some 6–8,000 U.S. ground forces,[11] a figure which later grew to over 10,000 as reported by Robert Hilsman who interprets the mission of such a force to be "to hold the ring against invasion from the north by regular North Vietnamese divisions and to man the northern borders against infiltrators while the South Vietnamese dealt with the guerrillas in the rear."[12]*

What did the President do? First, in the NSC meeting of November 15, he revealed again how deeply the Bay of Pigs disaster had con-

---

*In this one sentence Hilsman pithily summarized a plausible strategy which was rarely discussed throughout the remainder of the war.

ditioned his thinking about Indochina. He wondered aloud how he "could justify the proposed courses of action while at the same time ignoring Cuba."[13] Then, he went on to approve the additional military advisors and aircraft but postponed a decision on the commitment of ground forces. Whatever the intrinsic merits of this incomplete action, its greater importance was as a precursor of the Vietnam decision-making style. This emerges in Hilsman's description of it as "an interesting example of one type of gambit in the politics of Washington policy-making . . . [by avoiding] a direct 'no' to the proposal for introducing troops to Vietnam. He merely let the decision slide, at the same time ordering the government to set in motion all the preparatory steps for introducing troops."[14]

In this manner, the President avoided choosing between two contradictory estimates of the problem, made a partial decision and "kept his options open."

But did he? The net result was to increase our input into Vietnam without making a definitive difference, thereby simply ensuring a future need for more—the route of escalation without decision.

To be sure, there are occasions—and this may have seemed to be one of them—when it is wise to postpone decisive action until ready to act decisively. For example, in this case Kennedy might have deferred action and ordered a thorough study of whether and how U.S. forces might be employed, in what numbers and to achieve what objective. He might have raised the basic question: What kind of war are we really dealing with? What should be our basic premise? Should it be that the problem arises *primarily* from an internal uprising or *primarily* from an externally launched campaign of conquest? Is Vietnam the right place to get committed? But this is not what Kennedy did. Instead, until his death in November 1963, he oscillated between the two premises of war and insurgency. What Hilsman called a "gambit in the policy-making" became the standard *modus operandi* of our Indochina strategy.

Having escalated the numbers of American military advisors from 685 to 16,732 by incrementalism, Kennedy still had not faced up to the real issues, and shortly before this death, he gave his aide, Michael Forrestal, 100-1 odds that the U.S. could not win.[15] One wonders what he believed we were doing in Vietnam. Whatever it was, he could not change his policy until after his anticipated re-election a year hence.[16] As Arthur Schlesinger aptly points out, "Of course, he should have asked the searching questions long before. He should have realized the cumulative momentum of the policy of small concessions."[17]

Not surprisingly, the ambivalence spread throughout the Government, becoming a burden from which we were never completely relieved. The schizoid torment seeped outward and downward, affecting judgment at all levels. General Wheeler, Chairman of the Joint Chiefs of Staff argued that "the essence of the problem is military," but his recommendations were ambiguous. The President's Special Representative, Averell Harriman, as well as Assistant Secretary Hilsman and White House aide, Michael Forrestal, saw the problem as one of the civil war rather than external aggression. But Harriman himself was ambivalent. In May 1962, in the course of defining the logic of neutralizing Laos, he found it useful to argue that "It is necessary that the North Vietnamese stop their armed aggression." Thus, in *The New York Times Magazine* of May 27, 1962, Harriman even more specifically emphasized the external nature of the threat to South Vietnam:

> Both . . . Vietnam and Laos were faced with the clear and present danger of being overwhelmed by the Communists—the first by subversion and the second by direct military action. Despite the difference in the nature of the threat, *its source and strength were identical*. In Vietnam it was VC guerrillas, controlled and directed from North Vietnam who constituted the real heart of the immediate threat to the Republic and *not the local recruits* or disaffected villagers. In Laos, it was the Vietminh—Communist forces from North Vietnam operating with Russian support—and not merely the local Pathet Lao." (Emphasis added.)[18]

Yet, notwithstanding this clear attribution of the threat to military action by North Vietnam, in both Laos and South Vietnam, Harriman had, in October 1961, recommended to President Kennedy that the South Vietnam problem could best be solved in South Vietnam rather than by trying to find the solution by military action in Laos. No wonder President Kennedy was ambivalent!

Also ambiguously, the President's military advisor, General Taylor, was a supporter of and contributor to counter-insurgency doctrine in Vietnam, but in 1961 he had recommended deployment of some 8,000 American forces.

The pervasiveness of this ambivalence was not as apparent in the early 1960s as it is today. But with the voluminous evidence now available, it would be possible to go on layering examples of the never-resolved dichotomy between the aggression and insurgency theories—a choice consistently evaded. Roger Hilsman blames the ambivalence on "the pluralism of the American government," differences between the military and civilian agencies and the American mission's lack "of any clear line of authority and command that could control and coordinate the representatives of the often rival American departments and agencies. . . . [The] result was frustration for the advocates of both the 'military' and the 'political' approaches."[19]

There is some descriptive but little explanatory truth in this. It is misleading to load responsibility onto an amorphous sociological generality like "pluralism" or onto the Mission in Saigon when the needed line of authority and command existed and led directly from the White House as President Kennedy had spelled out in his letter of May 29, 1961 to all missions abroad. Indeed, the White House was itself the seat of ambiguity and conceptual pluralism.*

Here was the flaw—the conceptual flaw—at the very seat of power. The flaw was not in the concept of counter-insurgency itself, but in its use of this *language* to sublimate the failure of the high-level decision-making process. This was doubly unfortunate because a well-honed doctrine of insurgency and counter-insurgency should be a key element in America's kitbag. But even the best counter-insurgency doctrine and performance cannot do that which it was not designed to do—defeat an aggression. It is not the fault of American counter-insurgency doctrine that the concept was carelessly misapplied to an aggression it was not designed to meet.

The conceptual distance that, in 1961, separated the real threat in Vietnam from a common-sense "insurgency" can be measured by looking ahead from 1962 to the distance by which the concept was later stretched to encompass the actual measures carried out under its mantle. These included division-sized ground engagements, thick air cover and armed reconnaissance, heavy bombing by B-52s which "saw" their targets only as coordinates on a grid, daily strikes from aircraft carriers, naval patrols of the whole coast and amphibious landings. It included the fighting forces of several countries under a single command and under the umbrella of the Manila Pact (SEATO) and was often justified by reference to the Geneva Accords of 1954 and 1962.

Counter-insurgency! I recall attending an extraordinary night-time meeting in February, 1965, in the Command Center at CINCPAC Headquarters in Hawaii. I recall it particularly vividly because some

---

*It is true, as Gen. Bruce Palmer has argued in, *The 25-year War*, that under the Defense Reorganization Act of 1958, the Secretary of Defense was inserted into the chain of command between the President and the JCS (Joint Chiefs of Staff). But the President retained the constitutional power—which he used when he chose—to deal directly with the U.S. military or civilian authorities in South Vietnam.[20]

of us were in black tie, having been summoned there by Admiral Sharp from a dinner-dance in response to a message from the White House. The subject was air attacks to be made on Dong Hoi in North Vietnam in reprisal for an enemy attack on a U.S. military camp at Pleiku. The decision to make the strikes had already been made in Washington, the first result of McGeorge Bundy's recommendation for reprisals to be followed by sustained air assault on North Vietnam—known as "Rolling Thunder." As Political Advisor to the Commander-in-Chief, my only contribution to the meeting was a suggestion that as we were now obviously leaving the realm of counter-insurgency and entering the arena of conventional warfare, we should start thinking and planning our strategy and operations on that basis. Admiral Sharp's answer was to the effect that "No, we will make strikes like these but we will go on fighting a counter-insurgency."

And, indeed, we did go on *talking* of counter-insurgency and trying to cast our operations within the vocabulary of counter-insurgency long after the term had lost any relevance to South Vietnam. As late as the heavy bombings of Christmas 1972 we were still talking of "counter-insurgency."

Some insurgency! Some counter-insurgency!

One could say that Indochina was lost in the semantical limbo of a gambit called "Something other than war."

5

Out of the Jungle to Geneva

"We have Khrushchev's word he will work to establish Laos as a neutral similar to Austria."

W. Averell Harriman—Bangkok, May 5, 1961.

The Kennedy Administration was new and, in Laos at least, had not been bequeathed a workable strategy by the previous administration, but mankind has difficulty learning from history. The Department of State was at least trying when it expressed concern over Soviet intentions toward the ICC. For seven years, under the 1954 Geneva Accords in Vietnam, Hanoi's virtual paralysis of the ICC had made it impossible for the Commission to function in North Vietnam. Poland had used its veto in the Commission to stymie enforcement and the Soviet Union had provided public and diplomatic cover for both Poland and North Vietnam—not to mention the Pathet Lao. So, when an ICC-supervised cease-fire in Laos had been proposed late in 1960, it was no surprise that the USSR made a cease-fire contingent on firm agreement to a new Conference—thereby setting up a "cross-ruff" bridge game in which the cease-fire and conference could be alternately held hostage to each other. This procedure is what the Chinese Communists call "fight-talk, fight-talk." The U.S. at first demanded "an immediate cease-fire as an essential prerequisite for the successful execution of other proposals." This, the Russians summarily rejected, and by classic fight-talk methods, stalled the conference until we were worn down in May 1961.

One can sympathize with Secretary Rusk's poignant lament to British Foreign Minister, Lord Home, on April 15:

The long delay which has ensued with much talk of cease-fire is making them [our Laotian friends] even less effective militarily than usual. . . .

It is true that there are no major battles being waged, but in at least three rather critical areas the Communist build-up continues.

There is the matter of the Russian airlift. Although the President and I have been careful to discount publicly the increase in supply, it is a fact that in the recent few days a significant increase has been observed. . . .

With respect to the Russian response [to the crease-fire proposal], we find little encouragement leading us to believe that they have any intention of giving an early satisfactory reply. While delaying their answer, they make offhand remarks about the cease-fire being held off until the conference convenes. . . .

It should be remembered that when we agreed to the formula of the cease-fire and conference to begin with, we placed great emphasis on an immediate cease-fire. Weeks have gone by since we put forward this minimum requirement, and it has been largely ignored while they pursue their activities in Laos. . . ."[1]

Finally, on May 3 the Lao combatants made a vague cease-fire announcement while Secretary Rusk waited in Oslo for ICC verification before proceeding to the conference site in Geneva. Doubtful of prospects for verification and faced by mounting pressure for the opening of a conference, the Department of State concurred with Rusk on May 10 that he should proceed to Geneva "on the assumption that a cease-fire verified by the ICC or *other conditions satisfactory* to us will prevail by May 12."[2] (Emphasis added.)

President Kennedy so instructed him.

Over the next two days, in an exchange of cables, the escape clause "other conditions satisfactory to us" became first "a cease-fire reasonably frozen," then quickly melted down to "further cease-fire progress." Finally, a day later, statements by the Lao combatants, reported but not verified by the ICC, were found by Secretary Rusk "to meet our basic pre-conditions."

Throughout this progressive dilution of our conditions, Washington was not unaware of what was happening. The Department recognized that there was "continued Pathet Lao encroaching" and that the ICC "was rebuffed in its attempt to contact the Pathet Lao." On May 11, the Department cabled Rusk that

Communists obviously attempting to get conference started without formal and verified cease-fire, perhaps in part for purpose of merely making U.S. back down on this point. . . . Most likely they have decided that unformalized and unsupervised cease-fire will enable them continue using implicit threat of further military action during conference.[3]

Nevertheless, gradually, the United States had reduced its minimum conditions to a marginally ineffective and unverified cease-fire, thereby permitting the conference to open on May 16. Why? The United States was leading from weakness. Confronted with two alternatives—military action or negotiations—the side most prepared to continue military action has the advantage. The side most anxious to negotiate is in the weaker position. In 1961, U.S. military intervention was out of the question because of disarray among the non-Communist parties in Laos, because of our own military unpreparedness and because, in the wake of the Bay of Pigs, President Kennedy could not ask Americans to undertake a commitment 10,000 miles away. Hence, the U.S. found negotiations to be not just one alternative, but the only alternative to abandonment. Our strategy was, in Harriman's frequently-used words, "to transfer the Laos problem from the military arena to the political arena."

Sometimes, as in playing bridge, it is necessary to lead from weakness and this appears to have been such a case. But, in such cases, the important thing is to correct the weakness as quickly as possible so that it will be possible to change one's lead in the next play.

To strengthen the U.S. hand in Laos was one of the first tasks of Kennedy's roving Ambassador, Averell Harriman, who was instructed to explore the chances of an agreement. In doing so he visited not only the Soviet Union but our European allies as well as India, Thailand, South Vietnam and Laos. The substance of these explorations was the possibility of a neutral government in Laos, including Communist, anti-Communist and neutral elements—a "troika" in Khrushchev's idiom.* Harriman concluded that if such a government could be formed under Prince Souvanna Phouma, the Soviet Union would favor a neutral Laos.

After the prolonged efforts to arrange a cease-fire the conference opened on May 13, 1961. Then, after fourteen more months of on-and-off negotiations, cease-fire violations, Communist advances and a demonstrative deployment of U.S. Forces to Thailand, coupled with intense diplomatic activity offstage, the three factions in Laos finally agreed on a three-headed regime and a Declaration of Neutrality. The fourteen-nation conference in Geneva recognized the Laos Declaration, agreed on international guarantees of Lao neutrality, including withdrawal of all foreign forces and the establishment of an Inter-

---

*The word "troika" refers to an old-style Russian coach drawn by three horses. The word was adopted as a shorthand description of the three headed (right, left and center) government proposed for Laos.

national Control Commission to monitor implementation of the agreements.

The conference received much attention in countries around the world, all looking, as Secretary Rusk had said they would, to see whether or not the United States "would shy away from confronting Soviet power when the chips are down." The press summaries reported the tough warnings to the Communist side by Harriman and by his deputy, William Sullivan, a colleague who had entered the Foreign Service at the same time I did.

From occasional official summaries of developments it sometimes seemed that Harriman was more troubled by the right wing in Laos than by the Soviets in Geneva. At one point, he cabled the President and Secretary Rusk that "As far as Geneva's contribution to that objective [a peaceful solution] is concerned, it seems almost within our grasp and, as I have said, the most critical decisions are now in Laos."[4]

The difficulty was in making the facts on the ground match the formulae Harriman was weaving in Geneva.

The course of the negotiations was rocky. In May 1962, armed forces were deployed by the U.S. to Thailand in response to a Communist thrust toward the Thai border and as a demonstration of U.S. determination. But the most important aspects were handled in private talks which will be described shortly. If it would work, the concept of neutralization of Laos would impose order on the confused elements of the problem and on the unstructured instincts and inclinations of the new administration. Thus, neutralization and withdrawal of foreign forces from Laos would

(1) Validate Kennedy's political need to avoid a military commitment in Laos after shrinking from one in Cuba.

(2) Provide a buffer terminating infiltration into South Vietnam and relieving the Administration of the threat of North Vietnamese aggression.

(3) Make of South Vietnam a problem of "internal insurgency," an ideal testing ground for the new doctrine of "counter-insurgency."

A neutral Laos thus fit the political requirements of the Kennedy Administration and therefore became the keystone of U.S. strategy in Indochina. Moreover, successful neutralization would keep the U.S. from having to address the following dilemmas:

The politics of Laos (a chaos into which no one would wish to leap). There were

(1) A bumbling, swollen, politically and militarily ineffective right wing faction, primarily situated along the Mekong River lowlands.

(2) A Communist (Pathet Lao) dissident army, aided by Soviet parachute drops, located in the mountains where North Vietnam encadred, disciplined and used it as a facade for Hanoi's forces in Laos.

(3) A much smaller neutralist group whose main asset was a clever, patriotic Prince Souvanna Phouma who later, after overcoming his naiveté about the Pathet Lao (fronted by his half-brother, Prince Souphanouvong), became an accomplished political performer.

(4) A small neutralist army under a sincere but immature Major Kong Le who had defected from the Royal Army and occupied the Plaine des Jarres, a plateau between the right-wing lowlands and the Communist mountainlands.

(5) A still smaller left-wing neutralist (crypto-Communist) formation which had defected from Kong Le to become *de facto* allies of the Communists.

The concept of neutralization of Laos offered a slim chance for Prince Souvanna to blanket this chaos under the banner of "national union."

The military dilemma. However slim the chance of reunification, it was more attractive than the choice offered by the U.S. military at the time. Committed by the Manila Pact of 1954 (SEATO) to defend Thailand against a Communist threat through Laos, the military offered only two choices:

(1) Abandon Laos, with the possibility of having to fight later;

(2) Intervene in the jungled mountains, with no sure route of retreat, in open-ended numbers starting at either 60,000 or 140,000, gamble against Chinese intervention à la Korea, and demand advance commitment to use nuclear weapons if necessary.

Abandonment was unacceptable to President Kennedy and an open-ended intervention in such numbers was impossible, given the depleted state of our ready forces. As reported by Roger Hilsman, the conceptual poverty of our alternatives is suggested by a few of the ideas advanced:

(1) Secretary McNamara suggested arming training planes in Laos to use against advancing Pathet Lao. Secretary Rusk put this idea in its place with a recollection of Korea. "Air power is effective in support of men on the ground but indecisive when used alone."

(2) The military suggested parachuting troops into the Plaine des Jarres, an idea quickly abandoned when it emerged that the dropped forces would be vulnerable to annihilation for five days before the arrival of enough reinforcements to match the enemy and that the possibility of extrication was doubtful.

(3) Occupation, by only some 60,000 U.S. forces, of not only southern Laos but virtually the whole Laotian side of the Mekong River valley, an idea wisely discarded almost immediately, given the political turmoil in Laos at the time.

(4) "Limited responses," that is, enough to "deter aggression" but not enough to cause the Communists to think we had more ambitious motives, were rejected as the route to bloody, interminable jungle war.[5]

With all these unacceptable military options, neutralization understandably offered a welcome alternative course—a political rather than a military one, not Göttedämerung, not abandonment and not an inconclusive quagmire. Or so it seemed.

The Soviet Factor. There was a real need to test the meaning of Khrushchev's doctrine of "peaceful co-existence." As Averell Harriman said in his *New York Times* interview of May, 27, 1962, the Administration's decision "was based upon a willingness to accept Khrushchev's challenge of January 6, 1961 and to see the struggle in Southeast Asia pursued on 'political, social and psychological grounds.' "

Neutralization of Laos would be totally impossible without Soviet cooperation for, as Harriman went on, "it is necessary that the North Vietnamese stop their armed aggression."[6]

Khrushchev had offered us the opportunity to test him out in Laos. It was essential that the attempt be made.

Khrushchev first offered the opportunity of neutralization to Harriman when Kennedy sent the latter abroad as roving Ambassador in the spring of 1961. Harriman cabled Kennedy that Khrushchev had made it plain that he wanted no war over Laos. "After all," the Chairman shot at our Ambassador in Moscow, "Why take risks over Laos? It will fall into our laps like a ripe apple."[7] Presumably, this prophetic statement was discounted as an example of Khrushchev's well-known proclivity for aggressive banter. In any case, Harriman was convinced that the Soviet Union would cooperate in neutralizing Laos. Others in Washington were less sure but, as Roger Hilsman said, long experience "had given Harriman a sure knowledge of the Soviets."[8] Of course, Harriman could make no such judgments of China and North Vietnam about which there was much doubt. Nevertheless, he urged Kennedy to cooperate with the Russians and make sure that the blame for any failure fell on Peking or Hanoi—rather than on us. Indeed, one of the arguments for accepting Soviet assurances was that the Soviets wanted to restrain China. Harriman's judgment carried, as usual. According to Hilsman "By the time the talks began at Geneva, Harriman's advice was the government's decision."[9]

Convinced that there was no misunderstanding of Soviet intentions, Harriman had spelled it out clearly in a press conference in Bangkok on May 5, 1961. As our Embassy reported, Harriman said that he had "Khrushchev's word he will work to establish Laos as neutral similar to Austria, which we consider a very good example from our standpoint because Austria [is a] well-established neutral unhandicapped by interference from anyone."[10]

Finally, during the Kennedy-Khrushchev meeting of June 3–4 in Vienna, the Chairman told the President personally that Laos should not be an issue between them, that the goal was a truly neutral Laos and that he would work toward that goal. In the joint communique, he and Kennedy agreed "on the importance of an effective cease-fire." Although the ragged cease-fire was a continuing source of friction, Khrushchev's assurances continued to be the premise of our dealings with the USSR on Laos.

But it was not until September that the "t's" were crossed and the "i's" dotted on Harriman's understanding with the Soviet Union. The press reports from the conference during this period used tough language. Harriman and Bill Sullivan (later to become Ambassador to Laos) denounced the Communist side for violating the cease-fire, for blocking the conference and for trying to emasculate any measure designed to enforce the agreements.

Meanwhile, Harriman was engaged in serious private talks with the Soviet delegate to the Conference, Deputy Foreign Minister Georgiy Pushkin. Progress in these private talks was slow until mid-September, reports Professor Schlesinger, adding that agreement had been reached on only a few of 33 critical items. Then, there was a breakthrough. Harriman reached understandings with Pushkin covering the following essentials:

(1) Both countries would support a neutral Laos;

(2) "Neutrality" was illustrated by reference to Finland;

(3) The USSR would be responsible for compliance by the Communist side, including North Vietnam and the Pathet Lao. The UK and US would be responsible for the non-Communist side;

(4) The USSR would ensure that Hanoi would observe Lao neutrality to include preventing North Vietnamese use of Laos as a corridor to South Vietnam. Pushkin assured Harriman that North Vietnam was ready to live up to the agreement as were the Pathet Lao;

(5) The USSR would support neutral Laos against any political or military aggression by the Pathet Lao;

(6) The royalist, neutralist and Communist armies of Laos would be consolidated under a neutral government to be formed by Prince Souvanna Phouma;

(7) An International Control Commission (India, Canada and Poland) would monitor and enforce compliance with the agreements. But Pushkin assured Harriman the Soviets would seek to make the agreements so effective that the Commission would have little to do.

In a long, nocturnal, private talk in Pushkin's suite in Rome on September 13, Harriman tied up the package which quickly set the shape of the continuing negotiations at Geneva. Professor Schlesinger has reported a significant sidelight emerging from the Harriman-Pushkin meetings. Referring to the Soviet airlift of arms to the Pathet Lao which began in late 1960, Pushkin told Harriman that "apart from the Second World War, this [Laos] was the highest priority Soviet supply operation since the Revolution."[11]

Meditation on this statement of priorities casts a significant light on the role and importance of Laos to Soviet strategy as well as a measure of Communist determination which was, of course, later demonstrated. It should also be set in contrast to the view of President Kennedy who is quoted by Schlesinger as believing Laos "was not a land 'worthy of engaging the attention of great powers.' "[12]

But how long would the Communists permit a neutral Laos? Some feared it might last less than five years. No problem, thought Pushkin. Laotian neutrality would last much longer than that. In fact, according to one version, Pushkin waggishly forecast that Laos might well be the last country in the world to go Communist. But Harriman, an old hand at Soviet badinage, was equal to the challenge. He complained that Chairman Khrushchev himself had promised that the United States could be the last country to go Communist. Oh, well, was Pushkin's rejoinder, then Laos could be next to last.[13]

What could be better than a neutral Laos? The only thing the Soviets wouldn't agree to do was to recognize the 17th parallel boundary between North and South Vietnam. But, if everything agreed between Pushkin and Harriman were to be implemented, then the external threat to South Vietnam would disappear and any continuing difficulties in the South could be handled in the framework of the new counter-insurgency doctrine. There would be no need to deploy U.S. forces and hence no need to invite the backlash of the Bay of Pigs.

Indeed, this is the essential meaning of what Harriman told President Kennedy a month after his September understanding with Pushkin. In the third week of October, messages reported North Vietnamese violations of the Laos cease-fire and increased infiltration through Laos into South Vietnam, all of which could have triggered proposals for U.S. or even SEATO military reactions. It was at this juncture that Harriman, clearly disturbed by the prospect of a military reaction against infiltration, sent President Kennedy the October 26 cable briefly described in the Prologue and here quoted somewhat more fully: "I fully recognize importance of Laos attached to crisis in South Vietnam. It seems to me, however, that we should drive to conclude the negotiations and get an acceptable Souvanna Government, understanding regarding demobilization of forces and conclusion of Geneva agreement."

So confident was Harriman of the commitments he thought he had received from Pushkin that he went on to assure the President that "If agreement reached, both the Soviets and [Premier] Souvanna have committed themselves to block use of Laos territory against South Vietnam for what that may accomplish."

Having established this point, he went on to urge on the President his own conviction as to the strategy we should follow:

> Regardless of other considerations I continue to feel that the South Vietnam problem can best be solved *in South Vietnam* rather than by trying to find the solution by military action in Laos. I fear that if SEATO forces are introduced in Laos it will be difficult to prevent an extremely dangerous escalation and at best will have forces bogged down indefinitely.
>
> Introduction of forces into South Vietnam *would not be as dangerous or without terminus* and would have the possibility of far more world wide approval.[14] (Emphasis added)

Nowhere is our strategy at the beginning of the war in Indochina more neatly expressed. And two weeks later it had become the premise of a joint recommendation to the President by Secretaries Rusk and McNamara that the U.S. commit itself "to the clear objective of preventing the fall of South Vietnam to Communism." The memorandum recognized that "it will probably not be possible for the Government of Vietnam to win this war as long as the flow of men and supplies from North Vietnam remains unchecked and the guerrillas enjoy a safe sanctuary in neighboring territory."

Accordingly, Rusk and McNamara went on: "We should be prepared to introduce United States combat forces if that should become necessary [or] to strike at the source of the aggression in North Vietnam."

But, three paragraphs later the Secretaries note—as had Harriman—that the introduction of U.S. forces *into Vietnam* would not be so dangerous *after* an agreement neutralizing Laos. Then, after estimating that "there is at least a chance that a settlement can be reached in Laos," they went on to re-state Harriman's basic premise: "The prospective agreement on Laos includes a provision that Laos will not be used as a transit area or as a base for interfering in the affairs of other countries such as South Vietnam. *After* a Laotian settlement, the introduction of United States forces *into Vietnam* could . . . stabilize the position both in Vietnam and in Laos."[15] (Emphasis added.)

The concept of neutralization of Laos had pulled everything together. There would be no need to send forces into Laos. The problem of South Vietnam could be handled internally as Harriman had recommended—i.e., within the framework of the new doctrine of counterinsurgency. If it should become necessary to deploy U.S. forces, they would only be deployed to Vietnam—not to Laos—*behind* the protective screen provided by the Accords on Laos.

Based on Harriman's advice—and in turn on Pushkin's assurances to Harriman—our policy was set. Harriman had found the "political route" between abandonment and war or, to put it in his words, he had "transferred the problem from the military to the political arena."

This idea of containment by negotiation needed to be tried. If it had worked, it would have completed the definition of the territorial boundary between Communist and non-Communist power from the Baltic Sea to the Sea of Japan. It could have become the basis of real detente.

And, if it had worked, we would not have lost Indochina.

Book II ————————————————

The Gordian Knot

6

A Nest of Chinese Boxes

"The rule of three doth puzzle me. And practice drives me mad."

Anon.

As Harriman himself admitted ten years later, containment by negotiation failed in Laos. He might have added that the Soviets never made good on their promises to him to ensure performance by the Communist side.

On my first day at the Department of State after returning from Kabul late in July 1962, it was becoming apparent that the North Vietnamese were not going to withdraw their forces from Laos as prescribed by the Accords. Explanations were already being woven, and theories as to how the United States should react propounded. Not everyone was surprised.

There was the precedent of the North Vietnamese invasion of northern Laos just as I left Thailand in early 1953. It was an invasion never acknowledged or vacated as required by the Geneva Accords of 1954 but it burrowed deep into the flesh of Laos, implanting the Communist Pathet Lao arm of Hanoi's imperial plan for all of Indochina. Well—if Hanoi failed to comply with the Geneva Accords of 1954 why would they comply with those of 1962? If the Pathet Lao had failed to rejoin the Lao Government as prescribed in 1954—why would a coalition work in Laos in 1962?

On the other hand, if the Communists reneged we would be wholly justified and in a good position to launch a new strategy. Harriman had hinted at this in May, 1962. Writing in his *New York Times Magazine* article of current Communist ceasefire violations, he said, "If it signals an intention . . . to return to their previous efforts at military conquest, the bases of our current policy will, of course, have to be re-examined."[1] But would we really do it? As August and September of 1962 wore on and the North Vietnamese made no move to withdraw from Laos or even to acknowledge the authority of the International Control Commission, the atmosphere was turning brittle. The Geneva Accords were being deliberately aborted by total Communist non-compliance.

But, before describing the abortion, let me insert a parenthesis on the Geneva Accords themselves. Just as the force of gravitation defines the shape of a satellite's orbit, so did the Geneva Accords on Laos shape U.S. strategy in Indochina. Never implemented at all, the Accords were quickly turned inside out into their very opposite. It could be said that the neutralization of Laos and negotiation of the Laos Accords was the major strategic decision we made with respect to Indochina from 1961 until we departed in 1973. All else was either geared to it or was incremental, barnacled encrustation. That so little attention is devoted to Laos in studies of the Vietnam war and to the role of the 1962 Geneva Accords is more than an intellectual curiosity. It is a profound enigma. High-powered analyses of the Vietnam war have been written without more than a passing chronological allusion to the Accords on Laos. They are given only glancing notice in the *Pentagon Papers*. Official documents of the time do mention the Accords in relation to North Vietnamese infiltration but infiltration itself is treated as a peripheral operating problem to be dealt with pragmatically rather than as a key part of the whole strategic gravitational system which revolved around the concept—but not the reality—of the Geneva Accords.

It is a major premise of this book that the role of the Laos Accords in our strategy for Indochina—not just for Laos—was comprehensive, ubiquitous, determinative, enduring—and disastrous.

Actually, the Geneva Accords on Laos should be studied in the chancelleries and universities of the world as an extraordinary attempt to translate a theory of power and politics into reality by international relations engineering—and as a resounding failure, rich in lessons. The theory was that in a time of historic ideological conflict, peace and stability could be had by contractually building the ideological opposites into a structure in which they would be kept in regulated balance under the chairmanship of a third "neutral" element.

A question springs to mind. How can true ideological opposites meld, particularly when one side's ideology is dedicated to its own eventual worldwide triumph over all others? They can't, of course, and that lesson, if learned, would make the whole sorry experience worthwhile. But the question was finessed at the time by Khrushchev's supple doctrine that the ideological struggle would continue by other means—on "political, social and psychological grounds," a challenge which, on Harriman's recommendation, the Kennedy Administration accepted.

Thus, history would continue to move and troika neutralization would be a way-station on the road of ideological struggle. Meanwhile, the use of military means would be suspended. Of course, the unstated corollary is that at some time the historical ideological struggle for the World must reach a threshold at which the neutral solution will become outdated and then history may require the struggle to transfer back into a new subversive-military phase. Unless, that is, one happily assumes that the Communists will choose to let it all be decided by true, free self-expression which, if they were so inclined, they could have done anytime since World War II. In any case, troika neutralization provided what the Kennedy Administration wanted in 1961 so desperately—and not unreasonably—an operative mechanism for avoiding military engagement in Laos without abandoning it, or appearing to abandon it.

More of that later. For now, the main thing is to outline the essential structure and content of the Accords, which were put together like a nest of tightly fitting Chinese boxes, all constructed on "the rule of three," each enclosed in the next larger. Working from the center outward, we have:[2]

First—a Declaration of Neutrality by the newly fitted troika government of Laos, agreeing to

- the practice of neutrality;

- no foreign bases or foreign use of Lao territory to interfere in another country;

- no military alliances or protection from SEATO;

- withdrawal of all foreign troops and none to enter.

Second—a Declaration by the Conference, itself an artfully crafted mosaic consisting of the 4 countries of Indochina, as well as Burma and Thailand; then the neutral balancer, India, balanced between two groups of Communist and anti-Communist outside powers, each chosen to fit a special slot. The Declaration committed the signatories to:

- observance of the sovereignty, independence, neutrality, unity and territorial integrity of Laos:

- no threat or use of force;

- no interference in the internal affairs of Laos;

- no use of Lao territory to interfere in the internal affairs of other countries;

- no involvement of Laos in military alliances, and respect for its declared desire to eschew SEATO protection;

- no introduction into Laos of foreign forces in any form;

- no establishment of foreign bases, strong points or military installations of any kind.

Third—a Protocol which created the enforcement organ, called the International Control Commission (ICC), neatly balanced by Canada and Poland on the fulcrum of India which acted as Chairman. The Protocol provided the following:

- withdrawal of foreign forces in 75 days, i.e. by October 7;
  30 days—for Laos to set routes and exit points;
  15 days—for the ICC to get teams into place;
  30 days—for completion of actual withdrawal.

- withdrawal to take place only along designated routes and points with advance notice to the ICC of all withdrawals;

- entry of foreign troops prohibited;

- entry of arms prohibited *except* as needed by the newly unified Royal Government of Laos;

- supervision of the cease-fire by the ICC;

- violations to be reported by the ICC to the Co-Chairmen of the Conference who would assist and supervise compliance;

- possible violations to be investigated by the ICC, it being understood the ICC acts with the concurrence of Laos;

- ICC decision to investigate could be made by majority vote (to obviate a paralyzing Polish veto) and its reports could reflect differences among its members.

Fourth—the institutionalization of the Geneva Co-chairmen, Britain and the USSR, provided the West an opportunity to force issues into the open and the USSR with the opportunity to ensure that nothing happened contrary to its interests. At this level, issues reached the truth of world politics—power, where "the rule of three doth puzzle"—and the troika figure was dropped in favor of the cold reality of bi-polarism.

An amazing structure! Artfully designed and neatly executed, each piece fitting perfectly into place with no gaping joints or ragged edges. Only one thing was missing—glue. Glue in the form of a true meeting of the minds between the Communist and non-Communist sides was totally lacking. The understandings which Harriman had reached with Pushkin were violated the first day and any missed then were violated in the spring of 1963 when the Communist side pulled out of the neutral coalition government and set up a rival government in the Plaine des Jarres.

The facts are clear. What is more interesting—and more important—is the "way of thinking" by which the demolition of the Geneva Accords came to be interpreted in the United States Government as a "tacit agreement" reached by the U.S. and the Communist side— a "tacit agreement" which turned the Geneva Accords inside out, into their opposite, and then became a fundamental premise of the U.S. strategy that failed in Indochina.

7

From Geneva Back to the Jungle

"We must recognize that the North Vietnamese did not keep the Laos Agreement of 1962 for a single day."[1]

W. Averell Harriman, 1971

Governor Harriman was factually right in 1971 when he made the statement quoted above. He would have been historically right if he had said it in the autumn of 1962, chalked it up to experience and profited from it. Instead, we not only accepted what the Communist side had done, we clasped it to our bosom as a "tacit agreement" which we considered we had reached with the Communist side.

Before describing this tortuous process let me say that upon arriving in the Office of Southeast Asia Affairs at this moment I supported the idea of neutralization of Laos. I believed in geographical containment. Three years in Afghanistan, wedged between the Soviet Union and the non-Communist world, neutralized by Anglo-Russian treaty in 1907, had convinced me that landlocked neutral buffers can contribute to geographic containment—and to peace—when their international legal status corresponds to the facts on the ground. And, if in Afghanistan, why not in Laos?

It didn't take long in Washington for me to sense the tension between the facts on the ground in Indochina and the fiction so artfully woven into the Geneva Accords of 1962. Before going on leave in Illinois, I dropped into the Department about the time the Geneva Accords were signed. That had happened on July 23, the day the Department of State cabled Harriman President Kennedy's "very warmest thanks to you personally for all that you have done in these difficult and delicate negotiations."[2]

Exactly thirty-one minutes later the Department cabled Harriman to concert with Britain in setting up the ICC so as "to avoid any arrangement which would permit Soviets block ICC activity desired by West through its control over budgetary and funding process."[3]

To explain its concern, the Department referred to the Soviet Union's "unsatisfactory performance" during the interim operations of the ICC while the Geneva Conference was underway.

By the time I returned to Washington late in August, the leader of the Pathet Lao had announced that his side had no foreign troops to be evacuated! Soon afterward, my boss, Barney Koren, the Office Director, took me to lunch in the eighth floor dining room with Harriman. Having negotiated the Geneva Accords, Harriman was now Assistant Secretary of State for Far Eastern Affairs, in which position Kennedy expected him to demand performance from the Soviet Union on the promises made by Khrushchev and Pushkin. There was much buzzing in the Bureau about how the "Governor" was going to accomplish this. A certain mystique surrounded Harriman. I was told by more than one that Harriman had an extraordinary reputation for tough insistence on the execution of deals made with him. During the negotiations he had been tough on Lao royalist General Phoumi, who sometimes deserved it, and on some U.S. officials who didn't. Now, he would have the opportunity to capitalize on his long experience and vaunted rapport with the Russians in making the Geneva Accords work.

Although lunch was pleasant, I came away with an uneasy feeling. One or two things from that encounter stuck with me. The Governor welcomed me to the Bureau, noting that Barney was badly overburdened with four countries—Laos, Cambodia, Thailand and Burma. (South Vietnam was handled by a separate Working Group directly under the Governor.) He added, pleasantly, that I had come well recommended and he hoped that I would fulfill the promise forecast by John Steeves who had been with Harriman for a time at Geneva and then had been Deputy Assistant Secretary for the Far East. Early in 1962 John had been assigned as Ambassador to Afghanistan where we overlapped for the last four months of my tour as Deputy Chief of Mission. Before I left Kabul we had several talks about Southeast Asia, including Laos, concerning which John had disagreed with Harriman, thus lending a certain irony to Harriman's mention of John's recommendation. Arthur Schlesinger tells the story that one day, "the deputy chief of the Far East Bureau [Steeves] snapped, after reading a Harriman telegram from Geneva, 'Well, I suppose the next one will be signed Pushkin'."[4] Although John does not recall this, the story rings true.

But my uneasiness after this lunch stemmed from something else. My interest in the Foreign Service had always focused on the long tortuous frontier running from the thirty-eighth parallel in Korea to the Baltic Sea, dividing the maritime rimland countries of the non-Communist world and the Communist heartland empires. Along this frontier, Afghanistan seemed to me to have some strategic similarities to Laos because its independence depended on a rough balance between the great powers on opposite sides. There was no need to educate Harriman on this background, but I did remark that our experience in Afghanistan suggested that the key to making buffer neutrality work was ensuring that the powers on opposite sides be nearly enough balanced to make it unprofitable for one side to take advantage. I said that in Afghanistan there was some reason to believe we needed to do more to keep up our side of the equation. I do not recall a single word of Harriman's response but his tone was cool and, I felt, disdainful. The conversation moved on but I came away feeling that Harriman did not favor this kind of strategic view of Laotian neutrality or the comparison to Afghanistan. True, the analogy was not perfect (analogies never are), but I continue to think it was a valid comparison—the more so today, when both countries have been brutalized by their Communist neighbors who were pledged to respect their neutrality.*

Unfortunately, this kind of relative disadvantage afflicted the United States after the Geneva Conference, during the 75-day period prescribed by the Accords for the withdrawal of foreign military personnel.** Nevertheless, the Department of State, recalling the experience

---

*I made the same comparison a few months later in a talk to the Asia Society in New York, where it was better received. "Peaceful coexistence," I contended, "could bring balance only as long as there is an actual equilibrium of effort in the competition. This imposes a burden on the Free World to hold up its side in the competition . . . Afghanistan and Laos have something in common. Implicit in the 1962 Geneva Agreements on Laos is the idea that a unified, neutralized Laos would act as a buffer . . . In fact the country has not been unified . . . and far from being a classical buffer against conflict, Laos is an arena in which the competition is being carried on in microcosm." Published in *Asia*, Autumn ed., 1964.

**I do not forget that in May 1962, responding to a Pathet Lao lunge toward the Thai border, we sought to rectify our disadvantage by deploying ground and air forces to Thailand. The effect was to encourage the Communists to halt their advance and to strengthen our hand somewhat in the Geneva

continued on page 52

of being diddled by the Communist side as the Geneva Conference opened, struggled against a repetition as the Conference ended in the summer of 1962. The confrontation came quickly and the United States blinked.

The issue was the Communist total failure to comply with the very first requirement of the Geneva Accords—the withdrawal of all foreign military personnel—without which the neutralization of Laos would become a charade. The fact that North Vietnam did not withdraw is well known. What is at least as important and more interesting is the manner in which the United States rationalized this total perversion of the Accords just signed.

It started like this. Under the Accords, 75 days were allowed, that is until October 7, for the withdrawal of all foreign military personnel from Laos. The Lao Government was required, within 30 days, or by August 22, to designate exit checkpoints through which the ICC could monitor withdrawals. Checkpoints were required in each of the three political sectors—right, left and center. But, three weeks after the signing of the Accords no checkpoints had been named and the neutral government of Prince Souvanna Phouma was squirming in the toils of the built-in "troika." The Communist wing of the regime insisted that since they had no foreign military personnel there was no need for either ICC inspection or checkpoints in their area.* In response, the right wing threatened to designate no checkpoints for the exit of American military advisors.

continued from page 51
bargaining on treaty terms. With the signature of the treaty however, the bargaining value of these forces was largely dissipated, being overtaken by the political necessity for the United States to implement the treaty and by the resultant Thai desire for their removal. Indeed, so strong was the pressure to induce the successful implementation of the Accords (or the appearance thereof) that our relative position was even worse than before the Accords were signed when it was credible that we might walk out of Geneva.

*Perhaps this is what Pushkin had in mind when he assured Harriman that the USSR intended to make compliance so effective that the ICC would have little to do. In any case we were amply warned in advance of the danger of making ICC operations subject to approval in advance by all 3 factions of the "troika" Lao Government. Deputy Under-Secretary U. Alexis Johnson reports, in his book, *Right Hand of Power* that late in October, 1961 (just after Harriman had reached his private understanding with Pushkin) the issue became the subject of contention. Johnson, "having unhappy memories of the way North Korea and North Vietnam had hamstrung their international supervisors, wanted us to hold out for inspection provisions with more teeth." In a 3-way telephone conversation between Johnson and Kennedy (both in
continued on page 53

Souphanouvong had said on July 24 (to a British journalist) that the withdrawal would be conducted "in strict conformity" with the Agreements, "taking into account all existing objective difficulties.[6] It soon transpired that the principal "objective difficulty" was the "fact", as reported in the August 17 Cabinet meeting by Souphanouvong, that his Pathet Lao had no foreign troops requiring evacuation under the Geneva Accords! Asked to permit an investigation to establish the facts, Souphanouvong "replied there was no need for investigation since there were no troops in the [Pathet Lao] area."[7]

Then, the royalist leader, General Phoumi spoke up in Cabinet, disputing Souphanouvong and unequivocally asserting the well-known fact that there were many North Vietnamese military forces, Chinese advisors and Soviet pilots. If the Communist side would not name checkpoints then neither would the royalist side. He concluded, as reported by our Embassy in Vientiane, saying that "this question should be considered closed. He said the Geneva Accords [requirement] concerning withdrawal foreign troops within 75 days could not be implemented and that therefore the Geneva Accords are essentially worthless . . . He said it would be better if the three groups separated and began fighting as before."[8]

Phoumi's logic was impeccable, whatever may be said of his politics. The non-withdrawal of foreign forces made both unification and neutralization of Laos impossible and, with the ICC emasculated, the Geneva Accords were a hollow shell. But, as Phoumi knew, that was not a conclusion that the United States was prepared to allow—on the record at least.

The very next day, August 18, Harriman cleared out of the Department of State a cable expostulating that "Failure to provide checkpoints for Vietminh withdrawal borders on fantastic and we find it incomprehensible that at eleventh hour no checkpoints have been determined and none intended for Vietminh." The cable went on to instruct Ambassador Leonard Unger in Vientiane how to deal with this impasse. As for the Communist side, Harriman told Unger to

continued from page 52
the White House) and Harriman (in Geneva), on November 1, "Averell declared his judgment that we could not get a better deal and that to hold out would tie down or break up the conference . . . . The President told Averell to proceed." Johnson comments that Kennedy respected Harriman's advice and may "also have thought that he had reached an understanding with Khrushchev on Laos at their Vienna summit meeting, so that it was not necessary to spell things out in too great detail."[5] He might have added that Harriman probably also thought his understanding with Pushkin had the same effect.

argue that "If, as other side alleges, there are no Vietminh [North Vietnamese] in Pathet Lao territory, then they should welcome fullest ICC inspection; objection to inspection could only give world opinion every reason to believe Vietminh are present."[9]

This oft-repeated argument might be called the "victorious truth syndrome." It assumes the self-enforceability of truth once exposed to the world. From this it is concluded that the exposure of Communist perfidy and non-Communist fidelity to both truth and law will some-how wither the Communists and exalt us under the glare of "world opinion." This wistful American faith is the Achilles heel of the United States in dealing with the Communists. We forget that Communist power, unlike that of the United States, is not a butterfly pinioned against the backboard of "world opinion" by the arrow of Truth in the glare of hostile media.

The corollary of this—for application to our friends and allies—might be called the "clean skirts syndrome." It emerges in Harriman's instructions to Unger on how to talk to the royalist side: "Caution Phoumi exercise greatest patience . . . despite provocation from Sou-phanouvong . . . and importance we attach to his giving ample evidence . . . good faith where Agreements are concerned . . . Remind him that any violations must be attributed solely to pro-Communists, not to Phoumi group."[10]

Having urged on the Pathet Lao enlightened respect for world opinion and on the right wing a patient turning of the other cheek, Harriman launched an appeal to Soviet statesmanship, instructing our Ambassador in Moscow

"You should in concert UK Embassy seek urgent appointment with Push-kin or Gromyko and express orally and informally our grave concern at developments . . . You should stress that world expectations and hopes for peace stemming from Geneva Agreements likely be greatly dimmed if very first obligation called for by Agreements is not carried out. You should remind Soviet that it is responsibility of co-chairmen under Article 8 Agreement to see that parties carry out their obligations. You should urge Soviets take necessary steps so that Art. 3 can be complied with prior Aug. 22. Suggest you say that in light our mutual obligations make Geneva Agreements work we think it best take up problems like these in early stages so that later breaches may be avoided."[11]

Three days later, Secretary Rusk supported this plea in an embarrassingly gentle and generous personal talk with Ambassador Dobrynin:

The Secretary expressed concern about present difficulties in Laos re exit route issue. Secretary stated we know that Vietminh troops are in Laos, and the Geneva Agreement could break down because Souphanouvong not cooperating. We cannot believe this is known at the highest level in Moscow. Our two governments should see that the Geneva Agreements are carried out; this is of great importance to Chairman Khrushchev and President Kennedy. The Secretary said he hoped the Soviet Government would acquaint itself with the current situation; he wanted to be sure it was fully informed.[12]

Moscow did not hasten to respond to these appeals but the eventual effective answer was an oral statement to our Embassy in Moscow by Pushkin who sloughed off all the technical and legal rigamarole of the Geneva Accords and allowed that "the Vietminh would simply fade into the jungle."[13]

Finally, on August 21, Harriman instructed Unger to come down hard on neutralist Premier Souvanna:

"We have concluded that any proposal which does not provide for adequate checkpoints in Pathet Lao area is absolutely unacceptable as being wholly contrary to spirit of Geneva Agreements . . . At your discretion, you [Unger] authorized intimate to Souvanna we cannot carry on transactions with government which does not carry out the very first obligation required of it by Geneva Agreements."[14]

A few hours later, this was followed by another cable insisting

". . . on establishment adequate checkpoints in Pathet Lao areas as test of communists' and new Royal Laos Government's intentions live up to letter and spirit Geneva Agreements."[15]

Here the famous Harriman "toughness" found a fit target in the little neutralist Lao Premier, although under both the Agreements and the Harriman-Pushkin understandings the same reproof given Souvanna would have been more richly merited by the Soviet Union.

Against the background of these asymmetrical initiatives on the main issue, various collateral explorations were revealing the real meaning of the Accords in practice. For example, Col. Avtar Singh, Indian Chairman of the ICC, suggested that Souphanouvong's denial of any North Vietnamese presence be accepted at face value, thereby creating a presumption that any North Vietnamese reported later in Laos had entered in violation of the Accords as a basis for ICC investigation. This ingenious device was undermined by discovery that an ICC investigation of a Communist area would require "troika" approval by the Lao Government. So much for the "majority rule" provision in the Accords. As Ambassador Unger told Souvanna and reported to Washington "If ICC is at mercy of "troika" it will not be able to afford protection it was intended to provide."[16]

Later, Col. Singh turned aside Unger's suggestion that the ICC cite the North Vietnamese immediately for withdrawing unseen (if at all) in violation of the Accords. Again, Unger cabled Washington that "Singh's interpretation . . . means the ICC will not be a useful instrument to the U.S."[17]

Under pressure from the U.S., Premier Souvanna conceded there would be agreement on one checkpoint in each area. Washington responded that one checkpoint was totally inadequate for monitoring the departure of over 9,000 North Vietnamese. Yet, when Unger asked point blank whether one checkpoint in each area would be acceptable, the Department sidestepped, saying,

> You should, in no circumstances indicate the United States agrees to only three checkpoints (one in each zone) but you should reserve our position for any later action we might wish to take. At same time you should not press Souvanna and Phoumi in this matter to point where United States involved in blocking legal compliance by RLG with Articles 2 and 3 of Agreement. If compliance turns out in fact to be inadequate, we are thus free to weigh in later.[18]

This is an interesting example of the "open options syndrome" which is characteristic of incremental decision-making. By making the smallest possible decision, a government maintains maneuverability for future tactical use. The weakness of the "open options syndrome" is that options unchosen tend to dissolve in such a way that the power of decision is incrementally yielded to the cumulative weight of external events, as happened in this case. The next day, Souvanna announced three checkpoints, one in each area, a decision in which the U.S. tacitly acquiesced, not having approved. We not only did not "weigh in later" on this point but, as described later, we devised a sophistical rationalization according to which the North Vietnamese failure to withdraw became part of a "tacit agreement" thereby making us tacit accessories after the fact in the perversion of the Geneva Accords.

As for Prince Souvanna Phouma, Ambassador Unger reported that the Premier seemed content: "Souvanna seems not in mood to hold out for more points since he feels principle preserved."[19]

The same reduction of substance to form appeared in Ambassador Unger's background press conference on September 19. Said he, "U.S. position is of course that Vietminh should withdraw via ICC checkpoints, since Accords require this, but as practical matter Vietminh, *if* they leave, *may just slip away*. . . . Essential point is that they leave and thus one of the fundamental objectives Geneva Accords is accomplished."[20] (Emphasis added.)

On this basis, Pushkin's prediction that the Vietminh would "fade into the jungle" in defiance of the Geneva Accords represented a satisfactory, or at least acceptable, outcome. And in the end we did accept it, even including it in the "tacit agreement" we convinced ourselves we had reached with the Communist side. The meaning is that *sub rosa* frustration of the Accords preserves their principle and accomplishes their objectives. This sophistical reductionism soon became the solvent which dissolved the core of the Accords, leaving only the facade.

As the October 7 deadline drew nearer and voluminous intelligence showed no sign of North Vietnamese withdrawal, the U.S. had to consider whether to withdraw its own military advisors (now 666) despite Communist perfidy, or whether to keep them in Laos. Hearing arguments on both sides, Washington asked Ambassador Unger's views and recommendations. In his reply of September 22, the Ambassador recommended that the U.S. proceed with complete withdrawal—which we did. But Unger's cable is valuable more for its analysis and judgments than its conclusion.

First, he stated the opposite view forthrightly: "We could take the position that the Vietminh by failing withdraw have undermined one of the fundamental bases of the neutral solution in Laos and therefore the U.S. cannot withdraw its remaining military without some assurance compliance on Communist side."[21] He then identified the factor which made such a course well nigh impossible for the United States—the asymmetry of the rewards of open honesty and secret betrayal. If the U.S. did not openly withdraw its openly introduced military advisors, the ICC would surely cite it for violation of the Geneva Accords. But it was extremely doubtful that the ICC would cite North Vietnam for secretly retaining its clandestinely introduced army of thousands. The "troika" built into the Lao Government pyramided on the "troika" built into the ICC would prevent any ICC exposure of the Communist side.

The alternative course, said Unger, was to "carry the withdrawal to completion, receive blessing ICC and public opinion in many quarters concerning our good faith and determination live up to Accords."[22] A perfect description of the rewards provided by the "clean skirts syndrome."

In either case, the Ambassador argued, we must try to convince the Soviets that we knew what the facts were and publicize the Communist violations "so to embarrass Russians as to force them to put requisite pressure on North Vietnam to secure substantial if not total withdrawal."[23]

Hope springs eternal that the Soviet Union can be embarrassed by the truth as the U.S. can be! But, even if the Soviet Union were susceptible to this kind of embarrassment, our ability to produce it is limited. As Ambassador Unger hastened to point out, the limits on our ability to use sensitive intelligence publicly inhibits us from pursuing either course "to logical conclusion and not fall on our face from inability to document as necessary." This factor influenced Unger in his choice of the course of total withdrawal. "I am persuaded we should be able array enough facts to support strong *representations* envisaged in second course [withdrawal]. I am not so sanguine about our being able make case sufficiently strong and specific to defend *action* as grave as non-compliance envisaged in first course."[24] (Emphasis added.)

This trenchant point is stated with an exactitude approaching that of a mathematical equation: the public parading of truth is capable of supporting exhortation but not action. Put somewhat more metaphorically—words will float on words but action runs on the ground.

Nevertheless, having accepted the inevitability of total U.S. compliance, Unger recommended a maximum effort to focus public attention on the Soviet Union and to focus Soviet attention on our concern over North Vietnamese violations of the Accords:

> I also recommend we start immediately . . . make Russians painfully aware our knowledge Vietminh still in Laos in substantial numbers and showing virtually no signs any serious preparations depart. . . . Russians may be assuming either we are ignorant of Vietminh presence or do not feel able for some reason to raise it and therefore they feel no need to press North Vietnamese or Souphanouvong to get Vietminh out.[25]

If Unger implied here that our efforts with the Russians to date had been ineffective, he was right. Moreover, our continued exhortations, from 1962 to our final withdrawal from Vietnam in 1973, never caused the USSR to pressure North Vietnamese forces out of Laos. The Ambassador was closest to the truth when he opined that the Soviets felt no need to press North Vietnam.

Did we then have no effect whatsoever in getting some Communist compliance with the Geneva Accords requirement on military withdrawal? Not quite. Perhaps it was our pressure on the USSR that caused Souphanouvong to placate us with the brief soft shoe routine described below, which did not preserve the principles or achieve the objectives of the Geneva Accords. It did however, serve as a bit of staging which made it slightly less embarrassing for the United States as the curtain was lowered (having been barely raised) on the neutralization of Laos. It made it easier for the United States to sidestep the implicit showdown by finessing to the mere "facade of Geneva."

On September 29, the ICC was permitted to have a team at the Plaine des Jarres airfield to watch (but not identify) thirteen North Vietnamese officers, seventeen non-coms and five "experts" depart by two planes to Hanoi.

On October 7, Hanoi's news agency announced that North Vietnamese personnel "previously sent to Laos at the request of the Royal Lao Government have all been withdrawn from Laos." No such request had ever been made. The announcement made no mention of the Geneva Accords or the ICC.

Two weeks after the prescribed deadline, on October 23 the ICC was permitted to witness the departure by plane from Nom Ping in Nhommarath province of five North Vietnamese wearing no identifying uniform or insignia. Pathet Lao officials offered thanks and five village girls presented gift pillows.[26] The Pathet Lao and North Vietnam were not cited by the ICC for having violated the deadline.

On November 10, the ICC, unable to certify the departure of all foreign troops, repeated its performance of May 1961, simply relying on the statements of the three political elements. When the ICC report was received by the Soviet and British Co-chairmen, a British Foreign Office spokesman summed up the situation: "We know that at the time of the Laos cease-fire there were about 10,000 North Vietnamese troops in Laos. A number of those chose to withdraw secretly and only forty passed through the ICC checkpoints. It is not at all clear what happened to the remainder and how many may have remained."[27]

This was exactly the way the Communist side wanted it!

What to do? In effect, the neutralization of Laos which Khrushchev and Pushkin had promised to support had, with their connivance, been cancelled. Should we force a showdown over the massive violation? Those who favored this course argued that if we didn't make an issue of this case we would never be able to make an effective issue of any aspect of the Accords or of neutralization.

Don't force a showdown over technicalities, said others. To do so would only destroy the hope for gradually improving performance. This argument was explicitly formulated in Ambassador Unger's cable No. 469 of September 22 in which he said, "On balance, therefore, I recommend we carry MAAG withdrawal through to completion regardless of noncompliance by North Vietnam. Seems to me this course will put us in better posture press effectively toward primary objective i.e. withdrawal Vietminh from Laos."

But if massive violation is tolerated, how can hope for compliance rest on a foundation of non-compliance? And how could Laos be neutralized and unified while part of it was occupied by North Vietnamese troops? Those who opposed a showdown began to employ a specially crafted argument based on a distinction between the Geneva Accords as written and something called the "Geneva settlement." This ingenious distinction was expounded to me late one afternoon in October 1962 by the Laos desk officer, Charles Cross, who did not devise it but whose job required explicating it.

The Geneva Agreements, according to this interpretation, were an ideal, contingent, framework toward which we had to work. But realization would take time and was contingent on the outcome of the conflict in Vietnam. Meanwhile, the Agreements encompassed something else, more important but less precise. This was sometimes called the "Geneva settlement," later a "tacit understanding" by General Maxwell Taylor, and a "tacit agreement" by Roger Hilsman.

The theme of this "settlement" or "facade" was that both sides accepted the rough spotty division of power in Laos—which of course, nullified both the unification and neutralization of Laos which had been the fundamental objectives of the Geneva Accords. Neither side would push for conquest of Laos. Despite violations of specific clauses of the Accords, the basic balance in Laos would not be upset, *pending a settlement in Vietnam*. Meanwhile, the war in Laos would be put "on the back burner", another phrase that entered into the lexicon of Indochina strategy.

Here is General Taylor's concise capsulation:

> The Geneva Accord did not result in the withdrawal of the North Vietnamese troops supporting the Pathet Lao or the cessation of the use of the Ho Chi Minh trails to supply the war in South Vietnam. . . . There seemed to be a *tacit understanding* on both sides that the fate of Laos would be resolved in Vietnam. For that reason the Pathet Lao took as a primary objective the protection of the supply lines in the Laotian Panhandle, and maintained a *de facto* partition of the country on a north-south line which prevented any effective military action from the Mekong Valley against their communications.[28]

Taylor was quite right but his précis also contained its own obverse. For, if the fate of Laos was to be decided in Vietnam, then the fate of South Vietnam was to be sealed in Laos by the acceptance of this "tacit understanding" which encompassed—"as a primary objective" the use of the Ho Chi Minh trails in the eastern Communist part of the partitioned Panhandle of southern Laos. In actuality, the facade of Geneva became not only the framework of our policy in Laos, but the fulcrum of U.S. strategy for the remainder of the war in Indochina.

8

The Facade of Geneva

"Increasingly, it became clear that we had arrived at a tacit agreement—not on settlement of the Laos problem but on its temporary postponement."

Roger Hilsman, *To Move a Nation*.

Well, what was wrong with an unwritten "tacit agreement"? Answer: What was wrong was that it permitted Hanoi's eventual conquest of South Vietnam. Every North Vietnamese offensive from 1962 to 1975 was conducted within the framework of the so-called unwritten "tacit agreement," including the Tet Offensive of 1968 which caused the United States to reverse its course from incremental engagement to incremental disengagement. The "tacit agreement" also permitted the final offensive of 1975 when North Vietnam conquered South Vietnam.

I do not mean that the "tacit agreement" which became the "facade of Geneva" caused South Vietnam's defeat. That was caused by North Vietnam. Nor do I imply any inside American "betrayal." No responsible American official wanted to cause a North Vietnamese victory. The U.S. negotiated the Geneva Accords in good faith, intending to neutralize Laos and in so doing to help South Vietnam preserve its independence. But the difference between the Accords and the unwritten "tacit agreement" was not simply one of degree, or postponement or pragmatic untidiness. It was fundamental. Practically speaking, a North Vietnamese victory over South Vietnam was precluded by the Geneva Accords but it was quite compatible with the "tacit agreement." The Geneva Accords and the "Geneva settlement" were incompatible with each other. They had to be. Or, put another way, if the Geneva Accords, as written, had not excluded the practical possibility of Hanoi's conquest of South Vietnam, there would have been no need for the Communists to decide to postpone their implementation. It must be remembered that the concept of a "tacit agreement" was an American one, but the events that forced its formulation were a Communist initiative. The "tacit agreement" was the American way of rationalizing our acceptance of the Communist reversal of the neutralization of Laos.

To describe the sculpting of this ingenious rationale I shall shortly have recourse to the words of Roger Hilsman who, with Averell Harriman, co-authored it. Hilsman had been Director of the Bureau of Intelligence and Research (INR) in the Department of State until early in 1963 when he became Assistant Secretary for Far Eastern Affairs, succeeding Harriman who moved from the sixth floor to the seventh to become Deputy Under-Secretary for Political Affairs. A World War II veteran of guerrilla warfare (in Burma), Hilsman was a key advisor to President Kennedy on that subject as well as on Southeast Asia. As Director of INR during the Geneva Conference and for several months beyond, he had mobilized the research and analysis resources of the Department to provide Kennedy, Rusk and Harriman with timely interpretation and estimates of everything affecting the Laos negotiations.

The formula was actually cast in outline by Hilsman and Harriman before the 75-day deadline for troop withdrawal expired on October 7, 1962. But, though it already existed in the minds of policy-makers, the "facade of Geneva" was not fully marked out on the ground until the spring of 1963 when the Communist third of the "troika" government walked out and set up its own rival regime among the Pathet Lao military forces.

During the winter of 1962–1963 the "troika" regime barely held together as one of the many Laotian facades. No substantive progress was made toward real unification. The Pathet Lao army (itself a facade for the North Vietnamese army) was holed up in the mountainous eastern part of the country abutting on the Plaine des Jarres. For a time the tiny neutralist army of General Kong Le occupied the western Plaine des Jarres. The royal army controlled Vientiane and the plains bordering the Mekong River's left bank.

In February 1963, first a neutralist education officer was murdered, then the popular neutralist Colonel Ketsana, apparently by pro-Communists. On April 1, the ostensibly neutralist but actually crypto-Communist Foreign Minister Quinim (another facade) was killed by a neutralist sergeant in reprisal for the Colonel's murder. Next day, the Communist wing of the "troika", including Prince Souphanouvong, decamped for Pathet Lao military headquarters at Khang Khay. Despite appeals from the United States, the Co-chairmen and the ICC, the "troika" was not reconstituted. The *de facto* partition of the country was complete.

The Pathet Lao tried to force General Kong Le's neutralist forces to desert the neutralist Premier and applied pressure by cutting off supplies from Hanoi. Despite a small defection, Kong Le remained loyal to the neutral government in Vientiane, and his main force refused to defect. As a result, the neutralists and conservatives were thrown into an entente in self-defense against the Communist side.* Unable to dominate the "troika", the Communists had no further use for it. Instead, full partition and political polarization suited their purposes better. In June, they drove the small neutralist force back to the western edge of the Plaine des Jarres.

Now Hanoi's scornful refusal to withdraw its forces or comply with the Geneva Accords was formalized by partition. The Communists unilaterally controlled eastern Laos and they were virtually allowed to annex southern Laos. How could this result be conceivable within the framework of any understanding derived from the Geneva Accords since the Accords clearly excluded it? Here Hilsman lucidly exposes the intellectual process by which a concept can be converted into its opposite with much greater success than medieval alchemy achieved in transmuting lead into gold.

In a few remarkable paragraphs Hilsman reduces the grand concept of Geneva to a three-point, "tacit" rationale. Actually, there were three separate rationales, one for North Vietnam's failure to withdraw, its partition of Laos and failure to comply with the Accords; a second for U.S. meticulous compliance and third, an overarching rationale for the strategic meaning of the "tacit agreement" which is actually a reversal of the Geneva Accords.

The first rationale (for Hanoi's failure to withdraw), was presented to President Kennedy before expiration of the October 7 withdrawal deadline. Hilsman introduces it as follows:

> Just before the seventy-five day deadline on troop withdrawal, the National Security Council met again with the President. There was evidence that substantial numbers of North Vietnamese troops would remain past

---

*This was a political victory for the non-Communist side, a victory for which Harriman had angled. Hilsman quotes him as saying more than once, "If Souvanna's government of national union breaks up, we must be sure the break comes between the Communists and the neutralists, rather than having the two of them teamed up as they were before." (*To Move a Nation*, 153) Unfortunately, for lack of a realistic strategy, we were unable to convert this tactical political success into a strategic asset in the decisive struggle in South Vietnam. By contrast, the Communist side, even without this political advantage, had a strategy which enabled them to convert their position in Laos into a decisive strategic asset for their campaign against South Vietnam.

the deadline and pressure within the government had mounted to keep our own military advisors in Laos until the Vietnamese also withdrew. "How is it going," Harriman was asked. "Just about as unsatisfactorily as we expected," was his reply.[1]

Well, what did we expect? It was all very carefully worked out, Hilsman explained:

> We had put down what we expected in an informal "intelligence estimate" that Harriman and I used to brief the President. We felt, first, that the Communists would continue to pursue their goal of gaining control of all of Laos, but that for the *time being*, at least, they intended to do so *primarily* through political means and *generally* within the terms of the Geneva Agreements—the Geneva terms, that is, as conceived in very *elastic* *"Communist"* dimensions.[2] (Emphasis added.)

Here, we are being casually told that despite the signing of the Agreements only eight weeks earlier, despite Khrushchev's assurance to Kennedy and Pushkin's to Harriman, the Communist side was still not ready to support Laos neutrality! That the North Vietnamese would not totally ignore the Geneva Accords is insinuated but surrounded by a formidable defensive line of adverbial modifiers. For example, what does *"primarily* through political means" mean? No sooner asked than answered. Hilsman immediately explains that, "even though the Communists would *probably* rely on political means, the North Vietnamese would undoubtedly insist on maintaining *some* military presence in Laos."

But, if Laos was to be neutralized why would the North Vietnamese want or need to maintain forces there? For two reasons, says Hilsman: "to backstop the Pathet Lao and to maintain their hold on the infiltration routes into South Vietnam."[3] From this, one easily infers that the Pathet Lao needed backstopping because (despite total U.S. withdrawal) the North Vietnamese didn't intend to enforce neutralization but rather, intended to expand their area of control in Laos. One also needs no imagination to recognize that, despite the Geneva Accords, North Vietnam intended to use the infiltration routes to conquer South Vietnam.

But what was meant by "elastic Communist dimensions" as the criterion for compliance with the Geneva Accords? Obviously, from the Communist point of view, those dimensions had to be large enough to permit North Vietnam's conquest of South Vietnam. Later on, Hilsman confirms this. And, in the process, he gives a brilliant exposition of the kind of adverbial incrementalism by which we sought to force the reality of external aggression into the more limited dimensions of a guerrilla insurgency—that is, a problem small enough to be handled inside Vietnam rather than by military action in Laos, as Harriman had advised.

He accomplishes this in the course of estimating North Vietnam's requirements. For example, how much military presence would North Vietnam "undoubtedly" require in Laos?

"Our judgment," Hilsman tells us, "was that the Communists would make an effort to keep this military presence small and inconspicuous."[4] But what, for example, was "small" or "inconspicuous"?

Falling back on another adverb, Hilsman tells us that "our judgment was that the Communists . . . would use the infiltration routes *circumspectly.*" But what does "circumspectly" mean? Hilsman is ready with the answer which includes some further adjectival/adverbial fall-backs:

> By "circumspectly" we meant that they would continue to use the trails for infiltrating men on foot, cadres equipped with their own arms and whatever other, heavier equipment they could carry. We meant that they would use trucks where roads already existed and at the time of year that the roads were passable. But, we also meant that they would *probably* not make any *blatant* or *obvious* effort to turn trails into roads or to improve the roads except at places and in circumstances where they were fairly sure they could get away with it without being seen.[5] (Emphasis added.)

Hilsman does not explain the practical meaning "probably," "blatant" and "obvious," but the meaning emerges. It is easy to understand how the U.S. hoped North Vietnam would limit itself to such a low-key scale of guerrilla warfare. But why would it be in Hanoi's interest to do so? The North Vietnamese, Hilsman tells us, "were not willing to take that risk [of American intervention] . . . apparently because they felt *the main arena was Vietnam.* For this very reason however, the Communists wanted to keep on using the infiltration routes through Laos into South Vietnam."[6] (Emphasis added.)

He is absolutely correct and this is an important point. North Vietnam had an Indochina strategy in which eastern Laos (as well as Cambodia) was an instrument in bringing about Hanoi's conquest of South Vietnam. The United States believed the opposite. Instead of using Laos as an instrument in the defense of South Vietnam we told ourselves we had separated and "postponed" the Laos problem *pending* a solution in South Vietnam which was to be achieved *inside* South Vietnam and independently of events in Laos.

But what might force the Communists to raise the level of intensity? Even before warning that a U.S. attempt to retake northern Laos or threaten North Vietnam would have provoked Chinese intervention,

Hilsman makes his central point: "If the Americans attempted to take back territory already held by the Communists, even in the southern panhandle . . . the estimate was that the Communists would strenuously resist."[7] This thinking, of course, was consistent with the judgment that Hanoi regarded Vietnam as the "main arena." It follows that Hanoi regarded the infiltration routes as a strategic part of Vietnam, not of that part of Laos which the U.S. thought had been pushed to the "back-burner."

But knowing the Communist upper threshold of tolerance was not enough. We had also to know the lower level at which their scorn of a too limp U.S. posture might tempt them to escalate. As Hilsman explains it, "Our estimate, finally, was that the Communist side would stay at even this covert level only if there was continued evidence of an American determination to prevent their taking over the whole of Laos."[8] So under the "tacit agreement" the Communist side was able to squeeze the U.S. between two delicately calculated thresholds. If the U.S. tried too much or threatened the infiltration routes, the Communist side *would* escalate, but if the U.S. was too placid, the Communist side *might* escalate. In either case, the burden of preventing Communist escalation was on the U.S. By keeping up just the right pressure in northern Laos, the Communist side could divert the U.S. into concentrating on maintaining the delicate balance in that area while the Communists concentrated on the "main arena" infiltration routes.

With this exposition of the rationale for Communist misbehavior completed, Hilsman moves on to the rationale for strict U.S. compliance with the terms of the Geneva Accords. Why, if the Communist side was massively perverting the Accords, should the U.S. withdraw its military advisors?

The answer was presented by Harriman and Hilsman to the President at the same NSC meeting. Hilsman introduces his usually lucid explication as follows:

> Again the policy . . . had been worked out in the same informal process of exchanging guidance and specialist knowledge between the President, Harriman, Forrestal and the State Department group of research intelligence specialists [who worked under Hilsman's direction.] Harriman, especially felt strongly that the United States should comply with both the letter and spirit of the agreements in every detail, that its record should be absolutely clear. Our military advisors should be withdrawn promptly, and thereafter there should be no violation of any kind by the United States, neither "black" reconnaissance flights to confirm whether the North Vietnamese had actually withdrawn nor cloak-and-dagger hanky-panky. The Lao themselves would inevitably find out what the Vietnamese were

doing, and we could learn from them. Harriman wanted the political onus of any violations to fall on the Communists.[9]

What a perfect example of the interlocking "victorious truth" and "clean skirt" syndromes! Somehow, it was expected that the truth would be self-enforcing and that the political onus of violation would fall as heavily on the Communists as it would have fallen on the U.S. which would be strengthened by its demonstration of purity. But all of history tells us that in world politics—to the victor go the spoils. Hilsman continues in the same vein: "If the Geneva Agreements and the political solution failed in Laos, he [Harriman] wanted it to be the Communist side that had to pay the political cost, including the cost in terms of damaging their goals elsewhere in Asia and Africa, and not the United States."[10]

All in all, history since 1962 suggests that the United States has suffered more in Asia, Africa and Central America from its ineffectiveness in Indochina than the USSR has suffered from the exposure of its dishonesty.

Harriman and Hilsman carried the day in the National Security Council. Suspicions of Communist intentions were voiced by others but to no result. The decision came with relaxed unequivocation, as Hilsman tells us: " 'Well', said the President, swinging his chair around toward Harriman with a relaxed grin, 'we'll go along with the Governor.' "[11]

In this way was the "facade of Geneva" shaped in September 1962 from the "Harriman-Hilsman tacit agreement" so as to fit the "elastic Communist dimensions" which were known to include eventual control over South Vietnam as well as Laos. This was no fleeting tactical 'zig' in our long-term strategy. It became the strategy itself. Hilsman reports that "The United States continued this *basic policy* during the rest of Harriman's tenure as Assistant Secretary of State for Far Eastern Affairs, and we continued to follow it when I replaced him after he became Under-Secretary early in 1963."[12] (Emphasis added.)

Hilsman's third rationale is a post-partition exegesis on the "tacit agreement" which became our policy. By June, 1963, the troika coalition had broken up, the Communists had set up a rival regime under North Vietnamese protection and had openly driven the neutralists nearly off the Plaine des Jarres. The partition was complete—as was North Vietnamese domination of all eastern Laos.

Were we chagrined? Not a bit. Hilsman reports it with some satisfaction: "And then things settled down. Increasingly, it became clear that we had arrived at a tacit agreement—not on the settlement of the Laos problem but on its *temporary* postponement."[13] (Emphasis added.) But how long was "temporary?" He tells us quickly: "Until the matter of Vietnam was settled." What was the alternative? "The Communist North Vietnamese could . . . take [Laos] over within two to four weeks if they were willing to take the risk of an American intervention. . . . By using the more ambiguous guerrilla techniques they were applying to Vietnam they could probably have taken Laos over on a longer time scale with even less risk."[14]

The North Vietnamese were willing "to keep the use of the routes down to a level that was *less than fully provocative.*"[15]

But what did "fully provocative" mean? Here, we approach the nub of the unwritten Geneva "tacit agreement" or "settlement" or "understanding" or "facade." What is provocation? It is more than an empirical act or event. Provocation is a function of two variables—action by one party and reaction by another, in both directions. In an earlier paragraph, Hilsman had described the Communist behavior which he and Harriman expected and which the U.S. could regard as tolerable (not fully provocative) during a period of "tacit agreement" on a "temporary postponement." The criteria were: military presence ("small and inconspicuous") and infiltration ("circumspect and unseen"). By these standards, Communist behavior was never less than "fully provocative." In fact it soon became "blatant" and "obvious" and, more importantly, decisive.

The real "bottom line" of provocation is not the act of the provoker but the reactive threshold of the party provoked. By this test, "fully provocative" would mean an act which would provoke the United States to terminate the provocation, i.e., a North Vietnamese military presence or use of the infiltration routes which provoked us to terminate it. By this standard, North Vietnam consistently kept its use of the infiltration routes at a level "less than fully provocative" because the United States never allowed itself to be fully provoked to terminate the provocation. True, the U.S. was often provoked to reprisal and often reacted with vigor, ingenuity and sacrifice but it was never "fully provoked" *to end the provocation.* Why? Because we feared the consequences of shattering the "tacit agreement."

In effect, therefore, the U.S. commitment to the maintenance of the "tacit agreement" became the threshold of U.S. toleration for provocation. A built-in escalatory threshold of toleration! To preserve the "tacit understanding" or "facade" the U.S. consistently refused to allow Communist behavior, including astronomical escalation of infiltration beyond "guerrilla levels", to push it across the threshold of "full provocation." In this sense, until the United States withdrew in 1973, the Communists stayed within the limits of the Geneva "tacit understanding" as formulated by Harriman and Hilsman. Or, conversely, it could be said that, in a corollary of Parkinson's law, the dimensions of the "tacit agreement" expanded to accommodate whatever provocation threatened to demolish it. The United States refused to be *that* provoked. The infiltration routes were used to the level necessary to launch the Tet Offensive in 1968 which triggered the beginning of U.S. withdrawal, but not to the "fully provocative" level that would have required America to terminate the provocation.

The essential core of the "tacit understanding" was that North Vietnam was not to be effectively denied the use of southern Laos to invade South Vietnam. Because our own threshold of toleration was never defined except implicitly in terms of preserving the "tacit agreement," it became a function of the Communist threshold. What would have been a realistic threshold for the U.S. to adopt? I would suggest that the level of invasion through Laos should have been our threshold. When the infiltration reached the point at which it made the successful internal defense of South Vietnam impossible—the United States should have either intervened to stop this invasion or commenced a strategic withdrawal.

But, if the "tacit agreement" was the reversal of the Geneva Accords, what was the point in preserving even a facade? Having torpedoed the essence of the whole neutralization agreement, why would North Vietnam care about preserving the facade? Hilsman set forth a pithy and realistic appreciation of the Communist interest in preserving the "facade of Geneva" to screen the "tacit agreement": "Until the matter of Vietnam was settled there would be no progress toward a true government of national union, but the Communists would keep some token representation in Souvanna's government at Vientiane and thus avoid scuttling the Geneva Agreements *openly and irrevocably*."[16] (Emphasis added.)

How would the temporary suspension of the Geneva Accords end? Hilsman concluded his exposition by answering this question: "If the guerrilla struggle in Vietnam went *against* the Communists, Laos would quickly become the model for a truly neutral country in which the Communists participated in a coalition government without attempting to subvert it—at least for a while. But if the Communists *won* in Vietnam—they seemed to be saying—then they would regard Laos as part of the prize."[17] (Emphasis Hilsman's.)

In short, the Communist commitment to block use of Laos against South Vietnam, promised to Kennedy by Harriman in October 1961 was effectively amputated from the Geneva formula. What was left of the Accords was a dream which the U.S. and its allies might try to realize *if* they first defeated the North Vietnamese campaign to conquer South Vietnam. Meanwhile, it was only a dream and the victory would go to the side which could win on the ground—in the "main arena" which included the invasion route through Laos. Harriman and Hilsman had performed a real *tour de force* in formulating the definition of their "tacit agreement." They had anticipated every question. Except for one, that is. Was it possible to defend South Vietnam successfully against an invasion through Laos without blocking the invasion itself? Hardly.

What was the *quid*? That the United States would not effectively deny Hanoi the use of the Laos infiltration routes of invasion.

What was the *quo*? That Hanoi would postpone the takeover of all Laos until the decision was reached in South Vietnam. If, with the use of its invasion route through Laos, Hanoi still couldn't win in South Vietnam, then it would implement the Geneva dream—"at least for a while."

Hardly an equitable transaction, but to those who preferred a more limited goal over large scale intervention, Hilsman tells us Laos was a victory—of sorts.[18] He called it a "two-track policy." The derivation of the "two-track" strategy emerges from a sequence of map-diagrams which show how the 1962 Geneva neutralization of Laos was inverted by "tacit agreement" into its own negation.

The first diagram shows Laos as an integral, neutral state harboring no foreign forces, as prescribed by the Geneva Accords but never implemented. Had the Accords been enforced as written and signed (and as Pushkin promised Harriman) Laos would have played a decisive role as a buffer between North Vietnam, on the one hand, and South Vietnam, Cambodia and Thailand on the other. Hanoi's direct military access to South Vietnam would have been limited to the narrow Demilitarized Zone—a sector which could have been defended by South Vietnam with American support.

The second diagram shows Laos in the role to which it was consigned for the duration of the Vietnam war by the Harriman-Hilsman "tacit agreement." This diagram shows Laos partitioned roughly along an ill-defined and sometimes shifting north-south axis with the eastern part under Communist control, dominated by—and, in effect, occupied by North Vietnamese forces. The western part is under a neutral government, supported by U.S. economic and military assistance, but *not* by U.S. military forces. The ICC and Geneva Co-chairmen enforcement machinery has been reduced to impotence by Communist refusal to cooperate—a circumstance encompassed within our "tacit agreement", thereby making us accessories after the fact.

Although the "tacit agreement" covered the whole of Laos, the real "quid" and the real "quo" are the two dotted and lined sectors. The dotted area in the southeastern portion of the Panhandle contained

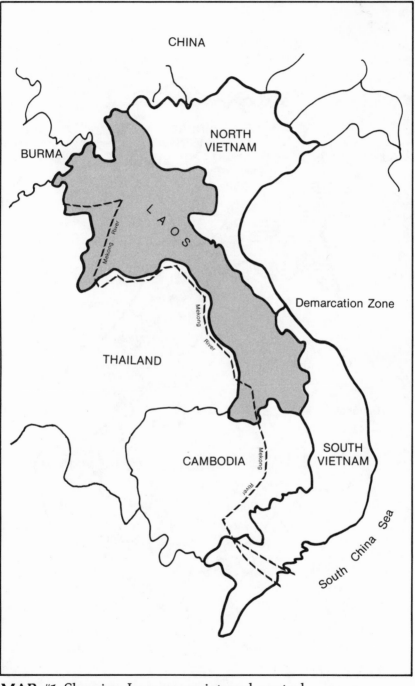

MAP #1 Showing Laos as an integral neutral
buffer per Geneva Accords

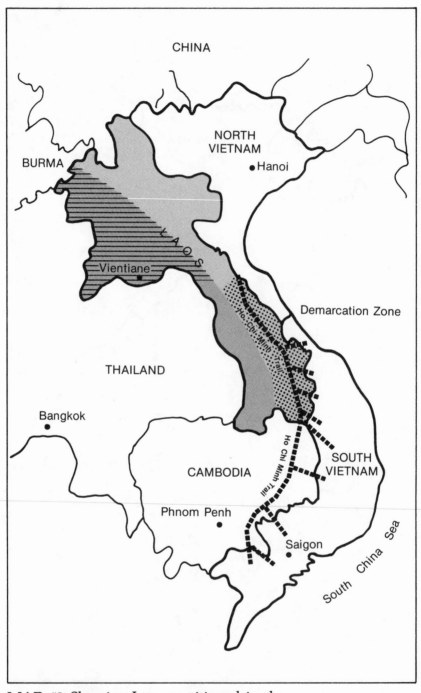

MAP #2 Showing Laos partitioned in the framework of the "tacit agreement."

the Ho Chi Minh Trail over which Hanoi infiltrated and invaded South Vietnam. In the process, the invasion was also extended through eastern Cambodia. The lined area in the northwest was the core of the neutral Laos regime which the U.S. supported. The nub of the "tacit agreement" was that as long as the U.S. did not try to terminate North Vietnam's control over the southeastern invasion route, Hanoi would not take over the northwestern base of neutral Laos. Within these limits there could be—and was—considerable fluctuation in the actual contours of the partition, including Communist pressure and feints on the neutral area. There was also U.S. aerial harassment of the continuing invasion along the Ho Chi Minh Trails, a campaign that, although well-executed by our pilots, was only an indecisive collateral harassment that did not change the terms of the war.

The ultimate victory of Hanoi was ensured by the operative imbalance between the two indicated areas. The one in the southeast was an indispensable tool for Hanoi's campaign to conquer South Vietnam. But the one in the northwest—while requiring strong U.S. assistance—made no effective contribution to the salvation of South Vietnam. Accordingly, our ultimate failure in Indochina was virtually assured as long as we persisted in waging our effort within the asymmetrical parameters of the "tacit agreement."

9

The Laos Strand

"In 333 B.C. Alexander the Great on his march through Asia, was shown at Gordium in Phrygia the chariot of the ancient king, Gordias, with its yoke lashed to a pole by a knot of which the ends were hidden. It was to be untied only by the conqueror of Asia. In the popular account, probably invented as appropriate to an impetuous warrior, Alexander cut the knot through with his sword. But earlier versions make him find the ends, either by cutting into the knot, or by drawing out the pole.

(Encyclopedia Britannica.)

In the foregoing chapters I have tried to indicate the key elements which defined the shape and direction of our strategy in Indochina—and of its eventual failure. Our courses in Laos, Vietnam and Cambodia were mutually incompatible. Instead of being smoothly intertwined, like three parallel strings, into a strong cord, they became knotted so that it was all but impossible to find the ends. Not until 1975 did Hanoi, with its final assault and conquest of South Vietnam, cut the knot through.

I wish that at this point I could tell how, after arriving on the job in September 1962 (as the U.S. withdrew from Laos and North Vietnam did not), with great insight and penetrating logic I either untied the knot or foretold the future. But it didn't happen that way. The knot was not yet complete and things were not as clear to me then as they later became.

At first, of course, I was a neophyte. It seemed that whatever I had learned of Southeast Asia in my earlier incarnation during the late 1940s and early 1950s was at best irrelevant. As with any new puzzle, however, it always takes time in a new job just to learn where the pieces lie, especially in such a focal office as ours that attracted the attention of everyone from the White House downward. It was sometimes said during the Geneva negotiations that John F. Kennedy was the Laos desk officer. But those days were mostly over, and the President was about to be distracted from unkept Soviet promises in Laos to Soviet lies about missiles in Cuba. In the Department of State new ideas are more often squeezed out by the hourly demands of operating an existing policy than squelched by suppression from the top—although the latter is not unknown.

More importantly, it seems to me now that my perception advanced at a glacial pace—some would say it went into reverse. (Later, one did say it.) Clearly, I was out of phase with the rhythm of U.S. strategy. Gradually, however, I did attain some insight and, still more gradually, formulated my own coherent (I thought) strategic concept. But I remained out of phase until the end of my official association with Southeast Asia in the summer of 1970—and intellectually out of phase until the end of the war in 1975. This probably accounts for the writing of this book.

During the winter of 1962 and the spring of 1963 I experienced a vertiginous sense of unreality surrounded by all of the elements in the one-sided Communist perversion of the Geneva Accords, including—

- the failure to withdraw from Laos,

- the reduction of the ICC to a joke,

- the break-up of the troika coalition,

- the Communist offensive to drive the neutralists off the Plaine des Jarres,

- the stark partition of Laos, and

- the persistent North Vietnamese slow invasion of South Vietnam through Laos.

It was as if Hitler had blown up the Arch of Triumph and then the Parisians had piled up the rubble and called it the "facade of Triumph!"

The sensation was a bit like motion sickness in a ship at sea. As long as one holds tightly to nearby interior objects fixed to the ship, one can maintain his posture relative to the "facade," provided one's stomach is strong enough for the pitching and rolling. But, if one raises his eyes over the ship's rail toward the horizon beyond, one loses balance. At least, so it seemed to me when I would try to look at the "big picture." For example, wholly within the framework of the "Geneva facade," all of the following were possible:

• If the Polish member of the ICC and the USSR covered up Hanoi's violations of the Geneva Accords, they were said to be really only protecting the *de facto* temporary partition of Laos which was part of our "tacit agreement." But to raise one's eyes above the rail of the "facade" to South Vietnam was to ask if Hanoi's use of the partition was compatible with our defense of South Vietnam's independence. And was the USSR's connivance compatible with the assurances of Laos' neutrality given to Kennedy and Harriman?

• If the Soviet Union gave arms to Hanoi, which in turn sent them for use in Laos, then Moscow was said to be only preempting and blocking Chinese influence and this was in our interest too—consistent with our "tacit understanding." But, if Hanoi was bent on conquest did it make North Vietnamese forces less hostile or dangerous to Southeast Asia to carry Soviet rather than Chinese arms?

• If Hanoi pressed its infiltration through Laos into South Vietnam, that was permissible under the "tacit agreement" (under which, we told ourselves, Hanoi would only infiltrate small numbers of pure guerrilla types.) Anyway, South Vietnam was a *separate* problem. In our "two-track scenario" South Vietnam was in the "main arena" while Laos was "on the backburner." But did the "tacit understanding" include Hanoi's agreement that *its* side of the temporary Laos partition was also "on the backburner?" Or did Hanoi regard its side of Laos as a strategic extension of Vietnam and therefore part of the "main arena?"

• If the United States and South Vietnam were to send ground forces into southern Laos against the infiltration routes, it was said that that "would destroy the "tacit agreement" and the "facade of Geneva." But to look strategically was to ask, "Why wouldn't the entry of North Vietnamese forces into the same part of neutral Laos also destroy the "facade of Geneva?" Answer: Because the function of the "tacit agreement" and the "facade of Geneva" was to act as a rationale for the total inversion of the actual Geneva Accords by the Communist side. Therefore, to look over the rail of the "facade" at the world beyond will only made one sick!

The making of images or facades seemed to me to be a large part of our decision-making process. When confronted with an event that required some response, the Far East Bureau often asked *not* what is the effect of this event on our policy or what does our policy tell us to do, or how should the policy be modified, but "What *image* do we want to project?" After a day or two of the Bureau's shaping the desired image, the time for substantive action might have passed or been overtaken by some other more immediate event. Worse yet, the flickering succession of images so blurred one's perception of reality that it was sometimes difficult to remember the reality of a week earlier or to re-create the reasons which seemed so persuasive then. During this period I developed the habit of writing draft memoranda which often were designed more to keep a grip on reality and continuity than to influence action. It helped to maintain my own continuity of thought and it kept me honest with myself—I think. Although most of the memoranda were never used, occasionally one would become the basis of an actual proposal—as happened in April 1963.

From September 1962 to April 1963 I attributed my dissatisfaction to subjective causes.Either I had not mastered the complex formulae of our policy, or perhaps I was too impatient. Maybe we were really just biding our time, paying out rope until the right moment when Harriman—affectionately known as"the crocodile" (whose snap I later experienced)—would present Pushkin's IOUs to Moscow and then force the Communist side back into line. Harriman's prestige was high and it was said in the Bureau that he would eventually bring the Russians around. I had seen him sternly admonish Ambassador Unger to be tough on neutralist Premier Souvanna Phouma with the object of making Souvanna tougher on his half-brother, the Pathet Lao leader, Prince Souphanouvong. In a memorandum of November 28, 1962, Walt Rostow, by now Chairman of the State Department's Policy Planning Council, reminded Secretary Rusk of Pushkin's promise to Harriman that the USSR would take responsibility for ending infiltration through Laos and went on to say that, before leaving on a trip to India "Governor Harriman urged us to keep the Vietminh issue—and continued Vietcong infiltration—at the top of the post-Cuba negotiating agenda with the Russians."[1] But the final test would be applying it directly to the Russians and when the time came Harriman would do it himself.

The test came in April 1963, a few days after Harriman had been promoted to Under-Secretary for Political Affairs and had been succeeded as Assistant Secretary for the Far East by Roger Hilsman, and shortly after the Pathet Lao had broken up the troika neutral regime, set up the rival regime at Khang Khay, and were heavily attacking the neutralists. Harriman went to London to consult with the British who, as one of the Geneva co-chairmen, had made serious but unavailing efforts to get the cooperation of the other co-chairman, the USSR, in arranging an ICC monitored ceasefire. On April 23, while Harriman was in London waiting for Khrushchev to set a date for a meeting, the Soviets flatly and publicly refused to cooperate.

On April 24, I sent a memorandum to Director Barney Koren. It seemed to me that now was the time to put the litmus test to Soviet promises. After all, the central political premise of the Geneva Accords had been the USSR's promise to Kennedy to support a neutral Laos and to Harriman to assume responsibility for performance by the Communist side. If they failed in this they would be cutting off our attempt to reach co-existence as Khrushchev had proposed. However, unpleasant it might be, the litmus test would be accurate and decisive.

I wrote to Barney,

Since the Russian action in torpedoing any possible effective co-chairmen action yesterday, the burden of proof now rests on those who argue that the Russians have both the intention and the ability to contribute toward implementation of the Geneva Accords. . . .

My own opinion is that the Russian commitment to the Geneva Agreements was always limited and that there never was a complete meeting of the minds between the U.S. and the USSR on the purpose of the Geneva Agreements. I believe the Communist side regards the Agreements as a satisfactory "facade" and is willing to preserve the "facade" since they have ample effective means to pursue their purpose of ultimate control of the whole of Laos, operating wholly within and behind that "facade"

The Soviet performance yesterday indicates that they have concluded . . . that the Free World is leading from weakness in Laos and is so desperate to maintain the Geneva "facade" as a screen for an "honorable retreat" from Laos that they need have no fear of forceful Free World intervention in Laos.

In this light . . . we should consider carefully just how important Laos is or is not to the U.S. and how far we will or will not go if necessary to prevent the absorption of Laos by the Communist bloc. For myself, I consider that there is no country in the world that is so unimportant that it cannot serve a useful purpose to the Communist bloc . . . and consequently there is no part of the world that is unimportant to the Free World.

As of today, Governor Harriman is waiting in London for the Russian reaction to his request for an interview with Mr. Khrushchev. . . . I think that serious consideration should be given to the possibility that Governor Harriman might withdraw his request for an interview with Mr. Khrushchev on the ground that the Soviet action yesterday has created an uncooperative and hostile atmosphere not conducive to successful negotiation. . . .

However, I recognize that the probability is that it will be decided that it is now all the more important that Governor Harriman proceed to Moscow. Therefore, I suggest that we pick up the gauntlet which the Russians have thrown down and test them to the very last ounce of their alleged commitment to the Geneva formula. . . . We might consider the following:

(1) Harriman visit to Moscow—
    a. Governor Harriman would suggest a cease-fire and an agreement by all sides to withdraw to the positions they held . . . and . . . a

Russian statement in unequivocal support of the (neutral) Souvanna Government.

b.   He would deliver no ultimatum . . . but warn of the necessity that the U.S. act . . . within a few days. . . . He would express willingness to stay in Moscow for several days if necessary to work out arrangements.

(2) If satisfactory arrangements were worked out in Moscow, we would proceed along those lines. If, however, the Soviets were uncooperative . . . or if it appeared they were not acting in good faith:

a.   Governor Harriman would return home;

b.   U.S. land and air forces would be ordered to Thailand on a contingency basis;

c.   There would be public statements relating this to the failure of the Communists to live up to the Geneva Accords.

The memorandum concluded with a discussion of possible Communist reactions and how we might respond by withdrawal of U.S. forces if the Communists complied with the Geneva Accords or by girding our loins if they maintained their aggressive posture.

Of course, such a recommendation had no chance of adoption because it would have made a litmus test of Communist intentions, the results of which would probably have been unwelcome. Still, I meant it seriously. At sea, one must find a prominent fixed feature—a base point—from which to calculate his position. After eight months of bobbing and weaving, the USSR had taken a position which seemed to me to provide a base point. Our whole strategy in Indochina was balanced on the neutralization of Laos and that, in turn, was balanced on the premise of Soviet support as promised to Kennedy by Khrushchev and to Harriman by Pushkin. By effectively walking away from its commitments, the USSR had provided us a prominent new feature on the horizon from which to plot a new course. Or, so I thought.

Harriman went to Moscow the next day and saw Khrushchev on April 26. The *New York Times* on April 27 headlined its front page report: "Khrushchev Fails to Give Promise of Help on Laos."

The following quoted paragraphs tell the story:

Moscow, April 27. Premier Khrushchev, in his meeting yesterday with W. Averell Harriman, gave no indication that he would try to restrain or could restrain the pro-Communist force in Laos, an authoritative source said tonight.

Mr. Harriman, the Under-Secretary of State for Political Affairs, was unable to obtain any commitment beyond a general affirmation of Soviet support for the 1962 Geneva Accords. . . .

Mr. Harriman said that Premier Khrushchev had "unequivocally reaffirmed" the Soviet commitment to support peace and neutrality in Laos. He added that the Premier had agreed *in principle* that the Control Commission should be permitted freedom of movement in Laos as provided for in the Geneva Accords. (Emphasis added.)

The *Times* then reported that "Mr. Harriman was understood to be satisfied with the nature of his talks with Premier Khrushchev and Foreign Minister Andrei Gromyko." It is difficult for me to understand why. The Soviet Union had refused to do anything to enforce the neutrality of Laos which Khrushchev had agreed to support *in principle*. Most important of all, Khrushchev had failed to do anything to enforce Communist performance under the Geneva Accords and, least of all, to execute whatever commitments Pushkin may have made to Harriman. Indeed, we do not even know whether Harriman called on Khrushchev to perform on Pushkin's promises.* While the Pushkin-Harriman understandings were an essential premise of the Geneva Accords as *written*, they were evidently no part of the Geneva "facade" or the Harriman-Hilsman "tacit understanding" that both Hilsman and General Taylor tell us we agreed upon with the Communist side. Chester Cooper, once an aide to Harriman, has offered, in his book, *The Lost Crusade*, a pregnant footnote to the whole Laos experience: "Whether indeed Pushkin ever informed his own Government of his compact with Harriman will probably never be known for certain; Pushkin died of a heart attack not long after the Laos talks and Moscow has never admitted to any knowledge of the arrangement."[2]

"Never be known for certain"! But how easy it would have been to find out! Did Harriman not report to Khrushchev at his April 26 meeting on the promises Pushkin made—and demand performance? Did Khrushchev deny Pushkin's promises or simply renege on them or shrug his shoulders? Harriman never said publicly (apparently not even to Cooper). We may never know this either. The Pushkin-Harriman understandings have dropped into an American "memory hole" as deep as the Soviet "memory hole."

*On the ground in Laos, as so often happened, the issue was lost in a miasma behind which the Communist side, having boldly extended the perimeter of contest, would temporarily fade into the mountain mists to emerge later when the non-Communist side had relaxed in renewed confidence in the "Geneva facade." In this case, the re-emergence occurred in May 1964 when they suddenly evicted the neutralists from the Plaine des Jarres.

Still, let us imagine for a moment the possibility suggested by Mr. Cooper. Imagine a Deputy Foreign Minister—not of a putatively independent jungle tribe but of one of the World's superpowers—who would blithely and irresponsibly engage the personal representative of the President of the United States in a series of understandings of great moment without telling his own government! Remember, this is the same Pushkin who, in October 1962, three months after signing the Geneva Accords, responded to our concern over the failure of Hanoi's forces to depart Laos by wisecracking that the Vietminh "will fade into the jungle." Imagine that the most highly integrated, totalitarian bureaucratic system in the history of mankind would leave such a loose cannon in a high position of responsibility without punishment! Would the Soviet Union deliberately attempt such a fraud on America's premier negotiator? One might as well imagine that Harriman fabricated his reports to Kennedy of Pushkin's assurances to him.

Mr. Cooper did not invent the idea, however. He is capsulating corridor speculation at the time. Another often heard variation on the same theme was implicit in the lament, "Ah, if only Pushkin had lived."

But, is it not most likely of all that Pushkin made his commitments to Harriman on instructions, and made them orally, knowing that his Government would need the flexibility to disown or forget them? Of course, it is. But that would raise the question of what were the USSR's real intentions and of what real value the Geneva Accords were and of how we should adapt our course to reality. As 1963 wore on, it became clear that the studied avoidance of these questions was part of the essence of the "facade of Geneva." By the onset of autumn I could cling to it no longer. It made me more than merely seasick.

I thought of seeking a transfer but I didn't believe that was the answer. Time was the answer—I thought. We were in an untenable position in Indochina and we couldn't stay in it. Inexorably, the logic of events would force us to shift in one direction or another—I thought. Either the aggression through Laos would force us to change our position there so that we could stop the assault, or the undermining of South Vietnam would force us to withdraw our military support. *We had to stop the aggression through Laos or we had to stop defending South Vietnam.* Either way—and I hoped it would be the first—the Gordian knot would be cut and our position rectified. Either way, we couldn't go on this way much longer. We couldn't have it both ways.

I was wrong. We went on trying to have it both ways for years, throwing in our wealth, our power, our youth, our prestige, to fill the gap.

Anyway, I stayed. Looking back, I think I didn't really want to change jobs for the same reason that keeps a reader of a mystery or suspense novel up all night. I was hooked. I wanted to see the solution. But I was right in one respect. I didn't belong in my position in the Far East Bureau. And it must have been evident to others because only a few months later, I learned of my impending transfer.

10

The Vietnam Strand

"But love is blind, and lovers cannot see
The pretty follies that themselves commit."
Shakespeare. The Merchant of Venice, II vi 36.

Compartmentalization was an essential part of our modus operandi in Indochina. Each country—Laos, South Vietnam, North Vietnam and Cambodia—was seen and dealt with according to separate rationales. I think my difficulty in coping with this intellectual compartmentalization was at the root of the sensation of "seasickness" which I experienced during this period. I didn't work directly on Vietnam problems at this time but was in close touch with those who did. They were organized as a special interdepartmental Task Force, nominally within the Department's Bureau of Far Eastern Affairs but with a complex State-Defense-CIA-ICA-JCS structure which required special direct ties with the White House.

Laos and Cambodia, on the other hand, were part of the Office of Southeast Asian Affairs. The separation from Vietnam is important, not for bureaucratic reasons, but for its symbolism of conceptual and strategic separation. In fact, the three Indochinese countries were strategically inseparable and the Communist side made its treatment of them dovetail as mutually supporting legs of a unified strategy. It was now clear to me that Ho Chi Minh's Communist Party intended to bring the whole of France's former Indochinese empire under its sway. It would have made better sense for the U.S. to create an "Indochina Task Force" but this would have been opposed by those who wanted to keep policy toward Laos and Cambodia separate from Vietnam where the military had such a powerful role. But I do not wish to over-emhasize the bureaucratic aspect (as we are inclined to do in the U.S. Government.) No bureaucratic arrangements could supply substantive coherence among policies which themselves sprang from a compartmentalized concept. This will become clear later. But, first, where did we stand in South Vietnam in the spring of 1963 as the "facade of Geneva" in Laos spread and enveloped our strategy throughout Indochina?

In one of his columns, Joseph Alsop quoted Averell Harriman as saying that Kennedy had told Harriman "to get whatever settlement he could on Laos, but that the U.S. really intended to make its stand in Vietnam."[1] Now, in face of the Geneva Accord's subversion by the Communists, it was time to make our stand in South Vietnam.

From 1961 to the summer of 1963, South Vietnam had been in the shadow of Laos. As the editors of *The Pentagon Papers* commented: "No fundamental new American decisions on Vietnam were made until the Buddhist unrest in the last half of 1963 and no new major military decisions were made until 1965."[2] Nevertheless, the numbers of U.S. military advisors rose gradually from a few hundred to 16,000 while the U.S. military provided fighter-bomber air cover and helicopter mobility. The extent of our involvement grew steadily during this period. That this could happen without major new decisions reflects a continuation of the October 1961 Kennedy style of incremental decision-making while treating Vietnam as if it were "something other than war."

It was recognized that the threat represented a combination of external and internal elements. Describing the Communist strategy beginning with 1958, Hilsman says that "A major attack was being launched. It was indirect but still it was aggression—through the guerrilla tactics and techniques of internal war."[3] At Fort Bragg in 1961, Walt Rostow had spoken of "a new form of aggression" by the Communists whom he characterized as "the scavengers of the modernization process."[4]

But while the element of external aggression was recognized rhetorically, the emphasis in action was placed almost wholly on the tactical internal aspects on the premises that

- the level of external infiltration was believed to be low;

- Hanoi would keep it low to preserve the fiction of an "internal war"; and

- a successful socio-political-military counter-insurgency in the South would allow Hanoi a quiet retreat while "saving face" and "salvaging prestige."

Accordingly, "internal war," not external attack, was the premise in our search for a strategic concept of operations.

The concept developed—broadly, a "counter-insurgency"—was built around three elements:

- a counter-guerrilla military capability
- separating the population from the Vietcong, and
- reform and development to build integrated, social, political and economic strength.

The centerpiece of the concept was the "strategic hamlet"—derived in part from the experience of an Englishman, Sir Robert Thompson, who had successfully applied it against indigenous Chinese Communist guerrillas in Malaya in the 1950s.

Guerrillas live off the countryside and require considerable support from the populace—voluntary, if possible, but forced, if necessary, as it was for the most part in South Vietnam (witness the very large component of terrorism, kidnapping and assassination in Vietcong tactics). Attacking guerrillas by means of superior conventional arms, infantry, artillery, aerial bombing or naval bombardment, damages the surrounding society more than the guerrillas who simply take cover and emerge only when circumstances favor them. The way to defeat such guerrillas, according to this concept, is to separate them from the population, sparing it from terrorist demands. The "strategic hamlet" was the answer.

Spreading outward, like an oil-blot on paper or cloth, from a secure area into less secure areas, the strategic hamlets, based on existing habitation patterns, were to be armed, fenced, trained, guarded and provided communications to enable them to hold out against attack until mobile military power could arrive. There was also a large element of what came to be called "nation-building" activities, local village democracy councils, special civic action teams to help in improved local administration, improved social services, economic, agricultural and educational assistance. It was important that the process proceed in an orderly manner at a measured pace, the perimeter expanding steadily and regularly so that it would not overreach or leave gaps vulnerable to penetration. By this means, the sociopolitical pacification part of the counter-insurgency program would be given time to move in behind the advancing security perimeter to do its part, thus strengthening the infrastructure of the South. Gradually, the enemy would be squeezed out and back by these advancing impenetrable, secure perimeters until eventually, according to the theory, Hanoi would suspend its effort, having been convinced it could not win.

But, to make success dependent on causing Hanoi to suspend its effort was tantamount to acknowledging that the prime mover of the war against South Vietnam was not internal but external. If so, then the so-called "insurgency" was not primarily a genuine insurgency or indigenous uprising. Rather, insurgency (the toreador's cape) was the simulated appearance of Hanoi's guerrilla tactics as distinct from Hanoi's strategy (the toreador's sword) which was territorial conquest.

It had worked in Malaya—where the situation was different in critical respects. As a sea-girt peninsula, Malaya was not bordered by a Communist, irredentist North Malayan state as South Vietnam was bordered by North Vietnam and the North Vietnamese-dominated part of Laos. Infiltration into Malaya was truly an insignificant trickle. Second, the guerrillas there belonged to a local Chinese minority, a distinction which set them apart from both the nationalist Malays and the Indian minority. Finally, in Malaya, the program was carried out under the guidance of the British who, having successfully governed the country for nearly a century, were well-situated to do it.

Still, despite the differences between Malaya and South Vietnam, the strategic hamlet concept had relevance for Vietnam if provision were made for the strategic external factor which weighed so heavily there as opposed to Malaya where it was virtually absent.* Unfortunately, this provision was not made. Instead, the external factor, which was often cited in public declarations to justify our presence, was virtually read out of the premises on which the strategic hamlet program was based. Thus, Hilsman, who at Kennedy's request wrote up the concept for the President** disparages the importance of external infiltration routes, arguing that

> The mistake so far had been to conceive the infiltration routes as the enemy's supply line and the regular Viet Cong guerrilla as the main body

*The external factor was also minimal in the Hukbalahap guerrilla uprising in the Philippines which was successfully defeated by President Magsaysay with U.S. help and the advice of Gen. Edward Lansdale whose advice was also sought with respect to Vietnam in the 1960s.

**Returning from a visit to Vietnam in January 1962, which included consultations with Thompson, Hilsman briefed the President on the concept. In his book, he reports: "The President was impressed with Thompson's ideas. . . . He told me to write the whole thing up as a formal report under the title, *A Strategic Concept for Vietnam* . . . . and kept me busy giving the oral version to his brother, the heads of CIA and AID." (Hilsman, *To Move a Nation*, p. 438.)

of his strength. But the true supply lines in a guerrilla war were the thousands of roads and trails radiating out like the spokes of a wheel from each of the sixteen thousand hamlets of South Vietnam. And the main body of the enemy's strength was the people of South Vietnam—at least potentially. What the strategic hamlet program was designed to do was to cut those true lines of supply and destroy the guerrilla's access to the main source of strength, the food and potential recruits in the villages.[5]

In other words, despite what he and others may have said elsewhere about North Vietnamese aggression, the real sinews of the war were considered to be internal—not external. That President Kennedy absorbed this conception of the war was evident from his pronouncement, quoted by Hilsman, that the external "infiltration trails are a built-in excuse for failure." But, if this were so, then why should success in the counter-insurgency campaign in South Vietnam be measured by causing Hanoi to suspend its supposedly minor role?

How far this view was from reality was revealed after Hanoi's final victory. When the North Vietnamese were able to shed the contrived image of insurgency with which they had masked their invasion, they frankly explained that as early as 1963 Hanoi had already concluded that the spokes radiating among the hamlets of South Vietnam could not support the war North Vietnam was planning. Before the death of Diem, Hanoi sent a mission under Col. Bui Tin (who, in 1975, accepted Saigon's surrender) down the Ho Chi Minh Trail to survey the situation. The conclusion was that the Vietcong were unprepared for an intensive campaign. As Bui Tin told Stanley Karnow: "We had to move from the guerrilla phase into conventional war. Otherwise our future would have been bleak."[6]

Based on this judgment, in the spring of 1964—a year before any officially admitted U.S. ground combat forces were deployed—Hanoi ordered the creation of a modern logistical system out of the Ho Chi Minh Trail in Laos. In effect this was a follow-on decision growing out of the decision in 1959 to create Group 559 to develop an infiltration route. It was required to support the deployment of regular North Vietnamese forces.

In any case, the strategic hamlet program was adopted by President Diem in March 1962 and was apparently off to a good start. Indeed, the situation improved considerably during the summer of 1962 and up to October, when the Communists seemed to have taken the measure of the hamlets. The new strategy began to show some weaknesses in execution. The South Vietnamese military tended to lean toward heavy-handed destructive military sweeps rather than on precise, efficient counter-guerrilla operations. Both the Vietnamese and the American military favored the use of aerial bombing, napalm and defoliants which some civilians believed would do more damage and generate more opposition than the value of what they achieved against the enemy. The Vietnamese Government multiplied the strategic hamlets more rapidly than it could support and supply them and in the process built many in exposed positions while leaving undefended salients into presumably secured areas. Worse, it appeared that President Diem's brother, Ngo Dinh Nhu, was deliberately pushing the expansion as a means of converting the program into a political instrument for strengthening the regime's control over the peasants.

The gains of the summer vanished and a downward slide set in as Communist attacks increased and government initiatives decreased. Several disastrous engagements (e.g. My Tho in October and Ap Bac in December) stimulated the suspicion that President Diem was deliberately encouraging the Army to avoid head-on engagements which might result in heavy casualties, preferring to let the enemy escape. Studies by the U.S. usually concluded that the hamlet concept was sound and that the fault lay primarily with the implementation. Failures were traced to weaknesses in Vietnamese administration and ultimately to President Diem himself and to his brother, Ngo Dinh Nhu.

In short, since the program was premised on internal war and was designed as an "internal strategy," its weaknesses were traced to "internal" causes. For example, Hilsman ruled out any significant external role in the downturn. In his book, he points out that our intelligence showed that in 1962 Vietcong regular unit strength went up from 16,000 to 23,000 in the face of losses, according to Vietnamese government claims, of 20,000, and an intelligence estimate that only 4,000 infiltrators at the most came down the Ho Chi Minh Trail.[7] He then dismissed any counter-claim of larger infiltration by reference to Kennedy's built-in dismissal of the trails as a "built-in excuse for failure."[8] Implication: Vietcong recruits are local, not infiltrated; if there were no local recruits, the number of VC would have fallen to zero.

Elsewhere, however, Hilsman was not so ready to accept uncritically Saigon's claimed estimates of enemy casualties. In his report to the President in January, 1963, when referring to peasant resentment toward the Government, he remarked that "No one really knows, for example, how many of the 20,000 Vietcong killed last year were only innocent or at least persuadable villagers."[8] So much for the 20,000.

As for infiltration, later information consistently forced the upgrading of infiltration estimates. For example, the cumulative estimate of infiltration made in April of 1964 for the period 1959 to 1964 had to be quickly revised upward in October. Even then, the recognized imprecision was so great that the new estimate had to cover a wide spread from a minimum of 19,000 to a 34,000 maximum.[9] Eventually, even the maximum figure proved to be too low as is evidenced by the 1972 Order of Battle report of 41,640 infiltrators during the period of 1959–1964.[10]

Now, let us bring this insight into a more narrow focus on the specific year used by Hilsman—1962—to make his point. Whereas Hilsman used the then current estimate of 4,000 infiltrators, today we know from the 1972 Order of Battle report that actual infiltration in 1962 was no less than 12,857—more than three times 4,000. This estimate raises VC strength in 1962 from 16,000 to 28,857, before subtracting VC losses.

If, instead of 20,000, actual VC losses were only 6,000 (which, in the context of Hilsman's scorn of the larger figure, is as reasonable an illustrative assumption as any), VC strength at the end of the year would stand at about 23,000, exactly the figure he gives.*

Whatever the numbers were, North Vietnam continued to send men in numbers sufficient to keep their style of war going, but this escalation was overlooked, so strong was the compulsion to sidestep the danger of "provocation"—to preserve and protect the "tacit agreement" and the "facade of Geneva."

Instead, the prevailing syndrome required looking inward, as with a microscope, into the internal symptoms of South Vietnam, rather than outward, as through a telescope, at the relationship of the internal symptoms to the external setting. On the plane to Saigon on the last day of 1962, Hilsman and Forrestal, undertaking a survey requested by the President, agreed to define the central issue as follows: "The issue was the political viability of the country and whether or not even the potential existed in South Vietnam to carry out the kind of tightly disciplined precisely coordinated political, social and military program that would be needed to defeat the guerrillas."[11]

*	Hilsman's Account	Alternative Account
VC-beginning 1962—	16,000	16,000
Infiltration 1962—	+ 4,000 (Current est.)	+13,000 (Final fig.)
Sub-total—	20,000	29,000
Est. VC losses—	−20,000 (Discounted)	− 6,000 (Illust.)
Remainder—	00,000 (Theoretical)	
VC at end 1962—	23,000 (Hilsman est.)	23,000 (Hils. est.)
Local recruits—	23,000	
(Implicit Conclusion)		

If the issue really were as presented by Hilsman, then doubt as to South Vietnam's viability should have led to a decision by the United States not to involve itself militarily in the defense of what was internally unviable. Instead, it led the United States into a regressively minute analysis of the internal weaknesses of South Vietnam in the hope of finding the ultimate microscopic fulcrum which might be corrected—at the instance of the U.S., of course. Hilsman concluded this portion of his analysis—as the U.S. Government did—by focusing on the ultimate internal fulcrum: "No matter how one twisted and turned the problem in other words, it always came back to Ngo Dinh Diem."[12]

This was the direction of movement when the Buddhist crisis, beginning in May 1963, accelerated things dramatically. In origin, the Buddhist crisis was unrelated to the war. It should never have occurred and once started it could have been quickly defused by repealing some old discriminatory laws governing religious groups. But Diem and Nhu, rigid and lacking in political finesse, not only refused to make the changes required but stubbornly reacted out of a blind fixation that the Buddhist leaders must be humbled. I do not intend here to review this sad episode. Suffice to say that it led to the world-publicized self-immolations by Buddhist monks, to mounting popular anger around the world, particularly in the United States, to the infuriation of the American press with Diem and vice versa, and finally, on August 21, to the attack on Buddhist pagodas by the Vietnamese Special Forces.

It led also to the unbridgeable gulf between the Vietnamese and U.S. leaderships which, in less than three months, resulted in the overthrow and assassination of Diem and Nhu. During part of the Buddhist crisis Ambassador Nolting was away from Saigon, and his deputy, William Trueheart, was Charge d'affaires. As a result of his experience of being stonewalled by Diem and Nhu in all his efforts to encourage a settlement, Trueheart became convinced that the war could not possibly be won as long as they were in power.* Other U.S. officials came to the same conclusion and with reason. This bitter confrontation influenced the White House in its search for a non-career diplomat, an American of political prominence, to send as Ambassador to replace Ambassador Nolting who was due to leave.

---

*A few months later, just before I left Washington, Trueheart returned to replace Barney Koren as Director of Southeast Asian Affairs. I did not serve with him long but I was impressed by the depth of the effect this experience had had on him when in our first discussion, he said simply, "Norm, I'm a dove."

Henry Cabot Lodge was the man and he arrived in Saigon just a day after the Vietnamese Special Forces attack on the pagodas and just two days before the fateful cable of August 24 which set the U.S. on a course toward the encouragement of Diem's overthrow.

The progression of events during the ten weeks from the cable of August 24 to Diem's overthrow on November 1 is infinitely complex in detail and vast in its political, moral, logical and human significance. Various accounts have been written. The one written by Roger Hilsman, with Harriman a co-drafter of the cable, is particularly revealing of how events were viewed at the time by the actors involved.

In essence, the August 24 cable recorded the U.S. conclusion that unless Diem would change his ways and get rid of his brother, we must plan on the departure of both from the Saigon government. The Vietnamese military were to be informed of this and advised that while we would take no part in planning action, nevertheless an interim anti-Communist government that brought about a change would receive U.S. interim support in continuing the war effort. This was an invitation to the South Vietnamese generals to carry out the *coup d'état* they were already considering. For practical reasons, the generals postponed action for over two months during which time, the Kennedy Administration agonized, debated and re-thought and reconsidered but, in the end, did not change the position of offering support to a post-Diem government brought to power by a *coup d'état*. Finally, on the night of November 1–2 it happened. Diem and Nhu were not only overthrown. They were slain.

Although I was not at the time privy to any of the decisive discussions it would have been hard not to learn a great deal from colleagues involved and to form some impressions. I formed two. First, it seemed to me that there was no hope in continuing to defend South Vietnam while Diem remained in office. Second, it seemed to me that the decision for the U.S. to involve itself to the extent of abetting Diem's overthrow should have been based on a solid conclusion that the war *could be won without Diem* rather than on the shallower judgment that it could not be won with Diem. I still feel the same way. I shall try to explain.

Earlier, I quoted Hilsman's statement of his and Forrestal's agreement on December 31, 1962, as to the "central judgment" to be made regarding Vietnam. Because of its importance, I shall quote it again somewhat more fully:

> Actually, the issue was bigger than just the personality of Diem, his dictatorial regime or his family. The issue was the political viability of the country and whether or not even the potential existed in South Vietnam

to carry out the kind of tightly disciplined, precisely coordinated political, social and military program that would be needed to defeat the guerrillas. On the plane going out Forrestal and I had decided that this would be the central judgment. We had since discovered that making a judgment on any aspect of guerrilla warfare was difficult—but this, clearly was the most difficult.[13]

It surely was the most difficult and it was a judgment never definitely made, one way or the other. From this central judgment—had it been made—would have flowed the answer to the key question: if the war could not be won with Diem, could it be won without him? And this question would have led to breaking down the Hilsman-Forrestal question into two component parts:

> First—Is the country really viable, with the potential to defeat the guerrillas?
>
> Second—Is the "political, social and military program" which the U.S. supported, even if thoroughly applied, "tightly disciplined and precisely coordinated," capable of defeating the kind of actual challenge which North Vietnam was putting to South Vietnam?

My own answers to these two questions, respectively, were "yes" and "no." Let me take them up separately.

First, was the country intrinsically viable? The proposition, as stated by Hilsman and Forrestal does not pretend to answer the question. Nor was it answered in the Washington discussions which led to the August 24, 1963 cable and took place from the time of the cable until the coup of November 1. Attorney General Robert Kennedy raised it in the September 6, National Security Council meeting as reported by Hilsman:

> The first question was whether a Communist take-over could be successfully resisted with any government. If it could not, now was the time to get out of Vietnam entirely rather than waiting. If the answer was that it could, but not with a Diem-Nhu government as it was now constituted, we owed it to the people resisting Communism in Vietnam to give Lodge enough sanctions to bring changes that would permit successful resistance. But the basic question of whether a Communist take-over could be resisted with any government had not been answered, and he [RFK] was not sure that anyone had enough information *to* answer it. (Hilsman's emphasis)[14]

Some questions, however, must be answered even without adequate information because there will never be sufficient exact empirical data from which an answer will emerge. These judgments must be made one way or another because if one does not choose an answer as an operating premise, events will force another—and perhaps less welcome—answer without a deliberate choice ever being willed.

Robert Kennedy's question was never answered. Instead, Hilsman tells us, "McNamara leaped on the Attorney General's question . . . and proposed still another mission to Vietnam to 'get the facts'."[15] The same day, Marine General Victor Krulak (SACSA)*, representing McNamara and Joseph Mendenhall from the State Department's Far East Bureau, flew to Vietnam and returned four days later to report to the National Security Council. Even though Krulak reported that the "shooting war" was going well, Mendenhall reported a virtual breakdown of civil government in the cities.** Robert Kennedy's question remained unanswered.

At the end of September, McNamara himself and General Maxwell Taylor made another "fact-finding tour" and returned to report that although the "shooting war" was making great progress, they recognized the existence of political tension associated with the growing unpopularity of Diem and Nhu. The NSC announced publicly that "the military program has made progress" but acknowledged repressive political actions which "have not yet significantly affected the military effort, but they can do so in the future."[16] Robert Kennedy's question still remained unanswered.

An answer would have provided a means to decide properly whether or not the U.S. should play a role in the overthrow of Diem. If South Vietnam was truly unviable and lacking even in the potential to cope with the Communist guerrillas, then the Diem-Nhu problem was only the tip of an iceberg. In this case, their overthrow would not solve anything, and if we collaborated in it, we would only be assuming further responsibility for a lost cause. Better to get out—as Robert Kennedy had mused. I remember Paul Kattenberg, then Director (soon to be replaced) of the Vietnam Task Force, who returned from Vietnam a week after the August 24 cable, desolate and convinced that in less than a year the people would gravitate to the other side. Therefore, he argued that we should withdraw gradually in order to avoid being forced out a year later. His advice was sound (although I did not agree with it), but only if Kennedy's question had provoked a negative response.

I did not agree because I doubted that South Vietnam was intrinsically unviable. Although I was not an expert on Vietnam I ques-

*Special Assistant (JCS) for Counterinsurgency and Special Activities.

**The President remarked, mockingly, "You two did go to the same country didn't you?

tioned crossing off as unviable any country of 16 million highly cultured people, particularly a people as venerable as the South Vietnamese. Partition does not make a country unviable: witness two Koreas, two Germanies and two Chinas, not to mention Poland which has maintained viability despite several historic partitions. In world politics today, viability depends not only on intrinsic internal factors but on all the external factors which go to create the balance in which a nation reposes. The United Nations is thick with intrinsically unviable states but they persist, for the time being, because they have reached a certain equilibrium among international forces and, in many cases, because they do not border on a Communist state. Without doubting the weaknesses of South Vietnam, I thought it possessed the potential viability of South Korea if only because it had an international position and strategic posture comparable to that of South Korea, including an internationally recognized cease-fire line against its Northern, Communist, irridentist antagonist.

Now, for the second question: was the counter-insurgency program supported by the U.S., even if skillfully executed, capable of defeating North Vietnam's challenge? This question was not specifically addressed as part of the decision to encourage the *coup d'état*, but an affirmative answer is implicitly assumed in the Hilsman-Forrestal proposition. It was assumed that the counter-insurgency concept was fundamentally sound—subject to ad hoc refinements—and would meet and defeat Communist strategy, spreading security like an oil spot outward until the guerrillas were squeezed against the border, at which time Hanoi, rather than come out into the open, would quietly suspend the war *sine die*. Hence, the internal war would eventually turn against the North Vietnamese, forcing them to abandon the external war.

If this hypothesis was right and if South Vietnam was intrinsically viable, then it made sense to abet the overthrow of Diem and Nhu so as to remove a roadblock to victory. But if either hypothesis was false, then our involvement in Diem's overthrow would saddle us with responsibility for the dismal aftermath. Unfortunately, neither of these hypotheses was examined to the point of formulating overt premises to serve as the foundation for deciding whether or not to participate in the overthrow of Diem and Nhu. Instead, we found the Diem-Nhu regime both unspeakable and impossible and, with characteristic American viscera, we leapt into the role of accessory in its overthrow, not seeing our passionate act as one that would itself commit us. Thus did Hilsman forecast to Forrestal, "all it meant was that we would have a second chance."[17]

But events forced the premises on us. Having abetted the overthrow of the Diem-Nhu regime we acquired a special responsibility for its successors and we became objectively committed (whether we believed it or not) to the hypotheses that South Vietnam was indeed viable and that the war was indeed winnable by the internal means of the counter-insurgency plan. And, come what may, we were objectively committed to make it come true.

I say we were *objectively* committed to all this because we were not consciously committed with deliberate forethought. On the contrary, President Kennedy did not apparently feel committed. It was just nineteen days after the *coup d'état* which he had abetted that, as is related in Chapter 4, he requested Michael Forrestal to study how we got into South Vietnam, what we thought we were doing and how we might be able to get out. Recounting the same conversation years later, *U.S. News and World Report* goes on to relate that the President raised again Robert Kennedy's question, which had never been answered: "Is it a viable situation? Can we see it through? What makes us think Vietnam can survive?"[18]

All were eminently sound questions which should have been asked and answered before. The answers should have formed the premises of our judgment whether or not to support the overthrow of Diem and Nhu. We were still embarked on two contrary courses in Laos and South Vietnam.*

Very few thought this way. Certainly not my old friend Bill Sullivan who served as Harriman's deputy during the negotiation of the Geneva Accords on Laos. Far from treating the Accords as a definitive test of Communist intentions in Indochina, most believed that the Accords were a design for the future, worth preserving, *in vitro*, as it were, if necessary until South Vietnam had been secured against both insurgency at home and Hanoi's aggression from outside. I, on the other hand, believed it was impossible to defeat the insurgency until the external component had been cut off.

A couple of days after Forrestal's departure to Cambodia, I was sitting with Bill Sullivan, eating lunch at Kitty and Al's restaurant in

---

*Even with the answers to his questions to Forrestal, it is unlikely that Kennedy, had he lived, would have reversed course in Vietnam. The same domestic political factors, after the Bay of Pigs, which led him into opposite courses in Laos and Vietnam would probably have prevented him from withdrawing in an election year, as he knew, according to Henry Brandon (*Anatomy of Error*, 30). By the beginning of a second term in January 1965 he would have been facing the same challenges (with the same advisors) that led Pres. Johnson into incremental escalation of American military deployments. Three weeks after his second inauguration he would have been confronted with the Communist Pleiku attack and McGeorge Bundy's recommendation for the sustained air campaign which became known as "Rolling Thunder."

the undeveloped area a block or so in front of the Department of State, an area now graced by an equestrian statue honoring the Argentine "Libertador," Jose de San Martin. We were sitting in the center of the room, crowded with a lunch-hour rush of patrons all trying to talk over the noise of each other as well as that of the radio behind the bar. It has always been difficult for me to sort out and listen to specific voices against the dissonant, layered background of masculine hum and shrill feminine laughter. It seems to me rather like trying to understand a radio program being jammed out by competitors filling up all the nearby frequencies. So, when Bill suddenly arose and walked to the bar, I looked up startled.

"Something's happened to the President," he said and shouldered his way to the radio.

Something certainly had happened. Within an hour we knew he was dead in Dallas.

The assassination of the President of the United States is a geological event that re-arranges the topography of the world. That was true of Kennedy's death. But the inertia of the American Government in motion is also awesome. With respect to Indochina there were changes of style and emphasis, but the basic pattern—the "tacit agreement" and the belief in "insurgency"—did not change except slowly and by the now-familiar methods of incremental decision-making.

The Vietnam and Laos strands of our strategy were crosswise and they were already tangling.

On January 30,1964, the second in a series of attempted and actual *coups d'état* occurred in Saigon. General Nguyen Khanh ousted General Duong Van Minh (Big Minh) who had led the revolutionary group which finished off Diem and Nhu three months earlier. Obviously, if the war had to be won in South Vietnam by internal means, we were on a very sticky wicket. What was needed was somehow to correct the self-defeating compartmentalization of our Indochina strategies, the idea underlying the following paragraphs quoted from a memorandum I wrote to Barney Koren on January 31, the day after the second coup:

> Yesterday's *coup d'état* in Saigon seems to me to illustrate again the urgent need for . . . extraordinary measures to force the communists to pull in their horns in Southeast Asia and to stop the spiraling deterioration of our position.
>
> South Vietnam—the second *coup d'état* suggests that the overthrow of Diem has left a highly fissionable situation and that there may be more coups before stability. . . . The prospects for winning the war are greatly reduced, whereas the prospects for further disintegration in South Vietnam are increased. While I am no expert on Vietnam, it doesn't seem to me

likely that we can beat this situation by actions solely within South Vietnam, short of a virtual takeover of the country ourselves.

Cambodia—It is perfectly obvious that the trend there is running against the U.S.

Laos—The Laos Panhandle remains wide open to use by the Communists all the way down to South Vietnam and Cambodia.

There is every need to reverse the trend. This cannot be done by half measures but requires the taking of real risks. . . . It has been a long time since the U.S. has bared its teeth in Asia—since the Korean War, in fact. It may be time to do it again.

The Laos Panhandle is the critical area because of its location touching on North Vietnam, South Vietnam, Thailand and Cambodia. It should be our objective to re-establish friendly control over the whole southern half of the Panhandle to prevent its use by the Vietminh, to cordon off Cambodia against direct Communist pressure, to protect the Thai frontier and to secure the flank (of the neutralist government) in Laos. It might be useful to consider ways of pressing vigorously on all sides to regain control of the southern Panhandle, utilizing Lao and South Vietnamese forces as well as Montagnard and covert units.*

We should be prepared in the event of resistance . . . to demonstrate with the Seventh Fleet off the coast of North Vietnam as well as to move American forces across the Mekong River into the Panhandle.

Our objectives would be calling off the war in South Vietnam with suitable agreements, withdrawal of all Vietminh and Pathet Lao from the Panhandle, full freedom for the ICC throughout Laos, including the Pathet Lao areas and, if necessary, the partition of northern Laos.**

There was no written response although Barney discussed the idea in the Bureau and I recall that it evoked some interest on the part of a couple of officials (one military and one civilian) in the Office of International Security Affairs (ISA) in the Department of Defense. In

*The Montagnard hill tribes of South Vietnam, bordering Cambodia and southern Laos, were good fighters and were being trained by the U.S.

**This memorandum shows some progress in thinking since the April 24, 1963 memo quoted in the last chapter. It accepts without mention the moribundity of the Geneva Accords and predatory intentions of the Communist side. It focuses on the Laos Panhandle as the strategic key linking all the countries involved. It fails, however, in its shyness to face up to the need for definitive U.S. action rather than merely "being prepared" and "demonstrating." At this stage, I was still under the spell of the "send-a-message syndrome" which, throughout the war, meant that by posturing in a certain way the U.S. could cause Hanoi to pull back. In this manner, the U.S. would "send a messagae to Hanoi" of what would happen if—in Dean Rusk's words—"Hanoi doesn't stop doing what it is doing and knows that it is doing."

retrospect, it is obvious that such a proposal could not survive, let alone be adopted although, as a matter of personal pride and principle, I wish that I had pressed it harder. Accordingly, the memo's only practical significance is in illuminating a casual remark made by Barney soon thereafter.

Late one afternoon about this time, Barney crooked his finger in the direction of his office, adjacent to mine. After some business, he leaned back and mentioned that our mutual friend, Ed Martin,* would soon be leaving Honolulu where he was Political Advisor to CINC-PAC. Ed was the third in the succession of Political Advisors sent by the Department of State to the Commander-in-Chief whose command included all U.S. forces in the Pacific and Far East. The first was John Steeves—the same man who had arrived as Ambassador to Afghanistan before I left Kabul for Washington. The second had been Sterling Cottrell, later the first Chairman of the Vietnam Working Group.

The job was created by agreement between the State and Defense Departments in the middle 1950s to provide a close, two-way operating liaison between the military and diplomatic components of U.S. policy and strategy in the Orient. The political advisor had access to the flow of political guidance from the Department as well as military communications with the Pentagon and the Far East. And he had personal access to the C-in-C, Admiral H. Donald Felt, who had set the practice of maintaining the closest of relationships with the Political Advisors assigned to him.

The "POLAD", as he was called in military acronymics, always travelled with the C-in-C in his extensive personal coverage of the area from Japan to Australia and from Taiwan to Thailand. Because the position was strictly advisory, some diplomatic officers questioned how effective it could be and preferred to remain in the straight line of advancement provided by the Department and the Foreign Service. There is something to be said for this point of view. However, one wonders how effective one person can be in the Department of State or anywhere else in the fantastically complex political-bureaucratic structure of the United States Government. In his book, aptly entitled, *The Diffusion of Power*, Walt Rostow, after eight years as Chairman of the Policy Planning Council, advisor to President Kennedy and Special Assistant for National Security Affairs to President Johnson, comments revealingly: "I do not believe the history of these years would have been substantially different if I had never set foot in Washington." Of course, the truth is that one cannot judge subjectively his

---

*Several years later to be Ambassador to Burma.

own objective impact. He can only register his own satisfaction (or lack of it) with his own effort.

"The POLAD job is one I've always wanted," mused Barney, who was already designated to be Ambassador to the former French Congo. (A couple of incarnations later, he got it.) "Have you ever thought of it?" I hadn't, really.

"Would you like it?"

Without waiting for an answer, he went on. "The Far East Bureau has been asked to name a successor to Ed and you seem to be the one. Roger [Hilsman] will send your name forward. Unless you object."

No, I didn't object. As I grew used to the idea it began to seem like just what I wanted—an opportunity to try to untie the Indochina knot from the other end of the string—the military end.

"You like to write long serious memos about policy and strategy. I think you'd like it," added Barney. He was right, and recalling my recent memo, I didn't mind this gentle, good-natured dose of realism. It was true—my only contribution in the Bureau, beyond the regular grist, had been a series of memos which said in various ways that our conceptual premises in Indochina were wrong. Now, my problem was to find a strategy that would gear the concept to the action, as George Kennan's "containment" geared our post-war concept of an expansive Soviet Union to action consisting of the Marshall Plan and NATO. Perhaps such a strategic link could be found on the military side. After all, an aggression is less likely to be disguised from or dissimulated by those who meet it on the ground than by those who read about it thousands of miles away. This was wishful thinking, I know now. But at the time it seemed plausible.

"Of course, I'd like to go. When?"

"Ed's leaving in late March. The Admiral is going to the Far East in early April and wants a new POLAD for the trip."

Two months! Yes, indeed, I'd go.

11

Cambodia Strand

" 'Prince Sihanouk, you are very young. You must choose between
the free world and the Communist world,' [said Secretary of State
Dulles in 1958.] Today, I pay homage to his grave. John Foster
Dulles was right. There is no nonalignment."

Prince Sihanouk in The New York Times, Sept. 5, 1981

So there we were, embarked on two incompatible courses, both
encompassed within the framework of the "facade of Geneva."
The first entailed tacit toleration of the slow, external invasion of South
Vietnam through Laos and the second entailed the internal defense
of South Vietnam for which we were incrementally assuming responsibility both by the logic of our strategy and by our role in the
overthrow of Diem. As a super-power, 10,000 miles from Indochina,
we were not (yet) devastated by this illogic because we were not
directly threatened and we could absorb the cost. But there was an
immediate and devastating meaning for Cambodia. The Cambodian
Chief of State, Prince Sihanouk, perceived it quite starkly. He was
convinced that North Vietnam would defeat South Vietnam and that
Communism would be the wave of the future in Southeast Asia. He
cultivated Communist China as an offset to a future unified, Communist Vietnam. To smooth the transition, he sought a new Geneva
Conference and treaty on Cambodia so as to stretch what we called
"the facade of Geneva" over his country. He made his meaning plain.

Sihanouk was an extraordinarily voluble man and his style of government included an almost continuous monologue which he kept
up while travelling around his country. In a way he was the obverse
of Diem who was a compulsive, inexhaustible talker in private conversation when he was imposing his theories and convictions on a
single listener whom he wanted to convert or overwhelm. But Diem,
a distant, ruling mandarin, was unable to communicate with his peo-

ple as a leader should. By contrast, Sihanouk conducted government like continuous theater in which he, as the only star, expounded his views on everything—simply everything—to his courtiers, political sycophants and political rivals, journalists, diplomats and above all, to "the children", as he rather patronizingly called his people. And "the children" responded, trooping after him even as the children of Hamlin trooped after the Pied Piper, to an equally tragic ending.

When one talks all the time one cannot always be consistent and Sihanouk certainly was not. His direction sometimes reflected his mercurial moods or his reaction to his interlocutor, and he sometimes doubled back on himself. Still, a few themes stood out fairly continuously. One was his belief that his small, defenseless country would have to rely on attracting world attention as a weapon of self-protection against its traditional rivals—Vietnam and Thailand. Specifically, he believed that he needed to engage the Cold War Great Powers in some kind of a stand-off agreement in the lee of which Cambodia could find a bit of derivative security.

Accordingly, beginning on August 20, 1962, the month after the Geneva Accords on Laos were signed, his main theme, repeated *ad nauseam* over the next couple of years, was the need for a new multinational Geneva Conference to recognize and guarantee Cambodia's neutrality. But this was already guaranteed by the 1954 Geneva Accords with monitoring by the ICC and collaterally re-insured by the 1962 Geneva guarantee of Laos's neutrality, also to be monitored by the ICC. In both cases, the ICC was totally ineffective and the neutrality promised by both was perverted by North Vietnam. Despite this dismal record, Sihanouk still thought that Cambodia deserved to have its own neutrality conference and treaty which would give him an instrument for focusing world attention on his country. And, despite the negative experience of the past there were some responsible officials in the Department of State willing to accede to Sihanouk's demand for a new round.

Were it not for Sihanouk's second theme, I suppose one could have said that a new international guarantee for Cambodia and a third equally ineffective ICC would have been harmless enough, even though unproductive. But his second theme was that South Vietnam was sure to lose, which is to say that North Vietnam was sure to win. In retrospect, one can say that not only was he right but also by his own behavior he helped to fulfill his own prediction. His "neutrality" was one-sided. The "enemy" from which he most wanted to be protected consisted of Thailand and South Vietnam, not North Vietnam which was already using Cambodian soil as an extension of the Ho Chi Minh

Trails.* Although his rhetoric was cleverly crafted to include all of Vietnam as a traditional threat, his own logic, had he realized it, should have led him to the conclusion that it was in Cambodia's interest to preserve the partition of Vietnam, that is, to preserve South Vietnam's independence. Whatever annoyance South Vietnam may have given Cambodia, it was hardly to be compared to the threat of an hegemonistic, united Vietnam to which Sihanouk trimmed his sails and from which his unhappy country now suffers.

Instead, when it came down to specific complaints and protests, it was South Vietnam that was his *bête noire*—not surprisingly, since he assumed North Vietnam would win. Occasionally, he would give voice to an oblique criticism which could be understood—by those familiar with his style—to refer to North Vietnam. But, day in and day out, his target was South Vietnam (and to a lesser extent, Thailand) whose occasional shallow and brief violations of Cambodian territory were slight alongside the virtual occupation of northeastern Cambodian provinces by North Vietnam. For Hanoi, northeastern Cambodia was an extension of the Ho Chi Minh Trails through Laos, a rest and training area for forces fighting against South Vietnam, a base for launching forays into South Vietnam and, later, the terminus of a major supply route through Cambodia from the port of Sihanoukville.

Prince Sihanouk's vision of the future emerged incrementally (as did everything in Indochina) as a hope that as the tide of Communism flowed over Southeast Asia, he could carve out a little niche in which "the children" could enjoy just a little cultural autonomy in the larger sea of regional Communist power. This was the shape and color of the "neutrality" Sihanouk sought. It was a specialized kind of "neutrality" which really needs to be enclosed in quotation marks because it was quite different from—indeed it was the opposite of—the kind of neutrality the United States had in mind when it negotiated with the Soviet Union and North Vietnam to neutralize Laos. For Sihanouk however, the best to be hoped for was to preserve the neutrality of a symbiotic lichen nestled in the roots of a large Southeast Asian Communist mangrove tree. Or, at least, so it seemed to me.

A third Sihanouk theme was a kind of schizoid dissimulation which may have served his domestic purposes but discredited him as a

---

*Years later—certainly by 1969—Sihanouk had changed his tune and not only publicly blamed Hanoi for violating his country but privately indicated his willingness to tolerate U.S. B-52 raids against North Vietnamese base camps in eastern Cambodia. Of course, by then, it was too late for Cambodia.

serious partner in serious international negotiations. He tried to draw
a curtain between his public remarks directed to his own people and
those directed to foreign countries. He talked all day long as he walked
in Phnom Penh or in the villages or paddy fields or schools and, in
the process, painted a pattern of purpose that contrasted with the
pattern he sometimes painted in official statements to the United
States. Inevitably, some of his remarks would be repeated to the press
or to foreigners. But he would be furious if a foreign government, a
few days later, would point out that what he said was incompatible
with what he had told that government's ambassador. He would reply
that what he said to his own people had nothing to do with what he
said to a foreign government. Admittedly, in most countries there is
a certain tension between the domestic and international postures
assumed by the government, but Sihanouk went much farther. He
would tell the United States privately that he knew we were not
responsible for a particular incident on his Vietnamese border and
the next day he would say the opposite publicly to some Cambodian
gathering. Yet, if we were to protest, he would tell us in high dudgeon
that we had no right to question his statement to his people. True
enough, no doubt, but the result was to create doubt as to the meaning
and value of what he told us.*

There was something feline about Sihanouk—something which baf-
fled by its inscrutability but constantly threatened by its capacity to
strike capricious, clawing blows. It took great patience and long study
of his history and words to establish a background of sufficient depth
to understand and respond to Sihanouk knowingly. Our Cambodian
desk officer could do that. As for me, I accepted him as a fact to be
dealt with but not as the innocent victim of our stronger allies—South
Vietnam and Thailand.

Still, despite Sihanouk's perversity, one had to give him credit for
attracting the attention of the Great Powers. First, the British, and
then later Britain and the USSR together as Co-chairmen of the
1961–2 Geneva Conference, supported the idea of a new conference
on Cambodia. Even in the Department of State, exasperated by his
one-eyed "neutrality," Sihanouk elicited significant sympathy which
sometimes seemed to rise and fall in proportion to our irritation with
President Ngo Dinh Diem in South Vietnam.

But no conference materialized, and in November 1963, Sihanouk
blasted the Western powers for ignoring his proposals. He demanded

---

*Since his fall from power and particularly since the Communist take-over
of his country, the Communist nations have shown a cool disdain for Sihanouk's fickle garrulity which he has tempered in adversity.

the cessation of American aid—to which the United States readily assented. This, in turn, led to a Philippines good offices mission to help Cambodia and the U.S. resolve their differences—a mission that seemed to me from the start to be doomed because the fundamental difference between us was that Prince Sihanouk was committed to the premise that South Vietnam and our cause in Indochina would fail. Such a difference cannot be easily compromised.*

Nevertheless, Under-Secretary Harriman, who was inclined to be more sympathetic toward Sihanouk than toward South Vietnam (even post-Diem), had directed a study of the aspects of a new 14-nation conference on Cambodia. It was quickly obvious to many of us that a new international guarantee of Cambodia's neutrality, coupled with a new troika ICC, would not be effective in improving Cambodia's security but rather, successful only as a political propitiation of Sihanouk, in the fond hope of making him behave in a more truly neutral way. However, relying on the general direction of Sihanouk's words and behavior, I doubted that it would work out that way. Indeed, such a guarantee could place in Sihanouk's hands another club to be used on the United States and its allies, South Vietnam and Thailand. I tried to reduce my reasoning to writing. Lacking any notes on this, I have tried to reconstruct the substance from memory:

Subject: The meaning of Sihanouk's demand for an international conference on Cambodia.

In deciding on our response to Sihanouk's proposal of a new conference we should try to analyze why he wants it and how he is likely to use the resulting agreement.

1. Cambodian neutrality was covered in the 1954 Geneva Accords and was reinforced by the 1962 Accords on Laos. Both treaties provided for the ICC to assist in enforcement. A new treaty would add nothing substantial to the existing situation.

2. Sihanouk does not seriously use the 1954 ICC, which is ineffective anyway because it is stymied by the Polish member's obstructionist veto. Majority rule has not increased the effectiveness of the ICC under the 1962 Accords. A new ICC would be no more effective, although it would create a new instrument available to Sihanouk for his purposes. What are his purposes?

3. Sihanouk seeks international attention for his country but when he gets it he focuses it against South Vietnam (and Thailand) rather than against North Vietnam which poses a greater long-range threat. Why does he do this?

*Moreover, the Philippines, as a close military ally of the U.S., was not well-situated to preserve the equidistance required in the effective exercise of good offices.

4. Because he expects North Vietnam to win and is preparing his posture to accommodate to that outcome. He would use a new ICC against South Vietnam (and Thailand)—not against North Vietnam (which the Polish ICC member would prevent anyway).

5. Cambodia's true interest should be to preserve the 1954 partition of Vietnam, thereby weakening the traditional power of a unified Vietnam which Sihanouk fears. This means preserving South Vietnam's independence, restraining North Vietnam and clearing North Vietnamese personnel out of the Laos Corridor where they border on Cambodian territory from which they attack South Vietnam. Instead, however, Sihanouk assumes North Vietnam's victory in advance and he acts to ready Cambodia for it.

6. What Cambodia needs more than a new treaty is removal of North Vietnamese forces from the adjoining Laos Panhandle.*

A little later—late in February, I believe—I sent Assistant Secretary Hilsman a short memo based on this reasoning, the essence being that since Sihanouk's problem did not spring from lack of treaty guarantees, it would not be solved by pyramiding another treaty and associated institutional paraphernalia on top of the failed existing ones. There was no response—at least not then.

In a nutshell, Sihanouk wanted to pull the "facade of Geneva" in Laos over Cambodia since he saw it as an instrument, not for stopping North Vietnamese expansion but easing the transition to accommodation. And perhaps, Sihanouk should not be blamed in light of the fact that the prevailing wisdom in the U.S. Government was that the "tacit agreement" on Laos, adumbrated by Hilsman, achieved a "postponement" somewhere between military intervention and surrender. The difference was that in the U.S. view, the "postponement" was to cover the gap until the "counter-insurgency" had saved South Vietnam, but in Sihanouk's view, the "postponement" was to cover the gap until North Vietnam won. As it turned out, Sihanouk's view proved to be the more realistic.

This was another time when we should have recalled and followed Harriman's prescription in May 1962 that if the Communists did not play fairly in the search for peace, "the basis of our current policy will, of course, have to be re-examined." But our policy was not re-examined, least of all by Harriman himself who seemed to favor

---

*It is only fair to admit my recollection may be more clearly crystalline than my words were in 1964. At the same time it is not unfair to note that today, Sihanouk, with the advantage of hindsight has shifted his field and is now willing to make common cause with anyone who will help against Hanoi's forces occupying his whole country.

repeating in Cambodia the same formula written into the treaty on Laos. Curiously, those who supported a Cambodia conference didn't argue that a new neutralization statute and ICC for Cambodia would work or would objectively improve Cambodia's security. Rather, the current seemed to spring from a felt need for tactical motion on our part to offset or compensate for setbacks in Laos and South Vietnam.

The study proceeded and various tentative drafts of treaty language were prepared, including clauses to cover enforcement and protection of Cambodian borders. At one point, I recall consulting with a member of the Vietnam Working Group, Joseph Mendenhall (the same man who had accompanied General Krulak on an inspection trip to Vietnam a couple of months before the overthrow of Diem). He and I agreed that since there might actually be a conference and a new treaty (the value of which we doubted), the U.S. should at least make the most of the opportunity to profit from the lessons of the dismal experience with earlier "troika" ICCs in Vietnam and Laos, composed of Canada, Poland and India. The pattern worked like a broken phonograph record. The Canadian would favor an investigation of a reported violation, the Pole would oppose any investigation in a Communist-controlled area and the Indian was pinioned between the two. The much-touted "majority-rule" adopted for limited use under the 1962 Accords worked no better in Laos where the ICC was subordinated to the triple-headed Government which applied the rule of unanimity. Moreover, the exercise of majority rule was rendered largely ineffective by the severe strain it placed on India whose overall policy of neutrality required it to maintain a position approximately equidistant between the other two—a virtually impossible feat.

Mendenhall and I experimented with designing an ICC for Cambodia which would substitute a totally neutral composition for the paralyzing Cold War troika formula. The idea was to have an ICC membership chosen from neutral countries uninvolved in Indochina and disinterested. As members we thought of one from Asia (Ceylon or Burma), one from Europe (Sweden or Austria) and one from Latin America (Colombia, or Venezuela or Peru) or from the Middle East (say, Egypt). There were various combinations. Such a commission would test Sihanouk's intentions but it would also provide him an opportunity. If he were really serious about wanting a new and, this time, effective ICC to monitor his country's neutrality effectively against all violations, including Communist ones, this would provide a new structure of use to him. If the Communist side opposed it, that would only be another litmus demonstration (if one were needed) of their intentions—a demonstration which I believe some preferred not to see made.

We were still consulting when, one day in February 1964, I was summoned to brief Under-Secretary Harriman on something which escapes me now. After I had finished, Harriman asked me casually how our study of a conference on Cambodia was coming. I told him where we stood and mentioned that we were working on some possible improvements in the ICC with the idea of making it truly neutral and therefore less vulnerable to Cold War paralysis. I mentioned that one idea was an ICC composed entirely of neutrals. He nodded and made some inocuous indication of interest. That was all—for then.

Work on the idea of a new conference proceeded desultorily as events raced ahead more rapidly than policies could be devised to handle them. We were in the process of negotiating the termination of aid programs in Cambodia and the withdrawal of our aid personnel, meanwhile coordinating with the Philippines in their effort to mend U.S.—Cambodia relations. Then, on February 11, 1964, mobs attacked the U.S. and British Embassies in Phnom Penh. On February 20, an accidental Vietnamese bombing of the Cambodian border interrupted Cambodian-Vietnamese talks designed to restore relations between those two countries.

I was scheduled to leave Washington at the end of March for Honolulu. Then, quite coincidentally, it was announced that Hilsman would resign at the same time. In his book he explains that his decision to resign reflected his belief that under President Johnson, the U.S. was, "obviously going to take the military path" whereas he, Hilsman, "was deeply convinced that the political approach was the wiser course", along the lines of President Kennedy's policy to "treat the problem of Vietnam as something other than war and to avoid getting American prestige so involved that the United States could not accept a negotiated settlement along the lines of the Geneva Accords on Laos— when and if the Vietnamese desired it."[1]

Of course, in Laos, North Vietnam had already accepted a settlement precisely "along the lines of the Geneva Accords on Laos" and then from the first day had totally refused to apply it.

Hilsman was to be replaced by William P. Bundy, well known to the Department through his many years in CIA and the Department of Defense. It was, all agreed, an excellent appointment, and I was sorry in a way that I would be leaving just as Bundy came to the Far East Bureau. Eight months later, in November, I would be sending him a lengthy memorandum containing my principal recommendation for a change to the course I thought we should follow if we were to continue to support South Vietnam. (See chapter 14).

My last day in the Department was as much symbolic as interesting. Hilsman took me and a couple of others to Harriman's office to report on some subject. It was late on a Friday afternoon of Hilsman's last week before leaving the Government and, coincidentally, my last week before leaving for Honolulu. When the regular business was finished, Harriman made some gracious remarks about Hilsman's work and his immediate departure. Suddenly, something reminded him of Cambodia and he whirled on me fiercely like the "crocodile" which was used to characterize him.

"What's this I hear about you going behind my back to oppose the ICC in Cambodia? I don't like it. You're trying to put out some unworkable new thing to replace the ICC. The Russians will never accept it. I've been in this business too long to stand for this. You're undercutting me and I don't like it. What is wrong with the ICC with majority rule?"

Rather taken aback by this explosion, I decided that the last question was rhetorical and that he didn't really want me to say what was wrong with the ICC. Moreover, if he didn't already know what was wrong with it there was little I could say this late on my last day, except to mention that I had briefed him on the Cambodian subject earlier and that I was sorry if I had wrongly understood his willingness to consider alternatives. The subject was dropped and we left his office shortly.

Walking back to Hilsman's office I described my earlier briefing of Harriman. Hilsman opined that the Governor had forgotten. He was probably right, but the incident provided an insight into one of the sources of U.S. policy. Back in his office, Hilsman put his feet on the desk and, in a tone of rumination, asked, "But, what *are* we going to do about Sihanouk and his conference?"

I said that Sihanouk's troubles didn't spring from lack of a neutralization statute or ICC enforcement machinery and that his troubles were not likely to be solved by another layer of what had already failed. As is evident from the quotation at the head of this chapter, Sihanouk himself has come to this view—a refreshing demonstration of an ability to learn from history.

I asked Hilsman if he had read the memo I sent him a few weeks earlier.

"Yeah", he replied with evident disdain. A few minutes later, we said goodby and wished each other well. I picked up my briefcase and went home to pack for Honolulu. It was time to go.

Book III

Incremental Agonies

12

The Scene in 1964

"On this side lay Scylla, while on that Charybdis in her terrible whirlpool was sucking down the sea"

Homer: *The Odyssey*.

Fresh—or, at least, newly-arrived—from Washington, I brought as baggage one key pre-conceived conviction—that the United States was embarked on three conflicting courses in Vietnam, Laos and Cambodia. We were, in a way, driving a troika of our own design, a troika whose three steeds pulled in opposite directions.

• In South Vietnam we were trying by internal means to defeat a slow invasion launched through Laos and Cambodia, but disguised as an "insurgency";
• In Laos we supported a disadvantageous partition behind a facade which veiled and tacitly condoned Hanoi's use of eastern Laos (and Cambodia) as the invasion route;
• In Cambodia, we were caught in the middle with Prince Sihanouk who adjusted his "neutrality" to accommodate the North Vietnamese victory he believed to be inevitable.

Governments are often compelled by circumstances to straddle contrary forces in world politics. This three-way straddle, however, was largely of our own making and it was a leitmotif of the American war in Indochina. Events in Laos and South Vietnam during the spring and summer of 1964 illuminated a series of agonizing dilemmas that resulted from this straddle:

• Should the United States continue to deal with Laos and South Vietnam separately as required by the "facade of Geneva" or together as required by the defense of South Vietnam?

• Should the United States deal with the problem in South Vietnam internally, as an insurgency, or seek to protect it from external aggression?

• If the United States would not stop Hanoi on the ground, could the United States, from the air, cause Hanoi to stop itself?

• In pressuring Hanoi to cease its campaign against South Vietnam should the United States risk escalating too far, thereby making it impossible for Hanoi to compromise, or not far enough, thereby failing to influence Hanoi at all?

• Should the United States act so as to create an image of determination which would impress Hanoi or should it act so as to stop Hanoi unilaterally?

• Should the United States take over de facto management of the war in South Vietnam or limit itself to providing the material and specialized resources while South Vietnam's Government exercised responsibility?

• In the face of the downward political spiral in South Vietnam and expanding Viet Cong operations should the United States refuse to carry out operations against North Vietnam for fear of a collapse in the rear? Or should it step up operations against North Vietnam as a means of bolstering confidence in the South Vietnamese Government and military?

I had hoped that the catalyst for resolving these dilemmas might emerge from the deepening contradictions of our posture in Indochina as seen from the military side. This was a misplaced hope. In fact, none of these dilemmas was resolved by deliberate choice.

There are two things about the American military:

First, they are superb in planning and executing military missions stated in terms that can be implemented by the military means at their disposal. Americans can be proud.

Second, they are absolutely devoted to the principle of civilian control—to a fault. For them, policy is the domain of civilian leadership. The impossibility of an extra-constitutional military takeover in the United States is never more evident than in a high military command headquarters.

This is as it should be. Policy belongs to the civilians. Execution is the domain of the military. But, there is a wide gap between policy and execution—a gap called strategy—that which gears means to ends. Unfortunately, this gap was never closed. The civilians did set the policy and the military accepted it with alacrity: to preserve the independence of the non-Communist states of South Vietnam, Laos and Cambodia. But by what strategy? There was the rub.

At first, in 1961, lagging on the inertia of the previous Administration's policies, the U.S. military had pushed for a regional strategy based on southern Laos as a buffer for South Vietnam, Cambodia and Thailand. In an October 9 memo, which recognized the probable need for at least three U.S. divisions, the JCS argued:

> To concede southern Laos would open the flanks of both Thailand and South Vietnam as well as expose Cambodia. . . .
>
> What is needed is . . . a concentrated effort in Laos where a firm stand can be taken saving all or substantially all of Laos which would, at the same time, protect Thailand and protect the borders of South Vietnam.[1]

The trouble with this, apart from the political turmoil in Laos and our own military unpreparedness, was that it came precisely at the time the U.S. was negotiating the neutralization of Laos at Geneva. Accordingly, the military quickly shifted field to get back into line behind the Kennedy Administration's policy based on counter-insurgency in South Vietnam and neutralization in Laos. But by the winter of 1962–1963 the neutralization of Laos had failed, as described in Chapter 7. Now was the time to review our policy as Harriman had once said we would. Why didn't the military propose a review of the role of southern Laos in a regional defense strategy?

Because, with incredibly fast footwork and deft handiwork, the civilian leadership had gathered up the rubble of Geneva and, as described in Chapter 8, even before the October 7 deadline, had begun to re-arrange it into something called "our tacit agreement" with the Communist side, or, better still, "the facade of Geneva." Sensing that the premises of "insurgency" and the "facade of Geneva" continued at the political heart of the civilian leadership's policy, the military tacitly accepted them as "given" and cast their recommendations in that framework. They would henceforth, assert their own contrary views and requirements in a context which they recognized as their own—that is, implementation. They would avoid challenging the civilians in the context of the political premises at the heart of policy. As the gap between ends and means widened in Indochina, the military adopted the practice of incrementalism, differing from the civilians primarily in pressing for a more rapid rate of incremental escalation.

This was well illustrated in March 1964 when Secretary McNamara, recommending new increments to President Johnson, carefully cast his proposals in the framework of the "tacit agreement." The new proposals, approved by the NSC on March 16, were based on the following premise:

In Laos, we are still working largely *within the framework of the 1962 Geneva Accords.* In Cambodia we are still seeking to keep Sihanouk from abandoning whatever neutrality he may still have and fulfilling his threat of reaching an accommodation with Hanoi and Peking. As a consequence of these policies, *we* and the Government of South Vietnam *have had to condone the extensive use of Cambodian and Laotian territory by the Viet Cong, both as a sanctuary and as infiltration routes* (Emphasis added).[2]

In fact, of course, North Vietnam was operating wholly outside and in contravention of the Geneva Accords while the "framework" within which the United States was operating was not that of the Geneva Accords but of their opposite, the "tacit agreement." This policy defined the limiting framework for the U.S. military.

Predictably, the Joint Chiefs of Staff found McNamara's memo to be weak tea and remonstrated to the Secretary of Defense. But—and this is the key point—the JCS did not revert to the concept of a concentrated effort in Laos which would protect Thailand and protect the borders of South Vietnam. They could not do so without challenging civilian policy. Instead, they tacitly accepted the policy and proposed to step up the incremental rate of escalation—to increase the ante, as it were. On March 14, three days before McNamara's paper was approved, the JCS wrote to the Secretary as follows:

> a. The JCS do not believe that the recommended program in itself will be sufficient to turn the tide against the Viet Cong in South Vietnam without positive action being taken against the Hanoi Government at an early date. They have in mind the conduct of . . . punitive actions against North Vietnam, specifically aggressive bombing. . . .[3]

By thus casting their recommendations within McNamara's framework, the JCS not only threw their weight behind the national policy but behind the implicit strategy prescribed by the civilians.

I had not seen either McNamara's approved memorandum or the JCS memorandum when, two weeks later, I left for Honolulu. By then, however, the focus of attention was shifting to political upheaval in both Laos and South Vietnam.

In Vietnam, instability was degrading both civilian and military programs. As a stimulant, Ambassador Lodge and General Westmoreland wanted strong air actions against North Vietnam and the Laos Corridor. Not everyone agreed with this logic, fearing that a deeper forward commitment might be undercut by political collapse in the rear. Another view favored greater U.S. involvement in the internal affairs of South Vietnam. This was a fundamental departure from counter-insurgency doctrine and from the report given the President on October 2, 1963 by Secretary McNamara and General Taylor on returning from their latest survey trip to South Vietnam, according to which, "this is a Vietnamese war and the country and war must in the end be run solely by the Vietnamese."[4] In January, McNamara told the House Armed Services Committee, "I don't believe that we as a nation should assume the primary responsibility. . . . It is a counter-guerrilla war, a war that can only be won by the Vietnamese themselves. Our responsibility is not to substitute ourselves for the Vietnamese."[5]

Nevertheless, in May, he cabled the participants at the May 30 Honolulu Conference to be prepared to discuss "a major infusion of U.S. efforts . . . where Vietnamese seem currently unable to execute their pacification programs . . . .

"We would therefore propose that U.S. personnel, both civilian and military, . . . be encadred into current Vietnamese political and military structure."[6]

Reporting on the Conference two weeks later, William Sullivan argued, "If we can obtain a breakthrough in the mutual commitment of the United States in Vietnam to a confident sense of victory, we believe that we can introduce this sort of executive involvement into the Vietnam structure."[7]

The editors of *The Pentagon Papers* commented that the dilemma ranged between two extremes: "one extreme would be our doing almost everything difficult for the Vietnamese and, the other would consist of limiting our own actions to provision of no more than material aid and advice . . . . Choice of a policy at any point on this continuum reflects a judgment concerning the basic nature of the problem, i.e., to what extent political and to what extent military."[8]

Actually, the choice as to the basic nature of the problem would have been better stated as between "internal insurgency" and "external invasion" and the distance between them was not a linear continuum but a fundamental qualitative dichotomy. Our failure to base our strategy on this fundamental distinction undermined all our efforts in Indochina throughout the war. Nevertheless, the editors were right to use the word "continuum" to describe policy as it was seen by key American officials. That is, in fact, the linear dimension in which the practice of "incrementalism" forced our strategy.

Meanwhile, in Laos, on April 19, a couple of right-wing generals had attempted a *coup d'état* to take over from neutral Premier Souvanna Phouma whom the U.S. supported. With American encouragement, Souvanna had made peace with the obstreperous generals, regained control and re-established the neutral regime. But the experience had provoked a loud and hostile clamor from the Communist

Pathet Lao who had withdrawn from the neutral government a year earlier and set up their own rump regime on the Plaine des Jarres. They, of course, would have preferred to see the break-up of the neutralist-conservative coalition.

Then, on May 16, the Pathet Lao, aided by North Vietnamese units, attacked neutralist forces in the western part of the strategic Plaine des Jarres. Before subsiding, the Pathet Lao had occupied virtually the whole Plaine and were threatening the town of Muong Soui at the intersection of Routes 7 and 13. The loss of Muong Soui would not only virtually evict non-Communist forces from the Plaine des Jarres, but the loss of the intersection would cut road contact between the administrative capital in Vientiane and the royal capital in Luang Prabang. The breathtaking speed and threat posed by the attack shocked Vientiane and galvanized American diplomatic and military authorities all the way to the White House. The two questions were: "How far will the Communists go?" and "What to do?"

Would the Pathet Lao go all the way to Vientiane and upset the neutral government? Many thought they had the capability to do just that. Or would they stop now, as the rainy season approached, contenting themselves with the present bite (as they had done last year) while saving another bite for next year and the year after that? Admiral Felt invited me to comment on a couple of military intelligence analyses which adopted the "annual bite" hypothesis. These reports also argued that the recent bite was bigger than expected because of an angry Communist reaction against Premier Souvanna Phouma for composing his differences with the right wing generals. I agreed with the "bottom line" of the two estimates that the Communists would not go all the way at that time. But, sometimes the bottom line is less important than the path one follows to it. I tried to put the question in the context of historical Communist strategy but, having done so, I failed to carry my own method rigorously to its logical conclusion:

> It is very difficult to make precise estimates of Communist intentions . . . because of the different role ascribed by them to Time in their plans. We try to make precise estimates of Communist intentions within a specified time frame but their objectives are not limited to precise time-fixing. Their objective in Laos is to take it over, completely, from stem to stern. When? Whenever possible. In how many bites? As few as possible but as many as necessary.
>
> We err in seeking to explain Communist moves as simple reactions to our moves or to other outside stimuli such as the April 19 coup . . . . Ever since Lenin the Communists have always made decisions on the basis of the total 'correlation of forces' in a long range historical context. . . .
>
> If I were making policy for the Communist side, I would assume that in signing the Geneva Accords of 1962 the United States was leading from

weakness because it did not want to become involved in a war over Laos. That being the case, it would be my hope to press wherever a soft spot could be found until I reached some hard obstacle. This would be the only way for me to judge the extent of the U.S. unwillingness to fight. This would be my way of calculating the size, location and timing of the bites . . . . It is my guess that the Communists . . . will leave something for another bite next year.

So far, so good. The conclusion was correct but the reasoning was incomplete, as was the answer. Having postulated the general Communist emphasis on the 'correlation of forces' I failed to apply the actual elements of the real 'correlation' in this particular case. In the Communist 'correlation' (which was regional in scope, comprising all of Indochina), Laos had a specific service to render to North Vietnam before it could be wholly incorporated into a Hanoi-dominated Indochinese sphere of influence. That service was to provide the invasion route to South Vietnam. Until South Vietnam could be conquered, it was necessary to avoid provoking the United States into direct action in Laos which might result in definitive blockage (as opposed to more harassment) of the invasion route on the ground.

I should, therefore, have concluded that as long as North Vietnam relied on the Ho Chi Minh trails for its slow invasion of South Vietnam, Hanoi would not risk provoking the U.S. by taking its last big bite in Laos. This, it will be recalled (Chapter 8) was the core of the Harriman-Hilsman "tacit agreement." South Vietnam was actually the penultimate bite on which a final Communist takeover in Laos would wait. In short, under our "tacit agreement", the last bite of western Laos could not be taken by Hanoi until South Vietnam had fallen.

Looking back, I think that I did not then realize how deeply ingrained in our thinking the "tacit agreement" had become. I had thought of it as a passing rationalization to cover a brief conceptual hiatus following the failure of the neutralization of Laos until the adoption of some new strategy. I was wrong. As is evident from Roger Hilsman's account (published in 1967) of the formula he and Harriman recommended to President Kennedy, the "tacit agreement" was a sophisticated, finely articulated doctrinal framework which, for lack of a new strategy, had become our strategy. How pervasively was becoming clear.

Even before the April–May crisis in Laos, the JCS had been urging ground and air reconnaissance into Laos to obtain intelligence on infiltration. They criticized our "self-imposed restrictions" as signalling "irresolution to our enemies." They wanted to impress Hanoi with our resolve to deny sanctuary.[9] (The emphasis on cultivating an image of determination was fast becoming a ubiquitous, narcissistic syndrome of all our Indochina thinking—in military as well as civilian quarters). Ironically, the State Department disapproved on the ground that policy required sensitivity to the political situation of Premier Souvanna and adherence to the 1962 Geneva Accords.

The May 16 Communist attack precipitated an interesting four day parenthesis in the career of the "facade of Geneva." The coincidence of crises in Laos and South Vietnam led to the creation of an inter-agency Executive Committee which actually considered the possibility of unifying our separate strategies for Laos and South Vietnam. On May 25, the Committee rejected a 30-day phased politico-military scenario and recommended a simple contingent "decision to use force if necessary." The Committee went on to recommend that "all functional and geographical elements should be treated as parts of a single problem; the protection of [all] Southeast Asia from further Communist encroachment."[10] This decision was to stand for four days.

On May 27th, the Government of Poland, a member of the ICC, advanced a proposal for a mini-conference of certain Geneva powers* to help resolve the crisis in Laos. The proposal was probably doomed by the troika principle from the start, but anything that seemed to make unnecessary more difficult decisions appealed to the Executive Committee. On May 29, therefore, the Committee reversed itself and cabled Secretary Rusk, then in Bangkok, its decision to explore the Polish proposal. The Committee explained:

> While we initially would seek to treat Laos question *separately* from North-South Vietnam problem, if satisfactory Lao solution not achieved basis should have been laid for possible subsequent actions that would permit our dealing more effectively with North Vietnam with respect to both South Vietnam and Laos.
>
> If Polish Conference not successful or in meanwhile Pathet Lao/Vietminh significantly advance toward Mekong from present positions, we would immediately deploy to Thailand an international force and initiate *selective* air strikes against Pathet Lao/Vietminh supply lines and installations.[11] (Emphasis added)

The Polish-proposed conference did not materialize. The Pathet Lao and North Vietnamese allowed the military situation on the Plaine des Jarres to simmer down a bit. The U.S. did not deploy forces or initiate air strikes at that time. And, despite what the Executive Committee had said on May 29, the U.S. did not revert to the idea of

*The Geneva Co-chairmen—Great Britain and the USSR, and the members of the ICC—Poland, Canada and India.

dealing with both Vietnam and Laos together. Instead, a high level U.S. conference was convened on June 1 in Honolulu which precipitated a new series of contingency incremental scenarios that filled the time until the Gulf of Tonkin incident in August.

The last week of July produced a fascinating illumination of the intricacies of the "Geneva facade" in the form of a cable from Ambassador Unger in Vientiane, Laos. The United States was becoming concerned over the increasing stridency of South Vietnamese Chief of State General Khanh's public talk of launching a direct attack against North Vietnam. Although he lacked the power to carry such an operation to a successful conclusion, the public threat to "go North" served as a tonic to the depressed spirits in South Vietnam. Washington feared that the tonic might become addictive and provoke hostile reactions around the world.[12] On July 26, the Department of State cabled Ambassador Unger saying that

> Primarily for reasons of morale in South Vietnam and to divert the Saigon Government's attention from proposal to strike North Vietnam, we are considering proposing to Ambassador Taylor that he discuss with Khanh air attacks on VC supply lines in the Laotian Panhandle.*
>
> It is assumed that the operation would be justified on grounds of infiltration of personnel and supplies through corridor in violation of Geneva Accords and that we would publicize relevant evidence from photography and POW interrogation. We would hope Souvanna would publicly support such rationale but at minimum would do or say nothing to undermine it.[13]

Given the opportunity to comment, Ambassador Unger did so at some length the next day.[14] After volunteering his own belief (confirmed many times during the war) that the effect of air attacks on infiltration would be "only marginal," he went on to oppose the operation on the ground that it "would probably bring to an end the possibility our preserving even *facade* of government national union *under* Souvanna and *Geneva Accords*." (Emphasis added)

The detailed clarity with which Ambassador Unger maps the layout of this facade warrants fuller exposition. He opens by pointing out

---

*It was all too characteristic of our planning to embark on new military courses for reasons that were primarily political, or even psychological, rather than military, thereby advancing (or withdrawing) an incremental military notch to gain an image-making point which dissolved almost as rapidly as it was created. Thus, while the cable went on to detail a program of strikes "the military objective of which would be to interdict and destroy facilities supporting infiltration", it added, in a quick parenthesis, that "the *political* objective might be achieved by fewer targets and/or sorties than indicated below." In short, image was the thing.

that "the fundamental attitude of Souvanna . . . that use of corridor, even though involving Lao territory, not primarily their problem, and anyway they have their hands full trying to protect heart of their country for defense of which corridor not essential." At first glance, one might think that Souvanna was giving the U.S. a free hand to act in the Corridor to protect South Vietnam rather than giving Hanoi a free hand to use the Corridor to invade South Vietnam. However, in the next sentence it is explained that "Our creating a new military as well as international political conflict over Corridor will be regarded by them [Souvanna and the Lao] as another instance Laos being involuntarily involved in struggle among big powers on matter outside Laos' own prime interests." How can occupation of a large part of a country's territory be "outside its own prime interest"? But Unger goes on to point out some additional consequences: "Why complicate our problem and risk creating dangerous military threat in central and southern areas where it does not now exist?" Except—of course— to South Vietnam. But so tightly were our Laos and Vietnamese strategies compartmentalized that it was quite possible to tolerate a situation because it benefitted the partitioned neutral half of Laos, despite the fact that it augured the eventual defeat of South Vietnam.

Continuing, the Ambassador estimated the Lao attitude: "Why does not the U.S. apply its power to source of problem and bomb Hanoi or move effectively in some other way against North Vietnam? North Vietnam is the cause of the trouble and ought to be the target. Moreover, we are not bound by international agreements there as we are in Laos." In this way, the insulation of Laos behind the "facade of Geneva" fed the natural inclination of the U.S. military to push for an intense and rapidly escalating air assault on Hanoi. As for the U.S. being bound by international agreements in Laos, this was a very special kind of asymmetrical bond as defined in the "tacit agreement". Thus, the Ambassador acknowledged that "There certainly has been no sign from Pathet Lao, Hanoi or Chicoms of any change in their attitude to encourage U.S. to believe they are ready to start living by Geneva Accords and end their interference in Laos." Nevertheless, the result of taking the proposed new measures in the Laos Corridor would be, in the Ambassador's judgment that "we may find ourselves turned entirely away from guiding principle of last two years under which we have accepted uneasy equilibrium of de facto division of Laos as best we could get for present and better than resumption of large scale fighting. . . . Action will also solidly link the questions of Laos and South Vietnam which at earlier date we appeared to be intent on keeping separate as possible." Although one might have thought it was North Vietnam which had linked Laos and South

Vietnam by using the former to invade the latter, it was the essence of the "facade of Geneva" to keep them separate, or put another way, to keep the linkage on "the backburner."

Despite all the foregoing, if the U.S. should be determined to go ahead, Unger suggested that we argue to Premier Souvanna that action against the corridor was fundamental in resolving the plight not only of South Vietnam but of Laos itself: "In other words, block corridor so that Government of South Vietnam can again assume full authority over its territory at which point North Vietnam can make no further use of corridor."

Although accurate, this statement would certainly frighten Washington off when taken together with the Ambassador's warning that "when it becomes clear air attacks do not halt infiltration" the U.S. might find itself pressed into "a major military effort aimed at pushing the North Vietnamese out of the Panhandle and eventually out of Laos."

Inevitably, Unger concluded, the proposed military actions in southern Laos would trigger "virtually irresistible pressures from Souvanna for similar escalation in this [northwestern] part of Laos" which, of course, contained Souvanna's capital. This conclusion leads us back to the basic equation of the Harriman-Hilsman "tacit agreement" which balanced Hanoi's continued control of the invasion corridor against Hanoi's provisional willingness to postpone conquest of Souvanna's base—contingent on the ultimate outcome in South Vietnam. The invasion corridor is allocated to Hanoi in return for a temporary existence permit to Souvanna's regime in Vientiane. Thus was the "facade of Geneva" intact in the summer of 1964.

The proposed air strikes were postponed, but it was not many months until the Corridor was subjected to aerial blows far in excess of those proposed in 1964. While the Ambassador's forecast that the ineffectiveness of bombing against infiltration would force us to try to drive the North Vietnamese out of the Panhandle did not materialize he cannot be blamed for that. His forecast was a logical one and he could not have anticipated that ineffective air operations would feed only incremental demands for more and heavier air strikes instead of triggering effective action on the ground.

Although I (like Ambassador Unger) was an amateur in military strategy, I thought (as I believe he did) that history had demonstrated the impossibility of forcing the capitulation of a determined opponent solely by air action. In World War II Germany was devastated from the air, but it required ground conquest from both East and West all the way to Hitler's bunker in Berlin to obtain German surrender. London, too, was hardly humbled by the Luftwaffe. In 1961, as related in Chapter 5, Secretary Rusk once put down McNamara's proposal to arm some training planes in Laos by reference to the demonstration in the Korean war that "Air power is effective in support of men on the ground but indecisive when used alone." If Germany, which was heavily dependent on a sophisticated military-industrial machine, could not be bombed to capitulation, how could it be done in North Vietnam, particularly when our own policy excluded overturning the government in Hanoi?

Because Admiral Felt seemed receptive to amateur strategic commentary (without being confused by it), I elaborated on this theme in a couple of memoranda done in the first week of June during and after the Honolulu Conference on Indochina. The following extracts (with bracketed comments from today's vantage point) not only illustrate the point but lead toward the major thesis of this book:

> In reading about possible actions against North Vietnam I have been deeply impressed with the importance of balancing air attacks on North Vietnam with the timely establishment of a strong military position on the ground along the Mekong River, including the Lao side. Air attacks on North Vietnam without such a position on the Mekong would be like trying to hammer out a hot piece of metal by hitting it with a sledge without any anvil. It might create a lot of fireworks but it won't work the metal. . . .
>
> Without a balancing position along the Mekong, I think air attacks would not be an efficient means for achieving a limited, precisely defined political objective. Such air attacks would be open to misinterpretation by both friends and enemies. They might be interpreted as an invitation to escalation, or as bluffing or as reprisals proceeding from frustration, or as the opening gun of the liquidation of North Vietnam or as part of a plan to seize all of Laos. The most difficult objective of all to prove by this means would be the return to some status quo ante in Laos. . . .
>
> Synchronized pressure by air and ground is a far more convincing demonstration of U.S. determination than air attacks alone. . . . A combined squeeze would make it much easier to bring the operation to an end." [Without coordinated air/ground actions, the war in fact became a sheer test of endurance.]

A week later, on June 8, I elaborated further on this theme:

> Without ever planning it, we seem to be on the way to a test of the effectiveness of air warfare in the jungle and probably under the most unfavorable conditions.
>
> We have no forces on the ground to exploit the advantages which air power should give us and we apparently have no intention to introduce ground forces, particularly during the rainy season. . . .

If we keep this up, "tit-for-tat", we will soon become more deeply engaged in air reprisals despite the fact that this will not restore our side to any of the territory it has lost.

If we keep on escalating the air warfare, we will shortly run into trouble with Souvanna on whom our present position depends and we might be forced to back down. [Although I disliked seeing our actions based on the "Geneva facade" I wanted it challenged openly and directly, if at all, not by incremental indirection.]

If, under these circumstances we are forced to back down, the ironic result will be that instead of having forced the Communists to cease and desist from their attack on Laos, we will be the ones forced to cease and desist. [I consistently overestimated the velocity of political pressures but the process did catch up with us, first, in the form of repeated "pauses" in the bombing and finally in our withdrawal from Indochina.]

The air campaign could be better justified, however, if it were an integral part of a regional plan, which would serve our purposes in Laos and South Vietnam as well as in the whole region of Southeast Asia. I strongly believe that before we get much more deeply involved in the present course, we should consider the dangers of being led, without planning into a course from which we may have to make a humiliating retreat.

An integral, regional strategy—this was the direction in which I thought events would propel the U.S. military. More specifically, I could not see how air attacks, unlinked to territorial defense, outlined and actually defended on the ground, could succeed. Surely, a highly disciplined Communist North Vietnam, backed by China and the USSR, would not bow to air power any more than Germany or England had done. This was particularly true since our own objective, which we assiduously communicated to Hanoi, was not to overthrow the regime. No bombing campaign that did not overthrow the regime would reach the threshold of North Vietnam's endurance, the point at which Hanoi would abandon its campaign to take over South Vietnam. If this was true, then it followed that an escalating bombing campaign would first reach our threshold of political endurance under the weight of domestic and international opposition. Without constructive results, apparently endless bombing would soon begin to appear wanton. When our threshold was reached we would have to execute what I thought would be a humiliating retreat. In the long run, we did retreat but, as so often happened, the "long run" was much longer than I expected.

Admiral Felt was interested enough to comment to the Chief of Staff, Lt. Gen. Verdi Beethoven Barnes, that I had a point and he asked that General Barnes review CINCPAC's own 20-point table of proposed graduated pressures. This list, which had been presented to the Honolulu Conference the week before, escalated to a contingent deployment of U.S. forces to Thailand but not to Laos, and then to intense air strikes and aerial mining of North Vietnam's harbors. Having reviewed the plan, Gen. Barnes replied that its validity depended on the answers to two questions, which he posed and answered:

a. Is the U.S. willing to escalate? Answer: Yes.
b. Is the U.S. willing to put ground troops into Indochina? Answer: "The last thing the U.S. Government desires to do and it hopes to get by without doing so."

Methodically applying these two answers with the rigor of a scholastic theologian, Gen. Barnes ratified the CINCPAC list, concluding that, "the only thing left is to intensify air and naval attacks to hurt North Vietnam until Hanoi desists from pushing the war in Laos and South Vietnam." A perfect demonstration of military acceptance and automatic application of higher civilian policy!

I do not mean to dismiss the point facetiously. Let me repeat General Barnes' key proposition in his own felicitous formulation:

Question: "Is the U.S. Government willing to put in ground troops? Answer: "The last thing the U.S. Government desires to do and it hopes *to get by* without doing so." (Emphasis added).

This antipathy toward the very principle of committing U.S. ground forces was almost universal in both military and civilian circles, deeply felt, visceral, automatic. Senior Army officers—Korean War veterans and charter members of the "Never Again Club"—had vowed never again to get committed in a ground war on the Asian mainland without advance authority to use whatever weapons, tactics and geography were required to win. Politicians shied away from mobilization and domestic budget cuts. Civilian experts were loath to commit U.S. ground forces to a "counter-insurgency" on the other side of the world in a country of doubtful credentials. So deep was this antipathy that questions were disposed of summarily rather than thoughtfully. Ill-considered and ill-timed JCS proposals to deploy forces in Laos in 1961 had contributed to an automatic disposition to assume that all proposals were tainted by the same flaws.

Deploying U.S. ground forces to Indochina was indeed, as Gen. Barnes said, "the last thing the U.S. Government desired to do." Accordingly, it was the very last thing the U.S. Government thought about. In fact, it tried not to think about it, hoping, as Gen. Barnes said, "to get by without doing so." This was the touchstone of in-crementalism—"to get by" without confronting whole decisions in their total dimensions. So accomplished had we become at this that we were able, eventually, to deploy over half a million men to South Vietnam without deciding in advance to do it or why, but with a different incremental rationale for each incremental bit. The JCS oc-casionally alluded in passing to the need for a regional strategy but carefully did not step out from behind the "facade of Geneva."

Although several concepts for the use of American ground forces had been mentioned, none was under serious consideration. Among them was one to provide ready reserves behind the South Vietnamese forces, another to provide security for airfields and key military in-stallations, a third to secure Saigon, a fourth to secure several coastal enclaves and still another to bolster the Vietnamese forces below the Demilitarized Zone at the 17th parallel. There were others. I had a different idea—establishment of a strong blocking position in south-ern Laos, the key to Southeast Asian defense. I had summarized it in a draft cable (never sent) of May 27, and Gen. Barnes no doubt had it in mind when he gave his accurate estimate of the U.S. Gov-ernment's negative attitude. My concept was simple:

It can easily be argued that intrinsically Laos is not worth the struggle. For obvious reasons, landlocked, feeble Laos does present us with a pe-culiarly difficult problem. But Laos has one great (but perishable) asset to offer us at this moment—an internationally recognized special politico-legal framework (the Geneva Accords) which provides us with the best possible legal, political and psychological justification for direct action. It also is the strategic key to Southeast Asia since it contains the main Com-munist access routes to South Vietnam; it could become a buffer insulating Cambodia geographically from Communist power and it is the main line of Thai defense. Therefore, I suggest that we consider utilizing the present occasion in Laos . . . to convert our present position of military weakness to one of military strength, with the hope of:
• protecting the Thai border
• choking off the North Vietnamese infiltration routes;
• insulating Cambodia;
• establishing a position near the DMZ in case of open North Vietnamese attack;
• gradually establishing a line which could be the basis of later negotiations either to re-establish the Geneva Accords or to establish a final partition.
I recognize the Communist side might refuse to accept any defeat in Southeast Asia or it might over-react. But this possibility is implicit in the whole problem of dealing with people who are dedicated to our burial. This is a problem to be dealt with but not a justification for acquiescence.

If we acquiesce today, we will only have to face this possibility later under worse conditions."

But we didn't face it. We tried to slide by it incrementally. Unlike Odysseus who opted for Scylla and eventually completed his voyage, we did not choose. We slid into Charybdis.

13

1964—No Sticking Place

Macbeth: If we should fail—
    Lady Macbeth: We fail?
But screw your courage to the sticking place,
    And we'll not fail.

Macbeth, I vii, 16.

It was during the evening of August 2, 1964, aboard the CINCPAC command DC-6, leisurely droning eastward near Wake Island, that I first heard about the North Vietnamese torpedo boat attack on the U.S. destroyer Maddox in the Tonkin Gulf. We were returning to Honolulu from the first official visit to the Far East of the new Commander-in-Chief, Admiral Ulysses S. Grant Sharp, Jr., who had recently succeeded Admiral Felt. The Admiral immediately directed the Maddox to stay on station, reinforced by another destroyer, the C. Turner Joy. As the Admiral told *Time* magazine, "You can't accept any interference with our use of International waters. You must go back to the same place and say, 'Here's two of us this time, if you want to try anything' . . . . Our ships are always going to go where they need to be. If they shoot at us, we are going to shoot back.' "

We did just that. Two days later there was a second encounter.* The following day, August 5, the United States Government, without hesitation or dissent, launched U.S. Navy reprisal air strikes on four North Vietnamese torpedo boat bases and one oil storage facility. Fair enough.

---

*There are different interpretations of what actually happened during the second encounter, but nothing alters the fact that at the time the decision to conduct reprisals was based on the conviction that the attack was deliberate. I was in the CINCPAC Command Center that day. The evidence was analyzed with care and detachment. When CINCPAC telephoned Secretary McNamara confirming the occurrence of the attack he was speaking his conviction.

That was the simple part of it. The real significance of the Tonkin Gulf reprisals lay in the escalatory momentum they launched and in their meaning as a "message to Hanoi" of growing U.S. toughness and determination. Certainly that was the intended implication of the Tonkin Gulf Resolution passed by Congress on August 7. But what would be the message as received in Hanoi? According to one school, the Tonkin Gulf incidents were so specialized and so far outside the central framework of the Indochina War that their value as a message was extremely limited and possibly misleading. Another school argued that however specialized the Tonkin Gulf reprisals were, they nevertheless carried an implicit warning which could be extended to cover Hanoi's support of the war in South Vietnam; provided the momentum were maintained.

I was inclined toward the first interpretation even though the two were not necessarily incompatible. It was a question of "follow-up" and "momentum." For example, Maxwell Taylor, by now Ambassador in Saigon, argued first that

> Our retaliatory action in the Gulf of Tonkin is in effect an isolated U.S.-North Vietnam incident. Although this has relation to . . . the larger problem of North Vietnam's aggression by subversion in [South] Vietnam and Laos, we have not yet come to grips in a forceful way with North Vietnam over the issue of this larger and much more complex problem.[2]*

Later, say the editors of the *Pentagon Papers*, he spoke of the need for "subsequent actions that would convey to Hanoi that, 'the operational rules with respect to North Vietnam are changing.' "[3]

Assistant Secretary of State William Bundy thought the "message" as received in Hanoi would read simply that "we will act strongly where U.S. force units are directly involved . . . [that] in other respects the Communist side may not be so persuaded that we are prepared to take strong action." He envisaged a need for a "combination of military pressure and some form of communication" to cause Hanoi to accept the idea of "getting out" of South Vietnam and Laos.[5]

Not surprisingly, the military saw the incident as launching a "momentum" against Hanoi which should be maintained and increased.

*In a still later cable (November 3) Taylor argued that in the future "it is to our interest to strike Hanoi for its malefactions in South Vietnam and not for its actions in the Bay of Tonkin against the U.S. Navy. We need to tie our actions to Hanoi support of the VC, not to the defense of purely U.S. interests. Hence, the excuse for actions should ideally grow out of events in South Vietnam and Laos. Such events are available for our exploitation now in the form of infiltration activities in the Laotian Corridor and North Vietnam. . . ."[4]

Arguing that what "we have not done and must do is make plain to Hanoi and Peking the cost of pursuing their current objectives and impeding ours", CINCPAC asserted that "Our actions of August 5 have created a momentum which can lead to the attainment of our objectives in Southeast Asia. It is most important that we do not lose this momentum."[6]

In the same vein, the Joint Chiefs of Staff wanted to "sustain the U.S. advantage gained." They warned that "Failure to resume and maintain a program of pressure through military actions . . . could signal a lack of resolve."[7]

As is apparent from the last chapter, I was doubtful of the whole idea of "inducing" Hanoi to call it off by escalating aerial pressures and, instead, was coming to believe that South Vietnam could only be defended by literally stopping North Vietnam on the ground. Accordingly, I took a somewhat different view of the "message" communicated by the Tonkin Gulf reprisals in a personal memorandum written on August 6, the day after the reprisals:

> Our naval air attack on the North Vietnamese PT bases was necessary as a response to a direct challenge and was well done. The initial political impact will probably be very good. . . .
>
> In the long run, however, . . . this is a rapidly depleting asset. After the initial effect wears off, it will have to be followed up by new actions. We should, therefore, reexamine our position and look ahead to see where we are going.
>
> The recent incidents offered us a lesson in the concept of 'getting the message to Hanoi.' For some months we have been trying to 'get the message across' . . . in Presidential speeches, diplomatic channels, third party channels, by stepping up operations in South Vietnam, by threatening to carry the war to the North, by armed reconnaissance in Laos and by naval patrols in the Gulf of Tonkin. After all this . . . the North Vietnamese boldly attacked destroyers of the most powerful fleet in the world. Did they fail to get the message? Did they misunderstand it? Or is this their calculated contemptuous reply?
>
> What is the message we have given the North Vietnamese? Perhaps it is only that the U.S. is prepared to escalate indefinitely in the air and at sea but not on the ground. Is this credible?
>
> For years we have made it clear that . . . we consider the war in South Vietnam as a semi-political insurgency to be fought by the South Vietnamese themselves by means of counter-insurgency. . . . We do not intend to fight in Laos. . . . It was precisely because of this that we signed the Geneva Accords in 1962. . . . The Communists must regard our threats in the air and sea as incredible. . . . For the sake of two small pieces of jungle in Southeast Asia would we risk a sea-air war which would still leave the Vietcong in South Vietnam, the Pathet Lao on the ground in Laos and Ho Chi Minh in power in Hanoi?

Communist strategy has always been based on control of land and people. To them it is incredible that anyone could risk a major war in the air
and at sea while still leaving the land and people under enemy control. . . .

We should re-examine not only the concept of 'getting the message
across' but the concept of forcing the Communists to 'cease and desist'
from their support of the PL and the Vietcong. The Communists have been
in this business around the world for over fifty years. They have coped
with international forces which invaded Russia after World War I and they
have coped with the invasion by Hitler in 1941. The Chinese Communists
have made the 'long march' from South China and lived in the caves of
Yenan for years under pressures from both Chinese Nationalists and the
Japanese. [I could have cited Vietminh resistance to France.] The determination of such people cannot be easily distracted. I do not believe that
by taking peripheral actions, we can force the Communists to 'desist'. We
can hurt the Communists elsewhere but this they will cope with in other
ways. The Communists are fighting for control of land and people. The
only way to detach them is to fight against them for the land and people.

By "fighting for the land and people" I did not mean to commit
U.S. forces to fighting a guerrilla counter-insurgency in South Vietnam which, tragically, we began to do a few months later. Rather, I
had in mind making a stand with U.S. ground forces below the 17th
parallel Demilitarized Zone of Vietnam and in southern Laos where
it would be possible to insulate South Vietnam against North Vietnam's slow invasion and allow the South's forces to concentrate on
reducing the Vietcong already in South Vietnam. But, in the wake of
the Tonkin Gulf incidents, the tide was running in the opposite direction.* It ran toward orchestrated, escalatory ladders of "uncom-
mitting" raiding types of operations, mostly by air and sea, designed
to pressure North Vietnam to 'cease and desist' while retaining our
options to escalate, de-escalate, pause, negotiate or withdraw 'hon-
orably.'

The United States had a magnificent and sophisticated weapon in
its air power. The question was—how to use it effectively to achieve
our objectives. To destroy key military targets? To immobilize North
Vietnam's economic power to supply the Vietcong? To cut rates of
reinforcement and re-supply or to pressure Hanoi politically? In fact,
we had no constant or consistent rationale. As a northwoods logger

---

*Walt Rostow, then Counselor of the Department of State, departing from
the conventional pattern, did talk of some U.S. ground forces below the DMZ
and in the Laos Corridor but only as part of his own radical plan of escalation
to *persuade* Hanoi of our determination—not for the purpose of insulating
South Vietnam by stopping the slow invasion in its tracks.

birls (spins) a floating log and then, before falling, leaps to another log and another while floating downstream, so did the argument for air strikes jump from one spinning objective to another. In retrospect it seems that although the rationale continually changed, we continued to rely more and more on the air weapon because that was what we really knew how to do best.

In a late September (1964) memo to CINCPAC's Deputy Chief of Staff for Plans and Operations, Lt. Gen. T. Ross Milton (USAF), my deputy, Charles Flowerree, and I questioned first the effect on Vietcong operations of air strikes on North Vietnam's industry, then addressed the possibility of cutting off infiltration by air. Moreover, Flowerree concluded:

> Air strikes on North Vietnam would not cause it to suspend military assistance to either of its two agents, the Vietcong and the Pathet Lao. Nor would the psychological impact of U.S. attacks cause North Vietnam's leaders to lose their desire to support the Vietcong and Pathet Lao. In fact, the effect might be just the opposite. As long as the Communist leadership remained in control it would wish to retaliate against the U.S. in some way.

In his response, pencilled on the memo, Gen. Milton succinctly expounded what was, unfortunately, a valid thumbnail statement of the core of U.S. military strategy:

> "Perhaps the only solid fact is our ability to damage North Vietnam as seriously as we like. It is also, perhaps, the only positive strategy we have. As a threat backed up by occasional demonstrations it might be a severe discouragement."*

In other words, our strategy was to "get the message to Hanoi" and air power was to be the messenger.

How to "get the message to Hanoi?" How to induce, persuade, convince or pressure Hanoi to "cease and desist?" This was the grist

---

*But, if air attacks would not cause Hanoi to back down, they also "would not impel Hanoi to escalate the conflict in South Vietnam," Flowerree continued. "One of the hallmarks of North Vietnamese policy (reflecting that of China) is the avoidance of actions which might lead to a massive U.S. commitment of forces to Southeast Asia." This pinpoints the irony of the "airborne message strategy" which was that while hawks thought strikes would cause Hanoi to back down, doves thought it would trigger a massive counter-attack and escalation to a great power conflagration. Both sides over-estimated the role that air power could play alone and under-estimated the determined constancy of Hanoi.

of strategic thinking in both civilian and military circles in the fall and winter of 1964–1965. The period was bracketed by the Tonkin Gulf reprisals of August and the Pleiku ("Flaming Dart") reprisals of February 7–12. "Flaming Dart" led directly, on February 24, to the opening of the "Rolling Thunder" bombing program which continued (with occasional pauses) until the end of the war.

There was a curiously insubstantial or "free-floating" aspect to the debates on "graduated pressures." Each argument could be turned inside out and made to prove something different. One sometimes had the sensation of being in a house of mirrors in which he met himself coming and going. I believe this was because the debate had no real shape which could be defined in territorial or military terms. We did not carve out the territory to be defended and then plan to defend it. Instead, we engaged in a psycho-political test of our determination against Hanoi's will.

At one end of a linear continuum was Hanoi's will and at the other was U.S. determination (together with South Vietnam's morale). Proposed actions were measured, like musical notes, by presumed relative positions along a wave-length scale of capacity to approach and undermine Hanoi's will (high register) or to protect and project U.S. determination (low register). Mounting from U.S. determination toward Hanoi's will, the tension was tightened like a one-stringed musical instrument but—and here was the flaw—there were no intermediate stops or sticking places to hold the tension on Hanoi or relieve it on the U.S., as a front-line on the ground would have done. Once a new action was carried out and the initial tension was dissipated, we had no new ground to hold and we were back where we had been before—except that there was a residual tension which accumulated at the bottom end, slowly exhausting American determination. There was no position at which we could "stand pat." All was "momentum"—movement up or down the scale.

There were two possible results. The string might break or one side might let go and the string would roll up flaccidly. It was not our object to break the string—we did not plan to overthrow the Hanoi regime and we expected to come to an understanding, explicit or tacit, with North Vietnam. We wanted Hanoi to cooperate by letting go, probably the most complex and unlikely result of all. To that end, infinite thought, effort and resources went into the precise measurement of graduated notes which would lead *just so far and no farther*.

For example, a week after the Tonkin Gulf, the State Department set down the guiding philosophy as "devising the best possible means of action that, for minimum risks, get maximum results in terms of South Vietnam morale and pressure on North Vietnam." To accomplish this, the Department called for "a short holding phase [of two weeks] in which we would avoid actions that would in any way take the onus off the Communist side for escalation."[8] The obvious purpose was to protect U.S. determination from a political backlash in the United States and the West.

Three days later CINCPAC argued that a "two-weeks suspension of operations is not in consonance with [the] desire to get the message to Hanoi and Peking. . . . Further demonstration of restraint could easily be interpreted . . . as a sign of weakness and lack of resolve."[9] There was something to be said for both arguments. But, what if both were right? What does it say for the rationale of our strategy if the requirement to protect U.S. determination and South Vietnamese morale and the requirement to increase pressure on Hanoi work against each other? Which, then, is the more important? The pressure on Hanoi or the determination to apply it?

Or, more importantly, what if both the State Department and CINCPAC were wrong in trying to base detailed military operations on esoteric, psychological imponderables? What reason did the State Department have to believe that the "onus" for North Vietnam's behavior weighed heavily on Hanoi? One recalls Harriman's insistence on U.S. simon-pure compliance with the Geneva Accords in October, 1962, despite total North Vietnamese violation. Why? As Roger Hilsman has told us, "Harriman wanted the political onus of any violations to fall on the Communists . . . including the cost in terms of damaging their goals elsewhere in Asia and Africa." (Chapter 8) This "onus" neither caused North Vietnam to obey the Geneva Accords nor did it visibly damage the Soviet Union's goals in Asia and Africa. When pursuing their interests Communists worry less about public "onuses" than we do.

On the other hand, what reason did CINCPAC have to believe that Hanoi's judgments and intentions were so shallow and flimsy as to be significantly affected by a two-weeks tactical phasing of certain U.S. military actions which were, in themselves, quite indecisive? Over the next three years we visited vast destruction on North Vietnam with no visible effect on their will, which survived, single-mindedly, to motivate the Tet Offensive of January 1968.

But it is unfair to single out CINCPAC for a vice that was endemic throughout the military and civilian elements of the Government. Throughout the Government, we were narcissistically cultivating various images of our own posture as well as hypotheses of the figure we thought we cut in Hanoi's eyes. These images were in a constant state of flux and contention and were being re-touched to reflect the latest statistics, the latest self-examination or the latest tea-leaf reading of a communique from Hanoi, Peking or Moscow. And, by extension, we read our own ways of thinking into our interpretations of Hanoi's thinking.

The flexibility of this one-string tactic lent itself to shifting, even reversible conceptual criteria. For example, given the weakening political situation in Saigon, should the U.S. postpone operations against the North for fear of a collapse in its rear or should the U.S. step up action against Hanoi so as to bolster South Vietnamese confidence? In August, Ambassador Taylor, in Saigon, urged that "we should be slow to get too deeply involved . . . until we have a better feel of our ally."[10] On December 2, President Johnson reinforced this in an instruction (possibly drafted by Taylor) saying, "we should not incur the risks which are inherent in expansion of hostilities until there is a government in Saigon capable of handling the serious problems involved in such an expansion. . . ."[11]

He then laid down a series of demanding standards to be met by the South Vietnamese Government prior to the launching of U.S. pressures on Hanoi. Following this logic, we withheld attacks on North Vietnam for several months, even ignoring serious Communist attacks on U.S. forces which merited strong reprisals. By this time, however, Taylor himself was beginning to doubt the practicality of making strong action against North Vietnam dependent on political events in Saigon. By January 6, 1965, as the political situation spiraled downward, William Bundy pointed out the self-defeating perversity of this reasoning in a memorandum to Secretary Rusk:[12]

> I think we must accept that Saigon morale in all quarters is now very shaky indeed, and that this relates directly to a widespread feeling that the U.S. is not ready for stronger action and indeed is possibly looking for a way out. . . . The blunt fact is that we have appeared . . . to be insisting on a more perfect government than can reasonably be expected before we consider any additional action.

On the other hand he acknowledged the risks of action:

> The alternative of stronger action obviously has grave difficulties. It commits the U.S. more deeply. . . . Most basically, its stiffening effect on Saigon political situation would not be at all sure to bring about a more effective government, nor would limited actions against the southern [part of North Vietnam] in fact sharply reduce infiltration or . . . be at all likely to induce Hanoi to call it off.

But, in the end he concluded that action against North Vietnam was needed because "on balance, we believe that such action would have some faint hope of really improving the Vietnamese situation and, *above all* would put us in a much stronger position to hold the next line of defense, namely Thailand." (Emphasis added)

Was this the strongest argument in favor of actions against North Vietnam? That it prepared us for a retreat (after failure in Indochina) to a new position in the rear? If it was, that did not bode well for a test of our determination. Unfortunately, this is only one of many evidences throughout the *Pentagon Papers* of a lack of confidence in the strategy of pressures on Hanoi's will. Curiously, very little consideration seems to have been given to other alternatives and the editors of the *Pentagon Papers* comment that ". . . in the end, the decision to go ahead with the strikes seems to have resulted as much from a lack of alternative proposals as from any compelling logic advanced in their favor."[13]

In any case, as so often happened, events had a way of taking the reins. On February 7 the Communists conducted coordinated devastating raids on a U.S. advisors' barracks in Pleiku and on a U.S. helicopter base four miles away. Nine Americans were killed and seventy-six had to be evacuated. This attack, which occurred while Presidential National Security Advisor McGeorge Bundy was in Vietnam, galvanized the U.S. within fourteen hours to launch a heavy air attack on North Vietnamese military facilities at Dong Hoi and Vinh Linh, north of the Demilitarized Zone in North Vietnam. Mr. Bundy's memo of February 7, recommending a strategy of sustained reprisals, confirmed the complete reversal of the equation which, for several months, had made military actions against North Vietnam dependent on political improvements in Saigon. Said Bundy,

> We emphasize that our primary target in advocating a reprisal policy is the improvement of the situation in *South* Vietnam. Action against the North . . . as a means of affecting the will of Hanoi . . . [is] an important but longer-range purpose. The immediate and critical targets are in the South—in the minds of the South Vietnamese and in the minds of the Viet Cong cadres. . . . (Emphasis in original)
>   . . . in all sectors of Vietnamese opinion there is a strong belief that the United States could do more if it would and they are suspicious of our failure to use more of our obviously enormous power. At least in the short run, the reaction to reprisal policy would be very favorable.[14]

McGeorge Bundy's memorandum was followed, in two weeks, by the Rolling Thunder campaign of progressive, sustained air attacks on the North. So, we were off in a test of our determination against their will. We were engaged in a continuing air assault against a regime (Hanoi's) which we did not seek to overturn or conquer, in order to persuade it to stop its campaign to overturn and conquer a state (South Vietnam) which we did not plan to defend on the ground, through a third state (Laos) via a corridor which, by our "tacit understanding" with the Communists, we would not close for fear they would take the rest of Laos which would fall into their laps anyway after their expected conquest of the South. How would we accomplish this? By incremental pressures played up and down a one-string tactic to demonstrate our determination and, in William Bundy's words, "to obtain [North Vietnam's] cooperation in ending Vietcong operations in South Vietnam."[15]

The eclectic plasticity of this one-string, tactical scale was miraculous in several ways. First, it lent itself to strategy by the cultivation of images—images of determination, of morale, of impending escalation, of moderation on our side and of Hanoi's imagined reactions on the other. Images were painted of Hanoi's protectiveness of its small industrial establishment and its independence of China, both of which conveyed an image of Hanoi's hankering to be reasonable. There were images of a pragmatic, avuncular USSR exercising its benign influence because of its jealousy of China. There were images to be cultivated in Moscow, in international public opinion, in Western Europe and—above all—in the United States. *The Pentagon Papers* demonstrate most prolifically that imagery was near the center of our strategy in Indochina. Ours was a strategy of mirrors.

Second, on our one-string incremental tactic, victory and defeat were not opposites but only different quantities on the same linear scale. Indeed, it was regarded as a virtue of any particular scenario that it blurred and smoothed out the differences between success and failure, thereby reducing possible damage to our image. For example, in expounding a proposed graduated "scenario" of a "Plan of Action for South Vietnam" in September 1964, Assistant Secretary of Defense John McNaughton listed in descending order of desirability the following "Chances to resolve the Situation":[16]

    a. To back North Vietnam down, so South Vietnam can be pacified.
    b. To evolve a tolerable settlement;
        i. Explicit . . . [at] a conference;
        ii. Tacit . . . including "de facto 'writing off' of indefensible portions of South Vietnam, etc.
    c. If worst comes . . . to disown South Vietnam, hopefully leaving the *image* of a 'patient who died despite the extraordinary efforts of a good doctor.' " (Emphasis added)

On January 4, 1965, McNaughton made a similar point more pithily, saying, "Our stakes in South Vietnam are:

a. Buffer real estate near Thailand and Malaysia and,

b. Our reputation.

The latter is more important than the former; the latter is sensitive to *how* as well as to whether, the area is lost.

. . . if we leave, be sure it is a departure of the kind which would put everyone on our side, wondering how we stuck it and took it so long.[17]

As George M. Cohan said, "Always leave 'em laughing when you say goodbye."

By March 24, 1965, McNaughton had quantified U.S. aims as follows:

70%—To avoid a humiliating defeat (to our reputation as a guarantor.)

20%—To keep South Vietnam (and then adjacent territory) from Chinese hands.

10%—To permit the people of South Vietnam to enjoy a better, freer way of life.

ALSO—To emerge from the crisis without unacceptable taint from methods used.[18] (Emphasis in original)

In his February 7 memo which resulted in the Rolling Thunder bombing campaign, McGeorge Bundy acknowledged that a policy of sustained reprisal may fail but "even if it fails, the policy will be worth it."* Why?

At a minimum, it will damp down the charge that we did not do all that we could have done. . . . Beyond that, a reprisal policy—to the extent that it demonstrated U.S. willingness to employ this new norm in *counter-insurgency*—will set a higher price for the future upon all adventures of guerrilla warfare."[19] (Emphasis added.)

In short, our strategy of graduated reprisals was designed more to blur the image of probable failure than to achieve success.**

Third, the lack of fixed, intermediate stops or "sticking places" made the possibilities of progressive refinement of escalatory scales almost unlimited. Warnings, actions, programs, could be started, stopped, reduced, or accelerated. They could be bunched up for rapid

---

*On a linear scale, he allowed a rather wide margin in estimating the chances of success between 25% and 75%.

**And our failure has, in fact, set a much *lower* ceiling on the price the U.S. is willing to pay to oppose subsequent Communist guerrilla ventures, *vide*, Central America.

escalation or they could be spaced out and subdivided into lesser increments depending on the image of the day to be projected. Thus, it might be theoretically possible to play the single string up and down almost indefinitely without snapping it. Theoretically, that is. Eventually, of course, U.S. determination flagged and we let go our end. But, in the winter of 1964–65, the potential weakness of the one-string escalatory ladder appeared to be at the other end where it was thought to approach our self-induced image of Hanoi's will.

As would be expected, the military generally urged rapid escalation toward high levels of pressure on North Vietnam in order to maximize the effect on Hanoi. They had good reasons and, had our objective been set in terms achievable by military means, they would have been right.

The civilians had reasons for applying other criteria. They knew that the terms of our Indochina war were being drawn along political lines traceable to our essentially political objective. As we never tired of saying in every forum and by every channel, our object was not to overturn or defeat North Vietnam but to cause Hanoi to cease its Vietcong campaign in the south and its support of the Pathet Lao in Laos. This was a political objective—even though some military means were used—because it required a *political decision* (not a surrender) by the government in Hanoi. Military means might be used but the decision in the end had to be made by Hanoi without having been defeated.

To accomplish this required, on our part, a fundamentally political calculation—how much military pressure is necessary to move Hanoi and how much is too much? How far could Hanoi be moved by attacks which it knew (because we had told them so) would not lead to their conquest or defeat? The corollary question was—at what point will our attacks become counter-productive by making it politically impossible for Hanoi to stand down even quietly (let alone publicly) from its campaign in South Vietnam and Laos? This was not only a political judgment in the province of the civilian authorities but it was probably the most delicate, difficult, complex and unlikely kind of judgment on which we could have made our objective depend. In retrospect it is clear that Hanoi never for a moment abandoned its campaigns. It grudgingly temporized briefly to negotiate the Paris Treaty of 1973 only because we were rapidly withdrawing and a treaty would hasten and shorten the interim before final victory.

This was not so plain in the autumn of 1964. Because it was a problem that had intrigued me, I had done some experimental drafting of a diagram to illustrate the problem. But it was a November 3 cable from Ambassador Taylor in Saigon which crystallized it—for me at least. Taylor was commenting on an October 27 JCS proposal (JCSM-902-64) of graduated measures to be taken in Laos and North Vietnam.[20] Although the JCS did not propose immediate action above the level of air operations against infiltration routes from North Vietnam, their proposal included graduated steps running up through naval quarantine and all-out air assault on North Vietnam, to commitment of U.S. and allied ground forces in Southeast Asia.

"I submit the following personal comments to JCSM 902-64, dated October 27, 1964," Taylor opened his November 3 cable. He commented on proposals at the lower end of the scale. Then almost as an afterthought, he appended a final brief paragraph. In it he raised casually—too casually, as it was not adequately absorbed in many quarters—the question of "how much is too much?" Taylor's paragraph is important:

> As a final word it is well to remind ourselves that 'too much' in this matter of coercing Hanoi may be as bad as 'too little.' At some point we will need a relatively cooperative leadership in Hanoi willing to wind up the VC insurgency on terms satisfactory to us and our South Vietnam allies. What we don't want is an expanded war in Southeast Asia and an unresolved guerrilla problem in South Vietnam.[21]

As is already evident, I doubted that Hanoi could be "persuaded" by incremental pressures from the air and sea to abandon its campaign in South Vietnam and Laos. But, since we seemed to be embarking on such a strategy, it was important to examine the calculus of "how much is too much." I took the JCS proposal* as the grist and Taylor's paragraph as my text for illustrating the kind of calculation that needed to be made. Let me emphasize the illustrative nature of the calculation shown in the diagram below (page 145) dated November 4, 1964. I did not presume to be qualified to make all the estimates implicit in it. The diagram could have been prepared differently, and indeed, I've shown two versions, one of which I prepared later, after, Admiral Sharp expressed some interest in this kind of exploration.

The idea was to speculate on the points in our escalation at which we might reach four significant thresholds. They were:

1. *Threshold of North Vietnam's stand-down*—The point we were seeking, at which our pressures would, in theory, become severe enough

---

*I used this particular proposal only because it was a current familiar one, based on authoritative military judgment. There were other similar proposals which would have served equally well. In this case, I have omitted the lower steps of the escalation since the problem at issue only appeared near the upper reaches.

to cause the North to cease supporting and directing the Vietcong insurgency.

2. *Outside limit of political détente*—The point which bothered Ambassador Taylor, the point beyond which increased pressures had a counter-productive effect since they would make it impossible for the North to come to an acceptable agreement with us. This point might be reached because of internal security problems or because of political pride or because of internal Bloc pressures. In any event, there certainly was a point beyond which no government could accept the humiliation of capitulating to its enemy without accepting complete defeat.

3. *Limit of Chinese tolerance*—This was the point at which Peking might think the situation was going so badly as to require intervention. This might come if the North were just about to meet our demand. Or, it might come if Peking feared North Vietnam was falling apart.

4. *International Political Pressure Point*—This was the point at which international pressures on the U.S. for a cease fire and negotiations would become irresistible. We couldn't discount this pressure because the United States is probably the most sensitive in the world to international pressure. I should also have specifically included domestic American pressure in the calculus.

Only one point is important. In both versions the very last critical threshold to be reached on the escalatory ladder is the one we sought, the point at which Hanoi would stop its campaigns in South Vietnam and Laos. In other words, before we could ever drive Hanoi to call it off, we would drive them to the point at which it would be politically impossible for the North Vietnamese to do so. In a sense, therefore, Ambassador Taylor's casual paragraph exposed a cardinal weakness in our strategy which committed us to a war of waiting—waiting for Hanoi's will to buckle under our military attrition—an attrition which would become self-defeating before it could succeed. At the same time, there was a reverse psychological attrition—a burden of waiting, endless waiting, levied on the American people—which worked to undermine our own determination.

But, in the autumn of 1964, the momentum of accelerating incrementalism took over, making this kind of reasoning unwelcome. The United States moved inexorably toward the strategy of sustained and escalating air attacks which, as was mentioned earlier, the editors of the *Pentagon Papers* said resulted "as much from a lack of alternative proposals as from any compelling logic advanced in their favor."

In the same cable, Taylor made another significant point already mentioned earlier in this chapter. He argued against relying on future Tonkin Gulf kinds of incidents to shape our strategy and urged that

Critical Thresholds (1)	Hypothetical U.S. Escalatory Ladder (JCSM 902-64)	Critical Thresholds (2)
	Commit U.S. & Allied Forces to Southeast	
North Viet. Stand- down*	Asia ↑	North Vietnam Stand- down*
	Amphibious & Airborne Operations on North's Coast ↑	Limit of Peking's Tolerance†
	All-out Air Attacks on North Vietnam	
Internat'l Pressure Point	↑ Increasingly Severe Attacks on North	Internat'l Pressure Point#
Upper Limit of Detente	Vietnam ↑	Upper Limit of Detente
Limit of Peking's Tolerance†	Naval Quarantine on the North ↑	
	Aerial Mining of North Vietnam's Ports ↑	
	Air Strikes on Infiltration Targets in the North ↑	
	Deploy Contingency U.S. Forces to Thailand & West Pacific ↑	
	Attacks on Lines of Communication in the North ↑	

*This hypothetically assumes that no other factors intervene before this threshold is reached. In fact, however, the three other thresholds listed below would be reached first. Hence, the threshold of North Vietnam's stand-down would never be reached. This is the point of the diagram.

†The second table of critical thresholds is an improvement on the first by taking account of China's patience which would probably not give way until North Vietnam's collapse was threatened.

#If, in the second table, I had labelled this threshold the "Psycho-political Pressure Point", thereby including U.S. domestic pressure, it would have been fairly prophetic because it was the crossing of this threshold after the Tet Offensive of 1968, that started the gradual U.S. turn-around.

our graduated military pressures, "should ideally grow out of events in South Vietnam and Laos. Such events are available for our exploitation now in the form of infiltration activities in the Laotian Corridor and North Vietnam."

He was right, and this insight could have provided a potentially effective "sticking place" along our linear scale of intensifying pressures—a place at which we could stand pat, hold something gained on the ground and, eventually, even negotiate a cease-fire. However, Taylor did not develop the point in this way. Indeed, he could not have done so without threatening to pull down the "facade of Geneva." No one knew its meaning better than Taylor who had called it a "tacit understanding" even as Hilsman had called it a "tacit agreement." In explaining the North Vietnamese failure to implement the Geneva Accords by withdrawing from Laos in the autumn of 1962, Taylor succinctly laid out the shape of the "facade" and the effect it would later have on our Vietnam strategy, an effect with which he was now coping as Ambassador in 1964.

> There seemed to be a tacit understanding on both sides that the fate of Laos would be resolved in Vietnam. For that reason, the Pathet Lao took as a primary objective the protection of the supply lines in the Laotian Panhandle and maintained a *de facto* partition of the country on a north-south line which prevented any effective military action from the Mekong Valley against their communications.[22]*

Now here, late in 1964, was our "tacit understanding" at work, precluding our termination of North Vietnamese use of the infiltration routes. Air attacks were tolerable because they only harassed but did not deny the North effective infiltration. Short term, harassing ground raids were also tolerable for the same reason, particularly if carried out by South Vietnamese, unaccompanied by Americans. But anything which portended a decisive U.S. operation on the ground which might effectively reduce infiltration below the levels required by the North was precluded by the "facade" because it risked provoking Hanoi to attack elsewhere in Laos. In a sense, therefore, the "tacit agreement" had become a kind of detour in our ladder of graduated pressures which by-passed the only "sticking place."

*Recall the similarity to Hilsman's version, quoted in Chapter VIII: "The North Vietnamese would undoubtedly insist on maintaining . . . their hold on the infiltration routes into South Vietnam. . . . If the Americans attempted to take back territory already held by the Communists, even in the southern panhandle . . . the estimate was that the Communists would strenuously resist."

The point seems not to have been addressed seriously in strategy planning but emerges, *sotto voce*, in many places. Commenting on a meeting of Cabinet-level principals on September 7, 1964, the editors of *The Pentagon Papers* remark

> From the September meeting forward, there was little basic disagreement among the principals on the need for military actions against the North. What prevented action for the time being was a set of tactical considerations [Domestic U.S. politics]. . . . Other concerns were . . . the desire not to upset the *delicate Laotian equation*.[23] (Emphasis added)

And what was the Laotian equation? The "facade of Geneva" at work.

On September 11, 1964 at a meeting in Saigon of representatives of U.S. missions there and in Laos and Thailand, it was recognized that U.S. advisors would be necessary to accompany South Vietnamese cross-border operations. But, the meeting accepted Vientiane's insistence that "such a flagrant violation of the Geneva Accords would endanger the credibility of our political stance in Laos."[24] Why should this be, in the light of the vastly more flagrant North Vietnamese violations of the Accords? Answer: Our "political stance" in Laos rested, not on compliance with the Geneva Accords, but on conformance with the obverse of the Accords, i.e., the "facade of Geneva."

A little earlier, as described in Chapter 12, Ambassador Unger had pointed out how incompatible with our posture in Laos was the desire to include—in the graduated pressures program—military operations against the North Vietnamese in the Laos Panhandle infiltration routes.

The point was neatly capsulated in another way on February 10, 1965, by William Bundy, who expressed doubt that any new negotiations on Laos "could in fact be pressed to the point of doing anything effective about the Corridor which, as a practical matter, Premier Souvanna regards as more our issue than his."[25] In short, the Corridor was primarily part of the Vietnam problem.

What could be more quixotic than embarking on a prolonged test of our determination against Hanoi's will with the knowledge beforehand that we were precluded by "tacit agreement" with the Communists from denying Hanoi its invasion route through Laos to South Vietnam? Given the nature of our limited objectives it seemed to me that a territorial defense line would provide the only possible "sticking place" at which we could stand pat and negotiate. Such a territorial defense line would have to be drawn so as to insulate South Vietnam against slow invasion through southern Laos.

In November, 1964, I wrote an exposition of this concept and made the following proposal. I sent it to William Bundy, Assistant Secretary for Far Eastern Affairs (having succeeded Hilsman) and his Deputy, Marshall Green, in the Department of State. I also gave a copy to the Commander-in-Chief, Pacific, Admiral Ulysses S. Grant Sharp, Jr., whose Political Advisor I was. This proposal, which is the subject of the next chapter, had its problems and there were arguments to be made against it. But a choice had to be made between drawing the line of defense and acceptance of the consequences of refusing to defend. A choice *had* to be made. Either choice would have been better than what we did do—which was to make no choice. As the paper itself states,

> The first step is to judge the importance of what is at stake. The lengths to which we must go must be related to the importance of our stake in the outcome. If the loss of South Vietnam is not unacceptable, then we should trim our effort accordingly—but, in that case, perhaps we should never have made the effort at all. If it is unacceptable, then logically we should be willing to risk much. . . .
>
> Options exist to be chosen. It is impossible to keep a full range of options forever open. History moves and options unchosen dissolve. Failure to choose can lead to the evaporation of options just as surely as choices can do, but without ever having exerted the power to choose. While we have kept our options open in Indochina, they have been steadily dissolving in South Vietnam, in Cambodia and Laos. We have less latitude today than we had a year ago. Soon we may have none.

14

The Necessity of Choice

"Once to every man and nation comes the moment to decide . . ."
James Russell Lowell, *The Present Crisis*, 1844

It is probably inescapable that to devote a whole chapter to the author's own lengthy memorandum written over twenty years ago will be regarded as self-serving. Nevertheless, I cannot avoid doing so. As I have said earlier, my purpose is not to render an "autopsy" on our whole Indochina war but to show how a policy first was formed by incremental accretion, then failed. My problem is that in the available records of decision-making, there is virtually no serious attention paid to the concept advanced here. It is not that the concept was studied, analyzed and rejected but rather that it was barely considered at all. A speculative historian might infer the existence of such a concept by analyzing the blank spaces in the record, much as scientists used to show the existence and characteristics of an unknown chemical element by studying the shape of the blanks in the pattern of known elements. But that is all.

Why? Because the mere evaluation of such a concept in 1964–5 demanded a deliberate, difficult and probably irreversible decision—positive or negative, and fateful either way. But, as is evident, the "way of thinking" which permeated our policy and strategy was artfully constructed so as to avoid addressing irreversible choices directly, to prevent large decisions from being taken, to dissolve difficult alternatives into miniscule increments—in short, "to keep our options open."

Under the circumstances, I have no alternative to using this memorandum in some detail. I have tried to do so honestly, claiming no more than it says and acknowledging its weaknesses. I have excised material of little relevance today. I have left the text in the present

tense, as it was written. Occasionally, I have interrupted the continuity to comment. The memorandum opens with a stark presentation
of two historical possible outcomes which hinged on America's immediate decision. The foreboding tone seems to me today—in the
light of subsequent history—to have been fully warranted.

MEMORANDUM

November 24, 1964

I. *Background*

   It is not often that so much of the world is balanced on a single fulcrum
as is now the case in South Vietnam. The watershed which we must pass
in the next few weeks or months is not only fateful for Southeast Asia and
U.S. interests there but it may be the apex of the Cold War confrontation.
The course and pattern of the cleavage between the Free and Communist
worlds will be largely determined by the role of the U.S. in Southeast Asia
in the next few months.* The outcome in Southeast Asia could be validation
and justification for all of the effort and treasure, blood and pain expended
by the Free World since 1946 in defending its independence against Communist aggression and subversion. Alternatively, it could begin the tragic
unravelling of the whole pattern of Free World strength, leaving us divided
and exposed in the future and making a mockery of twenty years of containment.

I must pause here to take account of the sharp dissonance between
the foregoing paragraph and the meticulous grinding and measuring
of "too much" and "too little" along the linear scale of "incrementalism" which has been described in previous chapters. By contrast,
the paragraph above sounds apocalyptic. I do not wish to explain
away this contrast. Rather, I call attention to it as a valid reflection
of the distance that separated my point of view from the prevailing
one which guided our strategy. I regarded the problem of Indochina
as a critical part of the Cold War cleavage. The 17th parallel demilitarized zone bisecting Vietnam was a critical sector of the Cold War
frontier which ran from the Baltic Sea to the Sea of Japan. This frontier
of containment had made possible co-existence between the Communist and non-Communist worlds since World War II. There was
an important gap in the line—Laos.

In this context the meaning and importance of Indochina extended
beyond immediate tactics, immediate results and immediate time—

*In fact, we passed the watershed just four months later, in March, 1965,
when we embarked on the gradual commitment of U.S. ground forces to
internal counter-insurgency rather than to the external defense of South Vietnam, following the familiar syndrome of "incrementalism."

far into the future and deep into civilization. Others might not agree—
viewing Indochina as a relatively unimportant hangnail dangling from
the dead hand of former European Empire, lacking in vital future
significance for the interest of the United States. Although there was
a case to be made for this view, what was needed was to choose and
then to act in accordance with the choice. Splitting the difference
satisfied the requirements of neither, but assumed that the only difference was a linear measure of degrees of violence and input. In fact,
the difference was qualitative, fundamental, essential and not susceptible to incremental subdivision. As someone once said, one of
the most difficult maneuvers to execute is to leap across a chasm in
two easy jumps.

The memorandum continued:

> Proposals for action in South Vietnam cluster around three foci. The first
> is to continue the present counter-insurgency without risking escala-
> tion. . . . It is argued that if the Vietnamese Government cannot restore
> political solvency then there is little the U.S. can do. . . .
>
> Actually, it is difficult to see how this concept can be anything more than
> rationalization for acceptance of impending defeat. . . . This would give
> us a dubious point in public relations gamesmanship—that is, the blame
> could be fixed on South Vietnam rather than on us.* But the defeat would
> be just as great.
>
> The second focus is the concept of exerting increasing military pressure
> (mainly by air) on North Vietnam to force cessation of support to the
> Vietcong.** This concept recognizes . . . that the Vietcong insurgency is
> not an isolated phenomenon but is directly related to external Communist
> support. . . . The trouble with it is that it is based on the very dubious
> premise that North Vietnam can be forced, by threat of severe damage
> inflicted from the air, to . . . give up its objective of extending its domination
> to South Vietnam. This assumes that the Communist determination is not
> great and that they are less able than Britain or Germany or Russia in World
> War II to absorb punishment. There is absolutely nothing in the history of
> Communism to support that view. . . . And what if the Communists refuse
> to capitulate? . . . There is a great likelihood that long before the point is
> reached at which North Vietnam ceases to support the Vietcong, it will
> have become politically impossible for Hanoi to make an acceptable agree-
> ment, or the Chinese will have intervened or we will have been dragged

*As the reader will recall from the last chapter, this is exactly what John
McNaughton and McGeorge Bundy began to do a few months later.

**This was the concept that underlay the Rolling Thunder bombing campaign
which opened two weeks after McGeorge Bundy's February 7, 1965 memorandum to President Johnson. (Chap. 13)

prematurely into a conference in which the only thing to negotiate is our withdrawal from South Vietnam.*

A third concept is that of seeking an international conference through which we can negotiate ourselves out of South Vietnam, which would be neutralized.** Of course, this is predicated on the unadmitted realization that neutralization is only a brief stop on the way to Communization. . . . How could a new conference guarantee compliance any better than those of 1954 and 1962? . . .

There is another concept—a fourth—which has not been much discussed in recent years, at least not with seriousness of purpose. And for well-known reasons. This is the concept of forcing a military confrontation in Southeast Asia, on land as well as air and sea, with the object of drawing a line—at great cost, if need be—between the Communist and non-Communist worlds. This concept involves admitting to ourselves that—

- the counter-insurgency program cannot win in the time available;
- the political renaissance of South Vietnam will take ten to twenty years and cannot be accomplished at all except behind a protective screen;
- a political-guerrilla war, inspired and organized by the Communist bloc and waged on the ground cannot be defeated from the air;
- holding on in South Vietnam requires integration of all our military and political resources in southeast Asia, including Thailand and Laos.

In short, it involves recognizing that our only chance of containing the Communists in Southeast Asia requires changing the nature of the war from the kind we are losing to the kind we could win, i.e., from a political-guerrilla insurgency to a full-scale military confrontation where we could be overwhelmingly superior.

It will be said that this would be an act of desperation. Perhaps, but a desperate occasion calls for desperate action. It will be said that the cost, human and material, would be unacceptable. But how does it compare with the cost of losing? It may be doubted that this proposal will succeed. But has it not a better chance than others? Let us, at least, consider this course seriously and analyze its many variations as carefully as we have studied all the variations of graduated but inconclusive pressures.

This was a plea to confront an important choice directly and to consider how to choose between two diametrically opposed courses. This first part of the memo ended with the segment quoted in the

---

*The reader will recognize here the essence of the argument made in the illustrative escalatory chart reproduced in the last chapter which, in turn, was an extrapolation from an observation made by Ambassador Taylor in Saigon.

**Thus, some officials wished to see Sihanouk of Cambodia get the conference he sought, hoping that it could be broadened to negotiate the U.S. out of Indochina.

penultimate paragraph of the last chapter—which I repeat here, to maintain continuity.

The first step is to judge the importance of what is at stake. The lengths to which we must go must be related to the importance of our stake in the outcome. If the loss of South Vietnam is not unacceptable, then we should trim our effort accordingly, but, in that case, perhaps we should never have made the effort at all. If it is unacceptable, then logically we should be willing to risk much—and not just money and equipment.

The second part of the memorandum tries to set forth why Vietnam is important. Here again, I have excised a number of distracting digressions. After all, one cannot write so many words without wandering. However, I have not altered meaning. There are places where I could do better today. But, in the light of subsequent history, I still subscribe to the main thrust.

II. *The Importance of Vietnam*

We have been deeply absorbed in operational tactics. But now, at the present watershed, we need to step back and view Vietnam and ourselves in the somewhat grander perspective of the World and History.

Since World War II, the U.S. has followed a fundamentally political strategy in Indochina rather than a military one. We have provided military assistance but in essence our strategy is not military. . . . We have sought to avoid using our own forces directly to establish some defended military position to protect the region. . . .

This strategy is predicated on the conviction that within a political framework, time can be made to work for us in Indochina as it has in some other places. This strategy seeks to avoid irreversible commitments and instead maintains flexibility in preference to establishing a military line. The disconcerting thing is that we are losing. Looking back over the post-World War II history of Indochina, it appears to be a general downward slope, notched occasionally by small plateaus representing periodic attempts to find a political formula for stability. Such notches would include the Geneva Accords of 1954, the early period of the Diem regime and the Geneva Accords of 1962.

Vietnam's Continental Role. Broadening the scope, our political strategy in Indochina stands in clear contrast to our essentially military strategy along the eastern shore of Asia—Korea, the Taiwan Straits, the island chain of Japan, Okinawa, Taiwan, Philippines, with the 7th Fleet and the 5th and 13th Air Forces, stretching from the Siberian coast to the South China Sea. . . . The Free World has been virtually excluded from the East Asian mainland but is clinging to islands, peninsulas and to the sea itself. In the southeast [however] we still stand in South Vietnam, not in military strength but in a political posture whose progressive undermining will soon force us to a decision.

Looking westward, along the south Asian underbelly, we find a situation more susceptible to the political approach. But there, unlike Indochina, we do not find Communists conducting quasi-military insurgency. [Here, I fell into the conventional loose use of the word "insurgency."] Spanning a wide spectrum from the closest alliance with the United States to the coldest correct contact, the states from Indochina to Turkey constitute a most important band in which we can and so far have successfully operated on the basis of a political strategy.*

The Consequences of Losing. The domino theory is valid in Southeast Asia. Indeed, it is no mere theory but a process well underway. The first domino was North Vietnam. The second and third are Laos and South Vietnam.** The tumbling of South Vietnam would give the final push to Cambodia and . . . the whole eastern flank of South Asia would be turned and India outflanked.

I must pause here to offer three elaborations in explanation of this telescoped, rather stark, forecast which some will regard as excessively fervid. First, in 1964, no argumentation was needed to prove the validity of the domino concept. President Kennedy himself had specifically and unequivocally expressed his conviction of its validity. Second, the later controversy over the concept reflects the danger of colorful metaphors. Opponents and adherents alike perverted the metaphor, either to dramatize and warn against too many perceived threats or to discount the existence of any threats. Of course, nations don't roll over with the inevitable automaticity of a row of dominoes. Nor did President Eisenhower mean that when he applied the expression to Southeast Asia. The essential meaning of the domino concept is that in international power politics, as in physics, a force once moving in a given direction will continue until deflected or stopped by a greater force. Moreover, such a force tends to gain momentum as it gains mass from sequential victories. As a result, the longer that counter-action is postponed, the greater the resistance needed to stop the force. The moral underlying the domino concept is derived from the historical observation that nations (especially democratic ones) tend to put off setting up the necessary counter-force until the initial

*At least so it seemed in 1964, fifteen years before the Russians saw an opportunity to extend their power by shifting to a military strategy in Afghanistan.

**Here, I carelessly reversed the strategic relationship between Laos and South Vietnam. As was explained earlier, the logic implicit in our "tacit agreement" required that Laos not be taken over completely until after it had served Hanoi's purpose in bringing about the defeat of South Vietnam. This, of course, is the way things actually worked out in 1975.

threat has attained a momentum at which it can only be stopped by a massive and destructive effort—for example, World War II.

Third, there is a tendency to extrapolate too literally from the image of immediate collapse of a row of dominoes to international politics where events occur on a different scale of time. Hitler's occupation of the Rhineland was not followed instantaneously by his takeover of Austria, by Munich and the Czech Sudeten takeover and by the invasion of Poland. But did the several-year phasing rob the sequence of its analogy to the domino process? And Hitler was a man in a hurry, unlike the Communists who have operated on the premise that since their ultimate victory is "inevitable," they can afford to take their time.

From 1954, when a separate North Vietnam was created, until the end of the Indochina war, more than twenty years passed, but this time-span does not invalidate the principle that there was a sequential and predictable relationship between events which—after allowing for the impressionism of the metaphor—could be reasonably described as a domino process. As to "turning the flank of south Asia," I was indeed reaching rather far but only to illustrate the historical significance of events. More time is required for the process to reach that stage, and when it does, perhaps a sufficient counter-force will be mobilized to stabilize the flank. But, it will require a greater counterforce than it would have required before Hanoi conquered South Vietnam, Laos and Cambodia.

The memorandum continues:

> It is implausible to say that the loss (including neutralization) of South Vietnam can be offset by . . . exercising the threat of our air-sea power to prevent further Communist advances. If all our resources cannot be used effectively to save South Vietnam today, then who will have confidence . . . tomorrow? If our resources are adequate to shore up Southeast Asia tomorrow, they should be adequate to save South Vietnam today.
>
> The Vietnamese are the most vigorous and potentially powerful people in Southeast Asia. It is idle to suppose that a unified Communist Vietnam could not extend its domination over Laos and Cambodia and seriously undermine Thailand.

In a brief aside, let me emphasize that I do not mean to sell short my friends, the Thai, who never lost their independence to Western colonization while all about them were losing theirs, who have demonstrated the vigor and productivity of a free socio-economic system and who, since Hanoi's conquest of Indochina, have responded both stoutly and generously to the challenges presented by the new Vietnamese Empire along their eastern border. But, like other applications of the domino concept, the effect of Communist pressure against Thailand from Indochina must be judged in the scale of Time.

The memorandum continues:

> Timing is critical. It can be argued that our task is not to win a military decision in South Vietnam but to maintain a *political* foothold in Southeast Asia until, in due course, the Chinese Communists mellow under new leadership and it becomes possible to reach some accommodation with them. The difficulty is that the accelerating rate of decline in South Vietnam does not offer us the time required for such a delaying action . . . which may be nearer to twenty years than to five.

Obviously, I did not then anticipate that in only eight years Richard Nixon would lay the groundwork for an accommodation with China. The main point here, however, was that it would be impossible for us to maintain a position in Indochina by means of a *political* strategy. The implication was (and this was the intended meaning of the whole memorandum) that we must shift to a true strategy of military containment or get out.

The memorandum continues:

> *The Corruption of American Purpose.* If South Vietnam is allowed to fall to the Communists or slip gradually under Communist control, the long-range effect on the American mentality and soul is likely to be devastating. Not only would this undercut the logic of twenty years of post-World War II foreign policy but it would undermine domestic faith in the honor and mission of our own nation. At first, there might be a false sense of relief from a burden shed and a companion sense of gratitude that the world had not suddenly become unlivable as a result. All the dire predictions would seem discredited. But over the next months and years, as the consequences were borne home, there would likely occur a subtle change to a mood of careless cynicism which would hardly support future sacrifices for the sake of Free World unity or strength.

I believe any reader who has lived through the score of years since 1964 will recognize the national malady from which we may only now be beginning to recover.

Part III was an attempt to define the structural conundrum of the existing strategy.

III. *The Problem*

With apologies to Winston Churchill, it can be said that in Indochina we are entangled in an insoluble problem, within a dilemma, tied to a contradiction and wrapped in irony.

The *problem* is to restore the internal political integrity of South Vietnam while North Vietnam is supporting a Communist insurgency against it.

[Again, I carelessly used the conventional but misleading word "insurgency" to refer to what was actually a slow invasion.]

The *dilemma* is that this must be done by exerting enough pressure on the North (without committing U.S. ground forces and without triggering Chinese intervention) to cause Hanoi to cease supporting the insurgency, but not so much pressure as would overturn the regime or destroy its ability to agree on stopping the insurgency.

The *contradiction* is that the very international settlement—the Geneva Accords—which ostensibly neutralized Laos and isolated it from the Cold War, in practice encompasses Communist domination of the Corridor by which the insurgency is fed from the North. [This was a clumsy attempt to isolate the essence of the "facade of Geneva" three years before the publication of Roger Hilsman's brilliant vivisection of the "tacit agreement" which he and Harriman conceived.]

The *irony* is that the resort to air assault on the North for the narrow purpose of forcing termination of aid to the insurgency in the South is an admission of the failure of the counter-insurgency. [I might, more accurately, have spoken of the "inapplicability" of counter-insurgency.]

We have treated infiltration as a subsidiary nuisance rather than as part of the essence of the problem. We have hoped that under the 1962 Geneva Accords the situation in Laos might be held in suspense, pending a resolution of that in South Vietnam, despite the fact that the suspension formula leaves the Corridor to South Vietnam in the hands of the same Communists we are seeking to defeat in that country. We have waited for progress in South Vietnam to bolster Cambodia's confidence in the Free World, but instead, Cambodia, responding to spiralling South Vietnamese decline, has turned increasingly against the Free World.

Having made all else dependent on the outcome in South Vietnam, we have encountered persistent deterioration there. . . . We are strong in the capacity for military confrontation but weak in the ability to cope with political insurgency [even though only simulated]. In Laos, we are in an advantageous political position which would provide justification for military action but, locked in the framework of a stalemate [the "facade of Geneva"] which contributes to defeat in South Vietnam, we are unable to utilize this advantage. We are strong in the air and at sea but today we are weak on the ground where the battle is being fought. . . . We are fragmenting our effort. Our separate policies for each country are tied in a Gordian knot which prevents utilization of our strength in those areas where we are strong but leaves us vulnerable where we are weak. Moreover, to cut the Gordian knot and change the war from a counter-insurgency—in which we are weak—to a regional military confrontation in which we could be strong, would require a major military commitment on the ground which we seem unwilling to make. [Or, as I should have said, unwilling to *decide* to make.]

The political structure of South Vietnam is virtually smashed by twenty years of Japanese occupation, anti-French and anti-Vietminh war and by Vietcong insurgency. Lenin once said that the Communists do not seek to take over the old state apparatus but rather that the old state must be literally smashed. While the Communists cannot claim the entire credit for it, the fact is that the political, social and institutional framework of the South Vietnamese state has been virtually smashed. It can barely carry on the minimum functions of bureaucracy. It is divided politically, socially, geographically, by religion and sect, and in the face of destruction is unable to muster a degree of unity sufficient to permit effective action against the common enemy. . . . Years are needed, perhaps twenty, to rebuild. A series of internal political upheavals probably will be necessary before a basis is found for the reconstitution of internal political integrity.

There is a fatal discontinuity between the political content and the military apparatus of the counter-insurgency. . . . With the Vietcong (as with all Communists) political guidance is one with military organization. The same cadre who lectures on politics in camp at night is leading his men through the forest next day. . . . But it is otherwise in South Vietnam where there is not only discontinuity but suspicion and distrust between the political and military areas. They are truly "worlds apart."

The U.S. concept of counter-insurgency imports its own bifurcation of political and military programs. . . . Our counter-insurgency is heavily military-oriented, emphasizing the military disciplines, tactics and paraphernalia of guerrilla war, supported by air. We are fifteen years too late. These techniques would have worked much better before 1954, if there had been real hope of independence and when Communist China was weak. But it is late for this approach.

Whereas the Communists can offer the chance to overthrow a moribund *ancien regime* and create a new one, what is offered to the non-Communist Vietnamese? . . . Only the chance to prolong briefly the tenure of a defeated regime—to defend an amputated half-nation.

But, this does not mean all is lost. This merely defines the scope and terms of the task. Several things are needed in South Vietnam:

1. Time—perhaps 10 to 20 years,
     —for socio-political development,
     —for beating the Vietcong,
     —for rebuilding confidence of the Vietnamese people.
2. A barrier behind which to gain and use time.

The U.S. should concentrate on what it can supply—namely a military position which will serve as a barrier of containment to gain the needed time. . . .

IV. *Proposal*

The following is the outline of the conceptual framework for an operation by which the U.S. could establish a military position which would serve as a containment barrier in Southeast Asia.

Before continuing, I should explain that I have shortened this section greatly. Whereas in 1964 this was the operative portion of the memorandum, in 1984 operational details have become less important, even academic; concept is all.

Establish a U.S. military position (supported, if possible, by friendly nations) south of the DMZ in South Vietnam and in certain points along the Laos side of the Mekong River and gradually link these positions by means of mobile patrols across the Laos Panhandle. The object would not be to invade North Vietnam. The fundamental object would be to establish a position of overwhelming mobile, military strength which would stand between Communist power and the non-Communist areas of Southeast Asia. . . . After all is said and done, the Communist threat to Southeast Asia is on the ground and failure to meet it there as well as in the air and sea can only lead to doubt as to our intentions.

Air attacks against North Vietnam in the absence of a backup position on the ground are likely to arouse widespread opposition around the world . . . because of the obscurity of our objective and the difficulty of knowing when it is achieved. However, air operations in support of a ground position are standard and well-understood. . . . Once in position on the ground . . . we would have established the limits of our objective by defining on the ground the line we intend to establish, thereby reducing the tendency . . . to expect a wider war. . . .

Using our ground position as the anvil and our aerial attacks as the hammer, our hope would be—
• to force a negotiated truce as soon as possible,
• to provide a screen behind which the counter-insurgency could be gradually won and political solvency established in South Vietnam. . . .
• to establish a position of strength for international bargaining . . . after the suspension of air attacks . . .
• to support interdiction of infiltration along the routes in Laos. . . .

The problem of bringing forces into South Vietnam would be relatively easy. In Laos . . . it would be highly desirable to have Premier Souvanna's request or . . . if that is impossible . . . his silent acquiescence. For this and other reasons it would be desirable to have a specific provocation to justify our entry.

The fundamental justification for our intervention already exists in the form of continuous, blatant and cynical Communist refusal to implement the Geneva Accords. Introduction of U.S. forces into Laos would . . . be carried out for the purpose of restoring the Accords to full operation. . . . The present stalemate in Laos does not work in our interest in Southeast Asia generally since it encompasses the unrestrained Communist use of the Laos Corridor to undermine South Vietnam which will lead to the ultimate upsetting of the stalemate . . . to Communist advantage instead of ours. . . . The boil must be lanced some day. . . .

It is not my purpose to argue against the original negotiation of the Geneva Accords of 1962. As an experiment in testing the meaning of co-existence and the possibility of successful negotiations with the Communists, the Geneva Accords have been extremely valuable for the lessons they have taught us. But times have changed. [I was wrong. In restrospect it is clear that we had not learned any lessons from the Geneva experience.]

The counter-insurgency in South Vietnam must go on and be strengthened. . . . The armed forces introduced in the northern part of South Vietnam would not be part of the counter-insurgency effort but would be an extra U.S. fighting element operating independently as a screen. The U.S. should not take over the direction and fighting of the counter-insurgency.

There is reason to hope that such a U.S. commitment might give confidence and encouragement to the Government of South Vietnam and to the many non-Communist elements now withholding their cooperation. . . . But whatever course we choose, it is possible that the Government of South Vietnam will crumble. . . . That would be a reverse for the United States but not appreciably worse if it happened after we had introduced armed forces on the ground rather than before. . . . We would face the same humiliation today if forced to withdraw some 24,000 military now in South Vietnam—greater than a division in numbers.

The Chinese Communists might introduce ground forces into Vietnam. . . . But a truce line cannot be established without first establishing a military line as was done in Korea.

The memorandum ended with a restatement of my continuing belief as quoted at the end of Chapter 13.

It might be said that introducing forces into South Vietnam would involve us in an irreversible commitment and thereby deprive us of the full range of options which are open to us otherwise. Options exist to be chosen. It is impossible to keep a full range of options forever open. History moves and options unchosen dissolve. Failure to choose can lead to the evaporation of options just as surely as choice can do, but without ever having exerted the power to choose.*

What finally happened is that our options *did* evaporate—in the same way that a bull is defeated by its inability to *choose* to fight on its own terms rather than on the terms of the toreador. That the U.S. should stop chasing the toreador's cape was the meaning of the memorandum.

What happened next however, was the arrival of a letter, dated December 9, from Marshall Green, reacting to what he described as "your labor of love on what we should do in Vietnam." He noted that he had sent copies to Robert Johnson, a member of the Policy Planning Council under Walt Rostow, and to Michael Forrestal, Averell Harriman's protege on the Vietnam Working Group, who had come to the White House in 1961, carried on liaison with the State

---

*The same point is expressed more elegantly in a different context by former French Premier Leon Blum in his book, *On Marriage*, "Life does not give itself to one who tries to keep all its advantages at once. I have often thought morality may perhaps consist solely in the courage of making a choice."

Department's Far East Bureau and later became Special Assistant to the Secretary of State.

"I think Bill Bundy and I would agree as to the merits of your proposal." With this rather cryptic introduction, he proceeded, in a few succinct paragraphs, to itemize the advantages and disadvantages, *as seen in Washington*, of committing U.S. ground forces—all without mention of the status of Laos or the Geneva Accords. Without reference to my suggested strategic concept of deployment—or to any other—he set forth the following pluses and minuses of U.S. ground force commitments—which I have quoted directly from his letter although, for ease of presentation and rapid comprehension, I have listed the points in tabular order.

The presence of U.S. ground forces:

(1) would convey a clear signal;
(2) would relieve South Vietnam forces for other duties and, above all;
(3) would strengthen our bargaining position should it ever come to negotiations.

We have not excluded this possibility. Indeed, our current plan provides for the possibility of putting a mixed force (hopefully including Filipinos and Commonwealth) in the Danang area. However, the top level is not prepared to cross this bridge yet. As you know better than I, the JCS has always been reluctant to get involved in any ground warfare in Southeast Asia.*

Seen in time sequence, the merits of taking a stronger stand against infiltration, including the commitment of ground forces, fall into this pattern:

(1) bucking up South Vietnam morale and getting South Vietnam factions to galvanize behind the government;
(2) reducing the flow of materiel from the north and to the extent possible, checking the flow of manpower from the north;
(3) conveying a strong signal of our determination to the enemy;
(4) discouraging the enemy from attacking South Vietnam in force once we start hitting Laos and even selected spots in North Vietnam south of 19° N;
(5) improving our bargaining position against possible negotiations, bearing in mind that international pressures for negotiations will increase if we go after the infiltration routes;

---

*He was right, here. But, as will become evident in the next chapter, neither Marshall nor I could have forseen the rigid, wall-eyed blankness which would do in the idea of a mixed force to be arrayed against invasion, whether north of Danang or across southern Laos.

(6) short of formal negotiations, putting us in a better position to take unilateral measures to withdraw power or reduce pressures if the Communist side unilaterally takes measures that would permit us to do so. This unilateral measures approach could lead to tranquilization and might indeed be a more effective means of controlling the situation over the long run than through the conclusion of specific agreements which we tend to regard as binding but which the Communists find it easy to circumvent.

There are of course a number of cogent arguments against the introduction of U.S. ground combat units, such as:

(1) facilitate Hanoi and the Vietcong in their campaign to portray the U.S. as the 'occupying' power as well as the real enemy of the Vietnamese people;
(2) cause the South Vietnamese to slough off the main task of defense to the U.S.;
(3) possible ineffectiveness of U.S. ground forces against the covert enemy, etc.

These were all important factors to be considered and the majority ostensibly weighed in favor of deploying U.S. ground forces. However, to me it seemed that their force and direction would depend on their application to some *particular* strategic concept of deployment, such as the one I had outlined, or another. Without some strategic, conceptual context they became abstract measures of the intrinsic value of ground forces *per se*—regardless of where or how deployed or to what purpose. Treated in this way, the deployment of U.S. ground forces became only a direct incremental transfusion of additional strength into the veins of the existing, self-defeating strategy. This is the essence of "incrementalism," which measures qualitatively different actions as quantitative inputs of strength on a linear scale. It is the opposite of treating the problem as entailing qualitative choices between radically different objectives and strategies. "Incrementalism" was like a transfusion of blood into a profusely bleeding patient, unaccompanied by the application of a tourniquet, or performance of an amputation or other conceptually decisive strategy.

I do not complain. Marshall is a friend for whose thoughtfulness years later I remain deeply grateful. Moreover, he had not only responded as fulsomely as he found possible but he had passed my proposal along to others to consider. Nevertheless, I was disappointed because I sensed the difficulty he found, at that time in Washington, in trying to address the strategic dichotomy directly. I had proposed a radically different strategy—a choice between "Yea" and "Nay," to replace the endless meticulous grinding and measuring of "too much" and "too little" along a linear incremental scale. The choices were as distinct as black and white. But, when put under the spectroscope of "incrementalism," choice is broken down into the infinite incremental hues of the political spectrum. The necessity of choice is diffused. How different the factors in Marshall Green's paragraphs appear depending on the strategy to which they are applied! Take paragraph one:

Would the deployment of U.S. ground forces always "send the same signal" to Hanoi regardless of which strategy was followed? Hardly. As 1965 opened, various concepts for possible deployment of U.S. ground forces were being discussed including 1) encadrement into South Vietnamese divisions; 2) a reserve force; 3) deployment to the central highlands; 4) beachhead enclaves and 5) defense of U.S. air bases. (The idea of deployment against the invasion across southern Laos to the Mekong River was rarely mentioned and quickly dismissed.) All these concepts could not send the same message to Hanoi. It seemed to me that infusion of U.S. ground forces into internal counter-insurgency would only signal a new transfusion into an incremental test of wills. But, U.S. forces deployed to bar Hanoi's access to South Vietnam through Laos would signal both the extent and the limit of our objectives and in the process also demonstrating our determination *by applying it*.

Sending American forces to relieve South Vietnamese in the highlands, or coastal enclaves or as a reserve force would bog them down as successors to the French. But to bar the slow invasion of the South would relieve the southerners to concentrate on the internal enemy— their proper job.

American forces dug in all over South Vietnam would have little use as a bargaining counter because the enemy would know we intended to pull them out and that we would be under great pressure to do so. But, U.S. forces deployed as a barrier to North Vietnamese aggression would create a strong position from which to negotiate a cease-fire—as in Korea.

Or, Paragraph Three: Here are listed, in incremental "time sequence," the advantages to be gained—not from blocking the invasion but from a "stronger stand against infiltration." If that meant only a comparative incremental infusion, then the "bucking-up" of the South would not last long. Similarly, the value of "reducing the flow" from the North to the South is diluted to an unknown degree by the phrase "to the extent possible." But a strategy which promised substantially effective insulation of South Vietnam against infiltration should be distinguished from the mere incremental tightening of a string which has no "sticking places."

As for "discouraging the enemy from attacking in force," our subsequent actual deployment of half a million U.S. forces in an internal war throughout the South, obviously did not deter an all-out attack such as the Tet Offensive. But, U.S. forces deployed in strength to face the enemy coming from the North would have been in a position, not just to "deter" but to *prevent* the build-up which made the Tet Offensive possible.

The idea of simultaneous unilateral withdrawals was, of course, seductive—a variation on "persuading the North Vietnamese to cooperate" with us in ending the Vietcong attack on South Vietnam. That the Communists find it easier to circumvent agreements than we do would tend to prove the unlikelihood of the Communists ever truly withdrawing unilaterally except as they did in Laos after the 1962 Accords—i.e., not at all.

The last paragraph mentions certain important contrary arguments which also need to be applied in a specific strategic context. Deployed in an internal war throughout South Vietnam, U.S. ground forces would indeed be vulnerable to the charge of "occupation," and they might take over from the South Vietnamese who might "slough off." Deployed against the external enemy however, they would be a friendly ally holding off an aggressor while the southerners dealt with the internal situation behind the screen. I do not believe that the United States should ever fight someone else's covert enemy but should face our own external enemy, forcing him to come out into the open. Ironically, as the Vietnam experience showed, whenever the enemy surfaced and fought, U.S. forces won the day.

15

Through the Looking Glass

"Beware the Jabberwock, my son!
The jaws that bite, the claws that catch:
Beware the Jubjub bird, and shun
The frumious Bandersnatch!"

Lewis Carroll, *Through the Looking Glass*, (Jabberwocky, st.I,82)

Marshall Green had held up the spectroscope of "incremental-ism," the approved "way of thinking" in Washington. Given the complex state of policy review in Washington during the interval between President Johnson's re-election and his January inaugura-tion, it now appears to me that Marshall could have done no differ-ently. Speaking of this period, the editors of *The Pentagon Papers* have this to say:

> At no time in this period was the NSAM 288 commitment [to preserve an independent non-Communist South Vietnam] brought into ques-tion. . . . Nor did it appear to U.S. decision-makers that we faced a stark choice between complete U.S. withdrawal from the struggle or a large scale introduction of U.S. ground forces. Nor did the leadership in Washington believe that a massive bombing campaign against the North need be se-riously considered—although such a program was proposed by the JCS. With all these alternatives implicitly ruled out at this time, the choice was both obvious and inevitable. Although it *did not take the form of a decision*, it was agreed that the U.S. should at an unspecified date in the future begin an *incremental* series of gradually mounting strikes against North Vietnam. The only real questions were precisely what actions should be taken and when?[1] (Emphasis added.)

Having ruled out the alternatives implicitly (why not explicitly?), how was it possible to embark on a course (which did not take the form of a decision) to take some incremental series of actions (not knowing what or when) to begin at some "unspecified date"?

How to fill in the blanks? This problem was given to a special NSC Working Group, chaired by William Bundy, which had struggled from November 2 to prepare a report for the "Principals" of the National Security Council.* After three weeks of laborious compromise, shaping and honing, the report was presented by Chairman Bundy on November 24, the same day on which I mailed my memorandum to him and to his deputy, Marshall Green.

In addition to Bundy and Green, the Group included Michael Forrestal and Robert Johnson of State, Assistant Secretary of Defense John McNaughton and representatives of the JCS and CIA. The Group's deliberations led to a "consensus achieved by a process of compromising alternatives into a lowest common denominator proposal which, although "precluding any real Presidential choice," President Johnson accepted after a December 1 meeting.[2] What the President approved was a very slight intensification (called Phase I) of what was already going on—naval patrols, small covert harassments along the beaches and in the Laos infiltration corridor, plus a reserved, contingent reprisal against some possible Communist spectacular attack. He also approved—in principle only—a Phase II program which would provide a slowly progressing air campaign against the North—contingent on prior internal reforms by the Government in Saigon.

As the editors of *The Pentagon Papers* explain, no formal NSC decision was taken because the course being adopted "did not constitute a significant departure from the actions authorized in . . . September."[3] Then what was the Working Group doing during November? Well, it rejected both of the outside alternatives: first, that the situation was so irretrievable that we must withdraw and second, that South Vietnam was indispensable to U.S. interests, thus requiring a massive intensification of the war. Thereafter, the Group had little left to do except to re-hone the *status quo* and tinker with the usual contingent ladder of escalatory pressures. The wide gap between the actions approved and the demands imposed by our rising commitments was frankly recognized in an intermediate draft (November 8):

> Yet . . . we cannot guarantee to maintain a non-Communist South Vietnam short of committing ourselves to whatever degree of military action

*The "Principals" were the NSC agency heads directly concerned with strategy on Vietnam, usually, State, Defense, JCS and CIA.

would be required to defeat North Vietnam and probably Communist China militarily. Such a commitment would involve high risks of major conflict in Asia, which could not be confined to air and naval action but would almost inevitably involve a Korean-scale ground action and possibly even the use of nuclear weapons at some point.[4]

The Working Group, however, underestimated North Vietnam's determination and overestimated the effectiveness of our actual and threatened pressures. In the face of all the facts, this syndrome became one of the most persistent of those that underlay our strategy of "incrementalism." There was no lack of contrary warning. The Working Group's intelligence panel took a decidedly pessimistic view, warning that Hanoi was willing to accept damage "in the course of a test of wills with the United States over the course of events in South Vietnam."[5] Nevertheless, William Bundy's final summary paper of November 29 included among its basically optimistic objectives the goal of getting Hanoi "to remove its support and direction from the insurgency in the South and obtaining their cooperation in ending Vietcong operations there. . . ."[6]

The same theme, in almost the same words, was on the lips of the other members of the Working Group, not to mention the Principals.

But why then, were the proposals made so mild—even timorous? Answer: "To keep our options open"—a second persistent syndrome of "incrementalism." Open for what? Open for the possible necessity to withdraw in the event of a political collapse in Saigon. The measures proposed were believed to be sufficient to give Saigon a breathing spell without risking failure. That was at the low end of the linear scale. At the upper end, the military pressed for immediate commencement of a rapidly escalating series of air attacks which, they argued, would be more likely than a slow escalation to curtail infiltration and cause Hanoi to stand down. How high, though, would the escalation have to proceed in order to succeed? The military didn't know. The weakness of their conception was that success was not in its power to achieve without either the cooperation of Hanoi or the destruction of North Vietnam. But this led back to the old underestimation of Communist determination. The JCS argued for the "reduction of the *rate of delivery* of support to the Vietcong to levels below their minimum sustaining level."[7] (Emphasis in the original.) Although everyone could agree on the desirability of that goal, the JCS proposal did not take into account the likelihood (and eventually, the reality) that Hanoi could incrementally increase the input at the top end of the supply and reinforcement pipeline enough to offset whatever attrition we could apply by air action.

As for using aerial pressure to cause Hanoi to relent, the JCS argued that sudden sharp attacks on airfields, petroleum and military establishments would demonstrate to Hanoi that "the U.S. intends to use military force to the *full limits* of what military force can contribute to achieving U.S. objectives."[8] Of course, in the next sentence, the JCS noted that the campaign "could be suspended short of full destruction of North Vietnam if our objectives were earlier achieved." But what if our objectives were not achieved? What then? On to the "full limits"—whatever that means? Just as a one-string incremental concept has problems at the bottom end, so might it lead to failure at the top as long as our strategy depended on obtaining Hanoi's cooperation in bringing the war to an end.

At the opening of the Working Group's deliberations, William Bundy called for "an action that would *show toughness*."[9] In the same vein, William Sullivan, Chairman of the Vietnam Coordinating Committee (and about to go to Laos as Ambassador), urged that "our first action be . . . one which *gives the appearances* of a determination to take risks if necessary to maintain our position in Southeast Asia."[10] (Emphases added.)

But the cultivation of image worked two ways. One element of the policy of graduated pressures was planned to be publication of new evidence which revealed Hanoi's infiltration to be much greater than previously believed. Not only designed as a warning to the North, these figures would also serve as justification in the U.S. and abroad for intensified action and as a boost as well to flagging morale in South Vietnam. On December 4, Chester Cooper, experienced in intelligence, presented a report he had been directed to prepare for publication. But by this time, the Principals (mainly Rusk and McNamara) had become skittish, fearing that too much public emphasis on increased infiltration would, as Secretary Rusk cabled to Ambassador Taylor, "generate pressure for actions beyond what we now contemplate."[11] As a result, publication was suspended to trim our image to the dimensions of our minimal plans.

Given such an atmosphere, it is not hard to understand Marshall Green's difficulty in addressing a radical proposal to block the invasion. At the time I did not know all the foregoing details which have been since published in *The Pentagon Papers*. Nevertheless, at CINCPAC Headquarters we were well-informed and, in retrospect, I believe that the impression I had at the time was not different from the impression I have tried to convey above. However, I didn't answer Marshall Green along these lines. The subject was complex, the situation fluid and time would be required. Moreover, his letter ended of a hopeful note:

Final decisions are yet to be taken on our future course in Vietnam/
Cambodia and we continue to need and welcome any ideas you may have.

Ironically, the "final decisions" were never "taken" (no fault of
Marshall Green), they "jis' growed." In reply, I did not argue the
issue further. Instead, I acknowledged the strong opposition in Washington to placing ground forces in Indochina. But, I added, "I am
nevertheless, convinced that in the long run this is what we will
probably have to do and therefore, that the sooner we get on with
the planning for it the better off we will be."

I sent him a revised version of Part IV of the memorandum, asking
him to pass it along to those who had received the first version—
Robert Johnson in the Policy Planning Council and Michael Forrestal
on the Vietnam Coordinating Committee. I don't know Johnson's
reaction. As for Forrestal, whose views were usually very close to
those of Averell Harriman, I expected that he would disagree. Accordingly, it was more than a little significant when, about a month
later, during a brief stopover in Honolulu on one of Forrestal's frequent trips between Washington and Southeast Asia, the subject of
my memorandum was raised in an unusual manner. One evening, I
was suddenly invited to Admiral Sharp's residence, three doors up
Makalapa Drive from mine, to meet briefly with him and Forrestal
who was spending the evening in the guest house next door. They
had been discussing my long memorandum. The substance of my
meeting with them consisted mainly of the Admiral's statement that
he planned to have the Command's J-5 (Plans) Branch make a study
and report on the proposal. Forrestal nodded agreeably but non-
commitally. The J-5 report was made orally a few weeks later. It was
negative. The reasons given, which I shall describe shortly, were more
interesting and revealing than the fact.

Meanwhile, the memorandum made its way around military circles
in Honolulu, including the Pacific Headquarters of the individual
armed forces as well as at CINCPAC. It was accorded polite non-
response from the Navy and the Air Force which were more interested
in naval and air operations than in a plan based on a ground war for
territory in which they would play auxiliary roles. The Army and
Marines were more interested. General John K. Waters, then Commanding General of the U.S. Army, Pacific, supported the concept
and sent a copy to the office of the Army Chief of Staff in Washington—without result. A World War II hero himself, General Waters
had a refreshingly uncomplicated view of war, the object of which
was to defend the territory of a friend against an external attack by
an enemy. He recognized the reality of political complexities and the

existence of internal problems and guerrilla activity inside South Vietnam. He also recognized the civilian authority to decide. But, authority is matched by a responsibility to decide—really decide, not indefinitely postpone a decision. Once the decision has been made and the military have been given their military assignment, defense becomes primarily a military function to be carried out within practical guidelines from the President. If the situation in South Vietnam were too confused to warrant a clear-cut civilian decision to defend South Vietnam against North Vietnam then the United States should stay out of it, rather than enter by a side-door, crab-like, without ever making the main decision.

Although General Waters' views were known both at CINCPAC Headquarters and in the Pentagon, they were not accepted. He told me that while there was some interest in my memorandum in the Army Plans Branch (G-5), the high command said such a concept would not get support. But he had advanced without success his own similar concept. After his retirement he finally published an article in the December 19, 1966 issue of *U.S. News and World Report*. In a few short paragraphs, with the authority of professional experience, he outlined a plan that was conceptually similar to the one I had amateurishly tried to set forth in Part IV of the long memo in the last chapter. Since this was substantially what he had been saying in December of 1964, I shall jump ahead a couple of years to quote a few excerpts:[12]

> The time has been long overdue for the United States to take the necessary . . . action on the ground . . . to isolate the South Vietnamese battlefields and interdict the enemy on the ground.
>
> The Ho Chi Minh Trail has never been cut, and . . . the enemy has had unlimited and free access to his various combat zones . . . on down through Laos and Cambodia. The back door has never been closed—and we are in a major war.
>
> The Navy has the sea blockaded. The Air Force has unlimited control of the air. On the ground, where the enemy strength lies, is where the key to victory is. The U.S. has not cut this lifeline.
>
> Route 9, beginning in the east of South Vietnam and extending across through Laos, provides a lateral route for the U.S. forces' rear supply. . . . The U.S. should block and interdict on the ground north of this.
>
> Coupled with [this] should be the assumption by Saigon of the war within South Vietnam. This will provide a clear, well-defined mission—the destruction of a cut off, surrounded and diminishing enemy within their borders. They will free their own country.
>
> As the North Vietnamese mass against our blockade . . . the U.S. should take whatever means are necessary to destroy them. To effect a break-

through of our lines would require a massing of enemy troops, a prime target of our air and ground weapons. . . .

The United States would not invade North Vietnam on the ground unless forced to do so by enemy reaction.

The General acknowledged the necessity to call up the reserves, extend enlistments, declare an emergency and cut back on other programs; then he called for the U.S. to make a choice and abandon reactive incrementalism: We must abandon the

"enemy act-U.S. react" policy and lay the future squarely on the line for our people and the people of the world. In the end it will save men, money and material.

He was right on the last point. The same issue of *U.S. News* reported that a Pentagon estimate in August 1965 had indicated a requirement of 350,000 troops to execute such a strategy. Actual U.S. forces in Vietnam at that time were about 100,000 and rising rapidly. By December 1966, the figure had reached 365,000—higher than the number estimated as needed to insulate South Vietnam. And we still had not blocked infiltration—that is to say, "slow invasion." Our forces were spread over South Vietnam, vulnerable to sudden guerrilla attacks by Communist forces who had come down the Trail. The "slow invasion" continued.

General Waters' approach was cold-shouldered—not only by civilians as might have been expected, but also by the Joint Chiefs of Staff whose attitude seeped outward and downward to other commands such as CINCPAC. I think that the military leadership's lack of interest in this concept stemmed from their tacit acceptance that the "facade of Geneva" lay at the political heart of the civilian leadership's policy and therefore had to be taken as "given." Recall how, in the face of massive Communist violation of the Geneva Accords on Laos, we adopted the sophistical formula, authored by Averell Harriman and Roger Hilsman, which Hilsman called a "tacit agreement" and General Maxwell Taylor (Chairman of the JCS from 1962 to 1964) called a "tacit understanding." Within this facade we accepted continued partition of Laos and we excluded the possibility of action to close southern Laos against use by North Vietnam for its slow invasion. That the military had reason to regard this facade as part of the civilian leadership's policy was evident in the NSC's approval, on March 17, 1964, of Secretary McNamara's draft paper, dated March 16, which stated that:

> As a consequence of these policies [Geneva Accords on Laos] we and the Government of South Vietnam have had to condone the extensive use of Cambodia and Laotian territory by the Vietcong both as a sanctuary and as infiltration routes. (See Chapter 12)

But, if the "facade of Geneva" did not limit the perspective of General Waters, the same could also be said of Lt. General Victor H. Krulak, Commanding General of the Fleet Marine Force, Pacific. He lived only two doors from us on Makalapa Drive and, in December 1964, our views on what needed to be done in Vietnam were comparably close. Of small stature but with a reputation for toughness, Krulak had been known as "Brute," since his Academy days at Annapolis but he was intelligent and intellectually flexible. You could talk to "Brute" and he would listen. My spirits rose on December 31 when I read his memorandum which opened with a flat statement that the idea of deploying mobile forces in strength across the Laos Panhandle and to the South China Sea had appealed to him since he first heard of it two years earlier. More than that, he also understood the perversity of the so-called stalemate in Laos and pointedly expressed his agreement with that portion of my memorandum which argued that it did not work in our interest.

He went on to analyze the proposal meticulously, criticizing particular points. More importantly, he gave it some professional military structure by estimating the size and configuration of the force needed to carry it out. In summary, he judged that about 2½ to 3 divisions would be required plus some Lao and South Vietnamese units, strong helicopter and air transport elements as well as air defense and close air support. Also needed would be sizable all-weather logistics bases on the South China Sea and in Thailand to support the force. He concluded that the project would require on the order of 100,000 men, a number that might have to be enlarged in the event of a strong North Vietnamese reaction in southern Laos.

This would be no "side show," he said. Quite so. At the time we had no U.S. ground combat units in South Vietnam and a commitment of this kind sounded rather spectacular. Of course, it rapidly came to appear more modest and then, even miniscule, as our unplanned incremental deployments began to rise. There is no war without risk, and General Krulak recognized the possibility (which was much on our minds at the time) that an unfriendly government might come to power in Saigon and demand our withdrawal. But, in such a case, he thought, we would be in a stronger and safer position with balanced U.S. forces on the ground than with unbalanced forces deployed as an advisory element in a counter-insurgency operation.

The United States did not, of course, adopt this strategy. General Krulak loyally accepted the decision and went on to devise his own version of an improved program (discussed in Chapter 16) for internal defense to which he thought the Marine Corps could contribute. I was grateful to both him and General Waters for demonstrating that the concept of territorial defense, as distinct from internal counter-insurgency, could have military value for U.S. ground forces in In-dochina.

In fact, as the situation worsened and Washington agonized over each incremental bit, there were some signs that a choice might be made soon. One encouraging sign of impending decision—or so I thought—was increasing interest in the idea of deploying an inter-national force of Korean, Filipino and Commonwealth troops as well as American. Marshall Green had mentioned in his letter that con-sideration was being given to putting such an outfit in the vicinity of Danang, nearly 100 miles below the Demilitarized Zone. He noted that the top level was not prepared to cross that bridge yet and that the JCS was very reluctant to get involved in ground warfare in South-east Asia. Still, the mere idea of joining with our allies in an inter-national force seemed to imply an incipient shift of thinking toward drawing a line against North Vietnamese invasion, and this would require a clear decision. Unfortunately, the concept finally collapsed because of unwillingness to adopt a strategy which could accom-modate it. It was too big a concept for the existing incrementalism but, when cut to incrementalist dimensions, it was too small for a definitive strategy of territorial defense.

Rear Admiral Donald Gay, Chief of the J-5 Plans Branch at CINC-PAC, and I discussed the Joint Staff version of an international force sent to CINCPAC for comment. Although not entirely for the same reasons, we agreed that the concept was flawed. One point had to do with the problems of deploying an international force that included countries already committed under SEATO regional contingency plans. I thought this was mainly a technical problem which could be worked out, but as will be evident, the military regarded it as having decisive strategic implications. While springing from an important and valid principle, the concept as drawn up seemed to me to have been devised to gain the political advantage of an international image while retain-ing the unilateral flexibility to "keep our options open" within the framework of incrementalism.

The mission of the international force was to be a relatively static one, standing in deterrence of an open offensive by North Vietnam, a most unlikely contingency. At the same time it would leave the way wide open to the very real and continuing slow invasion which was exhausting South Vietnam. At the same time, if foreign forces were to be deployed to fixed positions in dangerous inland areas (neither facing the international enemy, North Vietnam, nor with their backs to a safe retreat on the sea), they would almost surely be drawn, incrementally, into internal counter-insurgency operations. International forces should openly face an international enemy.

The Joint Staff concept was limited to South Vietnam. It did not extend to Laos—another sign that the idea did not presage a change in our customary strategy of dealing with these countries in separate compartments. As this point was very close to my heart, I wrote Admiral Gay that I questioned "the concept of winning in South Vietnam by whatever means while at the same time leaving the communists in control of their corridor in the Laos Panhandle."

Finally, the proposal seemed to make the introduction of U.S. ground forces contingent on prior agreement by other countries to join in. But this was upside down. It made the decision on what could become a major shift of strategy dependent on obtaining some marginal international reinforcement. Making the greater depend on the lesser really meant that no real shift of strategy was intended. It meant that the international forces would be simply injected as an additional transfusion into the veins of the existing incrementalism. But would it not be dangerous to ask our allies to participate in a strategy that we ourselves doubted? If we were to effect a piecemeal ground force commitment via the third country route, we would come under great pressure as the result of casualties, third-country reactions and domestic American doubt as to the value of fighting this kind of war. "In other words," I wrote to Admiral Sharp, "if we get involved in the wrong kind of war, we may be trapped into a political negotiation without ever having attempted the right kind of war."

Nevertheless, the idea of an international force at least had the advantage of focusing attention on the ground force question, a process which I thought CINCPAC should encourage because "The advantage of doing so is that in this way we could plan such a ground force commitment with definite objectives in view and carry it out at a time of our choosing . . . rather than running the risk of backing into an unplanned ground force commitment simply by the gradual accretion of third-country elements requiring foreign protection and eventually, U.S. augmentation." The Admiral acknowledged receipt of my note, probably after filing it mentally under the category of flank attacks on behalf of my own proposal which the J-5 Branch still had under study. If so, I suppose he was at least half right.

During the winter of 1964 to 1965 I had an acute sense of standing—standing as a citizen of the United States, that is—at an important hinge of history. Whether the door closed or opened depended on whether we decided to bar North Vietnam's slow invasion through Laos, or opted to liquidate our military involvement in Vietnam. I thought that the logic of 20 years of containment, as well as the interests of the United States and Southeast Asia, required us to do the former. Whatever course we would take would have to be decided in a short time—a few months at the most. During this period, almost every question which arose led, in one way or another, back to this one—the master choice.* This was reflected in my memoranda of the period.

The sensation of standing at an historical threshold was not new. In the summer of 1939, bicycling through decadent France and through Britain, belatedly renascent at the end of the feckless pacifist decade, one felt the hinge of history. It was a sensation experienced most excruciatingly on crossing the borders between quivering small countries and spoiling, resurgent Germany, where I could sense the schizoid internal split between traditional German Gemütlichkeit and Nazi Schrecklichkeit. That door closed, as everyone knows, on September 1 as Hitler stormed into Poland and as I sat—in comic incongruity—in a deck chair on a blacked-out Cunard liner in mid-Atlantic next to an anonymous Brooklyn girl who hummed "Blue Skies" as the ship's orchestra played. Both the United States and I escaped only for a 2½ year reprieve.

Or, in the spring of 1949, in Shanghai, as China's Red Army walked down the Yangtse Valley to surround the supine city, undefended, its harbor empty, the Nationalist exodus nearly ended, the American Navy and Marines gone, one could feel the door closing again.

This will sound overheated to some. But I must take account of the subjective factor. History does not occur in the abstract but is interwoven with the threads of its participants, great and small. My objective impact during the winter of 1964–1965 was too small to be measurable but, seeing the converging events of the time "writ large" as I did and, having an official position in the structure, I did not wish to be invisible. "You like to write long, serious memos about strategy," Barney Koren had said when he told me of my nomination to the post of Political Advisor. So, I wrote memos which were patiently accepted but not followed.

A cable from Washington, describing the two-phase program approved by the President on December 1 to cover the gap until the

---

*The one thing I didn't believe possible was that we would do neither—that instead of closing or opening the hinge, we would simply throw our weight to hold it half-open until we should become exhausted.

new Administration would take office in January, provided me an occasion to pontificate in a memo that "if we get through until January without some serious defeat in Southeast Asia, it will not be because of these measures." Admiral Sharp no doubt agreed with that but he made no comment on the punchline that followed:

If we are working for a contingent date of January 1, 1965, I think it is not too soon for the U.S. Government to re-examine its stake in Southeast Asia and, depending upon the result, to start contingency planning on how and under what circumstances we would commit forces on the ground. I deeply fear that our posture in Southeast Asia is now fully unbalanced because of our inability so far to find any acceptable means of coping with the Communists on the ground. We must do one of the following and do it soon:

Find a way to cope successfully on the ground;

Escalate to all-out air-sea confrontation with the Communists in the Far East;

Find a political formula for shedding our commitment in Southeast Asia.

To introduce some variety into my message, I was not above taking my text from the printed words of a pundit such as C. L. Sulzberger, in *The New York Times*, January 11, 1965. I sent the Admiral a copy of the article and commented briefly:

Sulzberger makes two points:

1. He argues that by delaying action over the last year or so, we have allowed our 'options' to dissolve so that we now have virtually no freedom of choice left. I think there is a lot of truth in this which, as you may recall, was the point made in the last paragraph of my paper on possible military action in Southeast Asia.

2. He then says that the only way out now is quiet negotiations with the Communists to enable us to get out of Vietnam quietly and gain time to strengthen our position elsewhere in Southeast Asia. I do not agree that this is the only option left to us, although I do agree that unless we act very soon in a decisive military manner in Southeast Asia, then Sulzberger will be right.

Well, what of my long paper? The dénouement, when it came, was swift. One day, late in January, I was invited to the presentation of J-5's report to an assembled group, including Admiral Sharp. As was customary, the report was presented by a colonel, equipped with a pointer and a rack of flip charts. It was a detailed report. It was oral and I have no copy, but the key points stick in my mind. First, the study concluded that a blocking movement through Laos on the ground would indeed make a decisive difference in South Vietnam, even though it would still leave a considerable guerrilla organization on the ground. I agreed.

Second, to do so would require an estimated 2⅔ combat divisions plus logistical and air support, an assessment similar to that of General Krulak. Emphasis was laid on the strong distaste in Washington, particularly in the Pentagon, for any decision involving a land war in Asia. As far as I recall, no note was taken of the possibility that without making a decision we might still become incrementally involved in a land war in Asia.

Third, the project would entail serious political problems, notably violation of the Geneva Accords on Laos. As with civilians, the military often emphasized this point in response to proposals to bar infiltration on the ground but slid over it in response to proposals for indecisive harassment. The "facade of Geneva" did not exclude harassment—only the decisive denial to North Vietnam of its invasion route.

Then came the blockbuster—although curiously, I had the sensation that everyone else had known it all along. The deployment of U.S. ground forces to stop Hanoi's slow invasion through Laos would undercut, and be incompatible with, certain regional contingency plans prepared together with our allies in SEATO. Since the U.S. was already committed to its SEATO partners to keep forces available to deploy against a North Vietnamese (or Chinese) attack across northern Laos toward Thailand, it must keep its forces free for that purpose. To commit U.S. forces, even unilaterally, in southern Laos against the invasion then going on would preempt our commitments to some future contingency.

Strategists are often criticized for trying to fight today's war with the weapons and tactics of the last war. But here we were being told that we couldn't fight today's real war because we had to keep ourselves in readiness to fight another future war which might (but probably wouldn't) happen at some future time. In fact, however, our SEATO allies—Thailand in particular—might have been more interested in winning the existing war than in keeping ready for the next one. Moreover, the forces which might have been deployed to defend South Vietnam against invasion through southern Laos would have been nearby, on the flank of any future North Vietnamese or Chinese attack through northern Laos toward Thailand. Indeed, they would have been better positioned to assist than were the half million American forces later incrementally deployed to South Vietnam. If the defense of South Vietnam required more forces than we had available, taking into account our other commitments, then the thing to do was to mobilize them as General Waters had argued and later wrote in *U.S. News*. Or, if the distaste for an Asian land war was to be controlling, then it was essential that we start immediately to shed our military commitment in Indochina *before* the logic of our strategy led us incrementally into an unplanned Asian land war.

As I left the briefing room, it seemed to me that perhaps Sulzberger really was right. Perhaps there really was only one way—to get out of Vietnam quietly and strengthen our position elsewhere in the region. For if, as I had just heard, we could not commit our forces against today's war in order to remain ready for some future war, then, in truth, we really *should* extricate ourselves from Vietnam and save our resources for the future. But I didn't really believe that because I didn't really think that the United States would make a decision on the basis of the logic I had just heard—which seemed to be just an incidental aberration.

But I was wrong. It was not an aberration. In December, the same formalistic logic had been applied in the Pentagon to kill the Joint Staff's study (mentioned earlier) of deploying an international force below the DMZ to deter an overt attack by Hanoi. The deed is described in *The Pentagon Papers* where it is reported that while the Department of State and other civilian agencies favored the idea, "the Department of Defense was less than enthusiastic." Assistant Secretary of Defense John McNaughton said that the idea had been shelved. McNaughton was reflecting the negative attitude of the armed services which had expressed their reservations in commenting on the Joint Staff study. The military objections, as recounted in *The Pentagon Papers*, consitute a preview of the CINCPAC J-5 report:[13] "They [the services] questioned its military utility due to deployments being framed essentially within a narrow deterrent contour."

Although true, the concept could have been enlarged to include aggressive interdiction of infiltration. But instead, "They recommended a continued adherence to the deployment concept in the approved SEATO plans, which in their totality were aimed at the military defense of all Southeast Asia." So, as long as the Communists launched no overt attack triggering the defense of all Southeast Asia by one of these SEATO plans, these plans could not be implemented, in effect immobilizing forces which might otherwise be available in the actual war we had on our hands. *The Pentagon Papers* editors note that "The Army, in particular, expressed concern regarding routes and modes of possible North Vietnamese advance into South Vietnam that differed from those assumed by the study's below-the-DMZ concept." The Army apparently believed correctly that an attack might come through Laos rather than over the Demilitarized Zone. Apparently, however, the Army did not propose extending the concept to include southern Laos. Instead, it preferred to stand on contingency SEATO plans which had virtually no prospect of being carried out because the Communists were far too smart to give us the pretext for carrying them out. The Air Force, too, pointed out "that the international force concept conflicted with the JCS concept for deterring and dealing with overt North Vietnam/Chinese aggression."

Note that these arguments, while being applied in this case to an international force, are stated in terms of strategic considerations which logically should apply to any unilateral U.S. deployment of ground forces directly against the North Vietnamese slow invasion. I had missed this point during the discussions at CINCPAC of the international force idea. I had thought that these arguments applied only to a multi-national deployment. But now it was clear that not only was the international force dead but, much more importantly, it had been done in by a logic which killed the idea of even a unilateral U.S. ground force strategy to insulate South Vietnam.

I did not grasp all this immediately, but gradually it became clear. The sequel to the briefing session came a few weeks later when I learned from a friend on the staff that a telephone call from the Joint Staff some time earlier had made it clear that the idea of a ground force deployment against North Vietnamese infiltration was out and no such recommendation would be welcome. One day, in Admiral Sharp's office I casually remarked, as was my wont, that time was growing short for planning how to use U.S. ground forces to protect South Vietnam. In a tone of good-natured exasperation, the Admiral shot back, "Norm, why don't you give up this idea? No one in Washington is going to consider it. They've got a lot of smart fellows back there. If there were anything to this idea of yours, some one back there would have thought of it."

I felt as if I had just walked through the looking glass.

Book IV _____

The Three Wars

16

Knit One: the Internal Pacification

Looking back on the whole war from a strategic standpoint, I have tried myself again and again to see what other broad alternatives we might conceivably have followed. Frankly, retaining in my own mind the "given" of our respecting the 1962 agreements on Laos, at least in high degree, I had not thought of the point you make. The more I now reflect on it, the stronger it seems. Surely we could have held a line across Laos and South Vietnam—perhaps in the area of the celebrated McNamara scheme—with significantly fewer men than we eventually employed within South Vietnam, far less American casualties, and in the end much greater effect and less bloodshed in the South itself.

William P. Bundy, in a letter to the author, June 16, 1975.

On March 8, 1965, the United States deployed two Marine battalions to Danang, a major base on the northern coast of South Vietnam, thus taking the first step in a fateful new phase of our war in Indochina. It was a phase which led, in three years, to the commitment of half a million American forces to fight throughout most of South Vietnam—without any strategic decision to do so.

Even though this process did not occur within the conceptual framework of the paragraph quoted above, I introduce Bill Bundy's 1975 judgment at this point because it was the last reaction—ten and a half years later—to my long proposal discussed in the last two chapters. In his letter, he was commenting directly on an article published four days later in *National Review*—the same article which provided the title of my Prologue and which restated the argument of the memorandum in chapter 14. I don't know what Bill Bundy thinks today and I do not suppose the quoted paragraph was his last word on the subject, but it does succinctly distill a point of view against which the massive deployments of the next three years should be studied.*

Actually, although the next phase opened on March 8 with the arrival of the two Marine battalions, it was signalled a couple of weeks earlier by the rather spectacular departure from Saigon of the erratic General Khanh after a year as a sort of Chief of State and after assorted *coups d'état* and attempted *coups* within *coups*—not to mention Khanh's making life unbearable for Ambassador Maxwell Taylor whom he threatened to declare *persona non grata*. With Khanh's forced departure there was some hope for the greater political stability that the U.S. had sometimes—but not consistently—argued was required as the condition for a greater U.S. military commitment.

A few days later I called at Admiral Sharp's office. On February 13 CINCPAC had cabled support for General Westmoreland's request for two Marine battalions to provide security for Danang Air Base and relieve four South Vietnamese Regional Force companies, a battalion and a tank platoon. Although Ambassador Taylor had warned this would lead to further deployments, the Department of Defense announced on March 6 that the Marines would be deployed for a "limited mission . . . to relieve Government of South Vietnam forces now engaged in security duties for action in the pacification program and in offensive roles against Communist guerrilla forces."[1] The Secretary of State said on national TV that even though the Marines would shoot if shot at, their mission was to put a tight security ring around Danang Air Base, thus freeing South Vietnamese forces for combat.[2] On March 8, they landed.

At the Admiral's desk, I expressed my concern that, whatever our intention might be, it would be impossible to limit the role of the Marines because they would be attacked and would have to respond. No, he replied, if the Marines were attacked they would defend themselves but their mission would remain limited to a precisely defined Tactical Area of Responsibility (TAOR). But, if attacked, their TAOR would have to be increased—and should be—I argued, because the Marines could not be kept in a permanent role of static defense against an enemy with the tactical initiative. Then, I rushed on to remind him that I was not opposed in principle to the deployment of U.S. ground forces. As he knew, I had urged such deployments for the

---

*It also illustrates that, Stanley Karnow to the contrary notwithstanding, reappraisals of wars are not to be discarded as mere "autopsies," that History is a living thing and that there is nothing dishonorable about profiting from the acuity of hindsight.

specific purpose of blocking Hanoi's invasion through Laos. What I did not favor was the unplanned piecemeal deployment of ground forces without a decisive, planned strategy to execute. This, I can see in retrospect, was stretching the diplomatic immunity of a civilian advisor pretty far.

"These are military matters, Norm. You just don't understand." The Admiral became busy with the papers on his desk.

Nevertheless, on March 17, I was irresistibly moved by a cable from JCS Chairman Wheeler to speak again. His cable had solicited views on four concepts for ground force deployments. "As you know," I wrote the Admiral,

> I have felt that the time would soon come when we would actually be seeking ways to introduce ground forces. General Wheeler's cable suggests that that time is nearly upon us. The ice was broken by the introduction of the Marines into Danang. The question no longer is *whether* to use ground forces in Southeast Asia but *how*. This involves many complex military factors but since the political and military are so inseparably intertwined, I will put in my oar.

I commented briefly on the four concepts, noting that while the "air base concept" had logistical advantages it had the disadvantage of presenting static defense targets to enemy attack while having no decisive effect on the war and providing no leverage for negotiation. The "highlands concept" for deploying U.S. forces to the central mountains might make a contribution to restricting infiltration but would not get at the main supply lines which could only be blocked farther forward, nearer the source. It also might result in a new Dien Bien Phu. The "beachheads concept," sometimes called "coastal enclaves," would secure coastal facilities but little else unless very large U.S. forces were to drive inland and put us in a quasi-French occupation position. Finally, of course, I favored the "blocking deployment to the Mekong River" provided it would not become entangled in international and SEATO negotiations. Logistics would be difficult but not impossible since we could supply from both South Vietnam and Thailand. We would be facing the real enemy and in the best position for international bargaining. The admiral suffered this memo in patient silence.

He was right. There were things I didn't understand. What I did understand, however, was that four weeks after the first Marines arrived, President Johnson had approved the deployment of two more Marine battalions and an air squadron. The eight-square-mile Marine TAOR around Danang Air Base grew in six months to more than 800 square miles. Another 100-square-mile Marine enclave had been created at Chu Lai to the south and still another 60-square-mile enclave had been created at Phu Bai to the north of Danang. Eventually, the Marine TAOR increased to 11,000 square miles. Marines in South Vietnam soon numbered 18,000 and by summer the 173rd Army Airborne Brigade was being deployed. On June 17, Secretary McNamara said that our ground forces would soon number 70–75,000.

As all this was happening, the other side was busy as well. Admiral Sharp points out in his book that by early June:

> Evidence indicated that the North Vietnamese were now capable of mounting regimental-size operations in many locations throughout the country and battalion-size operations almost any place. . . . Elements of one North Vietnamese regular army regiment had shown up in the northern zone of the second corps area and . . . perhaps two additional regiments were also in that area. It appeared that another North Vietnamese regiment was in southern Laos, capable of moving into South Vietnam quite rapidly. . . .
>
> Authorization had by now been given to go ahead with an increase of the South Vietnamese armed forces, but such action was deferred because the available men were needed to rebuild forces that had suffered heavy battle losses. Consequently, it was considered that a further increase in U.S. and allied forces was required at the most rapid rate.[3]

So, having postponed action and having failed to decide to stop the invasion, we now had to deploy U.S. forces to make up for the shortage of South Vietnamese forces fighting an *internal* war.

Sadly, although President Johnson and Secretaries Rusk and McNamara all knew that North Vietnamese aggression was occurring, they were still struggling to bridge the conceptual gap between an internal insurgency and an external aggression. Listen:

> *President Johnson:* "This is a different kind of war. . . . There are no marching armies. . . . Some citizens of South Vietnam, at times with understandable grievances, have joined in the attack on their own government. But we must not let this mask the central fact that this is really war."[4]
>
> *Secretary Rusk:* "The assault on the Republic of Vietnam is beyond question an aggression. . . . Between 1959 and 1964, 40,000 trained military personnel came down from the North. . . . More have come this year. Had all these crossed the line at once as the North Koreans did . . . nobody in the Free World could have doubted that the assault on Vietnam was an aggression."[5]
>
> *Secretary McNamara:* "In Korea, Communist aggression took the form of an overt armed attack. Today in South Vietnam, it has taken the form of a large scale intensive guerrilla operation. . . . The covert nature of this aggression . . . has now been all but stripped away."[6]

But the covert nature of the aggression had not been sufficiently stripped away to cause our leaders to see it clearly as the only proper target for our multiplying forces. Instead, U.S. troops were still being incrementally deployed to augment South Vietnamese forces in ambiguous counter-insurgency operations deep inside the country rather than to block the aggression they had identified. Nor had the contrived ambiguity been dissolved enough to relieve these three leaders of the compulsion to wrestle with themselves in public to exorcise it.

The U.S. Army's airmobile division was deployed to central South Vietnam in the highlands. General Westmoreland proposed his "search and destroy" concept of operations which he describes as "nothing more than the infantry's traditional attack mission: locate the enemy, try to bring him to battle and either destroy him or force his surrender."[7] Admiral Sharp supported Westmoreland in what "actually became the primary strategy during the remaining years of ground operations in South Vietnam." The Admiral goes on to report that the JCS asked him and Westmoreland whether forty-four battalions "would enable us to achieve our objective of convincing the enemy that he could not win." The Admiral reports that, "In response, General Westmoreland expressed the view that whatever we did would probably have little persuasive impact on the enemy, at least in the next six months, but that the forty-four battalions would be enough to prevent a South Vietnamese collapse and establish a favorable balance of power by year's end."[8]

While supporting Westmoreland's strategy, Admiral Sharp reports his own judgment that the real solution lay in the use of air power against North Vietnam: "The logical course would have been to unleash that air power against the homeland of the aggressor. Instead, we wasted our strength on inconsequential targets while planning to commit still more of our men to ground battle."[9]

To me it seemed that if General Westmoreland was right that "whatever we did would have little persuasive effect on the enemy" and if Admiral Sharp was right that new North Vietnamese battalions were rapidly arriving through Laos (and I believed both were correct), then the logical thing to have done would have been to deploy our forces to block the slow invasion and then use air power as a hammer to pound the enemy on the anvil of the blocking force.

In a way, the essence of the next three years of war, up to the Tet Offensive, can be distilled from the pattern and reasoning of these first ground force deployments in the first half of 1965. The rest is a string of incremental benchmarks. As a yardstick is marked with 36 inches, so our strategy during the three years from March 1965 to March 1968, when President Johnson withdrew from the Presidential campaign, was marked with 36 months, each of which was a statistic of our incremental force deployments—184,000 by the end of 1965, 385,000 by the end of 1966, 439,000 by April 1967, and approximately 500,000 at the time of the Tet Offensive January 30, 1968. And, like inches on a yardstick, they only led to the other end.

But the progressive commitment of American ground forces to South Vietnam must not be viewed in isolation from the two other principal elements of our war to preserve South Vietnam's independence—the internal pacification and reconstruction on the one hand, and the air campaign against North Vietnamese aggression on the other. Conceptually, these three elements had separate but interlocking roles. The internal pacification to separate the guerrillas from the population was to be screened by U.S. ground forces which could "seek and destroy" large invading North Vietnamese forces, while the air campaign would harass further aggression and cause Hanoi either to withdraw or to negotiate. Unfortunately, the three elements did not actually interlock effectively, rather like three spinning gears which don't mesh properly, resulting in a loss of power in the slippage.*

Or, to change the figure of speech, one can think of our strategy in Indochina as a piece of knitting, flawed at the center of the pattern by a "dropped" stitch. We "knitted" one stitch—the internal pacification, and we "purled" another stitch—the air campaign. But between these two we "dropped" a stitch—the groundforce campaign which (without discredit to our fighting forces but because of a conceptually faulty strategy) failed either to insulate the internal pacification against the invasion or to link effectively with the air campaign to the north. As a result, Hanoi continued its entry into South Vietnam through the hole left by the "dropped" stitch, culminating in the

---

*I have here omitted the superbly conducted and largely covert campaign on the northern Laos flank of the Vietnam war in support of the Lao regime and the doughty Meo tribes against North Vietnamese harassment. I do not mean to denigrate the intrinsic quality of this effort. But under our "tacit agreement" with the Communist side it was understood that North Vietnam would not take over all of northern Laos provided we would not deprive Hanoi of the use of southern Laos through which their slow invasion route ran. Since, therefore, by our "tacit agreement," the achievement of any decision in the northern Laos contest was suspended until after the conclusion of the contest for South Vietnam, its conduct had little effect on the main event in the South. The result, as former CIA Director William Colby notes in his book, *Honorable Men,* (p. 199) was that "the battlelines at the end of ten years of fighting, against an enemy whose strength increased from 7,000 to 70,000 in that time, were approximately where they were at the outset."

January 1968 Tet Offensive. The negative American public reaction to what was actually a U.S./South Vietnamese victory forced the U.S. to remove the "purled" stitch, i.e., the air campaign, thereby further enlarging the hole and further exposing the remaining "knitted" stitch, i.e., the internal pacification, to the enemy's continuing invasion.

Figures of speech always oversimplify but, after allowing for the oversimplification, they also provide ways to organize the study of complex processes. I have used this metaphor to organize an account of what happened from March 1965 to the Tet Offensive. The remainder of this chapter will deal with the first stitch—the pacification which—for all its weaknesses—was not the origin of South Vietnam's downfall. Hanoi's resort to the Tet Offensive proved the failure of the simulated insurgency. It was further demonstrated by Hanoi's 1972 resort to open attack and finally, in 1975, by the fact that South Vietnam fell only to an all-out invasion—not to an insurgency. Chapter 17 will deal with the air campaign, the failure of which, either to stop the invasion or induce a political decision by Hanoi to withdraw, resulted not primarily from its own inadequacy but from the "dropped" stitch—the ground campaign which should have been the centerpiece of the pattern. How the ground campaign stitch was dropped will be the subject of Chapter 18.

Internal pacification and development under conditions of guerrilla subversion are the essence of what is called "counter-insurgency." It is a highly complex and sophisticated subject which has spawned a substantial body of research and literature, much of it based on the Indochina experience. It is not the subject of this book but, by passing over it lightly, I do not mean to discount its importance. There was need in South Vietnam for programs of internal security and development and many excellent ones were applied as well as some that failed. The overall success of the effort is evident—as I have already indicated—from the fact that South Vietnam's internal socio-political structure did not collapse under either the Tet Offensive or North Vietnam's attacks of 1972 and 1975.

Accordingly, I balk at the use of the term "counter-insurgency" with respect to South Vietnam, even though I sometimes used it as a part of the conventional lexicon during the war. It focused attention on the enemy's use of irregular or guerrilla tactics and thereby obscured the essential political and strategic truth that the origin of the main threat came primarily from outside the country not from within. As a result, whatever reforms were accomplished, popular participation and social development were subject to continuous subversion and erosion by the slow strategic invasion of forces using irregular guerrilla tactics. By identifying and naming them "insurgents" according to *their tactics* rather than an invasion on the basis of their essential *strategic* nature, we tacitly accepted battle on their terms. We thereby committed ourselves to the waging of a permanent "counter-insurgency"—even "condoning" the simulated insurgency we opposed, as McNamara said in his NSC paper approved on March 17, 1965.*

From the end of World War II, pacification programs in Vietnam had been based on three core elements, in varying proportions: separation of the people from the enemy, political and social reform, and local participation. The last two are both difficult and slow processes, requiring as much as a score of years to work real changes in traditional societies. To gain the time necessary for these processes requires separation of the people from the enemy on a long term, country-wide basis.

It is "separation" that is my concern here. All of the programs applied by the U.S. and South Vietnam recognized the essentiality of "separation" to provide the opportunity for the other two elements to take hold and work. To succeed required converting space into time. In many respects much was achieved but, in the end, not enough, simply because we practiced separation on a "small-unit" scale—individual hamlets, villages, towns, valleys, roads, even districts. Later, when North Vietnam's role as an invader became accepted, we found it difficult to change course because by then we were trapped within a micro-scale strategy. Ironically, the essential problem had been identified as early as 1962 by Robert Shaplen, who wrote in *The New Yorker*: "In the long run, the Communists believe that time and space are in their favor. No matter what happens, the government cannot *patrol* a whole nation." So far, so good. In his next sentence however, Shaplen concluded that "Its ability to *control* it by winning the support of the citizenry will depend on whether or not it can come of age politically, as well as socially and economically." (His emphasis.)[10]

In a very long range sense, Shaplen is right, but given the long time required for a "traditional society" to "come of age," something is required to secure the space behind which the "coming-of-age" can happen. Because it is impossible to *patrol* a whole nation, a way should be found to *insulate* the nation as a whole. If doing so is impossible, then the Communists are right, i.e., both space and time do indeed work in their favor.

---

*Our failure to distinguish between tactics and strategy is a central point in Col. Harry Summers' incisive analysis, *On Strategy: A Critical Analysis of the Vietnam War*.

As I related in the last chapter, the Commanding General of the Fleet Marines in the Pacific, Lt. General Victor Krulak, was much interested during the winter of 1964–1965, in the idea of insulation by the deployment of U.S. forces across South Vietnam below the Demilitarized Zone and across the Ho Chi Minh Trails of southern Laos. However, when the first U.S. Marines did arrive at Danang, General Krulak described this deployment as follows:[11]

> The unit was restricted to protecting the Danang Air Base from enemy incursion, nothing more. It was not permitted to engage in day-to-day actions against the Vietcong, nor were the Marines allowed to leave the air base or to be involved with the local population—which is what counter-insurgency is all about. Soon the force was enlarged to . . . five thousand men, but it remained confined to the air base area, tied to . . . protection of the Danang Air Base. . . .

One can sympathize with his complaint that:

> This was never going to work. We were not going to win any counter-insurgency battles sitting in foxholes around a runway, separated from the very people we wanted to protect. Furthermore, . . . the airfield complex was cheek-by-jowl with the city of Danang, only a wire fence separating the base from two hundred thousand people—most of them suspicious of us, some of them hostile.

Nevertheless, as Krulak notes, "By April 20, 1965, the Marines were patrolling the hills about two miles west of the airfield and the countryside about four miles north of the field."

That the longest journey begins with a single footstep was recognized by General Krulak: "These tiny moves into the hinterland turned out to be the first steps in a massive expansion responding to the siren calls of seeking more favorable terrain and engaging the enemy."

But for Krulak the expansion of the numbers and role of the Marines could not be a mindless, brassbound inflation. The Marines *had* to have a mission. If they were not going to separate South Vietnam as a whole from the enemy by blocking his invasion route, then they would assist in pacification and development, doing their best to separate the people from the enemy on the small scale, hamlet by hamlet.

He illustrates the process with a telling description of the Marines' first experience of protecting the people in May, 1965. To secure the air base, our forces had to cover the Cue De River valley where the Vietcong operated in and out of Le My, a village of eight hamlets and about 700 people who were sick of the Communists but helpless, paralyzed by terrorism. After a difficult job of rooting the Vietcong out of the area, the Marines inaugurated a commendable program of rural development and social improvement behind their own protective screen. In the process, they attracted many more villagers from nearby Vietcong-dominated hamlets. Although the people were grateful, the district chief put his finger on the rub when he told General Krulak: "All this has meaning only if you are going to stay. Are you going to stay?"

Obviously, the Marines could not stay for years to guard this one village any more than they could stay around the Danang Air Base indefinitely, particularly in the face of increasing Vietcong operations throughout the country. The best Krulak could do was to assure the chief that some Marines would never be far away. In fact, despite guerrilla attacks and assassination, the Vietcong never again took over this particular village which, of course, benefitted from its favorable location. Many others were not so fortunate.

General Krulak sums up the lesson as follows:

> Ly Me was a microcosm of the entire war at this period, reflecting on a small scale the perspective of ten million rural Vietnamese in fourteen thousand hamlets. They always feared, and sometimes hated the Vietcong for their extortion, taxation, brutality and designs on local youth. They wanted and welcomed our protection but were terrified at the prospect of getting it and then losing it. The nearer we were to them and the more thorough our efforts, the better the system worked. This painstaking, exhausting and sometimes bloody process of bringing peace, prosperity and health to a gradually expanding area came to be known as the "spreading ink blot" formula.[12]

He wrote Secretary McNamara in November 1965, "We have to separate the enemy from the people and clean up the area a bit at a time." But McNamara, like Westmoreland, had commented on the ink-blot concept, "A good idea, but too slow."[13] In a way they were right, although they never followed this judgment to its logical conclusion. How long would it take, and how many men—including Americans—to provide security on a minute scale to 14,000 hamlets? General Krulak recognized the problem and acknowledged it as a strategic defect that "was unable to address the reality that the enemy enjoyed a privileged sanctuary in the ports of North Vietnam and in Laos, through which a growing cascade of deadly munitions was flowing."[14]

In the total context of our war in Indochina, pacification and development was a vast quilt of operations involving all the armed forces and many civilian agencies—the Embassy, AID, CIA, USIA and many

Washington agencies. Deployed suddenly to relieve South Vietnamese forces in a static security posture, the Marines had to *seek* their role, making it up incrementally as they went.

However, because of the rural population's apolitical provincialism, religious divisions and need for land reform, General Krulak found them to be vulnerable to Communist terror and difficult to organize for a national defensive effort. To exploit these weaknesses, the Communists made the people their main target. Krulak saw what was happening, but at the same time, he recognized that it would be impossible to succeed as long as the flow of reinforcement and weapons continued from North Vietnam. Since, plainly, our aerial campaign had not significantly impeded the flow through Laos, he recommended in December of 1965 that we should stop the flow at the source—Hanoi and Haiphong—through intensive bombing and closing of the ports.[15] Given that blocking the invasion on the ground had been ruled out, he had little other choice.

Because he had had the opportunity to comment on my proposal a few months earlier, General Krulak invited my comments on his. I agreed with the importance of provincialism, religious fragmentation, mal-distribution of land, etc., and all the things that Robert Shaplen had described as part of the "coming-of-age" process. But my concern was that these things take time—at least a decade (and I probably should have said a score of years)—thus requiring us to provide a long-term protective screen. I did not oppose heavy air attacks on North Vietnam's installations or closing the ports, but I thought that "it would be a mistake to rely too heavily on this program to accomplish a decisive attrition" of the flow of reinforcement. My reply to Krulak went on:

> The question is whether it would be more efficient to protect the people around their 14,000 hamlets or to protect the whole country by establishing a barrier which would isolate the battlefield in South Vietnam, for the duration of the pacification program—perhaps ten years. . . . We are confronted with a massive, multi-layered, long-range political-social-economic revolution in South Vietnam. Wiping out the so-called "main forces" will not solve the problem because the main forces can be augmented through infiltration and can feed on the simmering basic South Vietnamese revolution.

Krulak took his proposal to Admiral Sharp, who approved it, then to the Marine Commandant in Washington, Wallace Greene, who sent him on to Secretary McNamara who non-commitally sent him next to Harriman. At lunch in Harriman's Georgetown house, when Krulak mentioned closing North Vietnam's ports, Harriman knitted his eyebrows, waved his soup spoon and demanded, "Do you want war with the Soviet Union or the Chinese?" Of course, we know today that in 1970, five years after Krulak's lunch with Harriman, we did close the ports by mining them and the Soviet Union not only did not make war but continued SALT negotiations with us.

Finally, in the middle of 1966, General Krulak finally got a chance to bring the subject up with President Johnson who firmly steered him out the Oval Office.*

"The Marines never gave up," Krulak tells us. "To the very end and within the limits of the forces available, they strove to protect and emancipate the people. . . . And they went into the hinterland after the large enemy units—far more than they really wanted to but in response to strong pressures from MACV Headquarters." He concludes:

> This last challenge greatly drained the Marines, as it did other U.S. and South Vietnamese forces. As Soviet supplies and equipment continued to flow into the ports of Haiphong and Vinh, the North Vietnamese units became more effective. . . . More of their operating forces could be supported in the South, which in turn, generated a demand for even greater numbers of U.S.** troops to pursue General Westmoreland's search-and-destroy strategy. Those battles were fought too often on the enemy's terms. . . . Under those terms the attritional battle had to be more costly than we could prudently endure. . . . Thus, our self-declared victories in the search-and-destroy operations were not relevant to the total outcome of the war. Things were bad and bound to get worse unless our strategy was altered.[16]

Although I favored a strategy to block the invasion over Krulak's proposed heavy air campaign to interdict reinforcement, he was certainly right that our strategy needed altering—badly.

However useful the early Marine experience was to illustrate how incremental deployments failed to forge a tight interlock between military separation from the enemy on a country-wide scale and counter-

---

*The process by which General Krulak's proposal was disposed of reminded me of the process by which my proposal of December 1964 had been passed to Harriman's protege, Michael Forrestal, who suddenly appeared in Honolulu to raise it privately with Admiral Sharp who immediately directed a J-5 report which quickly rejected it for reasons which were quickly overtaken by the ruling syndrome of incremental deployments.

**At this point, Gen. Krulak appended a footnote remarking that during the first six months of 1966 at least 50,000 additional North Vietnamese were deployed in the South.

insurgency separation on a small scale, it was small by comparison with the overall pacification program which included all agencies and vast resources, human and material, civilian and military. Indeed, reviewing the whole period gives one the impression that the most important and time-consuming problem was organizational—who would be in charge? I attended a conference in Warrenton, Virginia in January 1966, a conference convened to review the pacification program. I was only in observer status from CINCPAC, but the large meeting convened representatives from a couple of dozen different civilian and military agencies. In looking over my notes on the two days of meetings, I find that 80% of the material has to do with discussions of coordination, management and control rather than with substance or strategy. At the outset, the question raised by one lead-ing participant was "how to defeat a war of liberation without over-whelming the local government?" There was no discussion of whether or not the problem in South Vietnam was primarily of internal or external origin. The same speaker went on to complain that the growth of our military commitment complicated the problem of "keeping the war within the framework of a counter-insurgency." There was no discussion of whether the increasing need for more military deploy-ments suggested that the problem was not an insurgency in the first place but an invasion. Near the end, another participant—a civilian in the Defense Department who shall remain nameless—made a brief peroration ending approximately as follows: "When history is written, Laos will be the great tragedy. We can't win while infiltration goes on. Our present actions are not a strategy—but a meatgrinder." The silence was deafening.

Eventually, the organizational contest was settled by putting the military commander—General Westmoreland—in charge and giving him a civilian deputy—Robert Komer, chosen from the White House staff. Once the question of "command and control" had been settled, the program went on to considerable success. There were some doc-trinal debates but three elements were consistently involved in all programs—separation, development and participation. The British experience during the Malayan "emergency" of the 1950s was studied closely and consultations were held regularly with a British Advisory Mission to the Vietnamese Government under Sir Robert Thompson who had been Secretary of Defense in Malaya. The British experience, while highly useful, as was Sir Robert's advice, nevertheless differed in several important respects as I have mentioned earlier. William Colby, of CIA in Saigon, later Deputy to Ambassador Komer in charge of the pacification and eventually Director of CIA itself, believes that "The British experience in Malaya had led them to conclude that the most important feature of rural village operation was a good, fair but firm central administration through which discipline could be imposed on local communities, cutting them off from contacts with the insurgents and thus starving the latter of recruits and even of supplies if possible."[17]

Colby's own conviction with respect to South Vietnam, however, was "that the guiding principle must be political. We had to enlist the active participation of the community in a program to improve its security and welfare on the local level, building cohesion from the bottom up rather than imposing it from the top down. Thus, in specific terms, we disagreed on the question of arming local communities. I advocated it and was, of course, heavily involved in doing so."[18] This point is important because it reveals another aspect of the importance of separation. In Malaya the British not only had the advantage of geographical and ethnic separation (the insurgents being Chinese) but of what might be called bureaucratic separation. Unlike the Government of South Vietnam, the British administration in Malaya was not part of an emerging traditional society trying to come of age, but of a distant, highly sophisticated European society, separated from the seat of indigenous weaknesses in an Asia "coming of age."

The importance of separation is that it insulates a benign but slow-moving process—pacification—against the hostile effects of an immediate and faster-moving malignant process—invasion—thereby buying time for the former to succeed.* The problem faced by the managers of pacification in South Vietnam was that there was no

---

*In March, 1968, six weeks after the Tet Offensive, I heard Sir Robert Thompson expound at a meeting in Bangkok. In commenting to Ambassador Leonard Unger (who had replaced Ambassador Martin) I argued that "there are inadequate forces of any kind to provide security for each hamlet, village, farm and individual. . . . I concur with Sir Robert that our aim should be to 'establish a permanent political structure, etc.' but he does not take into account that this objective is a long-term proposition requiring at least ten years and probably fifteen to twenty. . . . Who will provide security during this long time? If it means . . . chasing the North Vietnamese and Vietcong into the cities, through the paddy fields, into the villages and rooting them out of every hamlet political structure then I think this will frustrate establishment of a permanent political structure. Expansion of the war into every nook and cranny of South Vietnam . . . not only prevents the establishment of a permanent political structure, but destroys what little structure there already is. However, I should hardly criticize Sir Robert who is only following the same strategic error which has catapulted us since 1962 from victory to victory to our present position."

effective separation to fend off the mounting invasion. Under these circumstances, Colby had no choice but to emphasize the political factor, because whatever was accomplished within the villages of South Vietnam would almost surely come under some kind of enemy attack from outside.

What was needed was a program with real local roots which could survive without relying on the central government's fiat—a condition which, in a way, presumed the completion of the "coming of age" process—a local program into which the United States could inject some additional wherewithal. It was found, in prototypical form, in Qui Nhon on the coast of South Vietnam, by Peer De Silva of CIA. There, a team of local young men, armed for self-protection, had mobilized a village population for self-defense and for participation in a cooperative project to refrigerate their fish catch for export to more distant lucrative markets. Building on this, the concept was developed into something called People's Action Teams. With experience over the years it was further developed and applied throughout the country, under various labels, and by 1973, when the United States forces left, the Vietnamese were able to maintain it themselves.[19] The last vestiges of simulated insurgency were withering. This stitch was well-knit.

What had not withered but had grown, however, was the powerful North Vietnamese Army which during those same years had been enlarged, re-equipped by the Soviets and positioned to attack along the complex of roads which they had steadily built through Laos and Cambodia out of the original Ho Chi Minh trails in the jungle. Together with South Vietnam we had successfully established *some* provisional separation of the population from the enemy on the small scale. But doing so dug us wrongly into South Vietnam's internal structure, and this strategy would work only as long as we remained. If we withdrew, the provisional separation from the enemy would dissolve. This was the stitch we dropped.

Or to put it another way, this flaw had been observed in February 1964 by Mr. Lyman D. Kirkpatrick of CIA. Commenting to Director McCone on a report that he and De Silva had sent to Washington from Saigon, Kirkpatrick noted all the pessimistic factors in their report, then added on his own, "Finally, with the Laos and Cambodia borders opened, this entire pacification effort is like trying to mop the floor before turning off the faucet."[20]

South Vietnam was not the only country afflicted with the convulsive effects of what Walt Rostow had called the "revolution of modernism." Thailand, where I was transferred as Deputy Chief of Mission in the summer of 1966, had similar problems which were

exploited, particularly in the North and Northeast, by bands of terrorists led by Communists who had been trained in China and North
Vietnam. To coordinate our efforts in assisting the Thai Government,
Ambassador Graham Martin had obtained the assignment (on loan
from CIA) of Peer De Silva who became Special Assistant to the
Ambassador. Drawing on his experience in South Vietnam, De Silva
helped the Thai Government develop its own programs which included their version of the People's Action Committee concept in
South Vietnam.

Although Thailand is not the subject of this book, it does provide
an interesting contrast to South Vietnam. The Communist terrorists
(CTs) in Thailand were numerically small, in 1966 numbering perhaps
1000 in the far North and 1500 in the Northeast, with smaller elements
in the South. Of these, about 1400 were known to have been trained
in China and North Vietnam. It took several years for the Thai Government to refine its programs, train personnel and develop its bureaucratic structure for the purpose. Meanwhile, the terrorists had
some success, and by 1970, had increased slowly to perhaps double
the number of 1966. But the problem didn't escalate out of hand and
it still hasn't.

What Thailand experienced was a genuine insurgent manifestation
of the revolution of modernism—aided, of course, by Communists
trained abroad. What Thailand did *not* experience was a steady invasion such as South Vietnam did. Had South Vietnam experienced
only the indigenous percolation with peripheral external involvement
that Thailand did, the course of what then could have been properly
called its "insurgency" might have been comparable to that of Thailand. In this case, the techniques and methods of "counter-insurgency" could no doubt have been adequate to contain the violence
while ameliorating its social, economic and political causes.

The lesson is that genuine insurgency and invasion are qualitatively
different and are not simply graduated benchmarks of tactical violence
on a linear scale. But, so accustomed had the U.S. become to linear
measurement in South Vietnam that it was difficult to correct the
habit when it came to Thailand. While Thai pilots were being trained
in the United States, and until Thailand's own helicopters, on order,
were delivered, Ambassador Martin proposed lending a U.S. unit of
about 25 helicopters and pilots to provide the Thai some interim
mobility—provided that the U.S. machines were not to be assigned
to combat. The proposal was strongly opposed by Secretary Mc-
Namara who feared it would lead us into another graduated, endless
morass such as we were in in South Vietnam.

It didn't. Ambassador Martin was also a very determined man and eventually, McNamara consented. The Thai pilots completed their training, returned and took over their own unit of Thai helicopters when delivered. The American helicopters and pilots returned to Vietnam, as planned. Secretary McNamara had failed to distinguish between a genuine internal insurgency, largely contained within the country of origin, and external invasion, masquerading as an insurgency. He seemed to regard insurgency and invasion as merely quantitative benchmarks on the scale of violence. With this premise, escalation always seems inevitable, but such escalation exists only in the mind and eye of the beholder who then imposes it on the objective situation. The Thais were not invaded by anyone—and their *real* insurgency was brought under control.

17

Purl One—The Air Campaign

"I am convinced that, within the limits to which we can go with prudence, 'strategic' bombing of North Vietnam will at best be unproductive . . . that mining the ports would not only be unproductive but very costly in domestic and world support and very dangerous—running high risk of enlarging the war as the program is carried out, frustrated and with no choice but to escalate further. . . . I am doubtful that bombing infiltration routes north or south of 20° will put a meaningful ceiling on men or materiel entering South Vietnam. . . . [N]othing short of toppling the Hanoi regime will pressure North Vietnam to settle. . . . [A]ctions sufficient to topple the regime will put us into war with the Soviet Union and China."

Robert McNamara, June 12, 1967.[1]

"I strongly support our American concept of civilian control of the military. . . . At the same time, I believe . . . the civilian authority should consider carefully the advice of his professional military advisers. In his handling of the air war, however, Secretary McNamara arbitrarily and consistently discarded the advice of his military advisers. His insistence that we pursue the campaign on a gradualistic basis gave the enemy plenty of time to cope with our every move. He was, I submit, dead wrong."

Adm. U.S.G. Sharp, Jr., CINCPAC, May 1969.[2]

The air campaign against North Vietnam waged by the United States Navy and Air Force was probably the least bloody and most precisely—even surgically—executed air assault of comparable size in the history of air warfare. That it failed to achieve its objective is not the fault of the brave airmen who carried it out while suffering losses, but of the flawed strategy applied by both civilian and military leaders. Each of the two statements quoted above reveals an important truth, but taken together, they conceal an even more important truth about how we failed in Indochina. While the civilian and military leaderships differed on how rapidly and how much to escalate the air campaign against North Vietnam, the positions of both contained the same fatal flaw—which was to make of the air campaign an instrument to "persuade" Hanoi to stop the invasion for us rather than an instrument to support a combined ground-air strategy to block North Vietnam's invasion with our own resources. We needed that strong position on the ground across southern Laos.

Before continuing, I must say that our entire air effort in Indochina should not be considered as a failure. Aviation—in all the armed forces—played many indispensable roles, humanitarian as well as military. The pacification program depended on aviation for supplies, arms, food, reinforcements and quick help when under sudden attack. U.S. and South Vietnamese forces, seeking and pursuing North Vietnamese units, depended on air mobility as well as combat air support. In Laos, the Meo tribes, besieged by the North Vietnamese, depended on aviation for rice, cloth, medicine and ammunition as did the Royal Lao Army.

The subject of this chapter is only the air campaign against North Vietnam's invasion, in which I include both the assault against installations and resources in North Vietnam supporting the war and the attempted interdiction of the movement of men and materiel down North Vietnam through Laos and Cambodia to maintain the invasion against South Vietnam. This air campaign was one of the three principal elements of our strategy. All were supposed to be mutually self-supporting, as argued by the Joint Chiefs of Staff in a strong memorandum to Secretary McNamara on October 14, 1966: "The Joint Chiefs of Staff . . . believe our air campaign against North Vietnam to be an *integral* and indispensable part of our over all war effort."[3] (Emphasis added.)

The air campaign *should* have been integral but, in fact, was not well-integrated with the other elements of our strategy. The weight of its blows was dissipated ineffectively because of the lack of a strong U.S. blocking position on the ground. We talked much of exerting pressure against North Vietnam, forgetting that pressure is only effective when it is exerted against some stationary resistance. In the absence of a blocking resistance to the invasion on the ground, North Vietnam simply gritted its teeth, endured the air attacks and continued its slow invasion until U.S. patience ran out.

From the Tonkin Gulf incidents of August 1964 to the February 7, 1965 Communist raid on a U.S. barracks in Pleiku, the rule governing air attacks on North Vietnam had been based on occasional limited reprisals for spectacular Communist attacks. But McGeorge Bundy's post-Pleiku memorandum to President Johnson changed all that. Two weeks later, the Rolling Thunder air campaign against North Vietnam was begun. Paced with measured deliberation, the attacks were intensified slowly in the hope that they would serve as a warning of worse to come, thereby inducing Hanoi either to invite negotiations or unilaterally to terminate its intervention in South Vietnam.

By July, the ineffectiveness of the program was already being noticed by the military who argued that the pace had been too slow and the weight too light. The civilians acknowledged that a limited gradual program exerted less pressure on North Vietnam than a heavy one and was less likely to cause Hanoi to withdraw or negotiate. But they felt that all-out bombing would be disproportionate to our limited objectives and would risk widening the war.

The civilians tended to prefer to concentrate more air power against infiltration, believing that would make a more direct contribution to the war in the South. The trouble was that aerial operations against infiltration could only be described in unmeasureable terms such as "disrupt," "slow down," "harass" and "make more costly." Reports of damage done along the routes were available but were inconclusive indicators of how much reinforcement actually got through. Military estimates of the effectiveness of interdiction were often like Soviet 5-Year Plan statistics showing that production had risen by 50% over a previous period which had risen 50% over some unknown base figure. If, as was sometimes claimed, the interdiction was as much as 20% effective, then by putting 20% more into the top of the infiltration funnel, North Vietnam could sustain its losses to aerial interdiction and still achieve the same output in the reinforcement of the invasion. And, in fact, despite the intensification of interdiction, the infiltration of men through Laos and Cambodia into South Vietnam increased from 12,400 in 1964 to 37,800 in 1965, to 93,100 in 1966 and to 103,100 in the year ending December 1967, just one month before the Tet Offensive.[4]

Still, looking back on those days, I find it difficult to believe the unreal optimism felt by both civilians and military about the bombing campaign as an invaluable "bargaining chip." Backing away from his own July 1, 1965 proposal of a total quarantine of supplies into North Vietnam by road, sea and air, including mining the seaports, Secretary McNamara turned aside similar but stronger JCS recommendations, but he still recommended nearly doubling the number of strike sorties. In his July 20, 1965 memo to the President, he recommended intensified bombing which, together with some additional ground forces, "stands a good chance of achieving an acceptable outcome within a

reasonable time in Vietnam."[5] As for the terms of a "favorable outcome," McNamara set up a nine-point list of "fundamental elements"
which resembled a package proposal which an automobile company
executive might make to a union of workers who were sick of being
on strike.[6] Ten days later he assured the President that "even with
hindsight I believe the decision to bomb the DRV was wise and I
believe the program should be continued." So confident was he that
he emphasized the necessity of fine-tuning the bombing campaign
so as to dramatize to Hanoi the future threat while minimizing any
"loss of face" that might attend Hanoi's decision to negotiate—as if
Hanoi needed any help in "saving its face."[7]

As the months wore on and the bombing induced no favorable
response from Hanoi, Washington became uneasy—an early sign of
how, in such an ambiguous test of political endurance, time worked
for North Vietnam and against us. Secretary McNamara, on November 3, had proposed a bombing "pause" of several weeks to begin
before the Christmas holidays of December 1965. His reason (spelled
out in a November 30 memo) was to prepare U.S. and world opinion
for "an enlarged phase of the war," but only after first giving North
Vietnam "a face-saving chance to stop the aggression."[8]

As I have noted earlier in different contexts, this concept was mis-
taken in two respects. In the first place, it put the decision of when
and how to end the war in the hands of North Vietnam, because we
had assured Hanoi that we would not seek to destroy the country or
overthrow the government. Second, springing as it did from a common but shallow Occidental stereotype of a presumed Oriental ob-
session with appearances ("face") rather than substance, it grossly
underestimated Hanoi's determination.

It seemed to me that the evidence from all sides indicated that our
attacks were stiffening Hanoi's determination and there was nothing
to suggest that intensification would reverse this trend. Although
Admiral Sharp disagreed with me, calling this view a "questionable
assumption," our intelligence reports, plus those from British, French
and Canadian officials in Hanoi, indicated steadily increasing movement along the infiltration trails despite cratering by bombs, not to
mention public evidences of increasing North Vietnamese commitment to the Vietcong war in the South. It was my concern—reiterated
several times—that "if air attacks along the present lines are insuf-
ficient and if we are unwilling to step them up to the point of risking
Chinese intervention, then it is difficult to see where we are headed."

I believe it was at about this time in the autumn of 1965, that Admiral
Sharp suggested that I begin my own separate series of cables to the
Department of State for providing my views directly. Whether or not

this suggestion was in part motivated by a desire to redirect some of the flow of my memoranda into an alternative outlet I do not know, but I did pass it along to the Department of State. Not surprisingly, the reply delicately said that the Department felt that the Political Advisor could best play his role by giving his advice directly to the Commander-in-Chief rather than involving the Department of State in it. (I think Ambrose Bierce knew what he was talking about when, in his *Devil's Dictionary*, he defined "advice" as the "smallest current coin.")

After carefully analyzing the pros and cons, Secretary of State Rusk had opposed the 1965 Christmas bombing pause on what seemed to me the sensible ground that "In the absence of any indication from Hanoi as to what reciprocal action it might take, we could well find ourselves in the position of having played this very important card without receiving anything substantial in return. There are no indications that Hanoi is yet in a mood to agree to a settlement suitable to us."[9]

But McNamara—and Systems Analysis—carried the day. The pause began at Christmas and lasted until January 31, 1966. Whereas Rusk had reasoned from an empirical appreciation of Hanoi's actual attitude, the Systems Analysis approach treated the question of a pause as a computer game played in sterile insulation from political, ideological and psychological reality. Thus, Assistant Secretary of Defense John McNaughton had characterized the Rolling Thunder campaign as a "ratchet, such as the device which raises a net on a tennis court, backing off the tension between each phase of increasing it."[10] Similarly, McNaughton disagreed with Rusk's view of the pause as an important card that could only be played once or, at best, sparingly. He argued, with some mathematical—if not political—insight, that the pause card could be played any number of times "with the arguments against, but not those for it, becoming less valid each time"— as if the more we used the pause the better we could manipulate Hanoi's intentions.[11] The editors of *The Pentagon Papers* tell us that this argument "lay behind the Defense position that one of the chief reasons *for* a pause was that . . . it might set the stage for another pause, perhaps in late 1966."[12] Apparently, then, an accelerating sequence of pauses would lead to a permanent pause, a concept that is reverse "linear" escalation that proceeds automatically according to its own internal logic and has little to do with political reality.

Without the slightest hint of positive response from Hanoi, the pause ended after 37 days. Anticipating this result, virtually everyone concerned devoted himself to the production of lengthy interpretive analyses, elegantly structured and as nicely detailed as a medieval scholastic proof, on the subject of the period after the pause. Should it begin with a bang—a sharp sudden escalation—or a whimper—a slow and low key resumption where we had left off? The military favored the former. McNaughton and William Bundy both favored the latter—a two-week, slow take-off, designed to attract as little attention as possible—gliding from non-bombing into bombing—gliding, as we had always sought, through every transition in the war, in increments.

With the end of the pause, attention also focused on the future of "Rolling Thunder." The military argued against continued "gradualism" which, they said with some logic, dissipated the impact and allowed Hanoi to prepare in advance, e.g., by dispersing its petroleum reserves from large central storage areas near Hanoi and Haiphong to many smaller dumps around the country. The opposite view was that after a certain point further attacks would become counter-productive because they would strengthen Hanoi's determination—as if it needed strengthening. Moreover, there was the problem of our oft-stated intention not to destroy the country (as President Johnson put it) or to overthrow its regime, but rather to negotiate with it. What if we reached the ceiling imposed by this limitation and concluded that anything more might bring in China? What if we reached this point before the war in the South had been won and what if Hanoi still refused to budge but continued to send reinforcements to the South? What then?

The military tended to shy away from this point, asserting and reasserting their confidence that a properly conducted heavy bombing campaign would surely force North Vietnam to cease support of the war in South Vietnam. To some extent, they were trapped, having already accepted the civilian strategy of "persuading" Hanoi to back off. They could not overtly propose exceeding this parameter without challenging the policy adopted by the political leadership. In a sense, they too, were gliding from a precisely limited war into a more intense one. As their proposals escalated, it became necessary to consider at what point the escalation would change the nature of the war to something the United States had not decided upon.

This could be called the problem of the "upper limits." It had been implicit in the Rolling Thunder campaign since its inception in March, 1965. One lengthy, well-researched study in the spring of 1965 called for aerial mining of North Vietnamese ports, attacks on the northern railway system links with China and on northern highway bridges and, possibly, even flooding the Red River dike system on which North Vietnamese agriculture depended. Here, the problem of the "upper limits" stuck out like a sore thumb. Invited by the Chief of

J-5, Plans, Rear Admiral Gay, to comment, I tried to formulate the problem in the following terms:

> My principal comment on the study is that the measures recommended do in fact go a long way toward changing the nature of the war . . . which is not consistent with the premise on which the study ostensibly rests. In one paragraph it is stated that under current U.S. policy our military objective is limited to impeding North Vietnam's support of the insurgency, and that we are not trying to bring North Vietnam to its knees. I think that the logic of mining the ports and destroying the bridges north of Hanoi clearly verges on an effort to bring North Vietnam to its knees. Indeed, on one page, one of the advantages of attacking the bridges is stated to be 'disrupting the economy and weakening Hanoi's control of the population.' In another paragraph it is recognized that if these measures did not produce the desired results, it might be necessary to go on and attack the dikes. . . . I think we would be fooling ourselves if we pretend that we can set out on this course and remain within the logic of our present limited policy and objectives.
>
> Personally, I have never believed that North Vietnam could be induced to negotiate or to call off the Vietcong by air attacks. Accordingly, I am not surprised that our air attacks so far have failed to achieve that result, nor do I think that extending them as recommended in the paper will do so. . . .
>
> I am not opposed to these measures *per se*. . . . I think these measures could be justified *if* we were pursuing the policy of unconditional surrender, or the policy of overturning the North Vietnamese Government and supporting the unification of the country under Saigon, or *if* we were consciously moving toward a direct military confrontation with China.* I do not say that mining the harbors or hitting the particular bridges mentioned will in themselves produce this change but they lead clearly in that direction. Since I do not believe they will have the effect of causing North Vietnam to call off the Vietcong or to come to negotiations, I feel that once

---

*There is a serious gap here. I should have added a fourth possibility—the only one I would have favored—the blocking position in Laos. I'm not sure why I omitted it but, having used up my credit in pressing for such a strategy, I suppose I left it out here so as not to distract from the main point. In fact, a year later, Prime Minister Wilson of Britain made exactly the right point to President Johnson in objecting to the bombing of Hanoi's oil—which I did not oppose. Said the Prime Minister: "If you and the South Vietnamese Government were conducting a declared war on the conventional pattern . . . this operation would clearly be necessary and right. But since you have made it abundantly clear . . . that your purpose is to achieve a negotiated settlement, and that you are not striving for total military victory in the field, I remain convinced that the bombing of these targets, without producing decisive military advantage, may only increase the difficulty of reaching an eventual settlement." (*Pentagon Papers*, Vol. IV, 102).

we have carried them out, we will then be faced with another watershed decision as to whether to go on toward full-scale war or stop. I am not prejudging the answer that we would give but I think we should try to see the end of the tunnel.

Admiral Sharp argued in *Reader's Digest* that "a nation which is not willing to take calculated risks to achieve its objective should never go to war in the first place."[13] He was right. The fact is, however, that the U.S. did not really *decide* to go to war. I thought that the thing to do was to force the issue into the open so as to cause a decision to be made—either to stake out the territory we would defend or withdraw our forces. Simply to propose continual escalation without taking account of where it would lead only served to undermine the military's credibility.

Air strikes on petroleum reserves began on June 29, 1966 and were attended by both tactical success and strategic failure. As usual, the Air Force and Navy did a superb job, hitting all targets with a minimum of unintended damage. McNamara announced publicly that the strikes were necessitated by the fact that during the very restrained bombing of the first half of 1966, infiltration of men and materiel by truck over the Ho Chi Minh trails had increased by 120% and 150% respectively.[14] However, by the end of 1966 it was apparent that infiltration had continued far above the 1965 levels even after increased airstrikes. Analysis of intelligence by a special study group showed that given the nature of North Vietnam's system and the relatively small quantities of oil it required, "it seems doubtful that any critical denial of essential [petroleum supplies] has resulted."[15]

By October, McNamara had recommended (over the strenuous objections of the JCS) both another "pause" and a "stabilization" of the strike level. Convinced that no air action would stop the invasion or make Hanoi call it off, he shifted his field to a "barrier" concept consisting of a complex technological, largely electronic, anti-infiltration system running along the DMZ and across southern Laos to the Mekong River border of Thailand.

Before I continue, a parenthetical note on the "electronic barrier" is in order. The concept is not to be confused with a ground force action to block the continuing invasion, although the mere fact of the proposal did reflect an incipient recognition of the core of the problem. In fact, the concept, later to be known as "the McNamara Line," had more in common with the Rolling Thunder bombing campaign since both were designed to slow the invasion by *indirect means* not requiring the use of ground forces to deny Hanoi use of its invasion route through southern Laos. The latter, of course, would violate our 1963 "tacit agreement"—the "facade of Geneva."

Indeed, it was the need for ground forces in Laos to defend and operate the electronic system that caused CINCPAC to oppose it, arguing that it would require 7 to 8 U.S. divisions and would force diversions of logistic strength from our forces in South Vietnam. CINCPAC opposed the use of forces in such a "static defense" effort, even though it might have been argued that a successful static effort capable of blocking the invasion would have reduced our requirement for ground forces in South Vietnam, already climbing toward half a million. In any case, the military opposition to using U.S. forces in southern Laos caused the concept to be cut back to the electronic elements that could be delivered and exploited from the air, thereby reducing its value below the level necessary to make the invasion ineffective. In 1970 I visited the center at which the electronic system in Laos was controlled—a facility known as "Igloo White" at Nakorn Phanom on the Thai side of the Mekong River opposite Laos. The technological sophistication of the system, the precision of its functioning, the imagination of its underlying concepts, the expertise of the men who tended it and the bravery of the pilots who exploited it were all absolutely overwhelming. The tragedy that such resources, like the Rolling Thunder bombing campaign, should be poured out lavishly—not to stop an invasion but to "persuade" the invader to behave while "keeping our options open" to escalate, de-escalate or withdraw without irreversible commitment—is also overwhelming.

Although the President approved McNamara's proposed "stabilization," the pause did not materialize until February 8–14, 1967, during the Vietnamese Tet holidays. A memorandum prepared in John McNaughton's office in the Defense Department outlined a "pause scenario" which resembled one side of a game of double solitaire (at which the other player's seat is empty) as programmed by a computer, or alternatively, the mating dance of a male ostrich about to be scorned by the female.[16] After the pause, the President successively approved strikes on North Vietnam's one steel plant and its one cement plant, as well as authorizing the mining of certain inland waterways—but not the seaports. In May, the Hanoi thermal power plant was struck. Throughout 1967, the prevailing pattern was of Defense Department opposition to escalation, matched by JCS pressure to escalate. Following a delaying action, Defense would grant reluctant partial acquiescence on a few new targets, thereby relaxing the tension in a kind of analogue of McNaughton's "ratchet" concept which seemed to work better on the U.S. military than it did on North Vietnam.

Having failed to move Hanoi, the pressure which had been put on North Vietnam now began to backfire seriously against the United States. If the United States backed down the "hawks" would protest, but if the U.S. didn't back down the "doves" would protest. Admiral

Sharp says that what the military wanted was "to bring the economy of North Vietnam to a halt."[17] But the civilians worried about what would come next if, after destroying the economy, Hanoi still would not terminate the invasion. What the military also wanted was to abandon "gradualism" and, as the JCS had recommended in October 1966 (quoting its own message of November 1964), to administer "a sharp knock on North Vietnam's assets and war-supporting facilities *rather than* the campaign of *slowly increasing* the pressure which was adopted." (Emphasis added.) The Chiefs went on: "Whatever the political merits of the latter course, we deprived ourselves of the military effects of early weight of effort and shock, and gave the enemy time to adjust to our slow quantitative and qualitative increase of pressure."[18]

However, McNamara's conclusion in June 1967—quoted at the beginning of this chapter—was different. He was convinced that the only way to cause North Vietnam to settle would be to topple the regime in Hanoi which, as the JCS recognized, would have been beyond the parameters of our political decision. But although they recognized the "upper limit," the JCS avoided the implications of exceeding it when they made their proposals to destroy North Vietnam's economy. Four months later, in October 1967, McNamara proposed to end escalation for the reason that bombing had neither significantly reduced infiltration nor diminished Hanoi's will to continue the fight.

In their response on October 17, to a Presidential request for proposals, the JCS still did not address the problem of "upper limits" when they proposed a new sharply intensified campaign in the area of Hanoi and Haiphong, an escalation that would void most of the existing restrictions and include the mining of the seaports. In this proposal the Chiefs specifically reaffirmed their adherence to the four well-known civilian strategic limitations which defined the parameters of the campaign to cause Hanoi to stop the invasion:

> a. We seek to avoid widening the war into a conflict with Communist China or the USSR.
> b. We have no *present* intention of invading North Vietnam. (Emphasis in original.)
> c. We do not seek the overthrow of the Government of North Vietnam.
> d. We are guided by the principles set forth in the Geneva Accords of 1954 and 1962.[19]

The Chiefs asserted that "U.S. objectives in Southeast Asia can be achieved within the policy framework set forth." But, excepting the word "present" in point (b), the Chiefs nowhere hinted at the critical question of what next step might be required if the proposed measures did not succeed in causing Hanoi to back down. This, of course, was precisely what troubled civilian authority.

It requires some "special pleading" to understand what the JCS meant by being "guided by the principles set forth in the Geneva Accords of 1954 and 1962," since the actual terms of both treaties had long been virtual dead letters. Since the Accords on Laos of 1962 had been massively violated by North Vietnam from the date of signature and since the military operations of both sides violated them every day, the only realistic, operative meaning that can be attached to the Chiefs' avowal is that they would be guided by the "tacit agreement" (the "facade of Geneva") which we reached with the Communists in the spring of 1963. Having accepted this limit as well as the limitation of our objective to "persuading" Hanoi to stop the invasion, the JCS, like the civilian authority, was constrained to limit the bombing campaign to a linear escalatory program—limited at the top end by the commitment not to overthrow the regime in Hanoi and at the bottom end by the commitment not to block North Vietnam's invasion route through Laos on the ground.

In short, the military were logically constrained within the same conceptual limits as were the civilians and, having accepted the policy decision made by civilian authority, the military expected to be placed in charge of executing the resultant air campaign. But the civilian decisions were only contingent, incremental ones—*contingent on political judgments not already made but to be made bit by bit, every day.* Gearing the air campaign to a daily calculation of political judgment in Hanoi is a curious way to fight a war, but this is what we did and it was a quintessentially civilian task. Not surprisingly, the military chafed under the requirement that every sortie—later relaxed to every strike—be not only approved in principle in advance but precisely timed and minutely designed by civilians in the Defense and State Departments and the White House. The alternative, however, would have been to turn over political decision-making to the military, a course which the military themselves opposed in principle. One can sympathize with Admiral Sharp when he proclaims, in *Reader's Digest*, and as I heard him say many times in 1965 and 1966: "I believe that once a political decision is made to commit American troops to battle, we are morally obligated to use our military power in such a way as to end the fighting as quickly as possible."[20]

But the Admiral misses a key point. The very political decision itself had not been "made", but was being daily extruded on an incremental basis like toothpaste from a tube. I can hear Admiral Sharp scoff, "That's no way to run a war." He would be absolutely right. But what to do?

The military never found an effective way to challenge this kind of decision-making. To a considerable extent they were even accessories to it. Proposals to "bring the economy of North Vietnam to a halt," and ominous hints of no *"present* intention" to invade North Vietnam only served to generate doubt and suspicion. But, without challenging civilian control, what the military might have done was to propose or request that they be given a true military objective—an objective obtainable by military means—unlike the political objective of "persuading Hanoi," and unlike the politically-molded objective of "interdicting infiltration" without violating a "tacit agreement" with the Communists regarding southern Laos—a "tacit agreement" which was the direct opposite of neutralization as set forth in the Geneva Accords.

They need not have challenged civilian control to do this. They only needed to give the President the benefit of their military advice (if they believed it) that the war could not be won along the prescribed lines because the objectives were political ones which could not be achieved by our own military means.* They could have said that military means can stop or defeat an invasion but cannot "persuade" the invader to stop the invasion unilaterally without ever defeating him. Following Clausewitz, they might have said,

> We are embarked on opposing an invasion and it cannot be defeated by treating it as an insurgency or as a political test of will. *Tell us what objective we have that can be accomplished by military means.*

Speaking this way would not be a refusal to carry out orders but only the execution of the military leadership's highest responsibility— to advise the civilian leadership on military matters. If this failed to produce a military objective and strategy achievable by military means and if civilian authority was bent on its own course, the military would have had no choice but to accept the decision—but accept it only *after*

---

*General Bruce Palmer (ret.) writes in his excellent *The 25-Year War* (University Press of Kentucky, 1984): "Finally, there was one glaring omission in the advice the JCS provided the president and secretary of defense. . . . Not once during the war did the JCS advise the commander-in-chief or the secretary of defense that the strategy being pursued most probably would fail and that the United States would be unable to achieve its objectives. The only explanation of this failure is that the chiefs were imbued with the "can do" spirit and could not bring themselves to make such a negative statement or to appear to be disloyal." (p. 46) Without questioning either the "can do" spirit or the loyalty of our military leadership, I suspect that to some extent they were simply "taken into camp" by the civilians.

having given their best advice. In the last analysis, the military's remaining course lay in the prescription of Napoleon which General Westmoreland says he kept under a glass panel on his desk:

> A commander-in-chief cannot take as his excuse for his mistakes in warfare an order given by his sovereign or his minister . . . absent from the field of operations and imperfectly aware . . . of the state of affairs. It follows that any commander-in-chief who undertakes to carry out a plan which he considers defective is at fault; he must put forward his reasons, insist on the plan being changed, and finally tender his resignation rather than be the instrument of his army's downfall.[21]

Instead, we continued to plunk the one-string linear Rolling Thunder program, up and down, avoiding both the upper and the lower ends until North Vietnam's Tet Offensive on January 30, 1968 precipitated first a cutback of bombing to the 20th parallel and then complete suspension as part of a desperate effort to get negotiations going.

* * *

When I left Honolulu toward the end of June, 1966, the Rolling Thunder strikes against North Vietnam's oil reserves were about to take place. The strikes went well, but it was not a good time. An ominous unease had been seeping through the American psyche for a year. If our leaders, both civilian and military, were at odds over the relation between our ends and our means, the people seemed even more uncertain—although I must admit that they were more patient and steadfast than I had expected, given the circumstances. I participated in a few public symposiums, including one or two at the University of Hawaii, experiencing at first hand what McNamara had described as "a new school of criticism among liberals and 'peace' groups."[22] I found this experience to be deeply unsettling because of the heavily loaded anti-American casuistry which seemed to permeate the protest. Opposition to the war provided an ideal surrogate outlet for ideological hostility toward the United States. Two former leaders of the protest movement, then editors of *Ramparts* magazine, reflected in 1985 on this aspect of the late 1960's. They believed that, "The left was hooked on Vietnam. It was an addictive drug whose rush was a potent mix of melodrama, self-importance and moral rectitude. Vietnam was the universal solvent—the explanation for every evil we saw and the justification for any excess we committed. . . . We knew that bad news from Southeast Asia—the reports of bogged-down campaigns and the weekly body count by Walter Cronkite—was good for the radical agenda."[23]

While it was not surprising that the American "left" was performing in its accustomed role, there was something else even more unsettling—a widespread confusion among well-meaning Americans as to our objectives, even though our leaders from the President on down were forever repeating them. In his press conference of July 28, 1965, the President read a letter from the mother of a soldier in Vietnam. She asked, "Why?" Wearily, the President recalled his efforts to explain: "I have tried to answer that question a dozen times and more in practically every State in this Union. I discussed it fully in Baltimore in April, in Washington in May, in San Francisco in June. Let me again now, discuss it here in the East Room of the White House."[24]

But nothing worked. Explanations—honest ones—covered the land like snowflakes, each repeating the same message with crystalline clarity and geometrical uniformity—only to dissolve shortly after falling.

Why was it that the more our objectives and strategy were explained the more they needed explaining? There were many factors—Lyndon Johnson's style, an unfriendly press, Communist propaganda, American weariness with responding to the clarion call of containment, the distance and strangeness of Asia, growing nihilism and the breakdown of social structures, the revolt of youth against the "system." All were relevant but inadequate explanations. The fundamental vulnerability lay within the bosom of the strategy itself. There was a critical discontinuity between our objective and our strategy for achieving it—an hiatus of ends and means. Either the objective was excessive or the means were inadequate. Either way, the gap led Americans to question both. Those who believed the objective was too much were called "doves." Those who believed the means to be too little became the "hawks."

In a way, the "hawks" and "doves" had more in common with each other than they realized. They both knew the official strategy was not succeeding. The "hawks" wanted stronger measures in order to win. The "doves" wanted to stop all measures and cut our losses before we lost completely. At any given moment the Government was tacitly stuck with defending the precise combination of measures then being applied as just the right mix to achieve the objective without going an inch beyond it. But this argument was hard to defend, and our record did not inspire unbounded confidence in our ability to walk an invisible line between "too little" and "too much."

This was the root of the hiatus between ends and means. The President assured us that "these steps . . . are carefully measured to do what must be done."[25] But did we really know how much needed to be done? The critics charged that we were in a war of "unlimited objectives." They were wrong. Our objective was truly limited to the termination of an aggression, but the gears of ends and means were afflicted with a crippling slippage. We aimed to end the aggression—but aggression increased. We aimed to "persuade" North Vietnam to withdraw or negotiate. But our chosen means produced no sign of that. We aimed to reduce infiltration—more properly called invasion—through Laos but it increased. Finally, we had no front line to define our position and progress. We defeated the invaders countless times in small and large engagements up and down South Vietnam's 700-mile length—on the coast, in the mountains, the paddyfields and villages. But when the friendly forces moved on, new invaders moved in.

At times, it was easier to agree with both the "hawks" *and* the "doves" than with our official strategy because both knew that what we were doing wouldn't work. But curiously, neither of them proposed an alternative to one-string incrementalism. The "hawks" said to throw everything, including the kitchen sink, into an unworkable strategy because the goal was a good one. The doves said to slink away because, if the existing strategy wouldn't achieve the goal, then the goal itself must not be worth pursuing.

Why did we not just draw a line against invasion, marking off the territory we would defend—then defend it by our own military means? We could have established a line and stood pat until negotiations produced a definitive cease fire—a line separating the people of Southeast Asia from the depradations of the enemy—even as we did in Korea. We would not have needed to repeat our mistake in Korea of going too far north. In order to challenge such a blocking force North Vietnam would have had to abandon clandestine infiltration and would have had to mass for battle—would have had to fight on our terms. With combined ground and air power we could have stopped them as we stopped the North Koreans *and* the Chinese.

But, perhaps we couldn't have done it? Perhaps not. The point is that we never even considered it seriously. Why? Because we had fallen into an incremental way of thinking which made it unnecessary to think about things in terms which required big decisions. Had we seriously considered this possibility we might have decided against it. But the very process of thinking about it in these terms would have led us to recognize that the alternative to blocking the invasion was simple—the alternative was simply *not to block it and not to defend South Vietnam*.

This choice we did not want to face.

18

Laos—The Dropped Stitch

"In retrospect, I am more certain than I was in 1967 that our failure to cut the Ho Chi Minh Trail was a strategic mistake of the first order."

Ambassador Ellsworth Bunker, in conversation with the author—
April, 1983.

In South Vietnam, the American troops had to intercept and defeat North Vietnam's invasion forces *after* they had crossed the narrow 160-mile axis in southern Laos, *after* they had spread down a 700-mile sector of Laos and Cambodia, and *after* they had turned east to invade South Vietnam at countless, concealed points with an aggressor's advantage of secrecy and surprise. (See map. p. 218)

Laos was the "stitch" we dropped. Laos was "the strategic key to the entire area of Southeast Asia" as Eisenhower told Kennedy the day before the new President's inauguration in January, 1961. Neutralization of Laos was conceptually consistent with this because, *if effective*, it would have made a benign insulator of the "strategic key," surrounded by more populous states—North and South Vietnam, Cambodia, Thailand, Burma and, of course, China.

As we have seen, however, "neutralization" never happened. Tracing the effects of this inversion is a bit like tracing the inversion of the polarity of an unseen magnet beneath a tray of iron filings. Had the Communist side implemented it, the original concept of neutralization would have acted as the positive pole of a magnet, attracting the countries of Southeast Asia into a stable, coherent pattern around a truly neutral and integral Laos. The substitution of the Harriman-Hilsman inverted formula reversed the magnetic polarity so as to repel

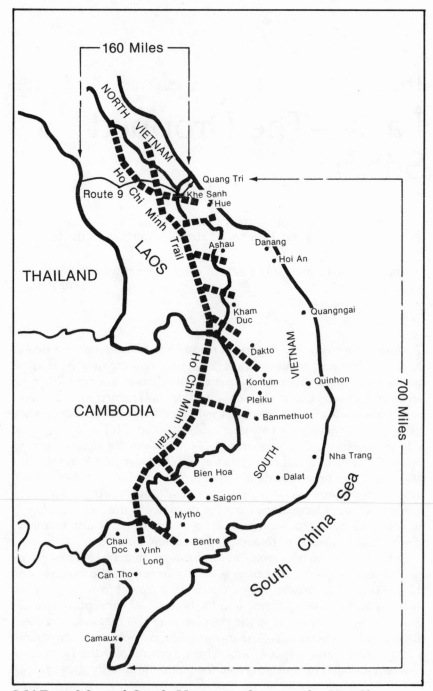

MAP #3 Map of South Vietnam, showing the Ho Chi Minh Trails superimposed on the major battles of the Tet Offensive in January 1968.

the elements into separate, mutually antagonistic patterns around the malignant force radiating from southern Laos. And, just as mariners must infer the presence of the North Pole from the behavior of a needle, so the effects of the inversion of neutralization can be observed in the behavior of the United States when operating near the silent, invisible wall around southern Laos.

To change the metaphor, this conceptual wall operated like a "given" premise in a geometrical theorem. Being given, it determines the nature of the problem. As succeeding derivative problems are posed, the "given" soon becomes taken for granted without the necessity of re-examination. A rare revelation of great clarity is William Bundy's reflection (quoted at the beginning of chapter 16) of how "the 'given' of our respecting the 1962 agreements on Laos, at least in high degree," obscured the likelihood that "we could have held a line across Laos and South Vietnam." But this crystalline revelation from one of the most perceptive and articulate of the responsible officials is the exception. The rule is that one is required to follow the players' tracks as they move gingerly around the force radiating from southern Laos.

For example, think of the generals, veterans of Korea who, as devoted members of the "Never Again Club," opposed any new U.S. land war in Asia. Consider how they shied away from a deliberately planned and defined ground action in southern Laos to block an invasion but went along with incremental injections of U.S. ground troops up to half a million (and would have gone higher if Westmoreland's final request to Johnson had been granted) in an unplanned and indecisive land war in Asia.

On the other hand, a notable exception appeared in January 1966 when the U.S. Military Assistance Command in Thailand (MACTHAI) proposed isolating the South Vietnam battlefield by cutting the Ho Chi Minh Trail. This concept argued that as long as Hanoi could move men and supplies in magnitude through southern Laos, it would have a significant advantage over the anticommunist side. "Not necessarily so," was the reaction of Admiral Sharp to this proposition when I later quoted it approvingly in a memorandum. The MACTHAI proposal emphasized the need to start preparing immediately for two-pronged, gradually expanding operations from both the west and east sides of the southern Laos Corridor. The idea of gradually extending our logistic system to support a gradually penetrating force was already being applied to support the combat operations of the Army's First Cavalry Airmobile division deployed in the western mountains of South Vietnam, over 90 miles from the sea. As Admiral Sharp points out in his book, the deployment was executed in stages, using the town of An Khe, only 35 miles from the coast as a staging area.[1] Curiously, there was no inclination to adapt the same sensible formula to the gradual extension of a blocking force against Hanoi's invasion through southern Laos. Significantly, the MACTHAI proposal noted that preparations would take at least a year and a half—that is, until the summer or fall of 1967, just a few months before Hanoi's Tet Offensive was to descend on South Vietnam.

General Westmoreland, too, was contemplating a similar possibility, but as I will point out later, not only conflicting U.S. policies but also the sudden reality of the 1968 Tet offensive prevented him from developing the concept further.

The MACTHAI plan won little friendly attention at CINCPAC or, for that matter, even at the American Embassy in Bangkok where it was regarded as empirebuilding by the U.S. military command in Thailand. This last probably contained an element of truth, but that should not have disqualified the concept from being judged on its intrinsic merits rather than on the basis of peripheral factors—whether military or diplomatic.

But failure to understand the "Laotian Equation" was not confined to the military, who had absorbed the habit from the civilian leadership. In early July, 1965, McNamara relayed a question from President Johnson to JCS Chairman General Wheeler, "If we do everything we can, can we have assurance of winning in South Vietnam?" A straightforward question from the Commander-in-Chief to his principal military advisor—a question of which Napoleon would have approved. Wheeler directed his assistant, General Andrew Goodpaster, to find the answer with the help of a special group assembled for the purpose. But the guidelines which defined the "givens" of the problem were given to General Goodpaster by Assistant Secretary of Defense McNaughton with the approval of Secretary McNamara. These were among the "given" premises:[2]

Manpower—A callup of the Reserves was ruled out, thus limiting the manpower resources and the strategies that could be considered.

Air Power—The Rolling Thunder bombing campaign would not be increased, nor would North Vietnam's harbors be mined.

Questioning the capability of bombing to "put a ceiling on infiltration," McNaughton continued: "My own view is that the study group probably should not invest time in trying to solve the problem by cutting off the flow of supplies and people by either of these methods." Having thus ruled out increased airpower to stop reinforcement by Hanoi, McNaughton moved on—somewhat obliquely, to bypass the use of ground forces for the same purpose:

Ground Forces—"I do not know what your thoughts are about the wisdom of investing time in the proposal that ground forces be used to produce some sort of anti-infiltration barrier."

By thus disdainfully discounting the importance of acting on the ground to block infiltration (and having already ruled out a Reserve callup), McNaughton managed to avoid charging the JCS with producing such a recommendation, and at the same steered around the problem of southern Laos without even mentioning it.

The search for an answer to the President also considered

Enemy Strength and Infiltration—Estimates of enemy strength and future infiltration were invited but, not surprisingly in the framework of the limitations prescribed above, the JCS response was perfunctorily optimistic.

Objective—"Winning . . . means that we succeed in demonstrating to the Vietcong that they cannot win."

Here is another example of forcing a military decision not by military power and prowess but by a test of *will* in a dimension of time. One should note how the word is used by the study group in its assessment of July 14, 1965: "Within the bounds of reasonable assumptions there appears to be no reason we cannot win if such is our *will*—and if that *will* is manifested in strategy and tactical operations." (Emphasis added.)[3]

What could be the strategy to accomplish this result? The JCS took McNaughton's broad hint and proposed neither to cut Hanoi's reinforcements by closing the ports nor by blocking the invasion on the ground. And why should they have proposed either? After all, if the result was to be determined by a test of endurance and will, it would not be necessary to seek a military decision only to hang on until North Vietnam and the Vietcong wearied. Accordingly, the assessment was predicated on a simple linear projection of existing conditions. It concluded with an estimate that the infusion of 35 U.S. battalions would be sufficient to maintain a minimum 4-1 ratio of friendly to enemy forces in accordance with doctrine on the need for numerical odds for the defenders against guerrilla warfare.[4]

Nor was Laos mentioned a week later when, after a visit to Saigon, Secretary McNamara recommended increasing the dosage of U.S. ground forces to 175,000 at the end of 1965 and to 275,000 in 1966. Strategy? "To take the offensive. . . . To compel the [enemy] to fight at a higher and more sustained intensity with resulting higher logistical consumption and, at the same time, to limit his capability to resupply forces in combat at that scale by attacking his lines of communication. The concept assumes vigorous prosecution of the air and sea anti-infiltration campaign and includes increased use of air in-country. . . ."[5] In short, an additional infusion into a linear war of incremental attrition—for both sides.

What might be Hanoi's response? "To send up to several regular divisions. . . . to assist the Vietcong if they see the tide turning and victory, once so near, being snatched away." Although he had no proposal on how to prevent Hanoi from sending these divisions, McNamara noted how ominous it would be if, as a result, we should be pressured "to 'counter-invade' North Vietnam and to extend air strikes to population targets in the North." Worse yet, even if we should succeed in "driving the Vietcong back into the trees" he fore-saw that "even in 'success' it is not obvious how we will be able to disengage our forces from Vietnam. It is unlikely that a formal agree-ment good enough for that purpose could possibly be negotiated—because the arrangement can reflect little more than the power sit-uation."[6]

He was absolutely right in this last estimate. So why did he continue to plod on, zombie-like, on such a course? Why did he not recommend graceful withdrawal which would have been consistent with his es-timate? Or, alternatively, why did he not at least examine the pos-sibility of ground action in southern Laos, to block the North Vietnamese reinforcements he anticipated? Because, as he had written in National Security Action Memorandum 288 of March 16, 1964, tiptoeing around the tacit inversion of neutralization, "as a consequence of operating *largely* within the framework of the 1962 Geneva Accords . . . we have had to *condone* the extensive use of Laotian territory by the Vietcong, both as a sanctuary and as infiltration routes." (Chapter 12) (Emphasis added)

The big question is this: where was McNamara leading the United States? The answer that springs to mind is that he was willing to let the result of the war hang on a test of endurance and will. In any case, he repeated this performance five months later in a November 30, 1965 report, increasing his estimate of forces needed to 220,000 at the end of 1965, 400,000 at the end of 1966 to which he added an estimation of an additional 200,000 in 1967. Why the sharp new in-crease? Because, as he said, of "dramatic recent changes in the sit-uation on the military side. They are the increased infiltration from the North and the increased willingness of the Communist forces to stand and fight, even in large engagements." He forecast that in 1966, North Vietnam would increase its strength in the South from 110 to 150 battalions. How to meet this challenge? He had to offer only his proposed new injection of troops to meet his hope that by the end of 1966, the enemy's "losses can be made to equal his input."[7]

Did McNamara really believe in a war to test endurance and will? One wonders. In December of 1965, in his "Prognosis Assuming the Recommended Deployments," be became grim:

> Deployments of the kind we have recommended will not guarantee success. . . . [The Communists] . . . believe that the war will be a long one, that time is their ally, and that their own staying power is superior to ours. . . . We expect them, upon learning of any U.S. intention to augment its forces, to boost their own commitment and *to test U.S. capabilities and will* to persevere at a higher level of conflict and casualties. . . . (Emphasis added.)
>
> If the U.S. were willing to commit enough forces—perhaps 600,000 or more—we could ultimately prevent North Vietnam and the Vietcong from sustaining conflict at a significant level. When this point was reached, however, the question of Chinese intervention would become critical. . . .
>
> It follows therefore that the odds are about even that, even with the recommended deployments, we will be faced in early 1967 with a military standoff at a much higher level, with pacification still stalled, and with any prospect of success marred by the chances of an active Chinese intervention.[8]

In July he had recommended deployments in order to "compel the enemy to fight at a higher level." Now he is saying that such increases in force strength would make it the U.S. whose capabilities and will are to be tested at higher and higher levels.

In another draft memo of November, 1965, McNamara had gone even farther, to forecasting that "despite our effort we will be faced in early 1967 with stagnation at a higher level and with a need to decide whether to deploy . . . forces probably in Laos as well as in South Vietnam."[9] At last—the possible necessity to act in Laos is acknowledged! But, only as a remote prospect, perhaps a year or more in the future. Still, if such an outcome could be foreseen in November, 1965, why not act sooner rather than later? Or, at least, why not recommend an urgent study of the prospects and problems of such an action and the development of a possible military plan? Or, if he believed that action in Laos had to be excluded by the Geneva Accords, why did he not recommend phasing out our commitment rather than staggering to eventual "stagnation at a higher level?" Why not start to go gracefully, sooner rather than later? Was it just the ultimate illustration of the incremental decision-making syndrome which seeks always to avoid or postpone difficult decisions or slice them into the smallest possible bits? Only McNamara himself can provide the true answer and he, so far, has chosen to remain silent.

Nowhere—apart from Roger Hilsman's exposition (discussed in chapter 8)—have I seen a more detailed and clearly drawn map of the protective conceptual field surrounding southern Laos than the one written to me in April, 1966 by our Ambassador to Laos, William Sullivan. His letter was sparked by an April 1 letter from me enclosing a long paper on Laos which I had been moved to write a couple of months earlier. I was beginning to experience again that unreal "Through the Looking Glass" feeling which, as will emerge later, I shared with Ambassador Sullivan, although from the opposite side of the glass.

As on former occasions my recourse was to try to describe reality as I saw it in sentences which had—I hoped—a fixed rather than a sliding import. The result was a paper, dated February 8, "The Strategic Significance of Laos." Copies were sent in several directions, including the State Department's East Asia Bureau where I believe Assistant Secretary William Bundy saw it and possibly Deputy Assistant Secretary Leonard Unger (former Ambassador to Laos and future Ambassador to Thailand). I did not trouble Admiral Sharp with it because the concept, at its core, was political rather than military; because a year earlier he had already vetoed the only course of action which might flow from it and because he was occupied with overseeing the air war against North Vietnam. Copies of the paper did go to Ambassador Graham Martin in Bangkok and Ambassador Sullivan in Vientiane.

On a subsequent visit to Honolulu, Martin commented favorably, which gratified me in light of my forthcoming transfer to Bangkok to be his Deputy. However, as I knew, he had not favored the MACTHAI concept of action in Laos advanced a few months earlier—for blocking the invasion coming down the Ho Chi Minh Trails. As it later turned out, he was more interested in the aerial interdiction of infiltration which I believed could only be accomplished if applied in tandem with a force on the ground.

Bill Sullivan and I disagreed on strategy in the war. He opposed blocking Hanoi's invasion on the ground in southern Laos. I favored it, believing that it was the only strategy that had a chance of success and that if we were unwilling to undertake it we never should have become committed in South Vietnam. As a result of having delegated the *real* decision-making power to Hanoi, I wrote, we were being forced inexorably toward other courses such as:

- Escalation of the air war to a level which exceeded our objective to limit the war and negotiate with Hanoi. . . .

- Amphibious invasion of North Vietnam—an idea which intrigued Sullivan. . . .

- Open-ended increases in ground force commitments. . . .

- Withdrawal under an unsatisfactory political formula.

The Laos Corridor being the "strategic key to Southeast Asia" (a proposition with which Sullivan specifically agreed in his letter), it seemed to me that the existing strategic pattern with respect to Laos was unsatisfactory. That pattern was not the one prescribed by the Geneva Accords of 1962 which was always unreal and bore no resemblance to the facts on the ground. The existing pattern made of southern Laos not only a deadly instrument against South Vietnam and Cambodia but an instrument which would finally lead to the destruction of free Laos. As long as we confined ourselves to aerial harassment and did not literally stop the invasion on the ground, the North Vietnamese would not—only for the time being—take over free Laos to the north and west, based on Vientiane. But there was a sequel that I thought followed logically:

> The obverse is that when the Corridor has served its purpose with respect to South Vietnam, the Communists will then be free to turn their full attention toward Vientiane—the capital of Free Laos. In other words, to paraphrase Lenin, the Communist route to Vientiane leads, not directly across northern Laos, but round about through the Corridor to Saigon and then back to Vientiane. [This is exactly what happened. In May, 1975 Saigon fell to an invasion through Laos and then the Communists turned on Vientiane, which fell a few months later.]

It was no doubt this paragraph which stimulated Bill's puckish opening acknowledgement of what he called "your April Fool letter containing the latest version of Hannah's Hegira,"* (the first version probably being the November 1964 paper which is the subject of chapter 14). "As you anticipate, I do not agree with it, although I do agree with your assessment of the Laos Corridor as the strategic key to Southeast Asia." In his view, as he explained, if we sent forces into southern Laos, Hanoi would retaliate in the northern part, driving westward from the Plaine des Jarres into free Laos, toward Vientiane.

---

*The Hegira—Mohammed's emigration, bearing the Truth of Islam, from persecution in Mecca to Medina—was the event from which the Mohammedan Era is dated, as the Christian Era is dated from the birth of Jesus.

Here Sullivan put his finger, with surgical precision, on the essence of the Harriman-Hilsman formula and on the *first* element of the invisible force which surrounded southern Laos, namely, that free Laos had been made hostage to Hanoi's control of the invasion routes in southeastern Laos. The outcome of the war would depend on which was to be the greater asset in the struggle for South Vietnam. Of course, the answer is clear today. Control of the invasion routes was the decisive asset of North Vietnam's conquest of South Vietnam. Our admirable campaign to assist and strengthen free Laos, superbly executed by Sullivan and many others, was a holding action which contributed little to the support of our cause in South Vietnam.

Sullivan went on to warn that action in southern Laos would require six to seven U.S. divisions—at least three to stop the invasion itself and at least three more to shore up the northern portions of Laos (and to bulwark Thailand) against the North Vietnamese attack he anticipated. One may wonder how it would serve Hanoi's aim of conquering South Vietnam to challenge the United States and its allies in an open conventional war along the Mekong River after the invasion route to South Vietnam had been closed. It would certainly have been an engagement better suited to America's strengths than the war we were actually fighting. Moreover, such an engagement might have left North Vietnam in the same kind of position North Korea had to accept—backed up against its own territory facing a defended, international cease-fire line. Nevertheless, even if Sullivan were right, these seven divisions (about 110,000 combat forces plus support elements) deployed to halt the invasion decisively seem rather modest alongside our eventual deployment of over half a million troops in an interminable, ambiguous "meatgrinder." And if the invasion had been blocked, most of these forces would not have been needed in South Vietnam. One must note the *second* corollary of the Harriman-Hilsman formula, namely, that defense of South Vietnam against invasion must be accomplished within South Vietnam—not in Laos where the aggression occurred—as Harriman had advised Kennedy in 1961.

Bill's next objection to action in southern Laos was that it would be provocative to the Russians who might decide to give material support to the Pathet Lao which, he said, they were not then doing, although they were giving important support to the North Vietnamese. It might also cause the U.S.S.R. to increase its political commitment to both Hanoi and Peking. I was reminded of the old premise regarding the Soviet Union which underlay the 1962 Geneva Accords—and the succeeding Harriman-Hilsman formula. The premise was that, as a spin-off from the rising Moscow-Peking rivalry, the

U.S.S.R. would restrain Hanoi's aggressive behavior in order to bar the expansion of China's influence into Southeast Asia—an objective which the Soviet Union was believed to share with us. As a corollary, it was said to be in our interest to encourage this latent Soviet moderation and therefore, not to force the Soviets into a more belligerent stance to protect its role as the leader of the Communist world. This premise, it should be recalled, was underwritten by Khrushchev's assurance to Kennedy of support for a neutral Laos and by Pushkin's assurance to Harriman that the Soviet Union would assume responsibility for Hanoi's implementation of the Geneva Accords.

Therefore, Bill chided me for neglecting to discuss the Soviet reaction to any possible U.S. action in southern Laos. In fact, however, the U.S.S.R. had completely reneged on its commitments under the Harriman-Pushkin understanding of 1962—if the Russians ever recognized or remembered the existence of a commitment. It had been obvious, as Sullivan acknowledged in his letter, that the U.S.S.R. was giving considerable material support to North Vietnam. Moreover, there was no visible evidence that Moscow was exercising any restraint on Hanoi. Accordingly, I considered that the special Soviet "restraining role" was already moribund—if it ever lived.

Nevertheless, Sullivan was right in the sense that I had neglected to take account of the lingering hankering on the U.S. side, even as late as 1966, to believe that Soviet moderation in Southeast Asia would contrast with a hostile Chinese role. In another context, Bill argued that mining North Vietnam's harbors might also tip Hanoi away from [moderate] Moscow toward [hostile] Peking.*

The U.S. fixation on a constructive Soviet role in Indochina was a key premise on which the Kennedy Administration had based its desire to negotiate the neutralization of Laos in 1961. While the U.S.S.R.'s total failure to carry out its commitments with respect to Laos had jarred the United States, nothing had destroyed our good old American optimism. Some even thought that Khruschev was unable to carry out his commitments to Kennedy (and Pushkin's to Harriman) because of the damage to his position resulting from his failure in the Cuban missile crisis. Accordingly, Premier Kosygin's visit to Hanoi in February, 1965 (while McGeorge Bundy was visiting Saigon) had fueled expectations of a stronger Soviet role. It was hoped that, in its effort to frustrate China's influence in North Vietnam, the

---

*Assistant Secretary of Defense, John McNaughton relied on Sullivan's judgment in making this point in his draft of a Presidential memorandum, dated May 19, 1967. *Pentagon Papers*, Vol. IV, p. 485.

U.S.S.R. would urge moderation on Hanoi, perhaps even leading the way to a negotiated neutralization of South Vietnam (à la Laos), with Vietcong participation in a coalition government.

Sullivan's letter did not go this far. Nevertheless, while noting that the Soviets might be "very sly" in fostering a takeover of Laos through the agency of North Vietnam, he saw no evidence of this. On the other hand he saw some indications that Moscow would still prefer that the North Vietnamese be "less aggressive in their 'liberation' operations."

Why it was assumed in some circles that restraining North Vietnam was Moscow's only possible way of preventing its loss of Communist leadership in Southeast Asia to China was perplexing. A much simpler and more obvious course was the one Moscow chose—to use its superior resources to outdo China in aid to North Vietnam, thereby encouraging Hanoi's alliance with and dependence on the Soviet Union and, at the same time, freezing out China. If Hanoi wanted to conquer South Vietnam and dominate Laos, the U.S.S.R. had no need to restrain it—beyond the perfunctory, cosmetic posturing required to divert the United States. It could—and did—simply provide North Vietnam with all the political and material support it needed and then profit from the eventual victory, to the disadvantage of *both* China *and* the United States.

How to account for the persistence of this vision of a Soviet moderating role? The answer, I suspect, is that once a force as vast and complex as the United States is launched on a course, it acquires a momentum so great that the premises on which the original action was based—the premise, for example, of a Soviet moderating role in Southeast Asia—become irreversible "givens" powered by the very strength of the force for which they provided the launching pad.

However that may be, the *third* element in the Harriman-Hilsman formula for southern Laos was the expectation of Soviet help in restraining North Vietnam within its borders. Sullivan concurred exactly with this proposition, giving it as his expectation that our "success" in the war would produce a tacit, unnegotiated withdrawal by North Vietnam in tandem with a Soviet undertaking "to guarantee and support North Vietnam within its current territorial confines." Subsequent history tells us that North Vietnam—with Soviet support—caused a different result.

In what I wrongly took, at the time, to be a brief rhetorical diversion from the subject of what to do about the invasion coming through Laos, Sullivan spoke of his preference for an amphibious invasion of North Vietnam at Vinh, some 150 miles up the coast from the Demilitarized Zone, rather than an overland operation across the Laos

Corridor itself. Although an audacious concept, as he said, it would not have stopped the invasion nor would it have provided a negotiable cease-fire line. It is apparent to me now that I underestimated Bill's real conviction regarding the Vinh concept. In a 1985 letter he has confirmed to me that his "current view is still that an invasion at Vinh would have been a better thing both militarily and strategically than Korean-izing the peninsula by a U.S. force all the way to the Mekong River." He goes on to say however, that "I was beaten down a couple of times. . . . when I proposed it in the late 1960s."

Then what could the alternative be? Having given up on Vinh, he went on, in his 1966 letter to lay out the "official line." The only alternative, he thought, was the Administration's attempt to do the job with "the current combination of forces," although in truth this was a combination whose "currency" was being weekly outdated by escalating numbers. Sullivan thought we should continue the current strategy of "chewing the enemy" in South Vietnam and attempting to harass him by air in Laos. The air campaign against North Vietnam would continue to be spectacular, even though it produced only marginal results. In other words—more of the same, meaning continued direct infusions of U.S. power into an incremental strategy whose success could only be measured by the arrival of Hanoi at the decision to withdraw quietly behind a "moderate" Soviet screen. Negotiations? Probably not, Sullivan noted, adding that he felt this was an additional reason for not acting, either in the Laos Corridor or at Vinh. Either of those courses would get us "too critically involved to permit a tacit dénouement." If we could "*slide* this thing out from under without the need for a conference" we would be better off "even though we won't have any very neat bundle of signed papers." Prognosis? "Has to be demonstrated." Long-range forecast? "A long, tedious, rather inconclusive haul in Southeast Asia."

He ended by expressing the hope that I would do a further revision of my paper, "bringing it closer into line with the facts on this side of the looking glass." I was gratified by the figure of speech which I had used myself several times. The question was which of us was on the clear side and which on the cloudy side of the looking glass?

On my side, the view was of a "regional line" which Bill did not comment on but clearly did not favor as I had described it in the paper I had sent him:

The concept is of a delineated, defended cease-fire line across Laos and termination of Communist domination of the southeastern Panhandle. . . . The idea of a "line" is sometimes criticized as being static and 'military' but experience since World War II indicates its usefulness as a prime condition of peaceful coexistence between two fundamentally hostile systems. . . . A line of this sort would simplify the problem of explanation to the American people who would find such a concept far easier to understand than our esoteric rationale which depends for its success on convincing the other side to cooperate by agreeing to negotiate its own withdrawal.

A regional line is related to our operations in South Vietnam where we face two tasks—defeating the enemy and pacification. . . . Our object is to "separate the Vietcong from the People" . . . But separation must be provided on a national scale at a line where the nation as a whole can be defended against aggression. By forcing the enemy to fight at the "gates" of South Vietnam, the main military action could be shifted away from the hamlets and villages.

Would partition of Laos be justifiable? Yes. It is partitioned anyway with no prospect of unification (except under Communist rule) and with no reliable cease-fire line.

Could the purpose be accomplished by air without ground forces? History and the evidence make it doubtful. . . . Moreover, our use of airpower is limited by our desire to negotiate with Hanoi.

Would Laotian Premier Souvanna agree? Not all at once but he has shown great capacity to adapt to changing realities. . . . Moreover, if the loss of South Vietnam would lead to a Communist takeover of all Laos, then the present framework in Laos is a dwindling asset to Souvanna. . . .

Would direct action be logistically feasible? Yes. The preparations would take time but this is not an absolute bar.

One may disagree with the forgoing concept of how we should have tried to end the war. The frustration of its consideration happened because the "givens" which enveloped southern Laos stalled all who approached, turning them aside on various tangents. For example, one idea, supported by General Westmoreland and Deputy Ambassador to Saigon, U. Alexis Johnson, was to constrict and gradually turn off the infiltration by the peaceful construction of a modern highway along Route 9 which spanned the infiltration corridor from South Vietnam to the Mekong River. The idea was to conduct the project under peaceful international auspices—the United Nations or one of its subordinate agencies. In this way, the project would be cleansed of hostile political or military content—a genuine multilateral effort to foster regional economic cooperation and development—hence difficult for the Communist side to oppose. Incidentally, in the process, construction would interrupt the movement of infiltration southward to South Vietnam.[10] This was an ingenious but foredoomed attempt to slide by reality. It made a familiar error in our strategy—underestimating the determination of Hanoi to conquer South Vietnam. President Johnson reflected this American misunderstanding of Hanoi's attitude when he described his San Antonio offer to North Vietnam of a multi-billion dollar regional development scheme as "an offer, old Ho can't turn down." What we failed to recognize or to admit to ourselves was that what North Vietnam wanted was to conquer South Vietnam and would oppose everything that stood in the way.

Another example of a tangential scheme to accomplish indirectly what we would not undertake directly was the "electronic barrier" concept, discussed in Chapter 17. This system worked—in the technological sense. It also worked in the sense that it did improve the effectiveness of our aerial harassment. But it did not work to the extent of reducing the continuing invasion to the level of ineffectiveness. It was another case of a feint at the real invasion but, having been deflected by the protective conceptual field surrounding southern Laos, it glanced off on a tangent—another attempt to accomplish something without really doing it. In a way, this was the leitmotif of our whole war, in which we sought to induce Hanoi to stop its invasion without actually being forced to do so.

Even in Bangkok, I found that except for those who had proposed the MACTHAI blocking plan, this unreal view of Laos made itself felt. In the fall of 1966, we were visited by that perennial consultant to Democratic Presidents, Clark Clifford, who was travelling the Far East searching new troop commitments from allied countries, such as Australia, New Zealand, the Philippines, Korea and Thailand. As a result of two days of almost continuous meetings, the Thai Government did agree to send a unit of some 12,000 Thai volunteers to South Vietnam.

What stands out most clearly in my memory, however, is a preliminary meeting that Ambassador Martin and I had with Clifford, immediately after his arrival at the Ambassador's guest house. Clifford explained the President's strong desire for greater allied support— later called "More Flags."

Ambassador Martin took note of all that Thailand was already doing to support our cause in Indochina, including support for Laos as well as for South Vietnam. He believed the Thai would want to do whatever else they could do. He went on to suggest that before approaching the Thai Government we should consider very carefully just what contribution the Thai could make that would fit most usefully into our overall strategy. He pointed out that the war was not only in South Vietnam but in Laos where the Thai were already helping the free Lao forces. The war was also passing through southern Laos in the form of infiltration to South Vietnam. Both of these manifestations of the war were closer to Thailand than was South Vietnam. Not only did the threat of Communist expansion in Laos threaten Thailand directly but, given its strategic position *vis-a-vis* Laos and its close cultural and linguistic ties with Laos, Thailand offered excellent opportunities to deal with aspects of the war which were difficult to get at from South Vietnam. In conclusion, the Ambassador simply suggested that we should consider where Thailand could make the most valuable strategic contribution—in Laos or in South Vietnam.

Clifford barely let Martin finish. His reaction was spectacular. Lacing his sentences with colorful language, Clifford made it briefly and pithily clear that he wanted to hear no more such talk. What the President wanted was more troops in South Vietnam. Because the President had done everything to support Thailand, the President now expected Thailand to support him. The need was in South Vietnam and that was where the President wanted Thai forces. End of subject. And, in fact, the Thai did provide a new injection of forces into the veins of our linear strategy of filling South Vietnam with forces to fight North Vietnamese invaders who kept coming down through Laos, often within a stone's throw of the Thai border.

So we continued to implement the same incremental non-strategy throughout 1967 and up to the Tet Offensive of January 30, 1968. In April of 1967, General Westmoreland requested 200,000 more troops on top of the existing ceiling of 470,000. On April 27, he accompanied the Chairman of the JCS, General Wheeler, to the White House to explain his rationale. Without reinforcements, he told the President, "we will not be in danger of being defeated but it will be nip and tuck to oppose the reinforcements the enemy is capable of providing" (down the Ho Chi Minh trails, one must note). Asked about the influence of this increased infiltration, he said, "Anytime we take an action, we expect a reaction."

The President then asked, "When we add divisions can't the enemy add divisions? If so, where does it all end?"

Westmoreland answered: "It appears that last month we reached the crossover point [the point at which the enemy loses forces to combat and other attrition faster than he replaces them] in areas excluding the two northern provinces. . . . Attritions will be greater than additions to the force."[11]

The General went on to characterize the strategy under the 470,000-man ceiling as a "meat-grinder" in which we would kill large numbers but barely hold our own. "Unless the will of the enemy is broken or unless there was an unravelling of the Vietcong infrastructure, the war could go on for five years." But, with a ceiling raised to 565,000, he could reduce that to three years and with 665,000 men—to two years. In none of these three cases did he indicate how the end might come—whether by unilateral North Vietnamese withdrawal or by negotiation.

What prospect could be more grim? This was the moment that Napoleon had in mind. Westmoreland could have told the President of his long contemplation of "moving into Laos to cut and block the infiltration routes of the Ho Chi Minh Trail" for which "in 1966 and 1967 my staff prepared detailed plans," and which both Ambassadors Lodge and Ellsworth Bunker had supported.[12] If the President found the prospect discouraging, the generals could have told their Chief of State (if they believed it) that the existing strategy would not work. They could have proposed an alternative—deployment of additional forces (fewer than the requested 200,000) to block the invasion in southern Laos. They could have explained that this would change the terms of the war from a test of endurance in an inconclusive bloodletting to a test of a great nation's military capability to define the space it intended to defend. Instead, they had a brief discussion of Cambodia and Laos in which Westmoreland reviewed for the President his operation plan called "High Port" which would have sent one South Vietnamese division into Laos with U.S. artillery and air support (similar to the later failed Lam Son 719 operation of February 1971). Clearly, not enough to do the job right, this plan would have resulted either in large scale U.S. reinforcement or withdrawal of the South Vietnamese division. The conversation ended inconclusively.

Meanwhile, Assistant Secretary McNaughton broke Westmoreland's request down into components and addressed them separately. First, he considered granting only 80,000 new forces (later he cut it to 30,000). The difference between this figure and the request for 200,000 did not reflect some significant strategic departure but only another application of the now-too-familiar incrementalism. If the military had only "more forces" in mind, the Department of Defense seemed to have only "fewer forces" in mind. As McNaughton said in a memorandum to McNamara, "providing the 80,000 is tantamount to acceding to the whole Westmoreland-Sharp request. . . . they will accept the 80,000. But six months from now, in will come messages. . . . saying that the requirement remains at 201,000 (or more)."[13] Neither the military nor the civilians had a new idea which would justify either more or fewer forces.

The only distinctive idea mentioned in McNaughton's lengthy May 19 Draft Memo for the President was a ground action in Laos which he quickly pronounced to be unwise (without study), on the basis of the advice of none other than Le Duan, a leading member of the North Vietnamese Politburo: Le Duan was quoted at length in the Department of Defense draft memorandum as having said, "The occupation of the Western Highlands is a tough job [for the U.S.] but the attack on central and lower Laos is still a tougher one. . . . In effect, an attack on central and lower Laos would mean the opening of another front nearer to North Vietnam and then the U.S. troops would have to clash with the North Vietnamese main force."[14] Le Duan put the point correctly. The question was clear. Was the United States prepared to meet the North Vietnamese main force to stop the invasion? We had said many times that we could beat the North Vietnamese if they would only come out and fight like a conventional army. But now, such a direct clash was being cited as something to avoid! If we really believed in avoidance, why should we have deployed ground forces in the first place? Because we had done so already, our logical course would then have been to begin to pull them out behind a rear-guard air action and a large military assistance program comparable to Nixon's "Vietnamization" two years later. But, if we were still ready to meet and defeat Hanoi's main force in open combat, the place to do it was in southeastern Laos.

The curious thing is that the planners of the Department of Defense did not see the prospect of engaging Hanoi's main force in southern Laos as a fundamental change of strategy but only as another step of linear escalation. That was all they were capable of seeing. McNaughton's understanding of Le Duan's declaration was limited to the following: "A brigade will beget a division and a division a corps, each calling down matching forces from North Vietnam into territory to their liking and suggesting to Hanoi that they take action in Northern Laos to suck us further in."[15]

So, in the end, we made a neat incremental decision—Westmoreland got 45,000 more troops and the ceiling was raised to 525,000.

In December, 1967, General Westmoreland reiterated the need for more forces—even as McNaughton had predicted. But this time, on February 12, 1968, the JCS stepped in and refused to approve any more deployments without a call-up of the Reserves[16]—an action that President Johnson would not take for domestic reasons. To go higher up the string of escalatory deployments was ruled out because the domestic political situation afforded no "sticking place." So we plodded on, putting in more forces, fighting bravely and well, defeating the enemy every day, and then doing it all over again the next day and the next—with no end in sight.

One man did disagree, however. Ellsworth Bunker, our new Ambassador to South Vietnam arrived in Saigon in April, 1967, just as the Department of Defense was studying Westmoreland's request for 200,000 more troops. Unencumbered with any responsibility for leading the United States into the strategic blind alley of incremental response to a spurious "insurgency" simulated by an invading army while waiting for the enemy "to get the message" and withdraw, Bunker looked at the problem from a fresh point of view. By June he knew that in the face of continued infiltration, the American people would not wait indefinitely while interminable bloodletting went on. He thought it silly to fight again and again in South Vietnam when, if we would cut off the steady, flowing invasion through Laos, the remaining enemy forces already in South Vietnam could be reduced as they withered.

During Secretary McNamara's July 7–8 visit to Saigon, Ambassador Bunker forthrightly made his point which was, in the words of the editors of the *Pentagon Papers*, "that the crux of the military problem was how to choke off the North Vietnamese infiltration."[17] Combining the political, military, strategic and moral aspects into one unified insight, he argued:

> What is involved, of course, are operations within Laos but I do not believe this fact should present insuperable obstacles. The North Vietnamese Government is a signatory to the 1962 Geneva Accords but its forces have been in Laos both before and since the signing of the Agreements. It is now using Laos as the main route for infiltration into South Vietnam. Is it not logical and reasonable, therefore, that South Vietnamese troops should oppose and combat North Vietnamese offensive action by whatever method can be devised in order to prevent the invasion of their country? . . . This is a matter which I believe we should pursue with the utmost concentration.[18]

General Westmoreland spoke next:

> We must convince the enemy that he cannot win, that *time is not on his side*. I believe that this strategy will succeed provided we step up the pressure. . . . The situation is not a stalemate; we are winning slowly but steadily and this pace can accelerate if we reinforce our successes. Therefore, I believe we should step up our operations in pacification in the south, increase the pressure in the north and *exercise new initiatives in Laos*.[19] (Emphasis added)

But what were the new initiatives to be? This only emerged gradually from the subsequent J-2 (intelligence) estimate of alarming increases of North Vietnamese reinforcements through Laos and Cambodia, and the J-3 (operations) estimate which detailed the deployment of "containment or anti-invasion forces" along the DMZ and "*opposite* enemy sanctuaries in Laos and Cambodia." (Emphasis added.)[20] In fact, "containment" was now rapidly becoming one of the key-words in our Indochina lexicon, along with "counter-insur-gency" and "pacification" and the "signal" to Hanoi. In this context however, it seemed that rather than containing the enemy, the de-fenders were containing themselves. As the editors of the *Pentagon Papers* remark, "The sum total of the briefings did not vary from what McNamara had heard so many times before."

So, we did not pursue the Ambassador's pristine, integral proposal at all, much less with concentration. The discussion at the conference quickly returned to more conventional terms, that is, to our usual strategy, waged in a dimension of time and aimed at matching our determination against North Vietnam's will.

But, Ambassador Bunker had one more string to his bow. In June, he had written a personal letter to President Johnson recommending that we move into southern Laos and cut the Ho Chi Minh Trail. It hardly need be said that this proposal got short shrift in Washington. The Ambassador later discussed it with me a couple of times in 1983 in Washington. Casting his mind backward, he said that he was even more certain in 1983 than in 1967 that our failure to cut the Trail was a strategic mistake of the first order. He agreed with what Eisenhower had told Kennedy, advice that Kennedy had ignored by overlooking the violations of the 1962 neutralization agreement on Laos.

Particularly interesting were Ambassador Bunker's recollections of the reasons given for the rejection of his recommendation, which he summarized in a letter to me of April 25, 1983:

> Three objections to the proposal surfaced. One, that it would be a vio-lation of the Geneva Treaty of 1962; two, that it might provoke a more active reaction on the part of the Chinese; three, that it would take two or three more divisions.
>
> My comment on the first objection was that it was true that it would be a violation of the 1962 Treaty but the other side had violated it almost from the day it was signed and were continuing to violate it. The Laotians through whose territory the Trail went would have welcomed our inter-vention. As far as the Chinese were concerned we could make it clear to them through our allies who had representation in Peking that we had no designs on China or North Vietnam but were simply insisting on the rights of the South Vietnamese to live under governments of their own choosing. As far as the extra troops were concerned we did put them in before the war was over.

I had one more letter from him, dated May 23, 1983, saying:

> In retrospect it is certainly a great tragedy that the recommendations to cut the Ho Chi Minh Trail—yours, Westmoreland's and mine—were not

taken up and acted upon by Washington. My recollection is that Bill Sullivan who was in Laos in June 1967 when I sent in my recommendation took a dim view of the idea.

I did not know then that General Westmoreland wanted to act in southern Laos, but he tells us himself in his book. "I still hoped some day to get approval for a major drive into Laos to cut the Ho Chi Minh Trail."[21] But the troops were unavailable. Where were the troops? Spread out over South Vietnam fighting the invaders who might have been blocked in Laos. How many would he need? "At least a corps-sized force of three divisions which I would be, for a long time, unable to spare from the critical fight in South Vietnam."[22] He never got them. Time and North Vietnam overtook him—and the United States—with the Tet Offensive, as he says in perhaps the saddest line of his book:

"When at last, in 1968, our strength had increased sufficiently. . . . President Johnson was so beset by war critics that he would take no step that might possibly be interpreted as broadening the war."[23]

In short—the opportunity came too late. Hanoi's Tet Offensive was to demonstrate that half a million troops inside South Vietnam could not stop an invasion through Laos. With the American people starting to demonstrate in greater numbers against the indecisive bloodletting, the Harriman-Hilsman tacit agreement—"the facade of Geneva"— still prevented us from taking what few options remained "open."

Book V _____

The Last Chance

19

Intermission at Tet, 1968

"Myself when young did eagerly frequent
Doctor and Saint, and heard great Argument
About it and about, but evermore
Came out by the same Door as in I went."

Edward Fitzgerald,*Rubaiyat of Omar Khayyam,* XXVII

North Vietnam's Tet Offensive changed everything. It also changed nothing. Both statements are correct. Effectively, the United States reversed direction, beginning to descend the incremental string of the strategy which had led it to this pass. There would be fits and starts, backing and filling and even some spectacular escalations in the coming seven-year descent, just as the seven-year long ascent had been marked by occasional pauses and sudden starts. But the eventual destination, from Tet onward, was our withdrawal from Indochina. In this sense, Tet was a watershed which reversed the flow.

In a conceptual sense, however, Tet changed nothing because it did not change our one-string strategy which had only one target—Hanoi's will—and included only two possibilities, linear escalation and linear de-escalation without creating any "sticking places" at which we could stand pat. Indeed, the desire to "keep open the option" of incremental withdrawal without serious damage to our "image" was explicit in our strategy of incrementalism. A strategy which includes both success and failure as mere benchmarks on a linear scale is semantic proof against the necessity of change in the face of failure. In this sense, Tet changed nothing.

What happened during the Tet Offensive has been described and analyzed in great detail, and I do not intend to add anything to that. It is sufficient to say that on January 31, 1968, North Vietnam fell on South Vietnam with suddenness and ferocity matching Hitler's invasion of Poland in 1939 and North Korea's invasion of South Korea in 1950 and with treachery matching that of Japan's attack on Pearl Harbor. Violating the holiday truce to which it had agreed, Hanoi set in motion an attack (prepared since September 1967 according to General Giap who planned it) launched and supplied over the invasion routes through southern Laos.

Thirty-four provincial capitals, sixty-four district capitals and all autonomous cities were attacked. The Communist side lost between 30,000 and 40,000 killed or captured and over 7,000 weapons. Hanoi committed nearly all of the Vietcong (who were decimated in the battle) and about 25% of the North Vietnamese Army forces in South Vietnam. The latter had been increased by 25 infiltrated battalions during the three months from November 1967.[1] South Vietnamese forces suffered some 2,000 deaths and 7,000 wounded. Five of nine South Vietnamese airborne battalions were rendered ineffective and many others were at half strength. Although the southern forces fell back in some disarray at first, they recovered and many units fought well. The Tet Offensive failed to collapse either the South Vietnamese armed forces or the socio-political structure of the country which, in fact, rallied under the blows of the savage, surprise Communist attack. Nevertheless, South Vietnam suffered grievously and was in dire need of great support to repair the damage.

The watershed of Tet, however, was not in South Vietnam but in the United States where the American people—accustomed to winning decisively and quickly and awash in the media's daily wading through deep blood and shallow analysis—had lost their stomach for an inconclusive bloodletting without any clear measure of success. It was this domestic revulsion that forced the Administration to reconsider its course.

The Tet Offensive thus precipitated a conceptual intermission which separated the first and second acts of the U.S. war in Indochina. The intermission lasted through most of President Johnson's last year in office—until the election of November 1968. I do not mean that military action ceased. Intense fighting continued. But 1968 was the year during which our strategic focus shifted from the incremental pursuit of success to the fashioning of a formula whereby we could begin the incremental descent toward withdrawal, while keeping our options open and our "image" bright. With the poet Omar, the United States could say, "I heard great argument . . . but evermore came out by the same door as in I went."

One thing was clear: the South Vietnamese forces needed to be rebuilt and re-armed. This much was accepted. But for the United States forces, there were three principal alternatives:

• The first was to escalate—a massive reinforcement by 206,000 additional forces, coupled with intensification of the bombing campaign. Recommended by the military leadership, this option was eventually rejected, partly because it would only have raised the conflict to a higher but still inconclusive plateau without leading to the negotiated settlement our strategy sought. It was also rejected because it would have required a Reserve call-up.

• The second alternative was to commence a unilateral de-escalation in the search for a conference with Hanoi to negotiate ourselves gracefully out of South Vietnam. This is the course we chose.

• There was a logical space for a third alternative—to abandon a failed strategy and shift our forces so as to block what was certain to be a redoubled effort by North Vietnam to replace its Tet losses. The interesting thing is that this course was not only not adopted—it was only barely mentioned, let alone considered. In short, we reversed course without changing strategy—indeed without even considering the most obvious alternative.

It was not for lack of perception of the nature of the problem that both the military and civilian leaderships apparently failed even to consider blocking North Vietnam's invasion routes on the ground. For example, the Chairman of the Joint Chiefs of Staff, General Wheeler, having been sent to Saigon by the President to survey the situation, returned to report on February 27, 1968, that: "To a large extent, the Vietcong now control the countryside." Additional forces were required, he said:

• to reinforce the South Vietnamese in the "security of the cities, towns and government structure";

• to "assist South Vietnam's forces to leave the towns";

• to meet the enemy in the north and western highlands (that is, behind the narrow Demilitarized Zone in the north and behind the country's long frontiers with Laos and Cambodia in the west).[2]

Coupling all these requirements together, he concluded that "MACV does not have adequate forces at this time to resume the offensive." However, rather than proposing to block the North Vietnamese reinforcement route to meet the problem, he recommended approval of General Westmoreland's request for 206,756 new forces which would have raised the ceiling from 525,000 to 731,756—a sheer linear escalation of forces—a massive injection of new blood into the veins of a failed strategy.

The reader will recognize, in Wheeler's description, the wages of a strategy based on what can be called "micro-security," that is, separating the people from the enemy on a town-by-town, district-by-district, hamlet-by-hamlet basis rather than separating the nation as a whole from the North Vietnamese invasion along a relatively much shorter line blocking the invasion through southern Laos. That it was part of Hanoi's strategy to force us into this posture emerged from a CIA estimate of February 29. The agency estimated that North Vietnam "will probably calculate that the U.S. [and Saigon] will be forced to defend the towns and the countryside will be left more vulnerable to Communist domination. . . . The total result of their campaign they hope, will be to so strain the resources of the U.S. [and South Vietnam] that the Saigon Government will lose control of much of the country and the U.S. will have little choice but to settle the war on Communist terms."[3]

In another appraisal, dated March 1, the CIA addressed the question of Hanoi's probable reaction to an increase of U.S. forces by 50,000, by 100,000 or by 200,000 over the next ten months. The Agency's conclusion: "We would expect the Communists to continue the war. . . . Over a ten-month period the Communists would probably be able *to introduce sufficient new units into the South* to offset the U.S. maneuver battalion increments of the various force levels given above."[4] (Emphasis added.)

That North Vietnam could do this had been foreseen in December 1965 by Robert McNamara who estimated that even with the then recommended new deployments of U.S. forces, we would "be faced in early 1967 with a military standoff at a much higher level" (see chapter 18). That the North could do so had just been dramatically demonstrated by Hanoi's heavy reinforcement (25 new battalions in three months) in preparation for the Tet Offensive. The Office of Systems Analysis in the Department of Defense made no bones about it. It was pointed out that although it had been our objective since 1965 "to make it as difficult and costly as possible for North Vietnam to continue effective support of the Vietcong and [to] cause North Vietnam to cease its direction of the Vietcong insurgency" we had failed. Said one report:

> While we have raised the price to North Vietnam of aggression . . . it shows no lack of capability or will to match each new U.S. escalation. . . . Our strategy of attrition has not worked.
> . . . The Tet Offensive demonstrated not only that *the U.S. had not provided an effective shield*, it also demonstrated that [South Vietnam] had not made real progress in pacification. . . .

We know that despite a massive influx of 500,000 U.S. troops, 1.2 million tons of bombs a year, 400,000 attack sorties per year, 200,000 enemy killed in three years and 20,000 U.S. killed, etc., our control of the countryside and the defense of the urban areas is now essentially at pre-August 1965 levels. We have achieved stalemate at a high commitment. A new strategy must be sought. (Emphasis added.)[5]

But no one apparently proposed any really new strategy. Least of all did anyone propose creating an effective shield against the continuing slow invasion that had made the Tet Offensive possible. A working group was created to manage the preparation of a report and recommendation to be presented to the President by the new Secretary of Defense, Clark Clifford. The underlying theme of the working papers submitted was a fine-tuning of the mix of military and political elements along the incremental scale. Like countless analyses and appraisals of the preceding years, the papers prepared at this time consisted of lists of options from which any one could be eclectically chosen to fit whatever the circumstances might suggest.

General Maxwell Taylor, by now a special consultant to the President, made a lengthy review and was able to produce only three choices—or "packages" as he called them. When unwrapped, the packages were found to contain first, 206,000 new forces for General Westmoreland, second, no new forces and third, some number (to be determined) between 206,000 and 0.[6] True, he did indicate that new strategic guidance might be given to Westmoreland with any of the three packages but he did not indicate what it might be. His basic premise was that no consideration was being given "at the moment to adding to or subtracting from our present objective," thus narrowing the scope of the problem to a mechanical calculation of how much more or how much less should be provided.

Assistant Secretary of State, William Bundy, advanced a "checklist" of alternative courses "that need preparation":

(a) Give the military the requested 206,000 extra forces;
(b) Limit our protection to main populated areas; [This idea reappears in a Department of Defense paper described later]
(c) Combine (b) with intensified bombing of the North;
(d) Give the military only enough new forces to meet their requirements for the next four months;
(e) Cut back all the military increases and continue on the existing strategy;
(f) "All-out option. Announce that we are prepared to hold in Vietnam no matter what developed."[7] [Unrelated to particular military steps, this seemed like a "straw-man."]

The Systems Analysis (Defense) paper mentioned earlier, which proclaimed that "a new strategy must be sought," flirted briefly with the idea of some new strategy but, by giving it a vague and ominous name, made it dismissable without discussion. Systems Analysis saw four alternatives, dismissed the first three with dispatch and favored the fourth—as follows:[8]

> 1. Give the military what they ask and change nothing else. [This, the memo rightly said, is only "another payment on an open-ended commitment. . . ."]
> 2. "Widen the war." [Without specifying what this meant, the paper discarded it as risking war with China and the U.S.S.R.]

In the course of rejecting this option, the memorandum presented a revealing comment: "The course of events already set in motion could lead to adoption of this alternative; increasing U.S. forces in South Vietnam would undoubtedly increase the possibilities of it." That is to say that increased forces would inexorably lead to an unintended expansion of the war, just as Secretary McNamara assumed (wrongly) in 1966 that the temporary loan of a squadron of helicopters to Thailand for a limited purpose would in some automatic, uncontrollable way, lead to an expansion of the U.S. role in the guerrilla war in that country (see chapter 16). In truth however, nothing leads more inexorably to unintended expansion than incremental deployments without any specific delimited and achievable military objective, but only as incremental pressures on the will of a determined enemy.

The Systems Analysis paper continues:

> 3. "Opt out of the war." [Dismissed automatically.]
> 4. Rebuild the South Vietnamese forces, "put a ceiling on U.S. forces, and prepare the world for gradually turning the war over to South Vietnam." [This course was analyzed more fully and it clearly was the preferred one.]

Thus, by ruling out escalation and withdrawal as well as some nameless other thing which might "widen the war," Systems Analysis was left with nothing but downward incrementalism.

The Office of International Security Affairs in the Department of Defense revealed most starkly the disjunction between diagnosis and prescription.[9] Its diagnosis was brilliant. Assuming the deployment of the requested new U.S. forces, ISA concluded that Hanoi could and would increase its own deployments to the South sufficiently to maintain a constant ratio of one North Vietnamese maneuver battalion to every 1.5 U.S. battalions. Projecting known combat statistics, ISA calculated that North Vietnam could continue to replace its monthly losses—mainly over the infiltration system (13,000–16,000), leaving only a relatively small requirement (4,000) for local recruitment. Having thus diagnosed the main problem as a continuing infiltrated invasion, ISA went on to suggest withdrawal of our forces to something called the "demographic frontier," that is, the heavily populated eastern coast and southern plains. Our forces would be available for spoiling raids into the "no-man's land." "Base areas and lines of communication *within South Vietnam* would be the subject of attack and disruption, *without extending the war to neighboring countries.*"[10] (Emphasis added.)

This strategy amounted to yielding a third of South Vietnam in order to withdraw the war to the point at which we could fight entirely inside South Vietnam without the temptation to carry it outside to the invasion coming through Laos—or Cambodia. Thus would Averell Harriman's recommendation to President Kennedy in October 1961 have been implemented! Despite the superficial appearance of a territorial strategy with shorter lines, there still would be no "sticking place" at which we could stand pat—no front line to separate the U.S. from our real enemy. The war would remain a militarily inconclusive test of political endurance. Another incremental step, but this time for an incremental withdrawal.

This vice of undefined "incrementalism" was not confined to Washington. To support the military case, General Wheeler asked General Westmoreland to list "specific goals" which would be achieved with the additional troops requested. The reply was a long litany of unmeasured and unmeasurable assertions of anticipated improved performance—"to reduce this," "to increase that," "to further one" and "to exploit the other." He concluded that, with the requested forces "it will be possible to deal with the invader from the north, and to face with a greater degree of confidence the potential tank, rocket and tactical air threat as well as the ever present possibility that he may reinforce with additional elements of his home army."[11] In short, we would be *tactically* better equipped to meet expected escalation from Hanoi. At the level of *strategy* however, Westmoreland did not seize the occasion to urge his long-postponed plans to deploy a "blocking force" because, as is related in Chapter 18, he knew that by this time, President Johnson "would take no step that might possibly be interpreted as broadening the war."

The final recommendation to President Johnson from the new Secretary of Defense, Clark Clifford, was a model of incrementalism. It included 22,000 new forces for General Westmoreland. It recommended a provisional Reserve call-up to put us in position to meet the remainder of the military request depending on further "week-by-week re-examination . . . as the situation develops." As usual, it called for improved performance by the South Vietnamese forces.[12]

Was there no recommendation addressed to the problem of the continuing invasion which the President's advisors had unanimously recognized, one that addressed the threat to South Vietnam coming through Laos? Perhaps, but to discern it required tracing the magnetic pattern imposed on the facts by the underlying Harriman-Hilsman "tacit agreement—the facade of Geneva." Clark Clifford's memorandum to the President called for a "re-statement of our terms for peace and certain limited diplomatic actions to dramatize Laos and to focus attention on the total threat to Southeast Asia."[13]

In a separate, annexed memorandum, the Department of State elaborated on this. The re-statement of our position, said the Department, should

> "include substantial emphasis on restoration of the Laos Accords of 1962 and on the preservation of the neutrality and territorial integrity of Cambodia under the 1954 accords. . . .
>
> There are strong diplomatic steps that could be taken to dramatize the situation in Laos. We could encourage (Premier) Souvanna to take the case to the UN where Laos and Souvanna have strong appeal. Concurrently, but we believe less effective in practice, Souvanna could press the British and Soviets to take action or even to reconvene the Geneva Conference of 1962.[14]

One hardly knows what to make of this. Did the authors of the memorandum really believe that "dramatizing the situation in Laos" by diplomatic means would actually "restore the Accords of 1962?" Obviously, they could expect no such thing. Why should Hanoi, at this time, restore the effectiveness of the 1962 Accords? Great effort and many lives had been expended by North Vietnam to develop the invasion routes through southern Laos and the sanctuaries in eastern Cambodia. The Tet Offensive had been launched by forces which had invaded South Vietnam by these routes. North Vietnam had kept its part of the "tacit agreement." It had not taken over free Laos in the northwest. How could we expect Hanoi to give up its *quid pro quo* just as it was proving its effectiveness in determining the outcome in South Vietnam? We could not.

Did the authors of the recommendation to the President not know this? Of course they did, as demonstrated during the Paris talks in October when we deliberately did not try to extract from Hanoi any commitment to restrain infiltration because we knew it was unenforceable. (See below) But, by mentioning the subject of Laos in a diplomatic context, they managed to touch the main point without actually tackling it—as if the war were a game of "touch" football rather than "tackle." The Harriman-Hilsman "tacit agreement" stood intact—unbowed by the blows of the Tet Offensive—the only part of the Geneva rubble that still stood.

As the editors of *The Pentagon Papers* commented, the final memorandum given to the President on March 4 recommended, "a little bit more of the same."[15] But the President's advisors reckoned without Lyndon Johnson. After mulling it over for three weeks, he agreed to the usual incremental deployment—raising from 22,000 to 24,500 the additional forces—and then, on March 31, proceeded unilaterally to limit U.S. airstrikes in North Vietnam to the area immediately above the Demilitarized Zone, to call for negotiations in which Hanoi "would not take advantage of the reduced bombing" and, most important of all, to withdraw his candidacy from the 1968 presidential campaign. By so doing, the President closed his personal "options" and, in the process, created only another temporary "notch" along the slope of our linear strategy.

It was not a true "sticking place" which, in war, is a position held on the ground at which one side (and perhaps both) can stand pat indefinitely against military pressure and political erosion, one like the 38th parallel Demilitarized Zone in Korea. Such a territorial "sticking place" is what our sliding scale strategy had been unable to supply in Indochina. President Johnson's maneuver carved out only a temporary political notch, limited—at the maximum—to the duration of his term of office, January 1969.

At the time, in Bangkok, I thought of it as a "ledge"—a level notch carved out of a high, steep mountain face which we had climbed over the preceding seven years. Having reached a point at which we wanted to go no further, but from which we could not suddenly descend, the President expended his political life to hack out a ledge on which we could stand and reconnoiter. As it seemed to me in a lengthy soliloquy begun in the summer of 1968, entitled "Ends and Means in Southeast Asia"

> March 31, 1968 may or may not have been one of the great watersheds of history. Only Time will tell. History reads the significance of today's challenges in the light of tomorrow's response.
>
> From March 31 we were poised precariously for a brief historical moment on ground purchased by President Johnson in return for the restriction on bombing at the 20th parallel and, far more important, at the price of his own political career. This space on which we were poised could be called "LBJ's ledge." We could not know whether this ledge was already over

the watershed into an historic national retirement from greatness or whether our occupation of it was only a tactical withdrawal preparatory to seizing better ground.

I realize that this—like the opening paragraph of the November 1964 proposal to block the invasion (see chapter 14), will strike some as apocalyptic. It is my belief that apocalypse is always latent in international and ideological competition and it should be a part of our calculation. Reduction to incremental bits does not dissolve the whole but only obscures it. Apart from that, even though historical judgments are forever subject to change two things seem clear. First, as I shall attempt to show, we did not successfully use LBJ's ledge to seize better ground. Second, the years since 1968 have manifested significant symptoms of American retirement, from which there are some recent signs of incipient recovery.

My 1968 analysis continued:

In either case, LBJ's ledge was narrow and short, limited by the remainder of his term of office. There was, of course, pressure to follow up the bombing restriction with a complete cessation. This would mean leaving the narrow ledge purchased by the President and seemed unlikely because of the intransigence of Hanoi which prevented the "talks" in Paris from becoming negotiations. Circumscribed by the President's term and by Hanoi's rigidity, LBJ's ledge provided us with a brief pause at a high pass, above the dust of battle, from which we could briefly scan the horizon to see where we were and how we got there.

By January, 1969, we would come to the end of LBJ's ledge and we would then have either to leap to better ground or withdraw further. There would be increasing pressure to move from the bombing restriction to a further de-escalation, unilateral if necessary. Any new Administration would have to move rapidly and vigorously in some direction if it would capture the initiative rather than be compelled to react to forces beyond its own control.

During the summer of 1968, many sequences of gradual phase-down or pull-back were proposed but all dissolved rather intangibly when they got down to the point of defining just what kind of situation would result in the end and how it would be reached. De-escalation became its own reward. The object was not to get to a particular end but simply to start moving down the course.

The hawkish proposals showed an equal lack of foresight. The logic of escalation, as it developed, had long been afflicted with the same sophistry. At every step, the question arose as to how effective new measures would be in either reducing the aggression or forcing Hanoi to withdraw or to negotiate. The answer was usually vague, saying that the new measure would "intensify the pressure," or "increase the cost," or "hurt the enemy," or "bring the war home" or "get the message to Hanoi." But why would the new measure be decisive? Such questions were turned aside by countering that, "No single measure is decisive—it is only persistent application of the total combination that will be decisive." No one explained why the addition of the most recent new measure would make the combination effective where it had not been so before.

What President Johnson did on March 31, 1968, was to seize control of both the escalator and de-escalator levers on our strategy and hold them in balance. He could do so only for the remainder of his term of office, because it was short. But when his term would end (if not before) the situation would change because our strategy *per se*, lacked an internal logic capable of controlling either escalation *or* de-escalation. Indeed, it fed both.

What was this gap between ends and means? To recapitulate, its origin was the gap between two different conceptions of the problem—an internal war to be dealt with inside South Vietnam—as Harriman represented it to Kennedy in October 1961—or an aggression to be stopped before it entered South Vietnam. The two conceptions were linked in North Vietnam's strategy which used guerrilla tactics in South Vietnam to simulate an internal insurgency, to mask the essential aggression and to diffuse the response of the defenders. This contrived ambiguity was the conceptual core of Hanoi's so-called "war of liberation."

But Hanoi's contrived ambiguity was matched by a kind of reflexive ambiguity on our part. Ambiguity flourished in the mottled shadows of the "facade of Geneva," including a Laos coalition which did not exist, under a neutralization which was fictitious, and a *de facto* partition through which the North Vietnamese aggressors entered Laos in the north and moved under the arboreal canopy of the jungle, emerging in South Vietnam as revolutionaries under the banner of the National Liberation Front! This phenomenon will some day be recognized as one of the most sophisticated political structures of our time—a structure which processed an advancing army as it passed from home base through an intervening "neutral" country to emerge in the victim's territory in the role of an internal insurrection. Our vulnerability to it was particularly complicated by the fact that it was partly of our own design and was tacitly ratified by the Harriman-Hilsman "tacit agreement."

This was the Laos disjunction that *continued* to orient the elements of our strategy long after the "tacit agreement" had become a subconscious "given." It was the origin of our failure in Indochina. Militarily, it was self-defeating. It led directly to the Tet Offensive (and would later lead to Hanoi's 1972 offensive). Politically, by making the war both endless and inconclusive, it corroded the support of our friends and the self-confidence of the American people, and after the Tet Offensive, caused the U.S. to reverse course in the search for a face-saving way out of Indochina. Now, in 1968, as the United States sought negotiations, the Laos disjunction was to appear in another form. As it had emasculated our military effectiveness and corroded our political stamina, it would betray us in negotiations.

The issue was the question of participation in the negotiations. Bilateral U.S.-North Vietnam talks had opened in Paris soon after President Johnson's dramatic speech. Our public representative, of course, was Averell Harriman, who had negotiated the 1962 "facade of Geneva."

The U.S. opening argument was for the withdrawal of all North Vietnamese forces from South Vietnam, to be matched by gradual withdrawal of American forces. Predictably, Hanoi not only refused to withdraw but even refused to acknowledge the presence of its forces in South Vietnam. This position was permitted by the disjunction in our strategy which had never forced North Vietnam into open battle to hold the invasion routes. We knew they were there and so did everyone else. But truth is not self-enforcing in the world of war where the only truth that counts is the truth that is made real on the ground. From the negotiating point of view, Hanoi was right. Because we had not forced a decision on the ground, we could not expect North Vietnam to open negotiations by giving away its principal asset—ambiguity—which we had not taken away from them.

Hanoi, for its part, demanded that the National Liberation Front participate in the South Vietnamese government. Our reply was, of course, that South Vietnam was an independent state whose people had the right to determine their own internal course. If the talks were to deal with internal affairs or with anything more than mutual military withdrawal by North Vietnam and the United States, then the Government of South Vietnam would have to be included.

As the talks to determine who would do the talking ground on through the summer of 1968, the deadlock seemed unresolvable. The shadowy National Liberation Front was only a veil, woven in Hanoi, to deceive the gullible as to the reality of North Vietnamese aggression. To admit the NLF to the negotiating table would mean that it was on a par with the legitimate government of South Vietnam. Conversely, it would reduce the status of the South Vietnamese government to that of the NLF. Since, the NLF was only the glove on Hanoi's hand this would mean, in effect, that North Vietnam had the right to participate in the internal management of South Vietnam's future—precisely what we had fought to prevent.*

Harriman at first opposed the admission of the NLF, but in the second half of October, as the American election approached, there were signs of increasing irritation with the government of South Vietnam's stance. Little appeared in public but, on October 31, President Johnson made a dramatic announcement without the concurrence of South Vietnam. After proclaiming the complete cessation of bombing in North Vietnam, he announced an agreement with Hanoi to proceed to substantive negotiations in Paris. In these negotiations, South Vietnam was "welcome" to participate while Hanoi would include such participation as they desired "on their side." Thus, did it become known that an understanding had been reached with Hanoi regarding admission of the NLF to the conference table.

The President's statement was unilateral because of what we said we hoped were only minor wording differences. Eventually, the government in Saigon publicly acquiesced in the formula we had negotiated with Hanoi, and formal discussions began at a round table. But what was at issue was fundamental and was recognized as such by South Vietnam. There were two reciprocal factors:

- First: Hanoi's refusal to acknowledge responsibility for the war in South Vietnam or to make any statement which might limit its ability to continue the war at will. Having waged war primarily through the "processing chamber" of southern Laos for years without being forced to admit its role and having finally forced the U.S. to negotiate at a disadvantage, Hanoi insisted on maintaining the forensic disjunction between itself and the war in South Vietnam.
- Second: the inability of the United States to compel Hanoi to accept negotiation on the premise of the well-known linkage between North Vietnamese invasion and the "internal war" in the South. Having ourselves accepted the strategic disjunction between the pacification effort in the South and the anti-aggression effort against the North—militarily, as opposed to rhetorically—we were unable now to force forensic acceptance in Paris of what we had not proved on the ground. We could not force negotiations on the basis of the truth that this had been a war of conquest and defense between North and South.

Under these circumstances there could be no agreed set of facts to serve as the premise for negotiations. Serious negotiations—even

---

*During all this preliminary posturing, on August 20th the U.S.S.R. invaded Czechoslovakia and, as everyone knows, eliminated the genuine growing "insurgency" against a crumbling, friendly regime.

between enemies considering only a temporary truce—require a minimum understanding regarding the facts, for example, the presence of each other's forces. But Hanoi denied the presence of its forces while the United States, betrayed by its own carefully maintained strategic disjunction, could not now join what it had for years kept asunder. To compensate for the lack of forensic symmetry, the U.S. delegation—obviously more determined than Hanoi to negotiate—fell back on a unilateral device which might be called "constructive inference." Following this technique, the U.S. delegate would assert the U.S. position together with our assumptions as to Hanoi's position. If the North Vietnamese delegation did not object, the U.S. delegation took silence as tacit agreement. For example, in private talks with Hanoi, the U.S. delegate often repeated the four points that underlay our willingness to negotiate and suspend all bombing. These four points were:

1. There would be no attacks by Hanoi across the Demilitarized Zone.
2. There would be no rocketings of cities.
3. The substantive negotiations would include the Government of South Vietnam while Hanoi could bring whom it chose.
4. The pattern of the negotiations would be a "your side-our side" formula.

Although Hanoi refused to accept these points, the U.S. repeated them several times to ensure that they were understood. My notes, based on official briefings in Bangkok at the time, record that the U.S. side was "confident of our judgment and we have reason to believe that they [the North Vietnamese] will comply." Our delegation's confidence in Hanoi's intentions was bolstered by an October 28 letter from Soviet Premier Kosygin assuring President Johnson that "doubts with regard to the position of the Vietnamese side are groundless,"[16] words that sounded much like Pushkin's assurances in 1961 to Harriman that Hanoi would comply with the Geneva Accords. Less than four months later, Hanoi would launch a brutal assault on the cities of South Vietnam, thereby exposing Kosygin's assurances as just as valueless as were Pushkin's to Harriman.

The shakiness of this understanding was implicit in the fact that the cessation of bombing and the negotiating pattern (both U.S. concessions) were to be made public but Hanoi's presumed willingness to spare the Demilitarized Zone and the cities was—initially—to remain private. Moreover, the subject of infiltration was not negotiated because of the difficulty of ascertaining compliance and proving violation. In any case, it would have been folly to suppose that

Hanoi would admit, let alone stop the steady invasion that continued to sustain its war effort. We did however, use the method of "constructive inference" to protect our right to continue aerial reconnaissance over North Vietnam, as well as to continue and even increase our bombing of the Ho Chi Minh Trails in Laos. We re-stated our promise to suspend bombing of North Vietnam in words which excluded reconnaissance. Since this re-statement was made "without challenge" it was presumed to be accepted.

We assured Saigon that we would support it in maintaining the "your side-our side" formula. But at the last minute, President Thieu repeated his demand for assurance that North Vietnam would deal directly with the government of South Vietnam. He was apparently doubtful of our ability to guarantee Hanoi's assurances. What Thieu asked, however, was incompatible with North Vietnam's consistent argument that Saigon must deal with the NLF.

Militarily, the arrangements of October 31 manifested a curious imbalance. Although we stopped all bombing in North Vietnam, the other side continued violations of the Demilitarized Zone and the shelling of southern cities. We did not retaliate by resuming the bombing because Hanoi would more likely respond by suspending negotiations than by suspending the attacks. By this time negotiations were more important to the U.S. than bombing. Unannounced by either side, however, the infiltrations down the Ho Chi Minh trails increased, as did our bombing efforts to stop it.

Politically, October 31 was a reversal of the course we had followed since 1954. The NLF was admitted to equal bargaining status with the Government of South Vietnam. The lengthy argument over the shape of the bargaining table was designed to provide each side with an argument to prove its point. Speaking of this dispute, a high-ranking spokesman remarked that "each side has its mythology"— a rather unbecoming sophistry!* In truth, we were trapped in our

---

*In an interview with *The New York Times Magazine*, August 24, 1969, Harriman afforded sophistical interpretation of what he called "this ridiculous performance of Saigon objecting to the shape of the table. . . . The round table historically has been a method of ending all dispute as to who has seniority; no one knows where the head of a round table is." But the issue was not seniority but recognition of equal legitimacy. The NLF was either a tool of Hanoi or it was an independent political force with as much legitimacy of status as the Government of South Vietnam. If the former, it had no place at the table. If the latter, then Harriman had reversed his position since the May, 1962 Bangkok press conference when he said that "VC guerrillas, controlled and directed from North Vietnam constituted the real heart of the threat to the Republic and not the local recruits or disaffected villagers."

own mythology of the last seven years, according to which there were three distinct wars in Indochina—one in South Vietnam, one in Laos and one of pressure against North Vietnam. Now, we were compelled to follow the same mythological strings to negotiate out of the maze that we followed into it.

Our acceptance of these bargaining terms was not just a de-escalation like the cessation of bombing, or a gesture toward peace like the commencement of talks in April. This was a fundamental strategic shift of direction—the first since the decision to treat Communist inversion of the Laos Accords as a "tacit agreement." After reconnoitering the situation for seven months, poised on LBJ's ledge, we saw the strategic divide and began a descent which led, in part, back down the way we had come.

"Where would it lead?" I asked in the analysis mentioned earlier. It continued:

> Possibly toward another in a long series of unsuccessful experiments with coalitions with Communists who are dedicated to taking them over or destroying them, as they had done in Laos in 1963. A tragedy—if so— a tragedy that after years of struggle we would reverse course and press toward a coalition between Saigon and the National Liberation Front which (if it were the right course) we could have done in 1962 or 1963 or 1964— 30,000 American lives earlier.
>
> Then, why do we not wait for the other side to seek peace on our terms? They cannot win militarily. How long can they stay in the game? There is the nub. They need not win militarily but they can stay indefinitely, maintaining a war at a level that required half a million U.S. troops. But we cannot keep half a million troops in South Vietnam indefinitely fighting an inconclusive war.
>
> How do they maintain a war indefinitely against the most powerful nation on earth? Simply by moving enough people, equipment and supplies through Laos and Cambodia to keep the war going. . . . By maintaining the ambiguity of the war, thus preventing a decisive U.S. counteraction which might define a line which would progressively insulate South Vietnam against seeping aggression—which would define on the ground the outlines of the kind of peace (or armistice) we seek in Paris.
>
> This is why we are headed toward coalition. In a way it has a certain historical logic. The Geneva Accords of 1962 encompassed a coalition which failed, opening the way for the aggression through Laos which brought South Vietnam to its present state. If we are not willing to go back and close the door left open in 1962, we must logically open—or allow to be opened—the next door—into South Vietnam. This is the course toward which we are headed on October 31, 1968.
>
> But perhaps it is not inevitable. Perhaps we are not irrevocably committed to seek a coalition with the Communists in South Vietnam. Possibly, we

have not even made a decision to do so—even though that is the logical consequence of the admission of the NLF to negotiations on a plane with the Government of South Vietnam. Indeed, it is quite probable that no such decision was ever made by the Johnson Administration. In the history of U.S. foreign policy there is an extraordinary element which we might call the "kernel of indeterminacy" which defies long-range strategic logic— as the Germans, Russians and North Koreans all know. If the decision of October 31 reversed the course of a whole decade, then another equally sudden decision can yet strike a new course. On October 31, we set course downward from LBJ's ledge, but in the time frame of war and world politics there will be occasions for new decisions. Obviously, a new period begins with the commencement of new talks under the leadership of the new Administration.

Is it too late to close the door left open in 1962—to leap to 'better ground'? As far as it concerns the objective situation in East Asia—NO. But what about the objective situation in the United States? From this point of view, it may be too late. . . . The Administration must take into account how far the bitter gap between promise and fulfillment over the last six years has undermined the belief of the American people in their own purpose and destiny. Once this balance is rendered up we must choose and, in such a choice, clearly the reconstitution of American unity of purpose and destiny must be the final desideratum.

20

Laos in 1969: Right Place, Right Time

"When the iron is hot, strike."

John Heywood, *Proverbs*.

Theoretically, the prospect of blocking North Vietnam's invasion through Laos had been foreclosed in early 1963 by U.S. acceptance of Hanoi's inversion of the Geneva Accords as a "tacit agreement" under which we could harass infiltration but could not deprive North Vietnam, on the ground, of its control over and use of the invasion route through southern Laos. From 1963 until 1968 the force and logic of events cried out for us to change course as the invasion mounted to the pitch of the Tet Offensive. In time, I thought then, we would change course. I was wrong.

In the past, the United States had not hesitated to change a losing strategy that has been overtaken by events. For example, theoretically the prospect of blocking a North Korean invasion of South Korea had been excluded by Secretary Acheson's January 1950 speech which put South Korea beyond our perimeter of strategic interest. Yet, confronted with North Korea's invasion six months later, the U.S. reversed this outdated position and sent an army to block the invasion. If we could change strategy to accord with changed reality in Korea, could we not do the same thing in Indochina? The principal difference between the two cases was tactical, not strategic—a question of whether the invaders enter all at once, openly or incrementally and clandestinely. Thus had Secretary Rusk argued plaintively before the House Foreign Affairs Committee on July 28, 1965 that "The assault on the Republic of Vietnam is beyond question an aggression. . . . Had all those [military personnel] crossed the line at once as the North Koreans did . . . nobody in the Free World could have doubted that the assault on Vietnam was an aggression" (see chapter 4).

But clear as this reality may have seemed, we did not change our position to accord with it. The Tet offensive of 1968 finally drained the U.S. Administration of the domestic support that would have been needed to make such a change—had the necessity to do so been recognized. Nine months after the Tet offensive began, President Johnson's October 31 announcement tacitly accepted Hanoi's tool— the National Liberation Front—as a separate participant in the Paris talks. Thus, in a little more than five years, our tacit agreement to Hanoi's use of Laos to invade South Vietnam had led to our tacit acceptance of North Vietnam's right to participate in arranging the internal political disposition of South Vietnam. Put another way, having in 1963 granted Hanoi the means to achieve its end, we were led, inexorably, in 1968, to grant the legitimacy (though not yet the realization) of the end itself. Far from having let our own ends determine our means, in fact, the means we chose led to Hanoi's attainment of *its* end. It was all quite logical—as the North Vietnamese representatives at the Paris talks soon began to insist as they demanded the removal of the Saigon government.

But for the United States, policy does not always proceed in logical progression. Any new administration—Democrat or Republican, but especially the latter—would have a brief period of flexibility during which it could alter course, within limits. And there certainly were limits in this case—the principal one being that any course chosen must lead openly and fairly directly to U.S. disengagement from Vietnam. Moreover, given our political and psychological exhaustion in 1969, the new administration would have to choose quickly and decisively. It would not have the luxury of open-ended incremental decision-making while "keeping its options open." The options we had tried to keep open over the preceding six years had suddenly been dramatically narrowed by events over which we had lost control. The new administration would have to make a large choice among a very few alternatives, all of which had to lead to American military disengagement.

The alternatives were few but, most importantly, the new administration would not be inexorably committed to follow in lock-step the course bequeathed it—picking its way by "tacit agreements," through the rubble of the inverted Geneva Agreements. Standing on the fast-crumbling ledge carved out by President Johnson, the new administration could embark on a daring escalatory gamble (highly unlikely), or it could begin slow de-escalation while negotiating toward some "satisfactory" political settlement (unpromising, given

Hanoi's arrogant rigidity), or it could embark on a dramatic military build-up of South Vietnam while gradually withdrawing behind a vigorous rearguard attack on Hanoi and "hanging tough" in Paris (the course actually chosen) or some variation on these.

President Nixon was aware of the necessity to shift from our syndrome of inconclusive incrementalism to a strategy of decisive choice between real alternatives. Late in the summer of 1966, he stopped in CINCPAC Headquarters following a visit to Saigon as part of a private world-wide trip. I had left Honolulu for Bangkok by that time, but Deputy Political Adviser Charles Flowerree was still there, and he has written to me a revealing recollection of Mr. Nixon's keen sense of the pressure of time on the President to decide.

> After being briefed at the Headquarters, Mr. Nixon asked to offer a few personal observations on some wider aspects of the war. Admiral Sharp was naturally pleased to give him the floor.
>
> At the outset, Mr. Nixon said he had been reflecting on what he would do were he in President Johnson's position at that moment. Whether or not Mr. Johnson wanted to seek another term in 1968, he would want to keep the office for the Democrats and this objective would be impossible to realize if the war was still dragging on at election time. The American people, Mr. Nixon thought, would not tolerate a long, inconclusive war; if Vietnam were not behind us two years hence, Mr. Johnson would be finished politically.
>
> Mr. Nixon went on to say that if he were in President Johnson's position, he would make ending the war before the '68 election his Number One priority. There were only two basic ways this could be accomplished:
> * seek the most honorable conditions possible for U.S. withdrawal, or
> * take the war directly to the North Vietnamese with the objective of bringing their country to its knees.
>
> Both courses of action would merit consideration, although it would surprise no one to learn that if he were president, he would incline toward the second. . . . As for direct action against the North, my recollection is that . . . the point he wanted to make was that he would not have ruled out any conventional type of military course that would contribute to bringing about Hanoi's capitulation.
>
> Mr. Nixon went on to say that this course of action would bring down a worldwide storm of protest on the president's head, but if the result was a quick termination of the war, the protests would just as quickly fade away. The important thing from President Johnson's point of view was for the United States to have found a solution to its Vietnam dilemma by the time the 1968 campaign began. [1]

Yes a new administration could consider taking "the war directly to the North Vietnamese" by blocking the invasion, then "stand pat" as we did in Korea until a demarcated, armed, territorial cease-fire line could be first established and then negotiated. By a quirk of circumstance, President Nixon gave me an opportunity to argue once more the case for such a course. My effort—which failed again—will be described in the latter part of this chapter. Although this concept was halfway implicit in two major initiatives undertaken by the Nixon Administration in Cambodia in 1970 and in Laos in 1971, in war, half-right can be all wrong. For lack of a unified, conceptual decision these two initiatives did not achieve a "leap to better ground."

Over a period of eight years any established policy and bureaucratic habit acquires tremendous inertia that is not easy to deflect. When the new administration pressed the military for new ideas, "all they could think of was resuming the bombing of the North," recalls Henry Kissinger.[2] He goes on to recall how at an NSC meeting on January 25, 1969, Chairman of the JCS, General Wheeler, assured the President that "everything possible was being done in Vietnam except 'the bombing of the North.' "[3] As Kissinger says, the Chairman "was only following inherited doctrine"—a doctrine which had been confirmed only a few weeks earlier by both Averell Harriman and Secretary of Defense Clifford.*

On February 22, Hanoi launched a violent offensive, dubbed "mini-Tet," of several weeks duration during which Saigon was rocketed and 32 attacks were made against major South Vietnamese cities in the first two weeks of March alone. These attacks, of course, were in brazen violation of our understanding (which Harriman had inferred in October from the North Vietnamese representatives' silence) that in return for the cessation of bombing there would be no such attacks. Nevertheless, rather than react precipitously, the Nixon Administration withheld any kind of retaliation for nearly a month while considering various possibilities. The JCS proposal to resume attacks against North Vietnam was not adopted (although justifiable in terms of our "understanding" with Hanoi). Instead, consideration was being given to striking some of North Vietnam's "base areas" along the Cambodian border from which the attacks were being launched and supported.

---

*It struck me as being in singularly poor taste that, on February 10, only three weeks after the new administration had entered into office and after Harriman had left the negotiations at Paris, he began publicly to berate it for not ending the war more quickly. "I think the time is coming when we will no longer have the right to ask American boys to die in Vietnam," he said. "You will hear me say more about it if the Nixon Administration doesn't get on with de-escalating the war." This, after spending some eight months in Paris without getting to serious negotiations while American boys were dying![4]

Although in Bangkok I was not privy to the debates going on in Washington, I agreed with the avoidance of precipitate resumption of bombing North Vietnam. Because bombing had never caused Hanoi to de-escalate, its resumption would only produce a storm of protest which would quickly force us to terminate it, ending up in a weaker bargaining position than we had been in before. "Our difficulty," I wrote to Ambassador Unger on March 8, was that "our negotiating position in Paris does not correspond with our military position in Vietnam. We seek withdrawal of North Vietnam's forces, restoration of the sanctity of the DMZ and observance of South Vietnam's frontiers, but we are not in a military position to force any one of these conditions."

What we needed, I argued, was "to establish a military position corresponding to what we seek in Paris, to the end that we would be able to 'stand pat' both in Paris and in Vietnam until the other side is ready to be reasonable."

To do so would require, I thought, limited but simultaneous ground and air actions with the former designed to establish positions we could hold after the air attacks ceased. Several brigades of U.S. and South Vietnamese forces would be inserted from South Vietnam into southern Laos at points selected by the military as effective for cutting the large movements of Communist forces and supplies into South Vietnam. No attempt would be made to drive across Laos to the Mekong River—at least not immediately. Simultaneously, air attacks against North Vietnam would be resumed. Even granting the justification by Hanoi's provocative offensive, there would be mounting protest against the bombing which would have to be stopped within a few weeks. But, while attention was being focused on the bombing, the ground forces, with close air support, would have—less spectacularly—established positions across some of the infiltration routes. By that time they would have engaged and/or captured enough North Vietnamese forces to bring into the open Hanoi's presence on the ground in gross violation of the Geneva Accords and to justify our presence to combat this illegal aggression.

To answer protests against our presence in Laos, I suggested,

> We would answer that since the North had demonstrated its unwillingness to adhere to the understandings in Paris in October, we had been forced to find other ways to accomplish the same result, that is, to compel North Vietnam to spare southern cities, to protect our own and South Vietnamese forces and to enforce a gradual scaling down of military activity in South Vietnam and to create a proper climate for negotiations. The rocketings of the cities are possible only because of North Vietnam's continuing use of the Laos Corridor.

What about Premier Prince Souvanna Phouma and his neutral government of truncated western Laos? Souvanna Phouma had become much tougher and wiser through the experience of the preceding six years than he was given credit for. Indeed, it seemed that his alleged sensitivity was sometimes invoked by American officials seeking reasons to avoid some proposed action. I suggested that when asked about the movement into southern Laos, "Souvanna could shrug his shoulders, saying that in the face of North Vietnamese perfidy in northern Laos in violation of the 1962 Accords, he is in no position to defend Hanoi's violations of the Accords in southern Laos." That Souvanna was capable of taking such a tough line was borne out five months later at a press interview with the official Lao daily paper, *Lao Presse*, when Souvanna, asked about North Vietnam's long-term objectives, said that North Vietnam "wants to dominate Laos and to transform it into a new type of colony." Asked about resolving the conflict through the Co-chairmen of the 1962 Geneva Conference (U.K. and U.S.S.R.), he said that "the Soviet Government had refused to cooperate with Great Britain to try to halt North Vietnamese aggression in Laos."[5]

In Bangkok, Ambassador Unger (formerly Ambassador to Laos), did not agree with my argument, but generously passed it along to the most logical recipient for military consideration—Chairman of the Joint Chiefs of Staff General Earle Wheeler, who in early March was with Secretary of Defense Laird on a trip to Southeast Asia. When General Wheeler departed Bangkok I accompanied him to his takeoff from U Tapao air base, near Sattahip, Thailand, on the coast of the Gulf of Siam. The General expressed interest in the memorandum and promised to study it.

As it turned out, the General's departure from U Tapao base proved to be more symptomatic of the future than the fact that he carried my memo in his briefcase. By agreement with Thailand, the United States had built runways and facilities at U Tapao to handle some of the B-52 bombers used against targets in Vietnam and Laos. The Thai retained control of the base, and it was agreed that targets struck from it had to be jointly approved either *ad hoc* or in accordance with agreed-upon categories and procedures. After the targets were selected in Saigon, B-52s were ordered from U Tapao or from Guam or Okinawa (and sometimes from all three) to conduct the strikes that were such excellent examples of precision management, navigation and control.

A week or so later, the Ambassador received a note from the Chairman of the JCS to which General Wheeler had added a handwritten note, saying, "I found Hannah's memo most interesting. I'm exploring it a bit." Unfortunately, I heard no further response to the concept that I had been proposing for so long.

More interestingly, on March 18, the day after the General wrote, B-52s struck North Vietnam's "Base 353" on the Cambodian border of South Vietnam, near the "Fishook" salient northwest of Saigon. This was the first U.S. retaliation—after a month of hesitation—against Hanoi's "mini-Tet" offensive which had begun on February 22. It was also the first of a series of similar strikes which were later characterized as the infamous "secret bombings" of Cambodia and continued until May 1970 when, with the "incursion" into Cambodia, the same strikes began to be made openly. Curiously, it was not the original intent to conduct the strikes in complete secrecy but to leave the publicity up to either Prince Sihanouk of Cambodia or to Hanoi. By not announcing this new air campaign, we sought to avoid *forcing* either the North Vietnamese or Cambodians, the Soviets or the Chinese, into public reactions they might not wish to make. As it turned out, none chose to complain publicly. As for Sihanouk, he had already indicated both privately (on January 10, 1968, to Chester Bowles, visiting Cambodia) and publicly (in a May 13, 1969 press conference) his tacit consent as long as Cambodian lives and property were not damaged.[6] Public announcement by the United States might well have forced him—for reasons of national prestige—to demand cessation, even though he favored the strikes. It is a testimony to the fact that North Vietnam completely controlled these areas, as well as to the skilled precision of the raids, that they continued so long without protest by Cambodia. It is also testimony to Hanoi's awareness of its own gross violation of Cambodia's territory that it did not protest damage to North Vietnamese facilities and personnel.

I learned of the secret bombing a little later—in June, I believe. As I indicated earlier, we followed an understanding with the Thai which prescribed the rules governing B-52 strikes from U Tapao. Targets in Cambodia were excluded. Late in the afternoon preceding a morning strike, Saigon would flash to our Embassy in Bangkok the coordinates for the next day's targets to be struck by planes from U Tapao. After checking the coordinates, the Embassy would flash back either a clearance or questions. One evening, a proposed target was pinpointed as being narrowly but definitely inside Cambodia, not in South Vietnam. When telephone conversation with Saigon failed to clarify the divergence, we disapproved the target. The same thing happened a few days later, precipitating an angry response from Saigon. The next day an Air Force Major General from Saigon was in my office in Bangkok to iron things out. Afterward, he told me the confusion might have resulted from differences between the grid charts used in Saigon and Bangkok and promised to send us new ones. This sounded like an unlikely mistake to be made by the U.S. Air Force. In any case, the new charts never came, but neither did any more proposals of targets in Cambodia. In retrospect, I assume that this incident contributed to the triggering of the new system of keeping two sets of books—one showing real targets and the other showing "cover targets."

I believe that this kind of double bookkeeping is a mistake that tends to poison confidence in the system. But I also believe that it was not entirely unique and reflected the persistence of an eight-year habit of the United States in Indochina—a habit of trying to accomplish things sideways—unnoticed—without doing them directly and thereby becoming committed—a habit of sliding by while "keeping our options open." It was a habit we had practiced since 1961 in the wake of the Bay of Pigs, as we tried to wiggle through Indochina, moving through one part (Laos) with a low profile and through another part (South Vietnam) with a high profile. The habit was continued by splitting the difference between insurgency and invasion, treating the problem incrementally as "something other than war" while waging "secret war" in Laos and finally, by pretending that the inversion—the negation—of the Geneva Accords on Laos was really a "tacit agreement" consistent with saving South Vietnam from invasion.

Although bombing North Vietnamese base areas along the Cambodian border was immediately helpful in defending U.S. and South Vietnamese forces, it could not be anymore decisive than had been the bombing of North Vietnam. The new administration had yet to make a large, substantive choice of long-range direction, either in Paris or in Indochina. In a May 14 speech, President Nixon addressed the subject of negotiations, proposing an 8-point program including cease-fires, international supervision, a specific timetable for withdrawal, free election, etc. It was more concessionary than anything previously proposed by any U.S. administration. But in his proposal, the President reverted to the shabby, self deceptive practice of offering to let Hanoi comply by means of a de facto "informal understanding" instead of by formal agreement.[7] Just as Harriman, in October 1968 had accepted Hanoi's silence as a tacit undertaking not to shell southern cities, so Nixon and Kissinger, in May 1969, proposed an "informal understanding" rather than open confirmed performance as the criterion for the withdrawal of North Vietnamese forces. The necessity to engage in this self-deception grew out of the fact that our military position in Indochina did not give us the capability to enforce any of the things we demanded in Paris. Hence, Paris was not the place for a long-range change of strategic direction.

What Nixon did effect in Vietnam was a gradual withdrawal of American forces, a course which, when linked with an intensive build-up of South Vietnamese forces, became known as "Vietnamization." In March the President had keyed future withdrawals to three criteria—South Vietnam's capability for self-defense, progress in the Paris negotiations and the level of enemy activity. While some such program was essential to enable the U.S. to define the terms of its own course, it became increasingly hard to enforce all these criteria. "Gradual withdrawal," really the old "incrementalism" in reverse, soon acquired its own momentum. As Kennedy had likened U.S. deployments to a first drink of liquor which would lead to another and another, so did Kissinger liken U.S. withdrawals to a mouthful of salted peanuts which would lead to another and another.[8] Nevertheless, because of years of "measured reactions" to enemy initiatives, the new U.S. Administration finally had to show that it could take a long-range initiative of its own.

After a meeting on Midway Island with President Thieu, Nixon announced on June 8, the first withdrawal of 25,000 troops. The day before, in Honolulu, the President had explained his plans to the U.S. military leadership who, as Henry Kissinger reports, accepted them "with heavy heart." Commenting on the military's loyalty, Kissinger goes on rightly to observe that "contrary to the mythology" the military rarely oppose their Commander in Chief.[9] The same characteristic was evident in the early days of the war when the military fell in quickly with the "given" premise of the civilian leadership that blocking the invasion on the ground was automatically excluded by our "tacit agreement" to Hanoi's inversion of the Geneva Accords.

I remember receiving a "Flash" cable one Sunday morning in Bangkok, instructing me (as Charge d'Affaires, the Ambassador being out of the country) to inform the Prime Minister of Thailand—our ally in South Vietnam—of the imminent announcement of the first 25,000 withdrawal. The cable was laconic, giving no explanation or indication of what troops would be withdrawn or what would happen next. The Prime Minister received me at his private residence together with Marshal Dawee Chulasap, the Chief of the Supreme Command. To ease the Prime Minister's consternation, I suggested that the forces to be withdrawn might be non-combat personnel. Marshal Dawee picked this up and jovially remarked that 25,000 cooks and commissary personnel could probably be withdrawn without affecting the military equation. As a matter of fact, we were both whistling in the dark; the U.S. would exit Vietnam as it had entered—incrementally. The fact was that gradual withdrawal, like other forms of "incrementalism," led nowhere but to the end of its own internal logic. Something else was needed to give us a military position we could hold long enough to convert it into a satisfactory negotiated settlement.

Fortunately, the President was scheduled to visit Bangkok late in July as part of a swing around Southeast Asia. I say "fortunately" because the year-long sequence of the Tet Offensive, the opening of talks in Paris, the cessation of bombing North Vietnam, the admission of the NLF to the talks and now, the commencement of U.S. withdrawals, had had an unsettling effect on our allies, particularly Thailand with its 1500 mile border with Laos and Cambodia. In Guam, on July 25, en route to Asia, the President enunciated what later became known as the Nixon Doctrine. As clarified later, the doctrine prescribed that:

- The U.S. would adhere to its treaty commitments. [Important to Thailand.]

- The U.S. would provide a nuclear shield. [Important but already generally assumed.]

- In case of "other types of aggression," the U.S. would offer assistance if requested but would look to the nation threatened to assume the primary responsibility of providing manpower for its defense.[10]

While this "doctrine" was intended to be a scaling back of future interventions, consistent with the national mood and with our expected withdrawal from Vietnam, it was sufficiently delphic to leave open the possibility of future direct U.S. military action if there were to occur another case of aggression masquerading as an insurgency. What the doctrine did *not* indicate was how any settlement of the Indochina war might be enforced after the completion of the U.S. military withdrawal. Something was needed to fill the gap—to cement a settlement when reached—something to prevent the settlement from washing immediately to pieces as did the Geneva Accords on Laos in 1962. I, of course, believed that this "something" should be an armed, demarcated and negotiated territorial cease fire line similar to the one in Korea. Although such a line had been excluded as a real possibility during the Kennedy-Johnson Administrations, what the Nixon Administration would do was still unclear.

In Bangkok, I attended the President's lengthy briefing of U.S. Far Eastern Ambassadors. It was a fascinating *tour d'horizon* covering many major foreign policy issues. About the future of Vietnam, Nixon said only that any satisfactory settlement must leave behind a government which would be able to stand for at least five years. It would be impossible to plan further, he stated, and he did not address the possibility of renewed North Vietnamese aggression. As we know now, in 1972 the President promised President Thieu a U.S. intervention by air in the event of a new attack by Hanoi—an assurance he was unable to implement in the wake of Watergate and the reneging of Congress on any further responsibility for Indochina.

Nevertheless, I believed the President recognized the problem. In April 1967, when he had visited Bangkok as a private citizen with Raymond Price (later a Nixon aide in the White House), I spent most of two days with him, at dinner in my house, visiting the King at his vacation palace, accompanying him to dinner with the Prime Minister and a number of other military and political leaders. Mr. Nixon was serious, asked good questions and above all was a good listener.

Most interesting to me during the 1967 encounter was a short discussion of Laos which took place in my office. He seemed to agree that Laos was the key to the Vietnam problem since it was through Laos that the North attacked the South. When I said that the aggression could be ended only by cutting it off in Laos he agreed but wondered about the political impact of that on the United States. I acknowledged that the rising domestic American opposition to the war as it was then being waged might have overtaken the practical possibility of dealing effectively with Laos. I remember wondering aloud whether "it might already be too late." He nodded—I thought— in shared concern.

This exchange came back to me on the last night of the President's state visit in 1969. It was a fairly large buffet dinner at the Prime Minister's residence. Marshal Dawee tapped me on the shoulder, saying that the President wanted me to join him with a group of Thai leaders to whom he was talking. "We have been talking of Laos," the President said. "I know you have some strong views on that subject. I'd like you to write them down along with your recommendations." I assented and said I would talk with the Ambassador about preparing a report. "I mean your *personal* views," he interjected, "and the Ambassador's." Forthwith, he spoke to Ambassador Unger.

Now for a brief personal digression. I strongly believe in discipline in the Foreign Service. The job of a Deputy Chief is to support the Ambassador, not to substitute his judgment for his chief's. It is the Deputy's responsibility to give the Ambassador his own best advice but in the end to accept and execute the decision of the Ambassador who is the President's personal representative abroad. Since, in this

270 THE KEY TO FAILURE

case, it was the President himself who had taken the initiative, I telephoned the Ambassador after the banquet to explain the circumstances. He understood. We had worked together in Bangkok for nearly two years and had got along well. We disagreed on one major point—the role of Laos in the Vietnam war and what to do about it.

One who has read this far might well ask why, having so consistently differed from the official strategy, I had not sought a transfer to another area more congenial to my views. In the first place, as I have said elsewhere, I didn't do it because I was "hooked." Like the midnight reader of a gripping mystery, I could not put Indochina down. I craved to know the end, and not only the end—that would become plain—but to know how we would get to the end. Second (and this can be judged better by my colleagues) I thought I could continue to play a useful role in the achievement of American ends even though I doubted the efficacy of the means chosen. Because I wanted the United States to succeed in preserving South Vietnam's independence and self-determination, I was willing to contribute whatever I could to that end—meanwhile hoping that we might improve our means.

Ambassador Unger had had his own experience as Ambassador to Laos during the first three years after the signing of the Geneva Accords of 1962, and as Deputy Assistant Secretary for East Asian Affairs before coming to Bangkok in 1967 as Ambassador. I should add that before his tour in Laos he had held my current position as Deputy Chief of Mission under the then Ambassador to Thailand, U. Alexis Johnson,[11] later successively Deputy Under-Secretary for Political Affairs and Deputy Ambassador to South Vietnam with Ambassador Maxwell Taylor. We had disagreed, as I have said, but this fact had not hampered our ability to work together to execute the policy of the United States—which is what we were both committed to do.

Ambassador Unger was generous in according a full hearing to divergent views. In this case, after a discussion with Mr. Kissinger, the Ambassador suggested that each of us separately draft a memorandum of his views. The next morning, as President Nixon walked across the tarmac to Air Force One, he paused momentarily to shake hands with me and to murmur—out of the hearing of the Indian Ambassador, the Dean of the Diplomatic Corps, "Don't forget. I want that report by the time I return to Washington." That meant in three days—by August 3.

It was done. Predictably, our views differed on the role of Laos— as they always had. I will not put words into the Ambassador's mouth today. The burden of his argument consisted of a lucid (as always) discussion of the problems and possibilities of action within a framework bounded on one side by abandonment of Laos and on the other by U.S. military intervention in Laos—both of which he (and most others) rejected. Given these limits, there was little with which I could disagree. It was the imposition of the limits in the form of "given" premises that I had disagreed with for several years, believing that they foreclosed serious examination of the real fundamental problem, thereby leading to a disastrous conclusion.

The first "given premise"—stated frankly and openly, not covertly insinuated—was the assumption that the United States did not intend to end North Vietnamese control of the Ho Chi Minh Trail, that this threat to South Vietnam would continue and that the United States would not intervene openly in Laos.

To me, this assumed away the issue as a "given" premise, thus making it unnecessary even to address it. It can be argued that history proves the accuracy of the premise but this leaves unanswered the question of what might have been the result if we had faced the issue directly instead of assuming it away. In any case, a history that ends in failure can hardly be adduced in support of one of the premises on which the failure was based.

Closely related was a second premise—that intervention by American ground forces to protect "free Laos" had been often rejected by the U.S. military and would not be supported by the American people. This, I thought, by-passed the question of U.S. intervention in Laos for another purpose, namely, *to preserve South Vietnam's independence* on which ultimately, the freedom of Laos depended. That the U.S. military, consistent with the Harriman-Hilsman "tacit agreement," had rejected intervention to save Laos alone was true but that didn't address the question of intervention to save South Vietnam. Moreover, this formulation also by-passed the question of whether it would be possible to preserve South Vietnam's independence while the Ho Chi Minh Trail remained open. It may have been true that by 1969, after years of unavailing expenditure of blood and treasure, the American people might not have supported what they would have supported in 1965. This, of course, tends to cast doubt on the value of continuing on the course which, since 1963, had brought us to this pass. In any case the president was in a better position than diplomats abroad to judge what the American people would or would not support.

The logical course which flowed within these limiting premises was the search for a middle ground between abandonment and direct

intervention. The standard "middle ground" was to continue operating "mostly" within the limits of the Geneva Accords while using
diplomatic means to press North Vietnam on its violations of the
Accords. The overt introduction of foreign troops into Laos could
shatter the existing system under the Geneva Accords and eliminate
Soviet support for the neutral Lao government. Therefore, in the
Ambassador's judgment, what was needed was to strengthen the
programs which we had been applying, beginning after 1962 when
we learned that North Vietnam had no intention of carrying out the
Accords.

Or, as the Ambassador aptly put it to me orally, it was in our interest
to "preserve the facade of Geneva." This was the logical conclusion
to be drawn within the given premises. It was the conclusion we had
consistently drawn from 1963 onward. It was the conclusion which
had led us to the Tet Offensive and beyond. It was a conclusion with
which I disagreed.

The reader will be familiar with my views which have appeared in
earlier chapters. I repeated them on this occasion. At this point, it
would seem appropriate only to summarize them briefly under three
headings:

I. The Role of Laos

Through the Geneva Accords we hoped to end the Laotian war and "put
Laos on the back burner." In fact, Laos has been the principal route by
which Hanoi has nearly conquered South Vietnam. Southern Laos is a
major asset which Hanoi will not give up. Laos is the strategic key to the
Communist push in Southeast Asia, used by Hanoi—as Germany twice
used Belgium—not only against South Vietnam but against eastern Cambodia.

The war in South Vietnam is an aggression. If it is not we never should
have entered it. Victory requires insulation of the victim against the aggressor—a proper role for U.S. forces, not counter-insurgency. This is
consistent with Vietnamization.

It is said that if the enemy does not "kick over the traces of Geneva"
then it is in our interest to continue to operate mostly within their limits.
But application of this "logical framework" has limited us to ineffectiveness
in dealing with the invasion. Massive air operations in the Panhandle have
failed to prevent the continuation of the invasion.

It is late in the game, but instead of calculating how much perfidy we
can tolerate in hope of an eventual "return to Geneva", let us identify what
in Laos is essential to a regional settlement.

II. The Proposal

The essential elements are non-Communist neutral rule in the Laotian lowlands east of the Mekong River thereby buffering Thailand; elimination of Hanoi's control of the southern Panhandle, thereby insulating South Vietnam and Cambodia against Hanoi's expansionism. Because the Panhandle route of aggression is strongly held by North Vietnam it could only be challenged successfully by strong U.S. forces. Engaging the North Vietnamese there would gradually shift the weight of the struggle from the weary South Vietnamese population to the remote, sparsely populated Laotian infiltration routes occupied by the North Vietnamese army. North Vietnam might move its routes further west or challenge us in strength in the Panhandle. In either case, they would become more vulnerable to our air power acting as the hammer against our ground forces acting as the anvil

III. Perspective

Our engagement of the North Vietnamese in Laos in massive violation of the Geneva Accords would force into the open Hanoi's invasion which it has never admitted. It would also establish a military position which could be converted into a cease-fire line on which we could base our negotiating position in Paris.

The Geneva formula was based on the premise that Moscow was ready and able to cooperate in supporting a neutral political settlement in Laos. That proved to be wrong. We must remain alert to respond when the Communist side might become ready for political settlement.

Until then, however [I continued], the only practical course is to continue to seek co-existence on the basis of a geographical detente—a "your-side-our side" frontier along a recognized line such as exists from the Baltic Sea to Southeast Asia and from the 38th parallel to the 17th. We need to fill in the last remaining sector of the line of co-existence. Failure to do so might start the unravelling of the whole seam of containment which has been painfully stitched together since World War II.

Americans are dillusioned with an *inconclusive war* but Americans are proud and do not like to come in second. The disillusion of 1969 would be nothing compared to that which would flow from failure.

What happened? The whole initiative reflected in these divergent memoranda (at least mine) sank like a stone in a bottomless sea. There was one small bubble. About two weeks later, Ambassador Unger remarked to me that he had heard from Marshall Green in the Department of State that Mr. Kissinger's office had sent copies of the memoranda to the Bureau of East Asian Affairs without comment.

What else happened?

On August 4, Kissinger met with North Vietnam's Xuan Thuy and Mai Van Bo in Paris and volunteered to discuss not only mutual withdrawal but Hanoi's Ten Points which demanded unilateral American withdrawal and disestablishment of the South Vietnamese Government. He would not, however, treat the Ten Points as if they were the Ten Commandments. The North Vietnamese denied that the Ten Points were like the Ten Commandments but were "the only logical and realistic basis for ending the war."[12]

On August 11, the North Vietnamese launched an attack against more than 100 towns and cities in South Vietnam.

On August 25, Ho Chi Minh replied to President Nixon's letter urging that both sides turn their faces "toward peace rather than toward war." He said that the "correct manner" to search for peace is for the United States to "cease the war of aggression and withdraw their troops from South Vietnam."[13]

On September 3, Ho Chi Minh died.

On September 10, Kissinger wrote to President Nixon that our ability to negotiate in Paris depended on the strength of our position both in Vietnam and in the United States. Vietnamization fed the American hunger to end it all, and we couldn't progress rapidly enough in South Vietnam to keep up with the pace of withdrawal. Therefore, time was again working against us. Although Hanoi was hurting, the North Vietnamese could settle down to a lower level of protracted warfare in order further to exhaust us psychologically.[14] Therefore, he told his staff, we were trying "to walk a fine line between withdrawing too fast to convince Hanoi of our determination and too slowly to satisfy American public opinion."[15] How could the President "force a rapid conclusion?" By a one-two punch of a generous negotiating proposal to be followed, if rejected, by mining Hanoi's ports and quarantining North Vietnam. Work began on both projects at once—a public statement which led to the President's November 3 speech, and a hard-hitting program of bombing and mining, known as "Duck Hook" and targeted for November 1 but never carried out.

On September 16, the planned withdrawal, by December 15, of 40,500 more American forces was announced.[16]

On September 26, in a press conference, President Nixon noted that in a 1962 speech, President Kennedy had asserted that Laos was potentially the key to what would happen in Thailand as well as in Vietnam and the balance of Southeast Asia. "Now, Laos relates very much to Vietnam," Nixon went on, "because the Ho Chi Minh Trail runs through Laos. It is necessary under these circumstances that the United States take cognizance of that."[17]

On October 17 and 30, Kissinger reiterated to the President his pessimism regarding the prospect that Vietnamization alone would work.[18] But he found that Vietnamization was the only alternative between (a) quitting quickly while dismantling the Saigon Government or (b) sharp escalation of bombing and mining (Duck Hook) which public opinion in the United States would not support long enough to succeed. It was the old problem—neither escalation nor de-escalation afforded any "sticking places" at which we could "stand pat" simultaneously in Indochina, in the United States and in Paris.

What did the President do? He made his speech on November 3rd. It was a good one. For the first time, he publicly accepted the idea of a total U.S. pullout. At the same time it was a strong speech. It made the moral case both for our original intervention and against a precipitous withdrawal which would "inevitably allow the Communists to repeat the massacres which followed their takeover in the North." The American response was deafeningly favorable. As Nixon tells us in his book, *No More Vietnams*, "Now for a time at least, North Vietnam's leaders could no longer count on dissent in America to give them the victory they could not win on the battlefield. I had the public support I needed to continue a policy of waging war in Vietnam and negotiating for peace in Paris until we could bring the war to an honorable and successful conclusion."[19]

Yes. Now was the time—the last chance—to carve out a "sticking place" by stopping the invasion in its tracks, where it occurred—in the Ho Chi Minh Trail of southern Laos. But we didn't.

1970 in Cambodia: Wrong Place 1971 in Laos: Wrong Time

"Lost time was like a run in a stocking. It always got worse."
Anne Morrow Lindbergh, *The Steep Ascent*

The new Administration would have one final chance to adopt a unified Indochina strategy to match Hanoi's. Having commenced a build-up of South Vietnam's forces to move in behind the gradually withdrawing American troops—"Vietnamization"—while negotiating in Paris, the Nixon Administration had a brief moment of opportunity, beginning in the autumn of 1969. Recognition of the need for an integral Indochina strategy against North Vietnamese aggression was implicit in the Cambodia incursion of May 1970 and in the South Vietnamese attack on the Ho Chi Minh Trail in February 1971. But, instead of combining the logic and force of the two operations into a single Indochina strategy, we executed them separately, in *incremental* sequence. As a result, we gained only temporary advantage from both, an advantage highly vulnerable to the erosion of time. We had bought a little time—not space.

Conceptually, the war was over, even though fighting would continue for years. This chapter is a brief account of how that happened.

In November 1969 our position seemed the strongest since the beginning of the Nixon Administration. We had withstood a military offensive by

Hanoi, as well as the Moratorium; the President had taken his case to the people and received substantial support.[1]

With these words Henry Kissinger confirmed President's Nixon's judgment of the strength of our Government's position in the autumn of 1969. But Kissinger also knew that in war a political image unsupported by a corresponding military position is a wasting asset. He knew that in a protracted war, "time was not on our side." He knew, he tells us in *White House Years*, that a satisfactory outcome "would be impossible unless we could convert our military position on the ground into a durable political structure."[2] He knew that the way to accomplish this was "to offer the most generous proposal imaginable—and then, if rejected, to seek to impose it militarily."[3]

But, it didn't work out this way. To Kissinger's credit he is able, in retrospect, to distill the cautionary lesson of "incrementalism," as practiced by the Nixon Administration, into one long but pithy sentence: "If we had offered at one dramatic moment all the concessions we eventually made in three years of war, and if the military actions we took with steadily declining forces over 1970, 1971 and 1972 in Cambodia, Laos and North Vietnam . . . had been undertaken all together in early 1970, the war might well have been appreciably shortened."[4] Had the Nixon Administration concentrated all this force, including the 1970 incursion into Cambodia and the 1971 Lam Son 719 operation into Laos, etc. so as to establish a position on the ground which could be converted into "a durable political structure," we might have accomplished even more than shortening the war. We might have ended it—made a definitive success of Vietnamization and preserved the independence of South Vietnam, Cambodia and part of Laos. Instead, he tells us, we followed what he obviously regards as the divergent course of Vietnamization, although reason suggests that nothing could have better supported and solidified Vietnamization than a position on the ground blocking the North Vietnamese invasion—a position which "we could convert into a durable political structure."

What did we do after November 1969: Two things; first, a major re-appraisal of "what was happening on the ground in Vietnam" and second, a baiting of the secret negotiating track in Paris. The re-appraisal was conducted by the newly created Vietnam Special Studies Group. Although there were some encouraging signs, the problem was, as it always was—how to measure progress—what criteria to use. For years, Secretary McNamara had agonized over statistical evidences of progress which seemed to dissolve before his eyes.

At the very time the Special Studies Group was grappling with the problem, Hanoi provided a strong clue to the answer—time and protracted warfare. North Vietnamese Minister of Defense, General Vo Nguyen Giap, architect of Hanoi's strategy, published a series of articles, the main thrust of which, Kissinger says, "was that a protracted struggle could defeat America's superior technology." It was not a new idea. Kissinger himself expressed it neatly: "It is a cardinal principle of guerrilla warfare that the guerrilla wins if he does not lose; the regular army loses if it does not win."[5] The side waging protracted warfare has only to keep the form and level of hostilities within the framework of its own capabilities, meaning a war of attrition against society, and keep it up, letting time work on the psychological determination of the conventional defender's society. Protracted war is waged in a dimension of Time, which is the arbiter of ultimate victory. Conventional war is waged in the dimension of Space, control of which defines the victory.

The Studies Group's findings were measured against a review conducted in South Vietnam by a special team under Kissinger's military assistant, Alexander Haig. The results were moderately encouraging but, as Kissinger notes, "No amount of study . . . could solve our basic dilemma. An enemy determined on protracted struggle could only be brought to compromise by being confronted by insuperable obstacles on the ground."[6] Although correct, Kissinger concluded that the obstacle could be created only by "building up the South Vietnamese and blunting every effort Hanoi made to interrupt the buildup—in other words, Vietnamization. "Time is fickle;" he says, "We had to use the breathing spell to strengthen ourselves on the ground."[7] Now, as valid as Vietnamization was as a pattern for the future, it could not erect an "insuperable obstacle on the ground" which could only be accomplished by blocking Hanoi's invasion on the ground. Unaccompanied by such a blocking move, Vietnamization could only have a moderate retardant effect on the attrition of protracted warfare waged in a dimension of time. As a result, the political advantage following in the wake of the President's November 3 speech was used, not to erect "an insuperable obstacle" but to buy a little time for the build-up of South Vietnam. "Time is fickle" says Kissinger. But, in reality Time is not fickle—it is relentless.

The time bought in November 1969 was also used for a new effort at secret negotiations in Paris. On February 21, March 16 and April 4, 1970, Kissinger met with Le Duc Tho, the fifth man in Hanoi's Politburo. To be as forthcoming as possible, Kissinger said the U.S. would withdraw *all* its forces (leaving no residual element) as part of a mutual withdrawal and, moreover, would not demand that Hanoi publicly acknowledge or demonstrate its withdrawal which, said Kissinger, could be *de facto*.[8] In so doing, Kissinger was repeating history, in effect allowing Hanoi the same tacit escape from compliance that Harriman's opposite number, Pushkin, at Geneva in 1962 had asserted later that year to explain away Hanoi's failure to withdraw from Laos. "They will melt into the jungle," one should remember Pushkin saying.

In February 1970, Hanoi was stronger than in 1962 and able to do its own reneging. In a hard lecture that illustrated the political side of "protracted warfare," Le Duc Tho demonstrated the application of the Leninist concept of the "correlation of forces" by using domestic American criticism of the war as his evidence of the American inability to outlast North Vietnam. He then insisted that the only subject for discussion was unconditional American withdrawal. Thereafter, he allowed, there could be discussion of political subjects which would lead to the removal of the leadership of the Saigon government.[9] A flatter "no-deal" could hardly be imagined.

The series of meetings ended on April 14 with Le Duc Tho denying any responsibility for military engagements in Laos and Cambodia but at the same time insisting that the "war in Indochina had become one . . . and would be fought to a finish on that basis.[10] For six months, the United States had expended its temporary political credit to re-study the situation in both Vietnam and Paris. Meanwhile, in March, the Chief of State of Cambodia, Prince Sihanouk, had been overthrown and North Vietnamese forces were breaking out of their bases in eastern Cambodia to threaten the capital. U.S. attention turned in that direction.

The United States had no part in the overthrow of Sihanouk who owed his downfall to his own blindness in the face of North Vietnamese aggression. In 1969, he had belatedly begun to take account of the incremental loss of his own country to expanding North Vietnamese base-camps, then had openly deplored such actions and had tacitly permitted U.S. air attacks on the camps in Cambodia. Late in February 1970, he went for another of his extended vacations in France. In March, public demonstrations against North Vietnamese expanding activities began in the border regions and spread rapidly. Sihanouk rejected advice to cut short his vacation. Brushing aside warnings to return home, he went from France to Moscow where he learned from Premier Kosygin of his own sacking by the Cambodian Parliament. Over-confident of his charismatic appeal to his people, he delayed again, this time to visit Peking. By then, it was too late. The anti-North Vietnamese fever had swept the country and demolished Sihanouk in the eyes of his people.

By April 3, Hanoi's base-camp forces had turned away from South Vietnam and were moving west against the small Cambodian army—

driving toward Phnom Penh, the Cambodian capital. By April 16, they were near it on the south, giving effective meaning on the ground to Le Duc Tho's scornful rejection, two days earlier, of Kissinger's proposal of neutrality for Cambodia and illustrating the force of his frank pronouncement that the conflict in Indochina—not just Vietnam—had "become one." By April 20, the United States had done just two things. First, it had covertly supplied the Cambodian army a mere 2,000 old, captured rifles. Second, President Nixon had announced the withdrawal from Vietnam of 150,000 forces to be completed over the next twelve months.

Between April 20 and 30, things changed. As North Vietnam moved toward the capital, it became evident that unless some action were taken quickly, the country would fall to Hanoi's control. U.S. and South Vietnamese forces would face not just base camps in the forest but a hostile Cambodia dominated by Hanoi and linked to it via the Ho Chi Minh Trail through Laos, Vietnamization would become only an obscene cover-story for a precipitate U.S. withdrawal followed by a North Vietnamese invasion from Cambodia. It was to meet this threat that the so-called "incursion"—Operation Rockcrusher—was launched into Cambodia on April 30 with both U.S. and South Vietnamese forces advancing to destroy the base camps.

Although surprised and doubtful regarding its underlying logic, I was initially cheered by the "incursion," thinking that having once "broken the ice" by attacking the North Vietnamese invasion forces outside of South Vietnam, we would roll them back into southern Laos. Quickly, it became evident that Operation Rockcrusher was no part of any such strategic shift designed to "Korean-ize" the war in Indochina. Instead, the operation was to be a large scale "in-and-out" raid designed to buy time by destroying the base areas. Hanoi would surely react by reinforcing and expanding its hold on the Ho Chi Minh Trail. In fact, before the operation was terminated, the North Vietnamese forces took the town of Attopeu in the Bolovens Plateau area of southern Laos, on the flank of the Trail. It was a town surrounded for years by North Vietnamese-controlled positions—a city which Hanoi could have taken but preferred to allow to wither on the vine as a token symbol of the "uneasy equilibrium" or the "tacit agreement" which the United States sought to preserve. Shortly afterward, the North Vietnamese also occupied the only other significant Bolovens town, Saravane, thereby consolidating the area. In anticipation of a possible extension of the incursion up into Laos, Hanoi took these towns to pre-empt any U.S. move which, of course, never came. The U.S. threshold of toleration automatically adjusted itself to accommodate the new level of provocation.

This North Vietnamese seizure of key points in the Bolovens Plateau confirmed CINCPAC's warning of Hanoi's increased pressure on Cambodia and utilization of the Ho Chi Minh Trail, suggesting to me that, in the words of CIA's Lyman Kirkpatrick (Chapter 16), after six years of trying to mop up the floor in South Vietnam while the hose of infiltration from North Vietnam continued to flow through Laos, perhaps we were finally ready to plug the flow. It seemed to me that we should begin to roll it up gradually northward from Cambodia into southern Laos until reaching a position at which it would be both militarily and politically possible to stand pat, awaiting either a political settlement or the definition of a cease-fire line. However, as so often happened, events took over—domestic American events.

Within the limits of its own conceptual framework, the incursion was a resounding success. During the two months penetration of Cambodia to a depth of 23 miles, as much as 40% of North Vietnam's war-making capacity in Cambodia was destroyed or captured along with vast documentary evidence of Hanoi's plans for the future. We had bought perhaps a year's time by administering this setback. But, ironically, this is the measure of the operation's failure as well as of its success. It bought a year's military time in Indochina but it lost political time in America. It bought a year's military time but it did not create a "military position on the ground" which we could "convert into a durable political structure." Nor did it confront the protracted struggle on the ground with an "insuperable obstacle" which could force compromise.

So the war continued to be waged in a dimension of time—not space. Our time was limited and shrinking; Hanoi's was practically unlimited. By the winter of 1970, North Vietnam was well on the way toward recouping the damage of the incursion. A major effort was applied to the development of the routes through the Laos Corridor to compensate for the loss of the Cambodian port of Sihanoukville which the new government in Phnom Penh had closed to North Vietnam's military use. By the end of the year, attention was beginning to be focused on the need for a new operation to follow up the incursion and buy more time. But this time, the new target would be in southern Laos. The logic of the inconclusive Cambodian incursion led directly—but too late—to the need to act in southern Laos in February, 1971.

By the time the United States was ready to turn to the invasion on the ground through southern Laos, the rules had been decisively changed. In the domestic upheaval unleashed by the Cambodia incursion, Congress passed the Cooper-Church Amendment which, as of December 29, 1970, *prohibited any U.S. forces from operating on the ground inside Cambodia or Laos.* The "toreador's cape" was no longer just policy—it was law. By exhausting its political credit on an indecisive delaying action in Cambodia, the administration had stimulated the erection of a legal barrier to our ability to wage a decisive action in Laos where we might have created a military position which could have been converted into a "durable political structure." Having finally focused on the toreador's sword, the bull had been reined in—prohibited from knocking the sword from the toreador's hand.

The immediate need for the February 1971 operation against the Ho Chi Minh Trail grew out of a calculation that the rapid withdrawal of U.S. forces—under great domestic pressure, heightened by the reaction to the Cambodian operation and coupled with Hanoi's intense reinforcement and re-supply—would soon result in a relative shortage of defense forces in South Vietnam. To compensate, it was decided to interrupt North Vietnamese reinforcement during the dry season and, in effect, to delay their schedule for another year. Perhaps, I suppose someone thought, doing so might even increase Hanoi's willingness to negotiate in 1972.

Since American forces were prohibited by law, the offensive into Laos would have to be undertaken by South Vietnamese troops. American forces could however, provide logistical back-up, artillery and air support, and evacuation services. The target of the operation was the knot of North Vietnamese supply lines which passed through an area of which Tchepone was the center. Tchepone was situated on Route 9 which ran from the sea across South Vietnam below the DMZ and across the border into Laos. Ironically, except for the limitation on American forces, the concept was similar to that of General John Waters, who had published it in *U.S. News and World Report* five years earlier (chapter 15). The plan was for the U.S. to secure control of Route 9 in South Vietnam up to the Laos border. South Vietnamese troops were airlifted into positions in Laos from which they were to drive to Tchepone. Then, they were to operate in the area, destroying North Vietnamese supplies and facilities and interdicting the infiltration routes until the rains started early in May. They were *not* expected to establish a permanent position on the ground. This operation, called "Lam Son 719," was designed to buy time, not to define a line in space on which to stand pat and wait for the other side to negotiate.

It is not my purpose to describe the operation or to analyze its conduct. It was seriously flawed—primarily by pitting a small South Vietnamese force against a force between two and three times larger—and it was terminated much earlier than intended. But it was not a complete failure. Some South Vietnamese units fought well and others not so well. There was poor planning. There were mistakes. The operation was hobbled by President Thieu's imposition of an absolute ceiling on the number of casualties that could be tolerated. Still, North Vietnam was hurt, and its plans were again delayed, although not by as much as had been hoped. We bought some more time.

The fundamental conclusion to be drawn from the operation's result is that after years of controlling and developing the lifeline of their invasion, the North Vietnamese forces in the Laos Corridor were too numerous, too well armed and too entrenched to be subdued by a South Vietnamese force of 16,000 operating in a strange and hostile environment. In fact, Hanoi even deployed some 40,000 forces from South Vietnam back into Laos to reinforce the regular Corridor garrisons.* As the essential key to the invasion of South Vietnam, the Corridor was too important to be lost. No wonder Hanoi was willing to put off its conquest of Souvanna Phouma's neutral regime in northwest Laos as the *quid pro quo* of retaining use of the southern invasion route—subject only to annoying but indecisive U.S. aerial harassment!

Hilsman and Harriman were right when they concluded in 1962-3 that the Communists, regarding South Vietnam as the "main arena," would want to keep on using the infiltration routes in the southern Panhandle and would "strenuously resist" any attempt to take them. Just how strenuously was demonstrated by North Vietnam's powerful defense against Lam Son 719 in February, 1971.** More importantly, Lam Son 719 demonstrated the extent to which the Harriman-Hilsman "tacit agreement" still defined the framework of the war despite seven years of failure and despite a change of political administration in Washington. The Congress enforced the formula on the United States by prohibiting U.S. ground forces in Laos. North Vietnam enforced it on South Vietnam. Harriman and Hilsman were still right in the sense that the war continued to fit the

---

*This reverse movement of North Vietnamese forces back to Laos from South Vietnam suggests how the launching of a major U.S. ground action to block the Corridor would have forced North Vietnam to shift its priorities, thereby abetting successful pacification and Vietnamization. While drawing U.S. and North Vietnamese forces out of South Vietnam, it would have left the South's forces free to sweep up the remainder of the simulated insurgency.

**The less than stunning success of Lam Son 719 is not a measure of what could have been achieved by a major U.S. blocking movement into the Corridor by forces determined to stay and large enough to do so—particularly if done before Hanoi had so heavily fortified the area—say in 1965 or 1966. Rather, it is a measure of the reversal of U.S. and South Vietnamese roles. Defense against external aggression was always the proper role for the United States.

framework they had devised in 1962–1963. It had been written thus and it was happening just as it had been written. The only question remaining is *why*. The Nixon Administration was not committed to the "facade of Geneva" and, on various occasions exposed its fallacies. Why then did it not break out of the self-defeating maze of the facade?

Among the "fatal flaws" of our policy from 1960 to 1968, identified by Richard Nixon in his book, *No More Vietnams*, the first two were that "We failed to understand that the war was an invasion from North Vietnam, not an insurgency in the South," and that "We failed to prevent North Vietnam from establishing a key supply route, the Ho Chi Minh Trail, through Laos and Cambodia." With hindsight, he is right. So why did the Nixon Administration not close the Ho Chi Minh Trail effectively? He goes on:

> The North Vietnamese invasion that began in late 1959 proved Hanoi's leaders had learned a lesson from the Korean War. North Korea's blatant invasion across the border had given the United States clear justification to intervene and had enabled President Truman to rally the American people and our United Nations allies to the defense of South Korea. North Vietnam, therefore, shrewdly camouflaged its invasion to look like a civil war. But in fact the Vietnam War was the Korean War with jungles.[11]

Or a toreador with a cape and a concealed sword!

So then, why did the Nixon Administration never act on this premise? Neither Nixon nor Kissinger answers the question directly. But is is clear that, side-by-side with its perception of the war as a North Vietnamese aggression, the Nixon Administration was able to entertain the opposite premise that holding Laos in a state of partitioned suspense (while the invasion continued) worked in our side's interest. Thus does Kissinger acquiesce in the asymmetrical political formula which had, for seven years, shaped U.S. strategy with respect to Laos—to Laos which was, of course, the key to blocking the invasion if it were to be blocked as it was in Korea:

> Hanoi was fighting essentially two wars in Laos, though both for the same objective of hegemony in Indochina. In the south, the Ho Chi Minh Trail was Hanoi's link to the battlefield of South Vietnam. In northern Laos, Hanoi supported the Pathet Lao but it was restrained, we thought, by fear of American or Thai response. It has sought to maintain just enough pressure on the Laotian army to prevent it from consolidating itself as an instrument of authority; it would be dealt with after the victory in South Vietnam. We did not, for our part, seek to disturb this uneasy equilibrium.[12]

The striking similarity of Kissinger's "uneasy equilibrium" to Hilsman's adumbration of the Harriman-Hilsman "tacit agreement" of

1962–3 is a tribute to the persistence of the equation as a tacit "given" of our policy and strategy from beginning to end—notwithstanding the change of administration.* Just as Hanoi was restrained in northern Laos by fear of an American reaction, so was the United States restrained in the southern Corridor by the desire to avoid a North Vietnamese riposte in the north. Meanwhile, the Corridor promised to lead Hanoi to victory.

Not only was action on the ground to block the invasion excluded by this formula but we went to great lengths, as Kissinger explains, to avoid anything that "would wreck what was left of the Geneva Accords, give Hanoi a pretext for further stepping up its aggression in northern Laos and fuel even more passionate controversy at home." He wrote to President Nixon that, "the North Vietnamese can overrun Laos at any point in time that they care to, providing they are willing to pay the political and psychological cost of upsetting the Geneva Accords."[13]

We were still caught in the rubble of the inverted Geneva Accords. Considering that the substance of the Accords had already been reversed, *de facto*, by North Vietnam, Kissinger's reference to "what is left" can only refer to the "facade of Geneva," which tied Hanoi's control over the southern Laos invasion routes to its temporary willingness to spare the neutral regime in northern Laos which, as Kissinger says, Hanoi would deal with after victory in South Vietnam— even as Hilsman had said years before. The principal cost to be avoided from Hanoi's point of view, was the triggering of a U.S. intervention which would interfere with the continuing invasion. Thus, North Vietnam's postponement of a takeover in northern Laos sprang, not from any fear of scarlet taint from violating the Accords but from a deliberate calculation of Hanoi's strategic priorities, which were to conquer South Vietnam *before* overthrowing the neutral regime of Souvanna Phouma in northern Laos.

Clearly, the Nixon Administration understood the design of the "facade of Geneva" and, as Kissinger says, "did not desire to upset this equilibrium." At first glance, one might think that this would have excluded the launching of Lam Son 719 into southern Laos. But Lam Son did not send U.S. forces into Laos—only South Vietnamese. By late 1970, when the idea of such an operation began to gestate, Congress was already enacting the limits of the so-called "equilib-

---

*It is also testimony to our persistent ability to believe two contrary propositions at the same time—a feat which approached that of Alice's Red Queen who sometimes "believed as many as six impossible things before breakfast."

rium" into law. Hence, there was no need to argue the merits of such a strategy as sending U.S. forces into Laos. The option of doing so had been closed by Congress. So, the "short straw" was drawn by the South Vietnamese forces.

In Laos itself, however, Souvanna had progressively become more realistic about North Vietnam and was much less inclined to defer to Hanoi's sensitivity about its exploitation and occupation of the southern part of his country. So, in response to the Department's request for his judgment as to Souvanna's probable reaction to the proposed operation, U.S. Ambassador G. McMurtrie Godley reported that the Premier would probably concur tacitly. Not satisfied with this, the Department instructed the Ambassador twice more to obtain Souvanna's formal reaction. Twice, Souvanna refused to veto the operation. In effect, he favored it.[14]

Disconcerting as it was to the Department of State to have the beneficiary of the "facade of Geneva" discount its value, the fact is that the "facade" was not seriously breached by Lan Son 719 since no large U.S. ground blocking movement occurred. A temporary incursion by a relatively small South Vietnamese force did not challenge Hanoi's stake in the Corridor decisively. This reflects, however, how far the U.S. and South Vietnamese roles had been reversed. As Kissinger says, "We were asking the South Vietnamese to conduct an operation that we had refused to take when we had 500,000 troops in Vietnam. . . ."[15] In short, South Vietnamese forces were being sent out of their country to defend against a powerful external attacker supported by the U.S.S.R. and China in order to protect their powerful American ally who remained behind, inside South Vietnam. Incongruous though it seems, that's what happened. Having failed to exercise our option to block the external invasion, it followed logically that when the option was foreclosed by a Congress impatient with indecisive warfare, we were left with only the option of staying behind to fight in South Vietnam. This straight-line progression of our compartmentalized and incompatible strategies in Laos and South Vietnam was encapsulated in Harriman's advice to President Kennedy in October 1961 that "the South Vietnam problem can best be solved in South Vietnam rather than . . . by military action in Laos." (See Chapter 5)

But the time for U.S. forces to fight inside South Vietnam was fast running out. Now—after Operation Rockcrusher in Cambodia, Lam Son 719 in southern Laos and the Cooper-Church Amendment in Congress, the options which the United States had kept open for years had finally closed, leaving us only the gradual but accelerating withdrawal of American troops, the build-up of South Vietnamese forces and a new attempt to negotiate. The first two were underway. The Nixon Administration sought to use the time bought in Lam Son to make a new try at Paris.

On May 31, 1971, Kissinger attended the first of a new series of "secret" talks. The continuing series of "open" talks served as a platform for public posturing and as a facade (another in the long series of Indochina facades) for the secret talks. Running fast against an even faster-running political clock, the U.S. was under heavy pressure always to make new concessions while Hanoi stood pat—confident of its position on the ground and time working in its favor. The new U.S. proposal included seven points:

1. *U.S. willingness, as part of an agreement, to set a date for total withdrawal.* [Hanoi demanded unilateral U.S. withdrawal unconditioned on any commitments by North Vietnam.]

2. *South Vietnam's political future to be decided by the South Vietnamese.* [Hanoi demanded that the U.S. replace the Saigon leadership.]

3. *A cease-fire throughout Indochina.* [Based on previous experience, this would be violated by Hanoi and be unenforceable.]

4. *No North Vietnamese reinforcement*—infiltration—to Communist forces in South Vietnam. [This deliberately sidestepped the continued presence in the South of large North Vietnamese forces. Moreover, in light of Hanoi's performance under the 1954 and 1962 Geneva Accords, Kissinger recognized the prospect of Hanoi's non-compliance again.]

5. *International supervision.* [Would be totally ineffective like the failed ICC under the Geneva Accords.]

6. *Neutrality for Laos and Cambodia.* [Already "guaranteed" under the Geneva Accords of 1954 and 1962, massively violated by North Vietnam and suspended in Laos by the Harriman-Hilsman "tacit agreement."]

7. *Return of POWs and civilian detainees.* [In return for our unilateral withdrawal, however, Hanoi would only agree to "discuss" prisoners without commitment.[16]]

All the old familiar elements of Geneva 1954 and 1962 were there and serving the same function—to provide a legal facade which, on one side would screen the U.S. retreat with "honor" while on the other side would screen Hanoi's pursuit of imperial dominion over all Indochina. I do not mean to ridicule the proposed terms that Kissinger tells us are not greatly different from those finally negotiated and signed in January 1973. By this time, we had no alternative option left—except to withdraw without any agreement at all. My purpose is to lay out the terms *as proposed* to serve as the measure of where we stood after ten years of war, to wit, *in the same place.* Except for one thing, that is. Because the Geneva Accords of 1962 required withdrawal of *all* foreign forces, including North Vietnamese, it was quickly necessary to fashion the "tacit agreement" to accommodate Hanoi's reversal of the meaning of the Accords. In 1971, however, what might be termed the "Kissinger corollary" of the Harriman-Hilsman "tacit agreement" was devised. Tacit provision for Hanoi's forces in South Vietnam was built into the very terms of the agreement which would specifically call for the removal *only* of American forces. In short, having got to this place by picking our way through the rubble of Geneva we found our way out by the same route.*

As the Johnson Administration departed in 1969, Presidential Advisor Walt Rostow offered a penetrating judgment of this failure more than two years before his successor, Henry Kissinger, advanced the seven points to Hanoi in Paris:

> We worked and got a good treaty on Laos in 1962 which required that all hands, including Hanoi, get out of Laos and cease transiting it. We had a side understanding with the Soviet Union that they would take responsibility for keeping Hanoi out of Laos, but Khrushchev could not or would not implement that agreement.
>
> It was perhaps the greatest error of this period that we did not insist toward the end of 1962 when the treaty came into effect and we knew that Hanoi was not honoring it—that we should have made it an absolutely fundamental, diplomatic and military position that it be scrupulously honored.
>
> Hopefully, we are going to have another agreement on Southeast Asia and, hopefully, we are going to have an agreement on missiles. And if there is one lesson I would draw, not only from the period of these eight years but from my experience in government since the end of the war, it is that we should insist when agreements are made that they must be most scrupulously honored.**

Although Rostow did not argue that forces should have been put into Laos, he nonetheless fingered our basic error—to have built our strat-

---

*Unlike the legendary inventor, Daedalus who, imprisoned in King Minos' Cretan labyrinth (which he had himself built), devised a radical new strategy—wings to fly out—we refused to adopt a radical new strategy to escape the labyrinthine rubble of Geneva. Like Theseus, we found our way out by rolling up the same thread by which we had been led in.

**Here, Rostow foresaw the problem we face today of Soviet violation of the Salt missile agreements.

egy incrementally on the rubble of the failed Geneva Accords: "I do think, taking the whole sweep of this problem, that if we put anything like the effort into the honoring of the 1962 Accords that we later put into saving Southeast Asia when it was near collapse in 1965, that we should have been better off—net."[17]

Nothing so damages a nation's credibility—its claim to be taken seriously—as does failure to insist on performance of promises or to find alternative effective means of gaining the substantive equivalent. In 1962, Hanoi saw us not only tolerate their violations of the Laos Accords but also do *nothing* to change the status quo. Now, in 1971, how could we change after ten exhausting years? We could not—at least we did not. And so, on May 11, 1971, after two years of North Vietnamese stonewalling in Paris, Hanoi's delegate, Xuan Thuy, said that his government would study our proposals carefully. Kissinger's delegation was "shell-shocked."[18] This is what we gained from the time that Lam Son 719 had bought.*

---

*On January 2, 1970, a year after Rostow had rendered his judgment and over a month before the Lam Son 719 operation, C. L. Sulzberger of the *New York Times* published a column on the role of Laos which was as notable for its rarity as for its historical accuracy and strategic perception. While exception can be taken to details, the essential points were valid:

"Perhaps the most significant American foreign policy failure over the past decade came neither in Vietnam nor at the Bay of Pigs but in Laos. Had U.S. diplomacy plugged the Laotian sewer already being exploited by Communist guerrillas ten years ago, the sordid drama that subsequently tortured external and internal U.S. relationships might have been avoided.

"Laos . . . is exceptionally important as the main military highway from North to South Vietnam. . . .

"By October 1960 the first Russians in history set foot on Laotian soil and Moscow swiftly mounted on behalf of the Pathet Lao, the fastest and most efficient foreign aid program it had ever attempted. [And, as Pushkin told Harriman at Geneva in 1961, apart from World War II, it was the highest priority Soviet supply operation since the Revolution.]

"When President Kennedy met Khrushchev . . . a conference had already started in Geneva . . . However, the United States was seeking to close the barn door on a horse that had fled.

"Dean Rusk told me at Geneva, May 14, 1961: 'We prefer a neutral Laos to a partitioned Laos. We don't sign something that is clearly a phony. . . .

"But the deal ultimately accepted, under the guise of *de jure* neutrality . . . actually accepted a *de facto* partition of the worst sort, leaving in Communist

There was little time left. The McGovern-Hatfield Amendment was gaining votes in the Senate. It would call upon the United States to set a specific date for withdrawal—unilaterally—thereby giving away whatever bargaining advantage there might be in the first of the U. S. 7 Points. On June 22, the Senate passed the Mansfield Amendment calling for withdrawal in nine months contingent only on the return of American prisoners-of-war. Perverse though these and similar demands might seem, there was a logic to them. We had waged a war in the dimension of time rather than space. We had not staked out any line in space we could stand on and convert into a "durable political structure." Now, when our time had run out, we were clearly leaving the ring. Why, asked many, why wait longer? Perverse, yes. Narrow, yes. And in some cases, not without an element of self-serving political animus—but also not without a certain logic. Why should we wait just to negotiate another Geneva-like facade?

The military withdrawal proceeded, and we would soon be unable to act on the ground with military force against any new North Vietnamese assault, even though our air power remained vast. The build-up of the South Vietnamese forces went on so well that some thought we should simply leave South Vietnam without again prostituting ourselves to obtain another agreement which would be only another facade. On January 25, 1972, President Nixon gave a public accounting of the secret negotiating history, exposing Hanoi's arbitrariness and perfidy. As usual, although this revelation briefly improved the Administration's public image, the effect was quickly dissipated. President Nixon's dramatic visit to China in February gave the U.S. some additional maneuvering room but did not change the

hands the entire Ho Chi Minh Trail down which North Vietnam's warriors are still marching . . . [This was the Harriman-Hilsman tacit agreement]

". . . The fault was bipartisan . . . the Eisenhower Administration tipped the apple cart in 1957 and failed to right it by 1960. . . . The Kennedy Administration was naive in seeking as the basis for 'settlement' precisely what its adversaries wanted.

"The vital strategic importance of primitive little Laos was insufficiently appreciated . . . .

"We have paid for the misjudgment. During the last decade U.S. aid to Laos has totaled possibly 1.75 billion dollars while all kinds of American paramilitary operations have been mounted there. Nor can any valid settlement of the Vietnamese war ever come until, as President Nixon said on May 14, 1969, Hanoi withdraws its troops from Laos, the 'traditional invasion route' down which they march into the south."

basic equation which was etched in military terms on the ground in Indochina.

Events raced ever faster toward an ultimate dénouement which had to be a complete U.S. withdrawal—with or without an agreement. On April 24, Hanoi launched a heavy attack, first against the Central Highlands of South Vietnam, opposite eastern Cambodia and southern Laos, then expanding up and down the country from the DMZ southward toward Saigon. Two days later, President Nixon announced the planned withdrawal of more troops which, when completed would bring our forces down to about 70,000. To offset this, U.S. air power in the region was augmented to support the South Vietnamese forces trying to stop the North's assault. This was Operation Linebacker, which was expanded on May 8 to include the bombing of Hanoi and the blockade of Haiphong and other ports by aerial mining. Despite the fears of many in government and the outcry of the media, Moscow took this calmly, not even suggesting postponement of Nixon's forthcoming summit meeting with Brezhnev in Moscow. Hanoi, which had been scornfully negative in the May 2 secret meeting in Paris, suddenly reversed field and became interested in resuming serious negotiations, especially because its first conventional invasion, led by tanks and conducted almost exclusively by North Vietnamese regulars, had been stopped by U.S. air power and South Vietnamese ground forces.

In a sense, the mining of the North's ports bore the superficial appearance of an effort to establish a geographic line to isolate the battlefield by cutting Hanoi off from some ⅞ of its imports and all of its oil—at least for a few months. As a tactic for slowing Hanoi and gaining some bargaining leverage in Paris—for buying time, in short— it was effective. That was all that was expected. Kissinger says we were looking for "a shock that would give the North pause and rally the South."[19] Despite the superficial appearance, the "line" of mines across the harbors of North Vietnam could not substitute for a "line" drawn against the invasion on the ground. It could not be converted into a "durable political structure" because we still said we had no desire to unseat Communist power in North Vietnam, a power that had already killed or wounded some 350,000 Americans.

But, if time erodes political positions, it also provides—in its own medium—pegs which, though short-lived—can, if properly exploited, provide useful temporary leverage. Such a peg was the American election to take place in November 1972. In 1968, in the wake of the politically devastating Tet Offensive, the uncertain prospects of the Democratic Administration had exerted pressure on the U.S. in the Paris talks and worked to the advantage of Hanoi. But now, in

1972, the shoe was on the other foot. The apparent certainty of another four years for the Republican Administration gave the U.S. a peg on which to hang in Paris and, by the same token, induce compromise by Hanoi. As Kissinger says, "The more we squeezed Le Duc Tho against what was more clearly than ever his self-imposed deadline (our Presidential election), the more forthcoming he was likely to be."[20]

Thus conscious of its bargaining position, the U.S. used it well. By October 8, Hanoi had virtually accepted the U.S. proposals that separated the military questions of cease-fire, withdrawal and POWs from the "political question" of South Vietnam's future. The latter question was to be settled by the "parties," that is the Government in Saigon and the recently announced Provisional Revolutionary Government which would remain armed and in South Vietnam. Although the PRG was only a facade for Hanoi, this formula meant that Hanoi had abandoned its demand that we engineer the overthrow of the Government of Saigon.

On the military side, the United States would complete its withdrawal in two months from the date of agreement; there would be a cease-fire in place under international supervision; there was to be no military reinforcement (infiltration); and POWs on both sides would be returned. Of course, we knew that the cease-fire would be violated, that North Vietnamese troops would remain in South Vietnam, that infiltration would continue and that the new ICC would be ineffective. But the United States—condemned by now to backing out by retracing its steps on entry—badly needed an agreement. It no longer had the forces in Vietnam to fight and the draft had been terminated. Willy-nilly, the United States was leaving Vietnam. Since we were leaving by the same route as we entered, it was important to leave South Vietnam in no worse a legal position than it had been in when we entered. Ostensibly, the proposed agreements accomplished that. As for Hanoi's expected future effort to conquer, President Nixon sought to meet that contingency by promising President Thieu to send "enough military aid to maintain the balance of power" and to respond "swiftly to North Vietnamese attempts to subvert the terms of the agreement. . . . Our military power was the principal disincentive to Hanoi's breaking the ceasefire."[21]

Using the approaching election to bargaining advantage, President Nixon refused to be stampeded during the breakdown of October. President Thieu surfaced new objections which we thought had been answered, and Hanoi denounced the U.S. in a slanted expose of the secret negotiations. After failed new efforts in Paris, Kissinger reported:

It is now obvious as the result of our additional exploration of Hanoi's intentions that they have not in any way abandoned their objectives or ambitions with respect to South Vietnam. . . . Thus, we can anticipate no lasting peace in the wake of a consummated agreement, but merely a shift in Hanoi's *modus operandi*. We will probably have little chance of maintaining the agreement without evident hair-trigger U.S. readiness, which may in fact be challenged at any time, to enforce its provisions.[22]

The deadlock deepened. Finally, on December 16, Kissinger publicly laid out what we wanted from Hanoi: an agreement that was "more than an armistice"; and from Saigon: recognition of the necessity to take it if we could get it. Two days later, heavy B-52 bombing of North Vietnam began. Even with the shrill excoriation from the U.S. media, academia and political circles, six days later Hanoi expressed its desire to resume talks. By January 13, 1973, amended agreements had been worked out. On January 14, Alexander Haig flew to Saigon with an ultimatum for Thieu based on our decision to sign with or without him. Thieu bargained further, and President Nixon used another of the briefly available pegs which time provides. He replied to Thieu's message the same day—January 17—rehearsing his arguments and ending with a request for a decision by Inauguration Day, January 20. Americans are good at *tactical*, fast-moving bargaining designed to achieve a specific quick result. Americans are poker-players. The Soviets—and perhaps Vietnamese and Communists in general—are chess-players. Thieu acquiesced calmly, waiting until January 21 (Saigon time) to get his reply under the wire—coupled with some simple requests for unilateral statements by the United States, which were made.

Henry Kissinger says in *White House Years*: "I believed then, and I believe now that the agreement could have worked. It reflected a true equilibrium, of forces on the ground. If the equilibrium were maintained, the agreement could have been maintained. . . . But for the collapse of executive authority as a result of Watergate, I believe we would have succeeded."[23]

Perhaps. But the facts are that Watergate did happen and Congress did savagely and irresponsibly cut aid to South Vietnam. In one sense, this caprice of politics could not have been anticipated. But, in another sense, the fact that the viability of the peace treaty depended on the contingency of one man's personal promise of intervention reveals the unsoundness of the political structure erected at Paris, just as similar "promises" undermined the 1962 Geneva Accords. Thus, when, a few months after the Paris Treaty was signed, Hanoi began to reinforce with some 70,000 men sent down the Ho Chi Minh Trails,

Mr. Nixon failed to react with bombing. "This," he acknowledges, "was a major mistake. . . . Hanoi's leaders found they could flaunt the terms of the Paris Accords and get away with it. . . . Also, although I did not know it at the time, I had lost the last opportunity I would have to use American power to enforce the peace agreement. . . . It was not a failure of presidential will—I was willing to act—but an erosion of congressional support."[24] From then on it was all downhill. Hanoi stepped up its plans by several years to launch its all-out invasion which conquered South Vietnam in April 1975.

All substantially true, but what if Watergate had not happened? What if Congress had not decided to cut and run? Suppose that President Nixon had actually used air power once or even twice to stop resumed North Vietnamese reinforcement? No doubt, North Vietnam could have been restrained for a few years—at least until the end of the Nixon Administration in 1977. But, it would be fatal to underestimate North Vietnam's determination—a principal error of the Kennedy, Johnson, and Nixon administrations. The U.S. could not intervene by air every time Hanoi made a move. President Nixon's failure to act in April 1973 hints at the difficulty of responding by air to ambiguous events on the other side of the world. In time, with continued U.S. aid, South Vietnam would have become stronger. But, ultimately, given Hanoi's determination, its support from the Soviet Union and, most important of all, its tacitly condoned strong military presence in Laos and in the hills of South Vietnam, the war would have resumed and the advantage would have remained with North Vietnam.

What then? There would be no possibility of the U.S. returning its ground forces to South Vietnam. This point is critical because, as Mr. Nixon knows, it highlights the fundamental weakness of our position from the very beginning. We had no territorially defined ceasefire line such as exists in Korea that we and South Vietnam had won and defended militarily. Mr. Nixon put his finger on the problem obliquely when he expostulated about Congress' refusal to appropriate aid to South Vietnam: "None would expect South Korea to be able to deter an attack from North Korea without the presence of 50,000 American troops. . . . Yet, they were unwilling to allow us to retaliate against a North Vietnamese invasion or even to provide the South Vietnamese with enough ammunition for their guns."[25]

There was a world of difference between Korea and Vietnam because North and South Korea are divided by a line which we and South Korea fought to establish. Having won it, we negotiated a ceasefire along it. Our 50,000 troops are our commitment to this line. Pyongyang knows that in the event of challenge we would reinforce and hold this line rather than abandon South Korea. There was no such defended cease-fire line in Vietnam or across the North Vietnamese invasion route through Laos.

Like a dispirited bull, the United States left the ring. The fight was over for the bull. But, the toreador from Hanoi still stood in the ring with his sword drawn and his cape tossed carelessly over his arm. Behind the fence stood thousands of his countrymen, armed and awaiting a signal. When the signal came, in 1975, the toreador dropped his cape and led the assault. Saigon fell on April 30.

"The toreador's cape" describes the strategy by which we fought a war in Indochina and failed without ever being defeated.

Epilogue

"No epilogue, I pray you, for your play needs no excuse.
Never excuse."

Shakespeare, *Midsummer-Night's Dream*

Far from an excuse, the epilogue is implicit in the play. As did
everything else in our Indochina war, the epilogue emerged incrementally—actually in three stages. The most spectacular stage was
North Vietnam's open, all-out invasion and conquest of South Vietnam in the spring of 1975, culminating in the fall of Saigon on April
30. The most revolting stage began with the occupation, on April 17,
of the Cambodian capital of Phnom Penh by the murderous Khmer
Rouge Communists (from whom North Vietnam seized power in
December 1978). The third, and conceptually the most significant,
stage began five days after the fall of Saigon with the proclamation
of a coalition government in Laos which served briefly as a transparent
facade for the Communist Pathet Lao Army which was the facade for
North Vietnam's continued drive for total power in Laos. On August
23, 1975, less than four months after the fall of Saigon, Vientiane, the
capital of Laos, also "fell," followed by the proclamation of the People's Democracy of Laos.

This third stage of the epilogue was the most significant because it
marked the collapse of the facade on which our strategy had been
based from early 1963. That strategic equation balanced the southeastern Laos infiltration corridor against the northwestern base of the
non-Communist Lao regime. The equation was converted into a tacit
bargain that the U.S. would not expel North Vietnam from the former
and Hanoi would postpone taking over the latter—pending the final
result in South Vietnam.

It is worthwhile to recapitulate the bare structure of this bargain.
Harriman and Hilsman calculated, and President Kennedy accepted

their judgment that "until the matter of Vietnam was settled . . . the Communists would avoid scuttling the Geneva Agreements openly and irrevocably." This became the "facade of Geneva" behind which the neutralization of Laos and the Accords themselves were suspended. So, when the United States undertook the struggle for South Vietnam's independence, Laos was not a neutral buffer as intended at Geneva, but a partitioned state whose southeastern sector was a pistol aimed by Hanoi at South Vietnam.

"If the guerrilla struggle in Vietnam went *against* the Communists," the calculation continued, "Laos would quickly become the model for a truly neutral country . . . at least for a while." This result could not possibly have happened because "the guerrilla struggle" was only a tactic of North Vietnam's campaign of conquest waged through southeastern Laos.

"But, if the Communists *won* in Vietnam . . . then they would regard Laos as part of the prize." This is what happened. After conquering South Vietnam in April 1975, Hanoi moved in August to claim the rest of the prize.

The most remarkable thing about this "tacit agreement" was its amazing persistence through all the vicissitudes of twelve years from 1963 to 1975, through the Kennedy, Johnson and Nixon Administrations—even until two years after the final withdrawal of the U.S. forces. Before proclaiming the "lessons of Vietnam" we need to contemplate the significance of this extraordinary equation. Even more, we need the retrospective recollection and judgment of leaders of all three administrations on the meaning and the historical significance of this "tacit agreement."

As Harriman noted, many years later, Hanoi did not comply with the Geneva Accords for one day, yet, the "tacit agreement" to suspend the Accords, which he and Hilsman fashioned, persisted for twelve years. In whose interest did it work? Starting out as a clever rationale to explain North Vietnam's failure to comply with the Accords, it became first a "tacit agreement" on the inversion of the Accords and gradually, the unspoken "given" premise of our strategy and operations, on the basis of which we "condoned" North Vietnam's infiltration. It not only survived but encompassed the Tet Offensive of 1968 because the U.S. did not allow itself to be provoked into overturning it. Toward the end of 1970, the essential substance of the U.S. side of it was written into law by the Congress. In February 1971, North Vietnam enforced it against South Vietnam. Never, was it again challenged. With logical elegance it measured Hanoi's conquest of Saigon *before* coming to claim the bonus prize in Laos.

"Our judgment," wrote Hilsman, "was that the Communists would use the infiltration routes circumspectly . . . for infiltrating men on foot, cadres equipped with their own arms." That was in 1963. By 1974, as Stanley Karnow reports, when North Vietnam's General Tran Van Tra returned from the South to participate in planning next year's conquest, he noted that "the Ho Chi Minh Trail was a 'far cry' from the primitive web of paths he had descended more than a decade earlier. Now, travelling by car, he cruised along a modern highway dotted with truck rest and service areas, oil tanks, machine shops and other installations, all protected by hilltop antiaircraft emplacements."[1] Despite all that, the U.S. never allowed itself to be provoked into challenging Hanoi's control of the Corridor. The "tacit agreement" expanded to encompass it all. It survived with the continuity of an "easement" in Anglo-American law, which, on the basis of long continued use, grants a right to engage in limited activity on the land of another, such as the privilege to maintain and use a driveway.

Why did the "tacit agreement" survive? Because it corresponded with the facts on the ground. Unfortunately, the facts were disadvantageous to the United States. The "stakes" of the bargain were asymmetrical. There were two beneficiaries of the "tacit agreement." Non-Communist Laos in the northwest was a strategically detached, benign beneficiary which could contribute little to a non-Communist victory in South Vietnam. Communist-controlled southeastern Laos was directly attached and indeed essential to North Vietnam's campaign of conquest over the South.

Caught in this asymmetrical trap and unwilling to break out of it, the U.S. had to throw in more and more resources to compensate for the imbalance. Underestimating Hanoi's determination to conquer and its better ability to survive the political and psychic erosion of protracted warfare, the U.S. increased its input incrementally in order to reach but *not exceed* the level caculated to be necessary to *persuade* Hanoi to give us what we had not won on the ground. But the actual level, or threshold of Hanoi's tolerance was measured by *time*, not by increments of military intensity. Accordingly, this kind of incrementalism in effect delegated to Hanoi the choice of when to end the war. They could give us what we wanted or wait us out. They chose the latter, leaving us eventually with no alternative but to withdraw—which we did.

But it is said that the U.S. was to blame for escalating the war in the first place, that had we not escalated neither would North Vietnam which would have continued infiltrating only "cadres on foot, bearing their own arms." This opinion assumes that the problem in South

Vietnam was really an internal insurgency to which Hanoi contributed only peripherally. In a letter of May 7, 1985 to the *New York Times*, Roger Hilsman says that "the U.S. escalated the war [in 1965] before it knew that North Vietnamese regular forces had been introduced." Of course, the fact that Hanoi concealed its escalation should not excuse it from culpability for escalating. But beyond that, we know today—and Hanoi boasts of the fact—that North Vietnam was bent on conquering South Vietnam from 1959 onward. We know they began developing the Ho Chi Minh Trails in 1959 for this purpose. We know that from 1959 to 1964, infiltration over this route totalled 44,000. Was this not the first escalation?

To be sure, Hanoi would have preferred to conquer at a lower level of military intensity—but they intended to conquer at whatever level and in whatever time span would be required. Hanoi began the escalation and the United States followed. Hanoi's incremental scale was based on its estimate of what was needed to win *in a dimension of time*. The U.S. incremental scale was based on calculating enough military intensity to cause Hanoi to back down but not so much as to make it impossible to negotiate. In this way, the U.S. became entrapped in Hanoi's virtually unlimited time frame. We bought time but no space. When we ran out of time, we had no militarily defined space "to convert into a durable political structure."

Fighting to defend territory is sometimes viewed as a throwback to the days of imperial expansion, especially when the quality of the society being defended leaves something to be desired. To draw a line on a map marking out the land to be defended does not have the emotional appeal of "winning the hearts and minds" of the people, or of "nation-building" or spreading democracy or wiping out corruption or feeding the hungry masses or preserving human rights. But it is not necessarily a sordid objective. It has the advantage of simplicity, of forcing a struggle into the shape of a clear contest of defense against aggression, a contest whose progress can be measured by the advance or retreat of a front line on a map.

Moreover, land is where people live. It is, therefore, the ultimate stake in world politics. Ideology, religion, truth, tolerance, love, freedom, justice, progress and prosperity—these are all things that measure the quality of human life. But they can only be pursued and practiced—and imperfectly at that—on a piece of land. By the same token, corruption, intolerance, oppression, poverty, etc., can only be reduced, over time, on a piece of defended land. One cannot "win the hearts and minds" of people until they have a defensible land to live in. Suppose the United States had disposed its half million forces in Indochina from the sea across Laos to the Mekong River, so as to block the North Vietnamese invasion. Given all the faults and weaknesses of South Vietnam's government and society from 1960 to 1975, who would argue that the condition of its people (and of Laos and Cambodia) would not be far better than it is today under Communist rule? Granted the unsavory aspects of South Korean government, who in the Free World would argue that its people would be better off today under North Korean rule?

In a military sense also, land is the ultimate desideratum. Control over air and sea is critically important and often essential but it is auxiliary to the main stakes. Nations and societies do not live in the air or on the sea. Air and sea power are useful to the extent that they can be converted to the control of land. To do so requires a strategy capable of making the conversion.

It may be argued that in expounding the inadequacy of our strategy in Indochina I have not taken up the moral purposive aspect. This is true. There are important questions untouched here. What business had we in Indochina? Was Indochina of critical importance to the United States? Was our purpose a morally right one? I believe Indochina was (and will again be) of vital importance to the United States; I believe our cause was morally right. At the same time, I recognize that others may seriously and honestly disagree. The fact that I have not dealt with this subject does not imply that it is unimportant. Rather, I believe a study of our war in Indochina as a case of unmatched ends and means has something to teach us about political and military strategy regardless of whether one agrees or disagrees with our purposes for intervening.

In war, moral purpose and practical efficacy, although categorically different factors, tend to merge. Success, particularly if relatively rapid, mutes moral outrage. Conversely, high moral purpose is corroded by inefficacy, by protracted and inconclusive bloodletting with no end in sight. This corrosion is not mere opportunism, but is instead a spinoff of the difference between the state and the individual in applying moral principles. An individual saint may make an absolute commitment to a particular moral objective and stoically accept whatever pain results. A state may support the same moral principle, but in application, the state is an institutional organization applying its institutional will to a large population for whose welfare it is responsible. The leaders must ask themselves how much they can demand of the people for whom they are responsible. They also must calculate how much burden can be borne without impairing the stability of the nation which is their supreme responsibility. Against this calculation, the leadership must calculate the probable efficacy of the strategies available to it. At this point, efficacy becomes a part of the essence of collective—as distinct from individual—morality. In our Indochina war, our leaders committed us to an inefficacious strategy of attrition for which our rival was well suited—and indeed chose—but we were not. The motives of our leaders as individuals were moral. But, on the level of the reason of state, to commit the people to war without an efficacious strategy violates the standard of institutional state morality. The result was that the inefficacy of our strategy corroded the people's conviction in the moral rightness of their cause.

If moral purpose and efficacy are, for a nation, reciprocal factors, then judgments based solely on the one without reference to the other will tend to become unhinged from reality. The Indochina war is one example. A different one was China. "Who lost China?" cried many in the early 1950s who focused on the inefficacy of our actions while avoiding the necessity to address the suitability of our purpose. In fact, China experienced a genuine internal civil war (or insurgency) which we could not have reversed.

On the other side, not content with this factual and rational response, there seemed to be a felt—almost compulsive—need to demonstrate the poverty of American moral purpose. The very question, "Who lost China?" was said to be a reactionary clamor for scapegoats. Some inverted chauvinists said the question reflected American arrogance. Sophists played a game with words, saying that "China was not ours to lose," much like saying that I cannot lose a friend because the friend was "not mine to lose."

In the spring of 1975, as North Vietnam's army raced toward Saigon, many Americans were repeating the same sophistry with reference to South Vietnam. "South Vietnam has never been ours to lose," they said. Surely a phenomenon of the magnitude and complexity of our war in Indochina has a meaning less shallow than this. Indochina is not China. China had an internal revolution. It was an error to think that we could intervene effectively. South Vietnam experienced a slow invasion masked as an insurrection. It was an error to think it could be treated as if it were an internal revolution. Eventually, we recognized the element of invasion, but we were so far committed to counterinsurgency that we could not change. We tried to split the difference. We tried to treat the problem of Vietnam as "something other than war."

To ask "Who lost Indochina?" is not a frivolous or arrogant question. Nor is it vindictive. Nor is it playing with words. We did lose something—a lot—in most ways far more than we lost in China. When mainland China came under Communist control in 1949, we lost a vast, historically and strategically important friend to hostile rule.* But as our actions in Korea demonstrated, we did not lose direction after the fall of China as we did after North Vietnam conquered South Vietnam. The argument about who lost China reflected differences as to what our policy *should have been*. Vietnam reflected a failure in *executing* policy, a failure that is far more devastating to Americans who pride themselves on succeeding at anything they undertake.

In China in 1949 we did not commit our forces to the defense of the Nationalist regime. The complaint of those who demanded, "Who lost China?" was that we seemed to have abandoned China without trying. This, they thought smacked of perversity or cowardice. But to *try* for years, at great cost, as we did, to save little South Vietnam and *fail* is different. Why did we fail? This is a different question from "Why didn't we try?" Was our effort in Indochina doomed from the start—an effort that should never have been made? Or was it a right effort miserably planned and executed? I believe the answer to the last question is affirmative and that is the substance of this exposition.

In our orgy of national self-flagellation for unaccustomed failure we have been told that we over-reached ourselves, that we are paying the wages of imperial ambition in Indochina and of Watergate in Washington. We have worn the "V" for Vietnam as Hester Prynne wore her "A" for adultress. Curiously—for pragmatic Americans— in our weakness for self-punishing explanations, redolent of Greek tragedy, we have given little attention to the methodical search for practical mistakes which could have been avoided, or to the study of alternative means by which we might better have sought to preserve South Vietnam's independence. It is almost as if we preferred not to discuss how we might have done it better in Vietnam for fear that we might find out—and that might somehow exonerate us for our sin. We fell into the compulsive habit of regarding Vietnam as a disgraceful symbol of a deservedly descending national trajectory. Thus, did the inefficacy of our means corrupt our belief in our ends.

But nothing in the American doctrine of counter-insurgency being developed in the early 1960s would have helped to stave off the fate that overtook Afghanistan in 1979—at the hands of the Soviet Union. It is revealing to view the American doctrine of counter-insurgency developed in the early 1960s retrospectively through the lens provided by the Afghan insurgency of the 1980s.

*The fact that the wheel of history has turned some distance since 1949 and our relations with China are improving does not invalidate the reality of the loss we experienced then.

In 1979, the U.S.S.R. put aside the concept of a "war of liberation", preferring to deal with Afghanistan directly by a military coup, underwritten by outright invasion. The Afghans responded with an insurgency, complex in detail but breathtakingly simple in concept. The sides are clear. The issue is clear. The Afghans want the Russians out. The struggle waxes and wanes as it shifts from town to valley to mountain-pass and back. It is sometimes terrorism and sometimes guerrilla war, with an occasional pitched battle. It is complicated by deep sociological economic and regional problems in one of the world's poorest countries. But resistance against the outside attacker is pervasive despite topography, tribalism, cliqueism and economic exploitation. The revolt remains an Afghan insurgency against Russian invaders and their sycophants. This is the stuff of which *real* insurgency is made—the kind of insurgency that makes the pulse beat fast. And what is more, this insurgency is being waged *against* Communists, thus undercutting the tired Western fatalism which underlay the American counter-insurgency doctrine—that insurgency is a Communist weapon.

That the Afghans today are fighting an insurgency derives from their structural relationship to their enemy, not from the fact that they may sometimes use terrorism or guerrilla tactics. They are the people of the country carrying out a "revolt or insurgency" against the Russians and the puppet regime fixed on their country. Their war will always be an insurgency even if they should later acquire the capacity to fight conventional engagements against the Soviets and hold territory behind a front line. By the same token the Soviets are fighting a counter-insurgency—which is the suppression of a genuine insurgency.

In Indochina, North Vietnam occupied the same structural position as the Soviets occupy in Afghanistan—the position of would-be conqueror. Hanoi's tactics varied because of its different strengths and vulnerabilities. North and South Vietnam were more closely matched than the U.S.S.R. and Afghanistan. Vulnerable to U.S. power, Hanoi needed a simulated insurgency as a screen to diffuse the American reaction. Because of ethnic and social similarities, Hanoi was able to carry out such a simulation. The United States accepted the challenge within these terms—rather than imposing its own terms of war.

My purpose has been to offer a little-noticed cross-section of our means for contemplation. My purpose is not to draw all the lessons of Vietnam—only one:

• The moral purpose of a just war can be corrupted by ineffective means.

- A government that commits its manhood to war has a *moral* obligation to be effective.

- This requires an effective correlation between ends and means.

Do the ends determine the means? No and yes. When chosen, the end should be compatible with the purposes of the nation. Thereafter, the means should be chosen for their efficacy in attaining the end. One thing is sure—the result actually achieved will reflect the means chosen.

- Great causes require great means.

- Small means achieve small ends.

- Uncertain means achieve uncertain ends.

- Our incremental means in Indochina achieved incremental failure.

Our means did not measure up to our ends. Instead of letting our ends determine our means, we chose our means on the basis of premises incompatible with our ends. We achieved exactly what those means could achieve. We chose our means on the premise that we had to compensate for the disaster at the Bay of Pigs; on the premise that the problem in Vietnam was an insurgency rather than an aggression; on the premise that Laos could be strategically separated from Vietnam; on the premise that North Vietnam was less than fully determined to conquer; on the premise that we could "persuade" Hanoi by attrition and on the premise that we could "signal" Hanoi to quit so as to avoid a smashing blow which we simultaneously signalled them we would not deliver. We achieved exactly what these means could achieve—frustration, exhaustion and incremental failure.

President Kennedy outlined our objectives to the American people in noble terms. The means he chose did not match the objectives he set forth. President Johnson, with the same advisors, poured out the resources of America in an attempt to correlate ends and means. President Nixon saw the discrepancy but did not follow through—except with his own personal assurance to South Vietnam, a promissary note he was unable to redeem.

Writing in the *Washington Post* on April 14, 1985, columnist Haynes Johnson offered the following allegory:

> The historical belief in the American mission in the world—the conviction that "God is on our side"—made the Vietnam defeat difficult to comprehend.

This statement is indeed a poignant evocation of how the Vietnam disaster has troubled the American soul. But—continuing the allegory—the difficulty in comprehension springs from a confusion of the roles of God and Man, which is to say, Ends and Means. If our cause was just—and it was—then God was on our side. But God doesn't do everything. Some things He leaves to men. In our Indochina war, men and means failed to measure up to the just end.

Speaking on behalf of the Kennedy Administration, Roger Hilsman in 1967 offered the following judgment:

> The neutralization of Laos and the Geneva Agreements of 1962 were, in my view, a triumph of statecraft. . . . No matter what happens in the future, to have steered past either abandoning Laos or letting it be the cause of a major military confrontation, to have succeeded in putting it to one side for the whole of his administration and beyond—this required not only wisdom on the part of a president, but nerve.[2]

However, taking full and honorable advantage of hindsight from 1987, a counter-judgment must be entered. The *concept* of neutralizing Laos was a brilliant stroke and the successful negotiation of the Geneva Accords as a *test of Communist intentions* was masterful. But, that being true, it follows that the *de facto* suspension, a few months later by "tacit agreement", of both neutralization and the enforcement of the Accords cancelled out the triumph. Worse, the artful subtlety of the tacit suspension left a shadowy "facade" behind which the Communist side used Laos as the indispensable weapon in its military conquest of South Vietnam. As it turned out, what was "put to one side" was not the problem of Laos but the very neutralization agreement which, had it been effective, would have been a "triumph of statecraft." There are no "triumphs of statecraft" in the tragedy of the United States in Indochina from 1961 to 1975.

The U.S. fought the war as a bull fights the toreador's cape, not the toreador himself. This strategy led not to our defeat but to our failure. The bull tired and was led away as the ring was occupied by an army of North Vietnamese toreadors who are still waving their capes in Laos and Cambodia. In the *real* Spanish bullring, one should note, a bull fights only once, and if he survives he is retired to stud. Why? Because by escaping the sword he has learned too much for subsequent toreadors to handle. Let us hope that in future international contracts from which we cannot retire, the U.S. will indeed have learned exactly why we failed in Vietnam.

Notes

Author's Preface

1. Arthur Schlesinger, *A Thousand Days*, (Boston: Houghton Mifflin Company, 1965), 547.

2. Harry G. Summers, *On Strategy; A Critical Analysis of the Vietnam War*, (Novato, California: Presidio Press, 1982).

3. Stanley Karnow, *Vietnam: A History*, (New York: Viking Press, 1983).

Prologue: The Toreador's Cape

1. U.S. Consulate General cable from Geneva, CONFE 785, October 26, 1961. (Cables or other documents not attributed to some other source are in the author's possession.)

2. Norman B. Hannah, "The Great Strategic Error," *National Review*, XXVII 23 (June 20, 1975):666–669.

3. Summers, *On Strategy*, 88.

4. Karnow, *Vietnam*, 17.

5. Ibid., 15.

Chapter 2: The Bay of Pigs and Indochina.

1. Nikita Khrushchev, "For New Victories of the World Communist Movement," excerpted in *Insurgency and Counterinsurgency: An Anthology*, (Washington, D.C.: Industrial College of the Armed Forces, 1962.) Edited by Richard M. Leighton and Ralph Sanders, 106.

2. Douglas Blaufarb, *The Counterinsurgency Era*, (New York: Macmillan Free Press, 1977), 54.

3. Edward R. Murrow, Memorandum to Under-Secretary of State, Chester Bowles, March 26, 1961.

4. Schlesinger, *A Thousand Days*, 249.

5. Arthur Schlesinger, *Robert Kennedy and His Times*, (Boston: Houghton Mifflin Company, 1978), 702.

6. Ibid.

7. Theordore C. Sorenson, *Kennedy*, (New York: Harper & Row, 1965), 644.

8. *Pentagon Papers*, Senator Gravel Edition, Vol. II, 33–34.

9. Hilsman, *To Move a Nation*, 134.

10. Ibid.

11. Cable from Secretary of State Rusk, at the U.S. Consulate General in Geneva, to the Department of State, SECTO 59, May 11, 1961.

12. Schlesinger, *Robert Kennedy and His Times*, 705.

13. Ibid., 703.

Chapter 3: Insurgency: What's in a Name?

1. *Insurgency and Counterinsurgency: An Anthology*, (Washington, D.C.: Industrial College of the Armed Forces, 1962), Edited by Richard M. Leighton and Ralph Sanders, 1.

2. Walt W. Rostow, "Guerrilla Warfare in the Underdeveloped Areas," *Insurgency and Counterinsurgency: An Anthology*, 7.

3. Ibid., 9.

4. U. Alexis Johnson, "Internal Defense and the Foreign Service," *Foreign Service Journal*, XXXIX 7 (July, 1962):20–23.

5. Lecture at Industrial College of the Armed Forces, Sept. 24, 1962. *Insurgency and Counterinsurgency: An Anthology*:15–28.

6. Hilsman, *To Move a Nation*, 415.

7. Summers, *On Strategy*, 83.

Chapter 4: Something Other Than War.

1. Hilsman, *To Move a Nation*, 525.

2. Ibid., 426.

3. Memorandum of Discussion at NSC meeting of November 15, 1961, Lyndon Baines Johnson Library.

4. Senate Foreign Relations Committee, *Background Information Relating to Southeast Asia and Vietnam*, June 1970, 189.

5. Lyndon Johnson, *The Vantage Point*, (New York: Holt, Rinehart and Winston, 1971), 58.

6. Rostow, *Diffusion of Power*, 282.

7. Schlesinger, *Robert Kennedy and His Times*, 722.

8. Hilsman, *To Move a Nation*, 536.

9. Schlesinger, *A Thousand Days*, 332.

10. *Pentagon Papers*, II. 68.

11. *Pentagon Papers*, II, 88.

12. Hilsman, *To Move a Nation*, 423.

13. Memorandum of NSC meeting of Nov. 15, 1961.

14. Hilsman, *To Move a Nation*, 424.

15. Schlesinger, *Robert Kennedy and His Times*, 722.

16. Henry Brandon, *Anatomy of Error*, (Boston: Gambit, 1969), 30.

17. Schlesinger, *Robert Kennedy and His Times*, 722.

18. Averell Harriman, "What We Are Doing in Southeast Asia", *New York Times Magazine*, May 27, 1962, 53.

19. Roger Hilsman, *Two American Counterstrategies to Guerrilla Warfare*, "China

in Crisis", edited by Ping-ti Ho and Tang Tsou, 1968; quoted in Blaufarb, *The Counterinsurgency Era*, 207.

20. Bruce Palmer, *The 25-Year War*, (Lexington: University Press of Kentucky, 1984).

Chapter 5: Out of the Jungle to Geneva.

1. Department of State cable No. 4874 to London, April 15, 1961.

2. Department of State cable TOSEC No. 33 to Osla, May 9, 1961.

3. Department of State cable TOSEC No. 47 to Geneva, May 11, 1961.

4. Consulate General Geneva cable No. 785, October 26, 1961.

5. Hilsman, *To Move a Nation*, 127–129.

6. Harriman, "What We Are Doing in Southeast Asia". *New York Times Magazine*, May 27, 1962, 54.

7. Hilsman, *To Move a Nation*, 130.

8. Ibid., 135.

9. Ibid.

10. Embassy Bangkok cable No. 1980, May 5, 1961.

11. Schlesinger, *A Thousand Days*, 331. For further discussion of the Harriman-Pushkin understandings see Rostow, *The Diffusion of Power*, 287–288.

12. Schlesinger, *A Thousand Days*, 329.

13. Chester Cooper, *The Lost Crusade*, (New York: Dodd, Meade and Company, 1970), 190.

14. Consulate General Geneva cable No. 785, October 26, 1961.

15. *Memorandum for the President*, November 11, 1961. *Pentagon Papers*, II, 110–113.

Chapter 6: A Nest of Chinese Boxes.

1. Harriman, "What We Are Doing in Southeast Asia", *New York Times Magazine*, May 27, 1962, 54.

2. *Declaration on the Neutrality of Laos and Protocol*, Signed at Geneva. Texts published in the Department of State Bulletin, August 13, 1962, 259–263.

Chapter 7: From Geneva Back to the Jungle.

1. Harriman, *Russia and America in a Changing World*, (New York: Doubleday, 1971), 145.

2. Department of State cable, TOSEC No. 38 to Geneva, July 23, 1962.

3. Department of State cable, TOSEC No. 43 to Geneva, July 23, 1962.

4. Schlesinger, *A Thousand Days*, 515.

5. U. Alexis Johnson, *Right Hand of Power*, (Englewood Cliffs. N.J.: Prentice-Hall, 1984), 325–326.

6. Embassy Vientiane cable No. 118, July 24, 1962. Extracted from an exclusive interview of Souphanouvong by British ITV reporter, Peter Hunt.

7. Department of State cable, No. 364, to Moscow, August 18, 1962, including extracts from Embassy Vientiane cable No. 249, August 17, 1962.

8. Ibid.

9. Department of State cable No. 205 to Vientiane, August 18, 1962.

10. Ibid.

11. Ibid.

12. Department of State cable No. 298 to Vientiane, August 21, 1962.

13. UPI Dispatch, Washington, October 4, 1962. Quoted in Arthur Dommen, *Conflict in Laos*, (New York: Frederick A. Praeger, 1964), 240.

14. Department of State cable No. 213 to Vientiane, August 21, 1962.

15. Department of State cable No. 216 to Vientiane, August 21, 1962.

16. Embassy Vientiane cable No. 255, August 19, 1962.

17. Embassy Vientiane cable No. 432, September 17, 1962.

18. Department of State cable No. 222, August 22, 1962.

19. Embassy Vientiane cable No. 280, August 22, 1962.

20. Embassy Vientiane cable No. 452, September 19, 1962.

21. Embassy Vientiane cable No. 469, September 22, 1962.

22. Ibid.

23. Ibid.

24. Ibid.

25. Ibid.

26. Arthur Dommen, *Conflict in Laos*, (New York: Frederick A. Praeger, 1964), 239.

27. Ibid., 240.

28. Maxwell Taylor, *Swords and Plowshares*, (New York: W.W. Norton, 1972), 218–219.

Chapter 8: The Facade of Geneva.

1. Hilsman, *To Move a Nation*, 151.

2. Ibid.

3. Ibid., 152.

4. Ibid.

5. Ibid.

6. Ibid., 154.

7. Ibid., 148–149.

8. Ibid., 152.

9. Ibid.

10. Ibid.

11. Ibid., 153.

12. Ibid.

13. Ibid., 154.

14. Ibid.

15. Ibid.

16. Ibid.

17. Ibid.

18. Ibid.

Chapter 9: The Laos Strand.

1. Rostow, *Diffusion of Power*, 288–289.
2. Cooper, *The Lost Crusade*, 190.

Chapter 10: The Vietnam Strand.

1. *Pentagon Papers*, II, 76.
2. Ibid., 18.
3. Hilsman, *To Move a Nation*, 419.
4. Walt Rostow, *Guerrilla Warfare in the Underdeveloped Areas*, address delivered at Fort Bragg, June 28, 1961. Printed in "Insurgency and Counterinsurgency: An Antholgy", 7.
5. Hilsman, *To Move a Nation*, 433.
6. Karnow, *Vietnam: A History*, 332.
7. Hilsman, *To Move a Nation*, 450–451.
8. Ibid., 464.
9. "Summary of Recent MACV and CIA Cables on Infiltration", Document No. 243, *Pentagon Papers*, III, 673–674.
10. *MACV Order of Battle Summary, February, 1972*. Military History Institute, Army War College, Carlisle, Pennsylvania.
11. Hilsman, *To Move a Nation*, 459.
12. Ibid., 460.
13. Ibid., 459.
14. Ibid., 501.
15. Ibid.
16. Ibid., 510–511.
17. Ibid., 512.
18. "Untold Story of the Road to War in Vietnam", *U.S. News and World Report*, October 10, 1983, 24 VN.
19. Rostow, *Diffusion of Power*, xviii.

Chapter 11: The Cambodia Strand.

1. Hilsman, *To Move a Nation*, 535–536.

Chapter 12: The Scene in 1964.

1. JCSM 717–61, October 9, 1961, *Pentagon Papers*, II, 74.
2. NSAM 288, March 17, 1965, *Pentagon Papers*, III, 500. See also Vol. III, 50–56.
3. JCSM 222–64, March 14, 1964, *Pentagon Papers*, III, 56.
4. McNamara-Taylor report to President Kennedy, October 2, 1963. *Pentagon Papers*, III, p. 19.
5. Secretary McNamara testimony before the House Armed Services Committee on January 27 and 29, 1964. *Pentagon Papers*, III, 36.
6. *Pentagon Papers*, III, 73.
7. *Pentagon Papers*, III, 78.

8. *Pentagon Papers*, III, 19.

9. JCSM 46–64, January 22, 1964, *Pentagon Papers*, III, 496–499.

10. *Pentagon Papers*, III, 170.

11. Department of State cable TOSEC 36 to Bangkok, May 29, 1964.

12. Embassy Saigon cable No. 214, July 25, 1964. *Pentagon Papers*, III, 512–514.

13. Department of State cable No. 89 to Vientiane, July 26, 1964. *Pentagon Papers*, III, 514.

14. Embassy Vientiane cable No. 170, July 27, 1964, *Pentagon Papers*, III, 515–517.

Chapter 13: 1964—No Sticking Place

1. TIME, Vol. 84, No. 7, August 14, 1964, 13.

2. *Pentagon Papers*, III, 189.

3. Ibid.

4. Embassy Saigon cable of November 3, 1964, *Pentagon Papers*, III, 591.

5. *Pentagon Papers*, III, 190.

6. Ibid.

7. Ibid.

8. Department of State cable No. 439, August 14, 1964. *Pentagon Papers*, III, 533–537.

9. CINCPAC cable to JCS, August 17, 1964; *Pentagon Papers*, III, 542.

10. Embassy Saigon cable No. 465, August 18, 1964; *Pentagon Papers*, III, 546.

11. *Pentagon Papers*, III, 91.

12. William P. Bundy memorandum to Secretary Rusk, January 6, 1965; *Pentagon Papers*, III, 684–686.

13. *Pentagon Papers*, III, 116.

14. McGeorge Bundy, "A Policy of Sustained Reprisal", February 7, 1965; *Pentagon Papers*, III, 689.

15. William P. Bundy, "Draft Position Paper on Southeast Asia", November 29, 1964; *Pentagon Papers*, III, 678.

16. John McNaughton, "Plan of Action for South Vietnam", September 3, 1964; *Pentagon Papers*, III, 559.

17. John McNaughton, "Observations Re South Vietnam", January 4, 1965; *Pentagon Papers*, III, 683–684.

18. John McNaughton, "Proposed Course of Action Re Vietnam", March 24, 1965; *Pentagon Papers*, III, 695.

19. McGeorge Bundy, "A Policy of Sustained Reprisal", February 7, 1965; *Pentagon Papers*, III, 690.

20. *Pentagon Papers*, III, 208.

21. Embassy Saigon cable, November 3, 1964; *Pentagon Papers*, III, 590–591.

22. Maxwell Taylor, *Swords and Plowshares*, 19.

23. *Pentagon Papers*, III, 111.

24. Ibid., 195.

25. William P. Bundy, "Memorandum for Mr. McGeorge Bundy", February 10, 1965; *Pentagon Papers*, III, 691

Chapter 15: Through the Looking Glass.

1. *Pentagon Papers*, III, 108.
2. Ibid., 111.
3. Ibid., 251.
4. Ibid., 217.
5. Ibid., 213.
6. Ibid., 245.
7. Ibid., 213.
8. Ibid., 679.
9. Ibid., 212.
10. Ibid.
11. Ibid., 255.
12. "A General Tells How U.S. Can Win in Vietnam", *U.S. News and World Report*, Dec. 19, 1966, 56–57.
13. *Pentagon Papers*, III, 258.

Chapter 16: Knit One: The Internal Pacification.

1. *Pentagon Papers*, III, 423.
2. Ibid.
3. Admiral U.S.G. Sharp, Jr., *A Strategy for Defeat*, San Rafael, California: Presidio Press, 1978, 89–90.
4. Press Conference statement, July 28, 1965. Dept. of State Bulletin, August 16, 1961, 262.
5. Before the House Foreign Affairs Committee, August 3, 1965.
6. Before the Senate Appropriations Committee, August 4, 1965.
7. William C. Westmoreland, *A Soldier Reports*, New York: Doubleday, 1976, 83.
8. Sharp, *A Strategy for Defeat*, 92.
9. Ibid., 91–92.
10. Robert Shaplen, *The Lost Revolution*, New York: Harper and Row, 1965, 187.
11. Victor H. Krulak, *First to Fight*, U.S. Naval Institute, 1984, 181–182.
12. Ibid., 185–186.
13. Ibid., 186.
14. Ibid., 194.
15. Ibid., 198–200.
16. Ibid., 201.
17. William Colby, *Honorable Men*, New York: Simon and Schuster, 1978, 176.
18. Ibid.
19. Ibid., 232 et. seq.
20. *Pentagon Papers*, III, 42.

Chapter 17: Purl One—The Air Campaign.

1. Draft Presidential Memorandum, June 12, 1967, *Pentagon Papers*, IV, 191.
2. U.S.G. Sharp, Jr., "We Could Have Won in Vietnam Long Ago," *Reader's Digest*, 119.
3. JCSM 672–66, *Pentagon Papers*, IV, 127.
4. *MACV Order of Battle Summary, February, 1972*. Military History Institute, Army War College, Carlisle, Pennsylvania.
5. "Notes for Memorandum from Secretary McNamara to the President," July 20, 1965, *Pentagon Papers*, IV, 622.
6. Ibid., 620.
7. "Secretary McNamara Memorandum to the President," July 30, 1965, *Pentagon Papers*, III, 388.
8. "Secretary McNamara Memorandum to the President," November 30, 1965. *Pentagon Papers*, IV, 33.
9. "Department of State Memorandum to the President," November 9, 1965. *Pentagon Papers*, IV, 34.
10. *Pentagon Papers*, IV, 33.
11. Ibid., 34.
12. Ibid., 34–35.
13. Sharp, "We Could Have Won," 120.
14. *Pentagon Papers*, IV, 107.
15. Ibid., 111.
16. *Pentagon Papers*, IV, 142–143.
17. Sharp, "We Could Have Won," 119.
18. JCSM 672–66, October 14, 1966, *Pentagon Papers*, IV, 128–129.
19. JCSM 555–67, October 17, 1967, *Pentagon Papers*, IV, 210–211.
20. Sharp, "We Could Have Won," 121.
21. Westmoreland, *A Soldier Reports*, 261.
22. *Pentagon Papers*, IV, 30.
23. Peter Collier and David Horowitz, "Lefties for Reagan," *Washington Post Magazine*, March 17, 1985.
24. Presidential Press Conference, July 28, 1965.
25. Presidential Press Conference, July 28, 1965.

Chapter 18: Laos: The Dropped Stitch.

1. Sharp, *Strategy for Defeat*, 91.
2. John McNaughton, "Forces Required to Win in South Vietnam," Memorandum to General Goodpaster, July 2, 1965, *Pentagon Papers*, IV, 291–293.
3. "Intensification of Military Operations in Vietnam—Concept and Appraisal," Study by JCS, July 14, 1965, *Pentagon Papers*, IV, 291.
4. Ibid., 295.
5. "Notes for Memorandum from Secretary McNamara to President Johnson," July 20, 1965, *Pentagon Papers*, IV, 298.
6. Ibid., 621–622.
7. "Memorandum for the President" from Secretary McNamara, November 30, 1965, *Pentagon Papers*, Doc. 262, IV, 622–623.

8. "Memorandum for the President" from Secretary McNamara, December 7, 1965, *Pentagon Papers*, Doc. 263, IV, 623–624.

9. *Pentagon Papers*, IV, 303.

10. Westmoreland, *A Soldier Reports*, 147–148.

11. From a McNaughton memorandum reporting the conversation, *Pentagon Papers*, IV, 441–442.

12. Westmoreland, *A Soldier Reports*, 148.

13. John McNaughton Memorandum to Secretary McNamara, May 6, 1967, *Pentagon Papers*, IV, 478.

14. John McNaughton Draft Memorandum to the President, May 19, 1967, *Pentagon Papers*, IV, 486.

15. Ibid.

16. *Pentagon Papers*, IV, 541.

17. Pentagon Papers, IV, 516.

18. Ibid., 517.

19. Ibid., 517–518

20. Ibid., 521.

21. Westmoreland, *A Soldier Reports*, 198.

22. Ibid., 148.

23. Ibid.

Chapter 19: Intermission at Tet: 1968.

1. JCS Memorandum, JCSM 91–68, February 12, 1968, *Pentagon Papers*, IV, 539.

2. Chairman JCS, General Wheeler, Memorandum, February 27, 1968, *Pentagon Papers*, IV, 548.

3. "Communist Alternatives in Vietnam," CIA paper, February 29, 1968, *Pentagon Papers*, IV, 551.

4. CIA Paper, March 1, 1968, *Pentagon Papers*, IV, 552.

5. Memorandum by Assistant Secretary of Defense for Systems Analysis, February, 1968, *Pentagon Papers*, IV, 557–558.

6. Maxwell Taylor, Memorandum, dated February, 1968, *Pentagon Papers*, IV, 553–555.

7. Assistant Secretary of State William Bundy, Memorandum, February, 1968, *Pentagon Papers*, IV, 553.

8. Systems Analysis Memo, February, 1968, *Pentagon Papers*, IV, 558.

9. Office of International Security Affairs, Department of Defense, Memorandum, March 1, 1968, *Pentagon Papers*, IV, 561–568.

10. Ibid., 565.

11. General Westmoreland (MACV) cable to CJCS Gen. Wheeler, March 2, 1968, *Pentagon Papers*, IV, 569–570.

12. Secretary of Defense Clifford, Memorandum of recommendation to President Johnson, March 4, 1968, *Pentagon Papers*, IV, 575 et seq.

13. Ibid., 576.

14. Department of State Memorandum (Tab E to Secretary of Defense memo of March 4), *Pentagon Papers*, IV, 582.

15. *Pentagon Papers*, IV, 585.

16. Lyndon Johnson, *The Vantage Point*, New York: Holt, Rinehart and Winston, 1971, 514–520.

Chapter 20: Laos in 1969: Right Place, Right Time

1. Charles C. Flowerree, letter to the author, December 26, 1986.

2. Henry A. Kissinger, *White House Years*, New York: Little, Brown, 1979, 238.

3. Kissinger, *White House Years*, 239.

4. Associated Press, *Los Angeles Times*, February 10, 1969.

5. *Lao Presse*, August 12, 1969.

6. Kissinger, *White House Years*, 250–251.

7. Ibid., 270.

8. Ibid., 284.

9. Ibid., 272.

10. Ibid., 224–225.

11. U. Alexis Johnson, *The Right Hand of Power*, Englewood Cliffs, N.J.: Prentice-Hall, 1985.

12. Kissinger, *White House Years*, 281.

13. Ibid., 283.

14. Ibid., 1480–1482.

15. Ibid., 284.

16. Ibid., 283.

17. White House Press Conference, September 26, 1969. State Department cable, unnumbered, Sept. 26, 1969.

18. Kissinger, *White House Years*, 285.

19. Richard Nixon, *No More Vietnams*, New York: Arbor House, 1985, 116.

Chapter 21: 1970 in Cambodia: Wrong Place
1971 in Laos: Wrong Time

1. Kissinger, *White House Years*, 437.

2. Ibid., 235.

3. Ibid., 308.

4. Ibid.

5. Ibid., 232.

6. Ibid., 436.

7. Ibid.

8. Ibid., 443.

9. Ibid., 444.

10. Ibid., 446.

11. Richard Nixon, *No More Vietnams*, New York: Arbor House, 1985, 47.

12. Kissinger, *White House Years*, 451.

13. Ibid., 453–454.

14. Ibid., 998.

15. Ibid., 999.

16. Ibid., 1018.
17. Walt Rostow, Interview with the *New York Times*, January 5, 1969.
18. Kissinger, *White House Years*, 1019.
19. Ibid., 1175.
20. Ibid., 1333.
21. Nixon, *No More Vietnams*, 169.
22. Kissinger, *White House Years*, 1435.
23. Ibid., 1470.
24. Nixon, *No More Vietnams*, 178.
25. Ibid., 189.

Epilogue:

1. Karnow, *Vietnam: A History*, 663.
2. Hilsman, *To Move a Nation*, 580.

Index